A Complete Nutrition and Lifestyle Plan
to Dramatically Lower Your Cancer Risk

The Strang
Cancer Prevention
Center Cookbook

Laura Pensiero, R.D., Michael Osborne, M.D., and
Susan Oliveria, Sc.D., M.P.H. | Foreword by Jacques Pépin

With my best wishes,

Michael O[signature]

McGraw·Hill

New York   Chicago   San Francisco   Lisbon   London   Madrid   Mexico City
Milan   New Delhi   San Juan   Seoul   Singapore   Sydney   Toronto

Library of Congress Cataloging-in-Publication Data

Pensiero, Laura J.
    The Strang cancer prevention center cookbook : a complete nutrition and lifestyle plan to dramatically lower your cancer risk / Laura Pensiero, Michael Osborne, Susan Oliveria.
        p.   cm.
    Includes index.
    ISBN 0-07-142404-0 (alk. paper)
      1. Cancer—Diet therapy—Recipes.   2. Cancer—Prevention.   I. Osborne, Michael.   II. Oliveria, Susan.   III. Title

RC271.D52P466   2004
616.99'40654—dc22   2004002918

1 2 3 4 5 6 7 8 9 0 AGM/AGM 3 2 1 0 9 8 7 6 5 4

ISBN 0-07-142404-0

Interior design by Monica Baziuk

McGraw-Hill books are available at special quantity discounts to use as premiums and sales promotions, or for use in corporate training programs. For more information, please write to the Director of Special Sales, Professional Publishing, McGraw-Hill, Two Penn Plaza, New York, NY 10121-2298. Or contact your local bookstore.

This book is printed on acid-free paper.

Contents

3. Phytochemicals ————————————————— 107
The New Functional Foods

4. Cooking for Cancer Prevention ————————— 125

5. Recipes ——————————————————————— 145

6. Prevention _____ 337

Lifestyle Modifications to Minimize Cancer Risk

Foreword

I**T IS ONLY IN RECENT YEARS** that doctors and cooks have tried to understand one another and have started to work together to integrate our eating habits and lifestyles into a regimen intended to keep us healthy and long-lived. Not that this is a new premise. The ancient Greek and Roman doctors, poets, and philosophers—from Hippocrates, Seneca, and Archestratus to the School of Salerno's humoral theory in the Middle Ages—incorporated food and medicine in a literature that taught cooking as well as medicine.

The yin and yang of the Chinese places great emphasis on food habits and well-being, just as French gastronome Brillat-Savarin's aphorism "Tell me what you eat, and I will tell you what you are" encompasses today's notion that health is tightly interwoven with our consumption of food.

Thomas Edison unknowingly defined the goal of the Strang Cancer Prevention Center better than anyone when he said that "The doctor of the future will give no medicine but will educate his patients in the care of the human frame, in diet, and in the cause and prevention of disease." Based on the latest nutritional research, there is no question that the quality of our food, the percentage of fat, and the amount of fiber from fruits and vegetables in our diet are all factors directly related to our physical health. The phytochemicals or "vegetable chemicals," which are the natural substances present in many fruits and vegetables, may be the plentiful and inexpensive pharmacy that we turn toward tomorrow.

The fusion of the cook and the doctor will be essential to comprehend that new source of health. Wouldn't it be great if we could make sense of the mass of nutritional information, often contradictory, that bombards us nowadays? Think of how invaluable it would be to have basic distinct guidelines that explain how eating fruits and vegetables can help to prevent disease and show us how to incorporate them without fuss into our daily fare.

This is precisely what the Strang Cancer Prevention Center provides in this book, and as a chef, home cook, and someone interested in good food and health, I am indebted to Laura Pensiero, Dr. Susan Oliveria, and Dr. Michael Osborne for providing us with the essential tools to better our lives and the lives of our family members and friends.

—Jacques Pépin

Preface

THE MAJORITY OF CANCER is related to lifestyle and therefore may be preventable. Good nutrition and exercise are of paramount importance. The Strang Cancer Prevention Center is dedicated to interdisciplinary research into cancer prevention and promotion of cure through early detection. Worldwide it is estimated that approximately 7.6 million people will develop cancer and 5 million will die of the disease annually. In the United States, more than 2 million develop cancer each year and about 560,000 die of the disease. One in two men and one in three women develop cancer in their lifetime. For the first time it is projected that more people will develop cancer than heart disease in this millennium. Research studies over the past fifty years have shown clearly that exercise and healthy nutrition are key factors in the prevention of cancer as well as cardiovascular disease. It is estimated that diet and obesity are responsible for about 30 percent of all cancer deaths, while a sedentary lifestyle is responsible for about 5 percent. Thirty-three percent of cancer deaths would be prevented by cessation of smoking and reduction in alcohol intake.

Understanding the risk factors and modifying lifestyles will do a great deal to lessen the individual risk of disease. The last half of the nineteenth century and the first half of the twentieth century have seen the conquest of a major scourge of the human race, infection, by prevention and treatment. Today the challenge is prevention of cancer and heart disease.

This book will show you how nutrition and lifestyle changes can give you the maximum benefit for prevention of cancer and other serious diseases. A healthy lifestyle will not only prolong life but increase its enjoyment as well, by enhancing its quality and quantity. A healthy diet and exercise lead to reduced stress, greater stamina, less fatigue, and better general well-being. I urge you to use the information here to stay healthy and get the most out of life.

—Michael Osborne, M.D.

Acknowledgments

W E ARE ESPECIALLY GRATEFUL to all the chefs who took time from their busy schedules to provide delicious and healthy recipes; without their help this book would not have been possible.

We are grateful to Dr. Andrew Dannenberg for his enthusiasm. A colleague and friend, he provided the strong mentoring and support needed to complete this book. Comments on the first draft from Paul Christos, Deborah Plutzer, Ivan Rico, and Rachel Weiss improved the book considerably, and we appreciate their help. Sincere thanks to Lynn Hoffman, who was integral to the revising and updating of the science sections of the second edition. We greatly appreciate Katherine Fenzel's painstaking work in formatting numerous documents to the publisher's specifications. Many thanks to our colleague Dr. Barbara Levine for her nutrition expertise. Harold Newmark's guidance and insightful comments during the writing of the section on phytochemicals helped to produce a concise and understandable chapter on this complex topic. Our colleagues Dr. Edward Giovannucci at the Harvard School of Public Health and Dr. Arline Salbe at the National Institutes of Health provided invaluable guidance for the science and applied nutrition sections, and we appreciate their help.

Sincere appreciation to our literary agent, Regula Noetzli, who always believed in the importance of this work and placed the second edition in the highly professional hands of McGraw-Hill. Many thanks also to Michele Pezzuti, our editor, who had the insight and creativity to help us present complex and diverse topics in an easy-to-understand manner.

Thanks also to All-Clad Metal Crafters Inc., which generously provided premium-quality cookware to complete the testing of each recipe.

Finally, we would like to thank Anne Fisher for her generous financial support to the Strang Cancer Prevention Center and the Anne Fisher Nutrition Center. We are also grateful to all the donors who have generously contributed to Strang.

Introduction

MY EARLY COUNSELING EXPERIENCES as a nutritionist and registered dietitian in a variety of hospital and clinic settings brought me to the realization that to make meaningful long-term changes in what you eat you need to have the necessary knowledge and tools to make these changes a reality. This recognition, along with advances in research supporting the role of diet in preventing disease, led me to expand my clinically based nutrition knowledge to include practical skills in the culinary arts.

I enrolled in the French Culinary Institute in the early 1990s and was well on my way to learning how to incorporate cooking and healthy eating as a teaching tool for nutrition education by the time I finished. To my clinical colleagues and my chef instructors at the institute it was a source of good-natured amusement that a registered dietitian would choose to study French cuisine. After I graduated, however, theoretical nutrition and diet therapy combined with a solid base in culinary arts, establishing the philosophy of NutriChef, a nutrition and culinary consulting company that I founded in 1995 and continue to direct today.

Although the recipes in this book represent many ethnic cuisines, the Mediterranean influence is the most profound. This is because of the naturally healthy ingredients, the simplicity of cooking methods, and the appeal that this cooking style holds for many people. These recipes, offered by Francesco Antonucci, Lidia Bastianich, Michael Chiarello, Barbara Lynch, Michael Romano, and Gianni Scappin, as well as many other Mediterranean-influenced chefs, will undoubtedly be part of your regular cooking repertoire. Their talents are displayed deliciously in recipes such as Venetian Peperonata, Tuscan-Style Cannellini Beans, Warm Pasta Vegetable Salad, Warm Shrimp and Barley Salad, Ratatouille Soup, Marinated Pork Tenderloin with Mashed Orange-Scented Sweet Potatoes, and Winter Vegetable Soup (*Ribollita*) (see Index).

The wide variety of recipes features plant food ingredients, which contain the cancer prevention substances phytochemicals. They work on a number of different levels—as antioxidants, as suppressors, or to help detoxify potential cancer-causing agents. Research is ongoing, but we do know that eating very colorful meals, containing a wide range of fruits, vegetables, whole grains, and legumes, will provide you with a broad spectrum of vitamins and minerals and a measure of protection against cancer and other diseases. Other high points of the book include tips (from increasing fruit and vegetable servings to decreasing carcinogens in cooking), shopping lists, and other how-to lists that provide you with knowledge and tools to get started.

Although my main focus continues to be ways to enhance healthy eating as a tasty way of life, my approach varies—from cookbook writing, recipe development and testing, and cooking demonstrations to nutrition education programs with clients at the Anne Fisher Nutrition Center, a research and clinical site at Strang Cancer Prevention Center. These wonderful and diverse people were unanimously clear when they said, "Please do not tell me what to do—tell me and show me how." This reflects the old Chinese proverb by Lao-tzu "Give a man a fish and you feed him for a day. Teach him how to fish and you feed him for a lifetime." My philosophy. Exactly.

The Strang Cancer Prevention Center Cookbook provides the sound scientific rationale for healthy eating and cancer prevention. It also shows in a clear, easy-to-understand way how to use nature's pharmacy of foods in everyday preparation, cooking, and eating. These are concepts that I believe can make all the difference in your ability to develop and maintain a healthy eating lifestyle.

There is a wealth of valuable information in this book. Eating healthy can play a vital role in staying well, and it is an evolving process of learning, cooking, and, most important, enjoying food and flavor.

Buon Appetito!

—Laura Pensiero, R.D.
www.nutrichef.info

IF HEALTHY EATING CAN IMPROVE both the quality and length of our lives, why is it that we often do not follow fundamental nutrition guidelines? In some cases a lack of information may be the problem. Although some of us are aware of the role that nutrition can play in keeping us healthy, far too many others do not have this knowledge. In other cases conflicting information has left many people frustrated and confused about what foods are good for them and which ones should be limited in their diets. In this book we have attempted to explain the complex relationship between diet and health in a thorough but easy-to-understand manner. At the same time we have made great efforts to separate facts from misconceptions or gimmicks that can be misleading.

As an epidemiologist, I try to determine what lifestyle or behaviors affect the risk of developing cancer. The writing of this book has been motivated by a strong desire to educate individuals about the importance of nutrition in cancer prevention. Communicating the importance that diet can have in promoting cancer, as well as the notion that people can modify their behaviors and lifestyle, is paramount. Individuals can reduce their risks of not only cancer but also other chronic diseases like obesity, diabetes, and cardiovascular disease if they maintain a healthy diet made up of lots of fruits and vegetables, whole grains, and foods low in saturated fat. I believe it is important for people to understand where these recommendations come from and the research studies that support them.

The public has many misconceptions about the role of diet in protecting against disease. Almost on a weekly basis there is at least one article appearing in a newspaper or on television dealing with nutrition. The public has been overwhelmed with the results of dozens of studies often in disagreement with one another. I have taken this opportunity to clarify these misconceptions by giving the reader the current valid scientific knowledge on the role of diet in promoting and preventing cancer, including the strengths and limitations of different types of studies. I hope that from the information included here, you can learn how to evaluate the studies that are reported and understand how they apply to your everyday food choices and reduce your own risk of cancer.

—Susan Oliveria, Sc.D., M.P.H.

1

The Science Behind Diet and Cancer

ANCER IS A DEVASTATING DISEASE, responsible for shortening lives and throwing families into crisis. Many people think it can't happen to them, but most of us know at least one family member or friend who has cancer. It is a very real disease that can afflict each and every one of us, although there are some people who are more susceptible than others because of lifestyle or heredity.

On the positive side, however, we can do something about reducing our risk for developing cancer even though there is no "magic bullet" to prevent or cure the disease. Believe it or not, the power to decrease our chances of getting cancer is at our fingertips—knowledge is this power. Information is readily available so that we can all learn what to do on a day-to-day basis to help prevent cancer. And we know diet is key to helping fight cancer; in fact, about 30 percent of all cancer deaths can be attributed to a poor diet. This might not sound new to many of us who have seen on television or read in the newspaper that certain aspects of our diet can protect us against cancer. The media conveys this information to us daily in the form of "headlines" and "sound bites." But we are also bombarded by conflicting studies and misinformation.

What should we believe, and, more important, what should we eat? What does a study really mean to you, and when should you make a change in your diet based on scientific findings? We begin by showing you how to understand the results you hear about each day and make the most of them to reduce your risk of developing cancer. Understanding the role of diet in cancer prevention is the first step toward making a change. We will then show you how to make those changes while enjoying a diet that is healthy, fun, and tasty with the help of professional chefs who have created a vast array of exciting and delicious recipes that are simple enough for almost anyone to prepare.

What Is Cancer?

Cancer is a proliferation of cells that grow uncontrolled and may eventually metastasize and spread, invading other major organs in the body. This multistaged process called *carcinogenesis* begins with the "initiation" of cancer cells. Initiation is then followed by "promotion," during which initiated cells are stimulated to grow by causal factors and they further progress. The entire process (initiation, promotion, and, finally, detection of cancer) takes from at least ten to thirty years.

Initiation of a cancer cell may occur through exposure to carcinogenic (cancer-causing) substances in our environment or may occur spontaneously. These substances have the potential to damage the cell's makeup and cause a genetic malfunction. If the process stops at this point, there is probably little danger of cancer developing. However, if these initiated cells are exposed to cancer "promoters," stimulation will occur, leading to uncontrolled growth and ultimately cancer. It is important to remember that it usually takes continued exposure to both initiators and promoters over a relatively long time for cancer to occur. Some carcinogenic substances have the ability to act as both initiators and promoters.

Since cancers take time to develop, aging (midlife and older) is probably the strongest factor increasing a person's cancer risk. This is particularly important for the U.S. population, where the average life expectancy has risen consistently over time. As the population ages, we might expect to see an increase in the total number of cancers simply due to longevity.

Cancer causes a significant amount of disease and mortality. It is the second-leading cause of death after cardiovascular disease in the United States. More than *2 million new cases of cancer will be diagnosed and approximately 560,000 people will die of cancer in 2004.* It is important to identify risk factors that can be modified to help prevent cancer.

Carcinogenic Process

The carcinogenic process follows essentially this path:

Exposure to carcinogens → Initiation of tumor → Tumor promotion → Progression → Precancerous cells → Malignant tumor → Metastasis

Here are some examples of carcinogens and promoters:

CARCINOGENS	PROMOTERS
air pollution	alcohol
chemicals	cigarette smoke
cigarette smoke	excess caloric intake
radiation	hormones
ultraviolet radiation (sunlight)	pollutants (like asbestos)
viruses	

Why Study Diet?

Although scientists have been able to identify both genetic and environmental factors as causes of cancer, we still have much to learn. Genetic factors are those traits that are determined by your genes or heredity. Environmental factors are all the things we are exposed to on a daily basis, including the air we breathe, the water we drink, the food we eat, and the lifestyles we choose. Many people believe that heredity plays a major role in causing most cancers. However, a major scientific report by the Office of Technology and Assessment of the U.S. Congress published in 1981 suggested that cancer is an avoidable disease and up to 80 percent of cancers can be attributed to environmental factors. These scientists estimated that 10 to 70 percent of all cancer was caused by diet. Since then these estimates have been refined, and we now believe that *diet contributes to 20 to 40 percent of all cancer*. Because some forms of cancer can be attributed to both genes and environment, diet may be especially important in individuals who have a family member with cancer.

The role of diet in cancer prevention has been the focus of intense interest, with hundreds of studies showing a link between diet and cancer. Initially diet was implicated as a cause of cancer based on observations that cancer rates varied among countries and that diets varied from country to country. Studies of migrants showed that people who moved to another country actually acquired some of the cancer rates of their new host country. For instance, a more-than-fivefold variation exists in breast cancer rates around the world. It has been shown that women who migrate from countries with a low incidence of breast cancer, such as Japan, to countries with a high incidence of breast cancer, such as the United States, acquire the higher rates of their new country. These observations implicated diet and other environmental factors as possible causes of breast cancer and implied that genetic factors were of lesser importance. (If inherited factors were solely responsible for breast cancer, we would not expect the rates to change so dramatically once women moved to a new country.) These studies also gave investigators hints as to the amount of time it takes for cancer to develop.

Studies of diet and cancer have been conducted in both animals and humans. Animal experiments are done in controlled situations where the investigator controls the animal's intake of the dietary factor of interest. Studies such as these often serve as the basis for studies in humans. Because animals are physiologically different from humans and because they are usually fed extremely high amounts of the dietary factor of interest, the relevance of these findings to people can be questionable. *Results of animal experiments do not necessarily apply to humans.*

Epidemiologic studies are conducted in large groups of people and seek to describe how much cancer exists as well as the causes or risk factors for specific cancers. *The goal of an epidemiologic study is to try to show a common factor in those people who have cancer and relate this to the biological understanding of how this factor might cause cancer.*

Epidemiologists calculate the risk of disease in those who are exposed to a certain factor as compared to those who are not exposed. These "risks" are often referred to as the "odds" of developing disease. They are a measure of the strength of the relationship between the factor and disease and of how important the factor is in causing or preventing disease. Examples of epidemiologic studies that had important public health impact on cancer prevention were those that showed a link between cigarette smoking and lung cancer. The risk (or odds) of lung cancer in smokers is about tenfold that of nonsmokers.

Despite the fact that we often hear in the news that a certain factor "causes" cancer, epidemiologic studies actually measure risk. Causation is difficult to prove, and the results of epidemiologic research cannot be used to predict that a particular person will or will not develop cancer. It is generally accepted that smoking causes lung cancer, but we all have heard of the person who smokes and lives to be a hundred years old! From a scientific standpoint it is difficult to say in every situation that if a person smokes he or she will get cancer. Thus epidemiologists will refer to a factor as increasing or decreasing risk and usually avoid the term *cause*.

Diet has been the focus of numerous research studies because so much preliminary evidence has revealed a link between nutritional factors and cancer. But it is even more complicated for epidemiologists to look at nutritional factors than at factors like smoking, because the relationship of diet with cancer is not as strong or clear-cut as the smoking-cancer relationship. Studying the relationship between dietary intake and cancer is difficult because it is hard to measure diet: we all eat differently, and our diets vary greatly from day to day. Our ability to remember what we eat is limited, and it is difficult to pinpoint what time period during our lifetime is important in influencing cancer development. Should scientists be interested in the diet consumed as a child, an adolescent, or an adult? Even if the time period of interest is during the adult years, is it the food we ate yesterday or five years ago that is important? We can speculate that the diet followed many years before a cancer diagnosis or the food eaten over many years is most significant. Various dietary factors may act during different time periods to increase or decrease cancer risk.

To further complicate the research, the total calories consumed and the amount of energy expended in physical activity can affect the results. Other lifestyle factors may be related to nutrition and the development of cancer as well. As an example, smokers often have a poor diet, and both smoking and diet are related to specific cancers. What, then, caused the cancer, the smoking or the poor diet? Recent developments in statistical methods and computing techniques have made it possible to adjust or control for these potential "confounding factors." In the above example, these statistical methods would allow us to study the effect of diet on cancer while controlling or adjusting for smoking. Thus, the effects of smoking on the cancer of interest would be statistically removed.

When, then, should a person make a lifestyle or behavior change based on research findings? We usually hear about the results of studies through the media: television, newspapers, magazines, or radio. When you see or hear these reports, be sure to understand who is being interviewed. Is it the author of the study? Try to balance the information by taking into consideration comments about the study reported by scientists or experts other than the authors. The media publicize a study when the findings are newsworthy and unusual. Avoid the news "headlines" and read or listen to the details, which will generally give a more fair description of the study results.

Most media reports are based on studies that have been published in major medical journals that have undergone peer review. This is a process whereby a scientist's research is scrutinized by other professionals in the relevant field of study and then a decision is made to publish or not based on the merits of the work. In most instances these news reports should be interpreted cautiously because the results are preliminary. *No definitive conclusion should be made based on a single study; instead the totality of the evidence is most important: what is the general consensus or conclusion based on the results of all the studies published about a particular topic?* Be careful of reports about anecdotal findings, where one person or a few people report their personal experiences. You should wait until medical experts reach a consensus.

Obtaining medical information, particularly with respect to diet, can be confusing and contradictory. Look at the big picture. For instance, many cancers can be attributed directly to poor diet, smoking, and obesity, while pesticides, medical x-rays, and food additives account for an extremely small amount of cancer. Some reliable sources of health information include the National Cancer Institute, American Cancer Society, Centers for Disease Control, and National Institutes of Health. These agencies serve the public interest. There are also health newsletters and books published by medical institutions that can be valuable resources for medical information. For a listing of medical, health, and nutrition information resources, see the Appendix.

Overview of Diet and Cancer

Scientists have attempted to assess the connection between cancer and many different aspects of diet, including foods such as fruits and vegetables, nutrients in foods such as fat, and other substances such as phytochemicals. As mentioned earlier, it is currently estimated that diet is responsible for 20 to 40 percent of all cancers. Fruit and vegetable consumption consistently has been shown to have a beneficial effect on cancer. High red meat consumption has been shown to increase the risk of developing colon cancer, while saturated fat from animal sources has been linked to prostate cancer. High intake of salty foods and cured foods probably causes stomach cancer, although in the United States this does not account for much cancer because stomach cancer is rare. It is also thought that excess calories early in life increase the risk of breast cancer, although the evidence is not conclusive.

Lifestyle factors related to nutrition, such as alcohol consumption, obesity, and physical activity, are also linked to cancer. Physical activity appears to protect against colon cancer and may be helpful for decreasing the risk of breast and prostate cancer. Obesity has been linked to many cancers, including endometrial, breast, kidney, colon, and ovarian. Alcohol consumption has been linked strongly to cancers of the digestive tract (oral cavity and esophagus) and liver. Also, tobacco consumption is most notably linked with cancers of the lung and oral cavity.

The process of carcinogenesis takes at least ten to thirty years, beginning with initiation of cancer cells, followed by promotion of these existing cells. Diet probably is important during the initiation phase, when certain foods or nutrients may serve to increase detoxifying enzymes that help stop the initial stimulation and growth of the cancer cells. At the same time, certain nutrients and foods may serve as promoters for already initiated cancer cells.

Fruits and Vegetables

Fruits and vegetables protect against cancer!

More than two hundred studies have shown that people who consume a diet high in fruits and vegetables reduce their risk of cancer, specifically cancer of the esophagus, stomach, mouth, lung, colon, rectum, larynx, and cervix. The evidence is strong, and there is a consensus in the scientific and medical community that fruits and vegetables protect against these cancers. Fruits and vegetables have also been shown to provide some protection against breast, bladder, pancreatic, endometrial, and kidney cancer and may have an effect on prostate and ovarian cancer, although the evidence is not as conclusive. *Studies have shown that people in the twenty-fifth percentile for consumption of fruits and vegetables are at twice the risk of cancer of those in the seventy-fifth percentile.*

Fruits and vegetables contain vitamins, minerals, and other nutrients, including vitamins A, C, and E, folic acid, and fiber. They also contain phytochemicals, naturally occurring substances found in plants that are thought to protect against cancer, including allium compounds, indoles, plant polyphenols, and carotenoids, as well as many others. It has been suggested that the vitamins, minerals, fiber, and phytochemicals found in fruits and vegetables have anticarcinogenic properties and help to ward off cancer (acting as antioxidants, detoxifiers, and blocking agents). Other anticancer functions include repairing damaged cells, inhibiting tumor formation, decreasing cell proliferation, and increasing immune activity.

Scientists are only beginning to explore the role of these phytochemicals. It is not possible at this time to measure the amount of most phytochemicals that people eat because we cannot isolate and quantify these substances in foods. Thus it is difficult to study the link between a particular phytochemical and cancer. We must rely on results from studies assessing the relationship between fruit and vegetable consumption and cancer risk. Furthermore, fruits and vegetables contain many substances, and it is probably not one nutrient or chemical that protects against cancer but a combination of these.

The beneficial effect of fruit and vegetable consumption on overall health is not limited to cancer. A favorable effect has been observed for other chronic diseases, including heart disease, cataracts, diabetes, diverticular disease, and stroke. Fruits and vegetables are also naturally low in calories and may be important in maintaining ideal body weight and controlling obesity.

Recent analyses have shown that Seventh-Day Adventists, who practice vegetarianism, have reduced rates of prostate and colorectal cancer as compared to the general U.S. population. It has been reported that vegetarians have lower overall rates of cancer than nonvegetarians, but the extent to which this can be attributed to diet is not clear. Individuals who adhere to a plant-based diet usually have other associated healthy behaviors (generally they do not smoke or drink) that contribute to this reduced risk of cancer. Their diets usually consist of adequate fruits, vegetables, fiber, and calcium and are generally low in total and saturated fat. Obesity is a risk factor for many cancers, and vegetarians tend to have weights that are within recommended guidelines; this may also explain their decreased risk of cancer. Some studies suggest that vegetarian women may be at decreased risk of breast cancer, although this remains to be confirmed.

Despite the healthful properties of fruits and vegetables, some consumers worry that they may contain "chemicals," such as nitrates and pesticides. *Nitrates* are chemicals that occur naturally in fruits and vegetables, as compared to *nitrites*, which are added to preserved meats and pickled vegetables to inhibit growth of microorganisms. Nitrates can be changed to nitrites with the help of bacteria present in the mouth or stomach. These nitrites can then undergo a process called *nitrosation* to form N-nitroso compounds. These N-nitroso compounds are carcinogenic in animals and presumably have adverse effects in humans.

nitrates → nitrites → N-nitroso compounds (nitrosamines)

It would seem reasonable to conclude that fruits and vegetables containing nitrates might promote cancer because of the potential for conversion to N-nitroso compounds. *However, the evidence does not support the assumption that nitrates found in fruits and vegetables are a cause of cancer. In fact, there is a strong, consistent, beneficial effect of fruits and vegetables on the risk of stomach, esophageal, and oral cancer.* This protective result is probably related to the presence of high levels of vitamins C and E, which help reduce the formation of N-nitroso compounds.

Pesticide levels in fruits and vegetables have been the concern of many advocacy groups seeking to limit our environmental exposure. Most pesticides are naturally occurring, produced by plants themselves as a defense mechanism, and present little danger to our food supply. Synthetic (man-made) pesticides used in coloring or preservation have not been shown to cause cancer. However, limiting exposure to man-made pesticides can be done by thoroughly washing produce or buying organically grown products. It should be noted that there is no proven beneficial effect of these organic products on cancer risk.

There is overwhelming evidence to support a recommendation for increased consumption of fruits and vegetables. Americans do not eat the suggested five to nine servings of fruits and vegetables daily. The average daily intake of fruits and vegetables is currently approximately four servings, and Americans do not choose from a sufficiently wide range of fruit and vegetable options. In 2000, only 23 percent of American adults consumed five or more servings of fruits and vegetables daily. From a public health standpoint, implementing this change would have a huge impact on decreasing cancer.

Protein

Foods high in animal protein include meat, poultry, eggs, and dairy products. The effects of animal protein (especially that obtained from red meat) on the likelihood of developing cancer have been studied extensively. The results have indicated that people who eat a diet high in animal protein derived from red meat may have an increased risk of colorectal, pancreatic, and prostate cancer. There is also some evidence to suggest that endometrial cancer may be associated with consumption of animal protein.

A possible explanation for this increased risk is that diets high in animal protein are also high in saturated fat (which is definitely associated with increased risk of cardiovascular disease) and/or that carcinogens (heterocyclic amines) may be created during the meat-cooking process (particularly frying or grilling until well done). However, other factors associated with a high-meat-fat diet may also be implicated, such as low fiber and antioxidant intake and high intake of cholesterol. It is difficult to separate these effects when studying the association between meat consumption and cancer risk.

While it appears that neither animal nor plant protein on its own is clearly associated with cancer, protein from plant sources is eaten along with the vitamins, minerals, fiber, and phytochemicals that make a plant-based diet very healthy. Also fish, an excellent source of protein, has omega-3 fatty acids shown to be important in many aspects of health, including prevention of cardiovascular disease.

Fat

Studies have indicated that people who eat a large amount of saturated fat derived from animal products may have an increased likelihood of developing certain cancers, including colorectal and prostate. Endometrial, kidney, and lung cancer are also possibly linked to a high saturated fat intake. Fat might induce certain cancers by affecting hormone levels and synthesis, increasing the body's exposure to bile acids, or promoting tumor growth. The breakdown of fat may produce free radicals, which are highly unstable molecules with the potential to cause cell damage. Also, high saturated fat intake may be a marker for low fiber, fruit, and vegetable consumption that could be more important in influencing cancer risk than fat.

It has been suggested that increased total fat intake is a cause of breast cancer, but this remains controversial. Initially, both animal and human studies supported an adverse effect of fat intake on breast cancer. Since then studies generally have been less supportive, and overall it appears that diets high in fat during midlife are not associated with breast cancer risk. The studies did not measure diet during puberty or adolescence, which may be the critical time period (because of the growth and development of breast tissue). Furthermore, these studies did not look at women with very low intakes of fat (less than 15 percent of daily calories), which may provide some benefit. Whether very-low-fat diets have a beneficial effect on breast cancer risk remains to be seen. But since a high intake of saturated fat can increase the risk for other cancers as well as heart disease, it is prudent to limit our consumption.

A few epidemiologic studies suggest that olive oil, one type of fat, may be beneficial in reducing breast cancer risk. This is a promising area of research, and work is ongoing. Omega-3 fatty acids (sometimes called *marine* or *fish oils*) have also been of interest because of the observation that some cancer rates are lower in populations where the diet is composed of a high proportion of these fatty acids, such as the Eskimos in Alaska and Greenland and the Japanese. Diets that contain a high proportion of these omega-3 fatty acids as compared to other fatty acids have been shown to slow or prevent the growth of tumors, particularly mammary and colon tumors in animals, possibly by inactivating hormones that promote certain cancers.

Fiber

Fiber has been identified as a potential preventive for colorectal, pancreatic, breast, oral cavity, and stomach cancer, but no firm consensus on this topic has been reached. Fiber may protect against colorectal cancer by increasing fecal bulk and normalizing the bowel function. Hypothetically this would mean that potential cancer-causing agents have less contact with the lining of the intestines. Fiber may also decrease or dilute the bile acids in the fecal matter that are thought to increase cell proliferation. Perhaps most important, fiber may be a marker for fruit and vegetable consumption (because fruits and vegetables are high in fiber), and the evidence for a protective effect against cancer risk is much stronger for fruits and vegetables than for fiber. Additionally, consuming healthy foods rich in fiber can provide a feeling of fullness and thereby promote the maintenance or achievement of healthy weight. Maintaining a healthy weight has been observed to be important in the prevention of colorectal, breast, endometrial, kidney, esophageal, oral, and pancreatic cancer, as well as in the avoidance of many other chronic conditions, including diabetes and cardiovascular disease.

Vitamins and Minerals

Vitamins and minerals are nutrients that are present in food but can also be obtained from supplements (pills and other forms). Since studies have consistently found that fruits and vegetables have a beneficial effect on cancer risk, it's reasonable to think that the vitamins and minerals contained in fruits and vegetables might protect against cancer. Research has investigated the role of particular vitamins and minerals and found that, while vitamins and minerals do not definitively prevent cancer, they have anticancer properties for certain cancers.

VITAMINS, MINERALS, AND CANCER

Antioxidants: Vitamins A, C, E, and Selenium

Carotenoids. Overall, a high intake of carotenoids (those that are vitamin A precursors and include beta-carotene) has been linked to a decreased risk of many cancers, including stomach, breast, colon, pancreatic, prostate, cervical, and lung.

Vitamin A (Preformed Retinol). Vitamin A has been shown to be modestly beneficial for breast cancer, although not definitively.

continued →

VITAMINS, MINERALS, AND CANCER (CONTINUED)

Vitamin C. Vitamin C has been reported to protect against esophageal, oral, stomach, laryngeal, cervical, and pancreatic cancer in people who have a high intake of this antioxidant vitamin, and some studies have suggsted that lung, breast, and colorectal cancer may also be reduced.

Vitamin E. Some forms of oral cancer and possibly lung cancer may be decreased if a diet high in vitamin E–rich foods is consumed. Some studies have suggested a beneficial effect on colon, prostate, stomach, cervical, laryngeal, kidney, and skin cancer.

Selenium. Some studies assessing the relationship between selenium intake and cancer have suggested a beneficial effect on colorectal, prostate, and lung cancer and possibly stomach, esophageal, and breast cancer.

Other Vitamins and Minerals

Calcium and Vitamin D. A link between increased intake of calcium and vitamin D and reduced risk of colon cancer has been proposed, although the evidence is not strong at this time. Additionally, there is some concern about a potentially increased risk of prostate cancer among men who consume a lot of dairy products or take calcium supplements.

Folic Acid (Folate). Folic acid appears beneficial in reducing the risk of both breast and colon cancer and possibly cervical and lung.

Magnesium. Magnesium deficiency may impair immunity or promote the cancer process. Further research is necessary, but initial studies have suggested a link between a low intake of magnesium and kidney cancer.

Iron. Recently there has been speculation that too much iron may be linked to cancer, especially in people who have iron absorption defects (called *iron overload* or *hemochromatosis*). Individuals with this condition may absorb up to two times more iron from food and supplements than those without this defect and store it in major organs like the liver, pancreas, heart, and brain. However, the evidence of a link between iron and cancer from animal experiment studies and human studies has been inconclusive.

Antioxidants, Free Radicals, and Cancer

Antioxidants act as scavengers of "free radicals," by-products of normal metabolism, before they can cause harm to the body. Free radicals are missing an electron (a negatively charged particle) from their chemical structure and are thus highly unstable, leaving them vulnerable to oxidation, the process whereby they take electrons and transfer them, leaving a new free radical. This is damaging to the body's cells and will continue as a chain reaction unless an enzyme or free-radical scavenger (antioxidant) stops the process.

If left unchecked, free radicals can cause oxidative damage: genetic damage, uncontrolled cell growth and cancer, heart disease and other degenerative diseases, and aging. Exposure to certain environmental factors, including radiation, ultraviolet light, alcohol, cigarette and marijuana smoke, air pollutants, smog, pesticides, herbicides, drugs, fried foods, inflammation, and very strenuous physical activity (such as marathon running), can promote the production of these free radicals. However, normal metabolism is responsible for most free-radical production.

The body has built-in defense mechanisms against this oxidation process, including enzymes and antioxidants that search for these unstable free radicals. It is thought that foods rich in vitamins A, C, and E, carotenoids, and phytochemicals work together as antioxidant free-radical scavengers.

Although many studies suggest that vitamins protect against certain forms of cancer, not all studies have been consistent in showing a beneficial effect. Nevertheless, because we know that diets high in vitamin- and mineral-rich fruits and vegetables definitely protect against many forms of cancer, it is prudent for all of us to eat the recommended five to nine servings of fruits and vegetables each day.

PROPOSED ANTICANCER FUNCTIONS OF SELECTED VITAMINS AND MINERALS

Carotenoids (Including Beta-Carotene)

Proposed anticancer functions: antioxidants; metabolized to vitamin A, which helps cell differentiation (cancer cells are characterized by lack of differentiation); may inhibit cell proliferation

Other functions: improves immune response; lowers cholesterol levels; may reduce incidence of heart disease, stroke, inflammatory disorders, and cataracts

Vitamin A (Preformed Retinol)

Proposed anticancer functions: plays a role in regulating cell differentiation; may prevent malignant transformation of cells; may enhance immune function

continued →

PROPOSED ANTICANCER FUNCTIONS OF SELECTED VITAMINS AND MINERALS (CONTINUED)

Vitamin C
Proposed anticancer functions: antioxidant; inhibits the formation of N-nitroso compounds (carcinogens implicated in stomach cancer); enhances immune system; plays a role in the synthesis of connective tissue proteins; may be important in inhibiting tumor growth and promoting cell differentiation
Other functions: may protect against atherosclerosis by interfering with oxidation of LDL (bad) cholesterol; may protect against cataracts

Vitamin E
Proposed anticancer functions: antioxidant; inhibits formation of N-nitroso compounds (carcinogens implicated in stomach cancer); modulates immune function to work against tumors; protects cells from malignant transformation
Other functions: may protect against heart disease (atherosclerosis) and cataracts

Selenium
Proposed anticancer functions: enhances antioxidant activity of vitamin E; increases immune response; produces enzymes that protect against oxidative damage; suppresses cell proliferation; may alter metabolism of carcinogens so they produce less toxic substances

Calcium
Proposed anticancer functions: regulates cell function (reduces proliferation and enhances differentiation of cells); may bind with bile acids and fatty acids to decrease the exposure of the colon to carcinogens and reduce the risk of colon cancer; may increase immune response
Other functions: reduces risk of osteoporosis

Vitamin D
Proposed anticancer functions: may retard formation or progression of tumors
Other functions: reduces risk of osteoporosis

Folic Acid (Folate)
Proposed anticancer functions: essential for DNA synthesis (low levels may cause errors in DNA synthesis and lead to genetic defects); may enhance immunity
Other functions: protects against heart disease and birth defects

Magnesium
Proposed anticancer functions: enhances immunity; competes with cancer-causing agents; a deficiency may trigger and/or promote the cancer process

Vitamin and Mineral Supplements

Studies that have looked specifically at vitamin and mineral supplements (as opposed to vitamins from food sources) have shown a decreased risk of some cancers: individuals who take vitamin E supplements may be at reduced risk of prostate cancer (and possibly oral and colon cancer); vitamin A supplementation has been reported to protect against breast and colon cancer; and vitamin C supplementation may decrease the risk of breast, colon, and bladder cancer. Selenium supplementation appears to reduce the risk of lung, prostate, and colorectal cancer, and it has been reported that folic acid supplementation can reduce the risk of colorectal and breast cancer. However, research conducted to date does not support a *strong* effect of vitamin and mineral *supplements* per se on cancer risk. Before vitamin supplementation is recommended for preventing cancer, its role in cancer prevention needs more research. One possible exception: vitamin supplementation may have a positive effect in people from countries that have high rates of stomach and esophageal cancer. Studies of vitamin supplementation (vitamin A, zinc, riboflavin, beta-carotene, vitamin E, and selenium) have been conducted in China, where the rate of both esophageal and stomach cancer is high. The results indicate that vitamin A, zinc, and riboflavin taken together reduce the risk of esophageal cancer, whereas beta-carotene, vitamin E, and selenium may be beneficial for stomach cancer.

The idea of taking a vitamin supplement to compensate for deficiencies in their diet appeals to many people. Although the chemical structure of a particular vitamin supplement is the same as that of the vitamin found in food sources, absorption and utilization by the body may be different. It is known that diets rich in foods containing certain vitamins and minerals help to prevent cancer; however, these foods may contain other substances, such as phytochemicals, that work in conjunction with vitamins and minerals to confer benefit.

In July of 2003 the U.S. Preventive Services Task Force stated that there is not enough evidence yet either to recommend or to caution against the use of vitamin supplementation as a means of reducing risk for heart disease and cancer. Nonetheless, nutrition and health experts do recommend taking a multivitamin as a complement to a healthy diet, the potential benefit outweighing any chance of harm as long as the doses of multivitamin supplements are moderate.

Other Dietary Factors

There has been much speculation about the role of alcohol, caffeine, salt, and "charcoal grilling" in causing cancer. What part do they play in our diet, and how do they increase or decrease our risk of cancer?

Alcohol

Studies have shown consistently that alcohol is the cause of many cancers, including breast, colorectal, esophageal, oral cavity, laryngeal, and liver. There have also been studies linking alcohol consumption to pancreatic cancer. It appears that the risk of cancer depends on the amount of alcohol consumed; that is, as alcohol intake rises, so does risk of cancer. With respect to breast cancer, as little as one drink per day increases the risk by 10 to 15 percent. Women who consume two drinks per day increase their risk by 20 to 25 percent.

It is speculated that alcohol acts as a tumor promoter. The ethanol contained in alcoholic beverages appears to be the promoting agent and may alter the liver's ability to metabolize carcinogens. Alcohol consumption is also associated with inadequate nourishment in moderate and heavy drinkers, which may indicate a deficient supply of the antioxidant vitamins C, E, and beta-carotene. Stores of folic acid and vitamins A, C, and E (which have cancer-fighting properties) may be depleted by alcohol consumption. Recent evidence shows that the increased risk of both breast and colon cancer that is associated with alcohol appears most frequently among those who do not consume the recommended amount of folic acid.

It has been shown that alcohol interacts with smoking to increase cancers of the oral cavity, larynx, and esophagus. In one large study of oral cavity cancer, a thirty-six-fold increased risk was observed in people who were both heavy drinkers and smokers.

Alcohol is responsible for an estimated 3 percent of cancer deaths. Reduction or elimination of alcohol clearly reduces the risk of developing many cancers. Moderate drinking is defined as about two drinks a day for men and one drink a day for women. A beneficial effect of moderate alcohol consumption on coronary heart disease has been observed, but this needs to be balanced with the associated increased risk of cancer.

Caffeine

Is caffeine really bad for you? Caffeine is a natural ingredient contained in coffee, tea, soft drinks, cocoa, and some medications. Considered a drug with biochemical and physiological effects, it can cause heart palpitations and raise blood pressure and cholesterol levels (usually at high levels of consumption) in some people. In the past, caffeine (in coffee) has been implicated as a cause of cancer, heart attacks, infertility, miscarriages, osteoporosis, and glaucoma. Because of its widespread consumption, the relationship between caffeine and disease has been studied extensively.

There is little evidence that caffeine or coffee in moderation causes heart attacks. Research into the relationship between coffee consumption (with or without caffeine) and breast, ovarian, bladder, pancreatic, rectal, and colon cancer has shown that coffee does not cause these cancers either. *The World Health Organization and the American Cancer Society both support the evidence that indicates no association between caffeine (or coffee) and cancer.* Two cups of coffee a day is generally acceptable and presents little health hazard for most people, although four to five cups a day may be a problem.

Furthermore, the totality of research studies does not show that caffeine is a risk factor for decreased fertility, birth defects, or glaucoma. Some studies have shown that caffeine intake may be a risk factor for osteoporosis, because it promotes excretion of calcium from the body, although the studies are conflicting. It appears that adequate calcium intake may balance any negative effect of caffeine consumption on osteoporosis.

Salt

Food additives have been accused of contributing to cancer, but in fact the research has not shown this to be true for any additive other than salt. Salted, smoked, and cured foods can increase the risk of developing some forms of cancer. A high intake of salted foods, including smoked and cured products, accounts for much of the stomach cancer observed throughout the world, especially in Asia. In the United States, stomach cancer is rare, probably because these foods are not a mainstay of our diet. Salted foods often contain nitrites, which can undergo nitrosation during the cooking process and produce N-nitroso compounds. These compounds are potent toxins and animal carcinogens. Also, salted Chinese-style fish, which is rarely consumed by Americans, has been linked to nasopharyngeal cancer in children. It is estimated that salt contributes to 1 percent of total cancer mortality. While no evidence suggests that salt used in flavoring foods affects cancer risk, salt is related to high blood pressure, so its use should be limited.

Cooking Process

The ordinary process of cooking can promote the formation of chemical compounds such as heterocyclic amines (from heating amino acids or proteins), polycyclic hydrocarbons (from charring meat), and nitrosamines (from gas cooking or barbecuing). The formation of these compounds depends on the type of food, cooking method (frying, broiling, or barbecuing), time, and temperature (above 100 degrees centigrade or 212 degrees Fahrenheit). So far studies have not directly measured the intake of these chemical compounds and are not conclusive, but it is reasonable to limit our intake because it is known that these compounds are cancer-causing. However, levels of intake shown to be carcinogenic in animals are many times higher than those consumed by people. The effects of moderate intakes are unclear, and research is ongoing.

In this chapter we have outlined what you need to know to understand how diet plays a crucial role in preventing cancer. With this information you can begin to make those changes that will ultimately lead to reducing your cancer risk. Now that you have the knowledge, you need to acquire the right tools to be successful. The next chapter tells you how to do just that.

2

Lowering Your Risk of Cancer Through Diet

IT IS IMPORTANT TO VIEW YOUR EATING HABITS as a lifetime commitment to good health, rather than a temporary inconvenience to endure until a short-term goal is reached. The word *diet* has too many negative, unpleasant connotations and is usually associated with bland meals, deprivation, hunger, and guilt. You don't have to starve to eat right, nor do you need to deprive yourself of many of your favorite foods. An occasional splurge will not ruin you as long as the exception does not become the rule. Extremes, either very high or very low, in certain nutrients such as calories, fat, protein, or carbohydrates are not the answer for a lifetime of good health, appropriate weight, and overall well-being. The key is moderation! After wading through all the gimmicks and "quick fixes," we will demonstrate that the real "secret" to healthy eating is to plan long-term goals based on variety, balance, and moderation—goals that you can both meet and maintain. It is essential to develop an eating plan that is right for you and your lifestyle.

Strang Cancer Prevention Center Guidelines for Reducing Your Risk of Cancer

These suggestions are adapted from the American Cancer Society Dietary Guidelines:

1. **Choose most foods from plant sources.** Eat five or more servings of fruits and vegetables each day. This will ensure that your diet is rich in vitamins A and C, as well as minerals and phytochemicals that may reduce the risk of cancer. Eat several servings from other plant sources, such as minimally processed whole-grain breads, cereals, and legumes (beans, peas, and lentils). If you follow these suggestions, your fiber intake will likely be within the recommended range of 25 to 35 grams per day.

2. **Moderate your intake of high-fat foods, particularly from animal and highly processed sources.** Limit meats, especially high-fat meats, such as some cuts of beef and pork. Eat moderate portions of other lean animal protein sources, such as chicken, fish, and low-fat dairy products. Processed foods often contain trans fats, which are not linked to cancer but do increase total and LDL (bad) cholesterol and decrease HDL (good) cholesterol.

3. **Reduce your intake of potentially carcinogenic (cancer-causing) substances.** Limit or eliminate the following from your diet:
   - smoked foods, which absorb some of the tars that arise from the smoking process and contain numerous carcinogens
   - nitrite-preserved foods, such as hot dogs, ham, and other processed meats. Nitrites can combine with proteins in your stomach to form cancer-promoting chemicals. Vitamin C–rich foods may help prevent this from occurring, so if you occasionally eat foods preserved with nitrites, be sure to consume a fruit or vegetable rich in vitamin C.
   - grilled foods (avoid charring)
   - salt-cured foods, such as bacon and many types of ham
   - alcoholic beverages. Regular alcohol consumption may promote certain cancers; heavy drinking is strongly linked to liver cancer. If you drink, it should be infrequently and in moderation.

4. **Be physically active; achieve and maintain a healthy weight.** Be moderately active for thirty minutes or more on most days.

5. **Eat a variety of foods each day.** Variety assures the intake of a spectrum of protective nutrients and phytochemicals.

6. **Moderate your sugar intake.** Although there is no evidence to support a link between sugar intake and cancer, limiting intake of sugar and other "empty calories" (calories without nutrients) leaves more room for foods rich in fiber, vitamins, minerals, and phytochemicals. High consumption of sugar-laden foods often results in excessive intake of calories and fat, making it difficult to maintain a healthy weight.

The first place to start making changes is with macronutrients, or energy (calorie)-yielding nutrients. Macronutrients include fat, carbohydrates, protein, and alcohol. The balance among them is an important factor in maintaining an appropriate weight and in preventing disease.

General Caloric Requirements

The following table gives the U.S. Department of Agriculture method of estimating your daily caloric needs: multiply your body weight (in pounds) by your corresponding level of activity.

	Sedentary	Moderately Active	Active
Males	16	20	30
Females	15	18	25

For example, if you are a 125-pound female who gets infrequent exercise (sedentary), you require approximately 1,875 calories daily (125 pounds $\times$ 15), which allows for a maximum fat intake of about 63 grams (based on a target of 30 percent of calories from fat; see Table 2.1 on page 24).

It should be noted that the actual number of calories needed to maintain a stable weight may vary among individuals by as much as 30 percent due to factors that influence metabolic rate, such as frame size, muscle mass, fitness level, decreased requirements with age, and genetic variations. If you weigh more than 30 pounds over your "ideal" body weight (see Figure 2.1 on page 22), use your ideal body weight to calculate your caloric needs.

Keeping tabs on your fat intake until it becomes second nature to you is an easier way to make healthy changes in your diet than making more complex calculations of caloric and nutrient contents. Initially, however, it is a good idea to get an approximation of your caloric intake (over the course of a few days) until you are confident that the fat allowance is indeed no more than 30 percent of your total calories. You can do this fairly simply by using recipes from this book, which give caloric values, by checking labels, or by consulting any handy calorie counter or nutrition software program. Consultation with a registered dietitian will provide the most accurate estimate of your calorie requirements.

BMI

Body mass index (BMI) is a method of determining fat or mass. BMI is calculated by dividing weight in kilograms by height in meters squared. It derives a single value that can be compared to standards established by scientists. Health researchers and practitioners are leaning increasingly toward BMI as a more reliable indicator of "ideal" body weight than height/weight charts. Keep in mind, however, that BMI, like other methods, can be influenced by muscle mass (a person with a high muscle density will yield a higher BMI, although his or her body fat may be quite low).

FIGURE 2.1 BMI (BODY MASS INDEX)

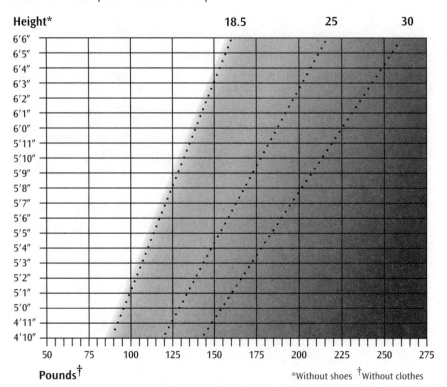

■ Healthy Weight BMI from 18.5 up to 25 refers to a healthy weight.

■ Overweight BMI from 25 up to 30 refers to overweight.

■ Obese BMI 30 or higher refers to obesity. Obese persons are also overweight.

Source: Report of the Dietary Guidelines Advisory Committee on the Dietary Guidelines for Americans, 2000, page 3.

The BMI ranges shown in Figure 2.1 are for adults. They are not exact ranges of healthy and unhealthy weights. However, they show that health risk increases at higher levels of overweight and obesity. Even within the healthy BMI range, weight gains can carry health risks for adults.

Here is how to use the chart. Find your weight on the bottom of the graph. Go straight up from that point until you come to the line that matches your height. Then find your weight group.

The Fat Facts

Americans have a love-hate affair with fat. It is one of the principal components of living cells, is essential in the diet, and certainly adds pleasure to eating; however, too much fat puts people at risk for significant health complications. In the 1990s fear of fat became a national obsession. Despite a decade of low-fat diets, Americans got fatter than ever, adding eight pounds to their average weight. During this period heart disease and diabetes rates soared, and they are still on the rise, especially in children. The popularity of high-protein diets brought dietary fats (any kind) back in fashion, but they have not dropped obesity rates, and the long-term health implications are not known. What is one to do?

To lower your risk of both heart disease and cancer, it is recommended that you limit your fat intake to 30 percent of your total calories, with the predominant amount coming from healthy plant sources. (Because individuals require different amounts of calories, fat intake is expressed as a percentage of caloric intake rather than as a certain number of grams of fat.) The guideline of 30 percent should not be used for individual foods but for your whole day or even week. If your average fat intake in a meal is 50 percent of calories, you can offset it by limiting two or more subsequent meals to 15 to 20 percent. In addition, you may have a day where your fat intake is at 50 percent of calories; you can come out even if you balance total fat intake for the next two days at 15 to 20 percent of calories. This amount allows for moderate portions of animal protein and limited amounts of added fat in cooking and seasoning of food and even an occasional rich dessert. It is also important to note that, for some people, underlying medical conditions warrant fat intakes lower or higher than 30 percent of total calories.

The best way to stay close to your fat-intake guideline is to assess your daily target for maximum amount of fat in grams. Once you know the number of grams of fat you can consume each day, reading labels and making decisions become much easier. To assess your daily fat intake:

1. Determine your daily calorie requirements (via the guidelines under "General Caloric Requirements").
2. Multiply your total calories by 0.30 (30 percent of total calories).
3. Since each gram of fat has 9 calories, divide the number you get in step 2 by 9.

   Example: *If you require 1,800 calories a day: 0.30 × 1,800 = 540 (fat calories). 540 ÷ 9 calories per gram = 60 grams of fat per day.*

If you don't want to do the math, refer to Table 2.1 after assessing your caloric requirements.

Table 2.1 Fat Gram Allowances

Daily Calorie Intake	Max. Daily Calories from Fat (at 25%)	Max. Fat Grams at 25% Calories Fat	Max. Daily Calories from Fat (at 30%)	Max. Fat Grams at 30% Calories Fat
1,100	275	31	330	37
1,200	300	33	360	40
1,300	325	36	389	43
1,400	350	39	420	47
1,500	375	42	450	50
1,600	400	44	480	53
1,700	425	47	510	57
1,800	450	50	540	60
1,900	475	53	570	63
2,000	500	56	600	67
2,100	525	58	630	70
2,200	550	61	660	73
2,300	575	64	690	77
2,400	600	67	720	80
2,500	625	69	750	83
2,600	650	72	780	87
2,700	675	75	810	90
2,800	700	78	840	93

To figure out the percentage of calories from fat in a meal, recipe, or food product:

1. Determine the number of grams of fat.
2. Multiply the grams of fat by 9 (every gram of fat has 9 calories)—this will provide the total calories from fat.
3. Divide this number by the total number of calories from the meal or food.
4. Multiply by 100, and you will have the percentage of calories from fat.

Example: *If a recipe contains 300 calories and 10 grams of fat: 10 grams fat × 9 calories per gram = 90 calories from fat. 90 fat calories ÷ 300 total calories = 0.30 × 100 = 30 percent calories from fat.*

Beware: fat grams (and their calories) add up quickly. A tablespoon of olive oil in a homemade salad dressing will cost you 14 grams and 119 calories; a small serving (4 ounces) of meat, fish, or poultry can be 10 to 15 grams; each teaspoon of butter, regular margarine, and other oils is another 5 grams. That's why it's important to moderate your intake of lean protein sources and added fats even when they are "healthy" fats.

The "Nutrition Facts" labels of commercial food products contain information on the fat content of particular foods in the "Total Fat" section that you can use to choose products that fit into your total fat allotment for the day. Be sure to adjust for the portion size you actually consume. See "Lowering Fat in Your Diet" later in this chapter for more information on keeping your fat intake on target without lots of gram counting.

Not All Fat Is Created Equal

Dietary fat is composed of two major types of fatty acids: saturated and unsaturated. Unsaturated fatty acids are further classified as either polyunsaturated or monounsaturated. Foods that contain fat usually have a combination of all three fatty acids, although they are generally classified by the predominant fatty acid. While keeping in mind the fact that all fats are high in calories and excess calories can lead to overweight—which is associated with cancer and many other health problems—the bottom line is that some fats are good for you. Saturated fats and trans fats are bad for your health, while—in moderation—monounsaturated and polyunsaturated fats are good for your health and enhance the quality of eating.

SATURATED FATS. Saturated fats are "saturated," or loaded, with the hydrogen atoms they carry. Make an effort to limit these fats. A diet high in saturated fat can lead to high blood cholesterol levels and may be associated with increased risk of certain types of cancer. Saturated fats are usually solid at room temperature and are the visible fats you can see in foods such as bacon. Although saturated fat comes in the highest ratios in foods of animal origin (beef, lamb, pork, veal, poultry, and full-fat dairy products), some vegetable-based products, such as coconut and palm oils (used in commercial baked goods) and solid vegetable shortenings, contain saturated fat. Coconut and palm oils, in fact, derive approximately 86 percent of their calories from saturated fat. While saturated fats raise total blood cholesterol levels more than dietary cholesterol does, they tend to raise both the "good" HDL and the "bad" LDL cholesterol.

CHOLESTEROL. Cholesterol is a waxy fatlike substance. Your body needs some cholesterol to help form cell walls and hormones. But too much cholesterol in your bloodstream can cause fatty deposits to build up on artery walls. This can lead to heart attacks and strokes.

Blood cholesterol comes from two sources. Your liver makes all the cholesterol your body needs. Blood cholesterol levels are also related to the foods you eat, particularly foods high in saturated fat. Surprisingly, the cholesterol found in food has less influence on blood cholesterol levels than does saturated fat. This type of cholesterol is called *dietary cholesterol* and it is found only in foods of animal origin, such as butter, dairy products, and meats. So it's not such a big deal when a food label says *cholesterol free* for a product such as peanut butter or vegetable oil, because these foods have always been cholesterol free. Don't be confused: cholesterol free does not mean fat free! Some plant foods that are high in saturated fat, such as coconut and palm oils, do not contain cholesterol.

Even though no relationship between dietary cholesterol and cancer has been established, you should limit your intake of foods that contain substantial amounts of cholesterol because they generally contain high levels of saturated fat, which has been associated with cancer.

TRANS FATS. Trans fats are produced by heating and "loading" vegetable oils (polyunsaturated fats) with hydrogen, a process referred to as *hydrogenation*. This makes them harder and more "shelf stable." Trans fats are found in commercially prepared baked goods, margarines, snack foods, and processed foods. Most commercially prepared fried foods, like doughnuts, french fries, and fried chicken, also contain a good deal of trans fat.

Trans fats are worse for cholesterol levels than saturated fats because they not only raise LDL (bad) cholesterol but also lower HDL (good) cholesterol.

Until recently there was no easy way for American consumers to determine how much artery-clogging trans fat was in their food. In 2003, however, the FDA announced regulations adding a new line to the nutrition labels found on commercial foods to show the amount of trans fat in every serving. Food companies need not comply until January 1, 2006, but many are conforming earlier to stay competitive in the marketplace. Additionally, many food companies and fast-food restaurants are eliminating trans fat from some of their most popular products. Avoid this type of fat by assuming any commercial deep-fried food or baked good contains them unless there is information to the contrary. In the case of store-bought goods, if the manufacturer has not yet listed trans fatty acids on the nutrient panel, check the ingredient list for partially hydrogenated oil (partially hydrogenated soybean and cottonseed oils are quite common, but other types may also be used).

UNSATURATED FATS. Olive oil is a type of unsaturated fat called *monounsaturated*. Olive oil is the predominant dietary fat source in Mediterranean countries like Greece, Italy, and Spain. The rate of breast cancer in these countries is lower than that of the United States (even though the overall total fat intake is about the same). A few epidemiologic studies suggest that olive oil may be beneficial in reducing breast cancer risk, but research in this area is continuing. It has been shown that monounsaturated fat (in place of saturated fat) has a positive effect on blood lipid (fat) levels. Monounsaturated fat reduces "bad" low-density lipoprotein (LDL) cholesterol and elevates the levels of "good" high-density lipoprotein (HDL) cholesterol, reducing the risk of heart disease.

Another type of unsaturated fat, polyunsaturated, is made up of omega-6s, found in vegetables, and omega-3s, which are most often present in fatty fish. Some plants have the potential to provide omega-3 fatty acids. The body can convert linolenic acid, a type of fat found in canola oil, flaxseeds, soybeans, walnuts, and some leafy green vegetables, into omega-3 fatty acids (see pages 29–30 for a comprehensive listing of omega-3 food sources). Moderate dietary intake of omega-3 fatty acids, found in substantial amounts in salmon, bluefish, swordfish, trout, tuna, and striped bass, may have a protective effect against heart disease and certain types of cancer.

Interest in omega-3 fatty acids has been based on the observation that some cancer rates are lower in populations where the diet is composed of a high proportion of these fatty acids. When compared to diets that contain omega-6 fatty acids from vegetable oils like corn and safflower, diets that contain a high proportion of omega-3 fatty acids have been shown to slow or prevent the growth of tumors, particularly mammary and colon tumors in animals, possibly by inactivating hormones that promote certain cancers. Other beneficial effects of omega-3 fatty acids include reduction of LDL cholesterol and triglyceride levels and lowering of blood pressure. They may also improve symptoms of inflammatory diseases like rheumatoid arthritis and ulcerative colitis, as well as immune function.

The omega-6s and their effect on cancer risk have also been a focus of research interest. It appears that certain polyunsaturated fats may actually increase the risk for some cancers; however, this has been shown mainly in animal studies, with little support from human data.

The relationship between omega-3 fatty acids and omega-6 fatty acids is competitive and interrelated. When dietary intake of one is out of proportion, the other can control important biochemical reactions in the body. Researchers believe that a one-to-one ratio of omega-3 to omega-6 may be important in the prevention of heart disease. The American diet contains about ten omega-6s to one omega-3. This disproportion may lead to the overproduction of hormones, which in turn can cause formation of blood clots, promote the buildup of plaque on artery walls, and disturb immune function. A healthy immune system is vital to warding off certain types of cancer. Here are some ways to increase your omega-3 intake.

- Include an omega-3-rich fish source in your diet two to three times per week.
- Sprinkle whole flaxseed on rolls, muffins, or breads before baking or add it to waffles, pancakes, muffins, or quick breads. For more information about flaxseed and its uses, contact the Flax Council of Canada: (800) 817-9894, or visit their website at flaxcouncil.ca.
- Substitute ground flax flour for up to 10 percent of the flour in baked goods. Because of its high fat content (omega-3s), cut the fat in the recipe by up to one-third by replacing the moisture with water, juice, or fruit puree.
- Use all oils sparingly and use olive, canola, flaxseed, soybean, and walnut oils more frequently than other vegetable oils.
- Limit omega-6-rich foods, such as salad dressings, margarine, and mayonnaise.

Avoid fish oil capsules unless prescribed by your physician. The most concentrated source of omega-3s, these supplements can cause overdose, which may lead to excessive bleeding, increased risk of hemorrhagic stroke, adverse drug interactions, and, in some instances, high cholesterol.

PROPOSED ANTICANCER FUNCTIONS OF OMEGA-3 FATTY ACIDS
Proposed anticancer functions: slows or prevents cancerous tumor growth; stimulates the immune system; inhibits cancer-promoting hormones
Other functions: lowers blood pressure; reduces serum triglycerides and low-density lipoprotein cholesterol; increases clotting times; alleviates symptoms of psoriasis, rheumatoid arthritis, and ulcerative colitis

Fatty Acid Food Sources

HIGH IN MONOUNSATURATED FATTY ACIDS

Best Sources

canola oil*	olives/olive oil

Good Sources

almonds/almond oil	lard†
avocados	margarine†
beef fat†	palm oil†
hazelnuts	peanuts/peanut oil

HIGH IN POLYUNSATURATED FATTY ACIDS

Omega-6s (Linoleic Acid)

corn oil	soybeans/soybean oil*
cottonseed oil	sunflower seeds/sunflower oil
safflower oil	walnuts/walnut oil*
sesame oil	

Omega-3s

Best Sources

anchovies	sablefish
Atlantic bluefish	salmon‡
catfish‡	sardines
herring	whitefish
mackerel	

Good Sources

pompano	striped bass‡
shark	swordfish
smelt	trout‡
squid	tuna

Moderate Sources

carp	ocean perch
cod	pollack
flounder	sea bass
grouper	shellfish: clams, oysters, mussels,
haddock	lobster, shrimp, scallops
mahimahi	snapper

Plant Sources of Omega-3s (Linolenic Acid)

canola oil
flaxseed/most flaxseed products (flour, bread)/flaxseed oil
leafy green vegetables (kale, spinach, Swiss chard)
soybeans/some soy products/soybean oil
walnuts/walnut oil

Some fats are undoubtedly better than others with respect to prevention of heart disease and cancer, but your total fat intake should be moderate. This will help keep you at an appropriate weight and will lower your risk for many chronic diseases, including heart disease and cancer. Does this mean the less fat you eat the healthier you will be? Not necessarily; it is possible to eat too little fat. Fat serves several vital functions in the body. Fats carry vitamins A, D, E, and K across the intestinal wall into the bloodstream. In fact vitamin E is found predominantly in fatty foods of plant origin. Essential fatty acids, such as linolenic and linoleic, which are provided only through the diet, are needed to make hormones and maintain healthy cells. Over a

---

*Also contains significant amounts of linolenic acid (omega-3).

†Fatty acid ratio is greater than 40 percent monounsaturated but also contains greater than 40 percent saturated fatty acids.

‡Wild or sea-caught versions of these fish have significant levels of omega-3 fatty acids. Keep in mind that farm-raised fish are fed grains (rather than feeding on marine plants) and therefore may contain omega-6 rather than the protective omega-3 fatty acids.

long period of time diets with less than 10 percent of calories from fat can put you at risk for vitamin and essential fatty acid deficiencies. Diets high in saturated and hydrogenated fat (the kind found in commercial snack foods and baked goods) can also lead to essential fatty acid deficiency if they are low in monounsaturated and polyunsaturated fats. The bottom line is to go easy on the fat-free and other processed foods. Moderation and variety are the keys to balancing your fat intake.

Lowering Fat in Your Diet

A little planning and good decision making when shopping, cooking, and dining out will help you decrease the amount of fat you eat. By using good-quality cooking equipment, some of today's hottest chefs have refined the art and techniques of healthy cooking. A sampling of their methods includes high-temperature oven roasting (for meat, fish, poultry, fruits, and vegetables), searing food in nonstick or cast-iron pans to achieve flavor and browning, and using fruit and vegetable purees to replace some or all of the fat in soups, sauces, and baked goods. By applying some of their basic techniques and making healthy substitutions for high-fat ingredients, you can substantially cut the amount of fat in your diet and never miss it.

COOKING AND BAKING
- Trim the fat off meat and limit portion sizes.
- Bake, broil, roast, boil, braise, sear or sauté (with minimal oil or stock in a non-stick or cast-iron skillet), steam, or grill rather than fry.
- Roast firm-fleshed fish, such as snapper, halibut, or cod, "en papillote" (in paper). Inside the fold of parchment paper, sprinkle the fish with fresh herbs and a splash of white wine (or broth). Seal at the edges with egg whites, folding over repeatedly. Well-sealed foil can also be used. This method of cooking really concentrates the flavors of the herbs and fish, allowing you to forget all about fat.
- Use a rack in the pan when cooking meats to allow fat to drip down.
- Use nonstick pans and bakeware to limit the amount of fat in cooking and baking. Use a limited amount of fat (about 1 teaspoon per serving) to sauté or sear food in a nonstick pan.* Heating oil before adding the food will help you achieve good browning and flavor with a minimum of fat.
- "Sauté" foods in broth, water, or wine instead of butter or oil.

---

*Use a well-seasoned cast-iron pan to limit the fat when searing or sautéing.

- Steam or oven-roast vegetables.
- Prepare soups and stocks at least a day in advance so that fat can be skimmed off the top more easily. Add starches such as beans (cooked), peas, potatoes, or rice when preparing soup. Cook until tender, then puree all or half of the soup. The starch will give it a creamy consistency and will thicken the soup.
- Limit the use of butter, margarine, oils, cream, regular salad dressing, lard, commercial baked goods (containing hydrogenated fats or tropical oils such as palm and coconut), and shortening.
- Try nonfat powdered milk in baking. Low-fat baked goods typically do not brown well. Adding 1 or 2 tablespoons of dry milk will help you achieve a golden brown color.
- Halve the amount of fat called for in savory recipes, such as soups, stews, sauces, and casseroles.
- When baking, use fruit purees made from apples, bananas, or prunes or substitute a portion of the all-purpose flour with soy or flaxseed flour, which contains "healthy fats," to replace part of the added fat. Replace unsweetened chocolate with unsweetened cocoa powder: for every ounce of chocolate, substitute 3 tablespoons of cocoa. Because fat adds flavor to baked goods, enhance flavor by increasing or adding ingredients such as citrus zests, various extracts, and sugar when you cut fat from a recipe.

SUBSTITUTE ...
- fish, poultry without skin, and lean meats for higher-fat meats
- nonfat or 1 percent milk for whole milk
- low-fat or fat-free sour cream for the full-fat versions; 1 or 2 percent milk or half the amount of fat-free sour cream for cream in "cream" soups and sauces
- 1 cup of milk mixed with 1 tablespoon of cornstarch or ¾ cup of evaporated skim milk mixed with 1 tablespoon of all-purpose flour for cream in cooking. Whisk the mixture into a soup or sauce and bring to a boil. Reduce the heat and maintain a low boil until creamy and slightly thickened, about two minutes (the cornstarch or flour will prevent the milk from breaking when heated).
- one whole egg plus two egg whites for two whole eggs in cooking and baking
- reduced-fat cheeses, such as cottage, part-skim mozzarella and ricotta, farmer, soy, for high-fat cheeses; and lower-fat versions of Swiss, cheddar, goat's milk, and cream cheeses
- soy sausages for regular sausages to add flavor (and protein) to a soup or stew; smoked turkey or lean smoked ham in bean soups that call for hocks
- fruit or vegetable salsas, chutneys, or flavorful mustards for mayonnaise on sandwiches

- pureed 1 percent or nonfat cottage cheese or yogurt cheese for mayonnaise as a sandwich spread or as a base for dressings, adding fresh herbs or seasonings, such as tarragon, thyme, parsley, cilantro, saffron, curry, cayenne, tomato paste or pureed sun-dried tomatoes, and a pinch of olive or anchovy paste (see tip on page 34 for making yogurt cheese)
- pureed 1 percent or nonfat cottage cheese for ricotta cheese in cooking and baking
- acidic dairy products, such as yogurt or buttermilk, for part of the liquid ingredients in baking to help prevent gluten (a protein found in flour) from developing and tenderize the baked goods
- turkey or chicken breast (skin removed) or tuna salad (prepared with a small amount of olive oil, reduced-fat mayonnaise, or mustard) for high-fat luncheon meats such as bologna, ham, or salami
- fresh fruit, pretzels, baked tortilla chips with salsa, raw vegetables, air-popped popcorn, low-fat cheese, whole-grain low-fat crackers, flavored rice cakes, cereal, or sorbet for high-fat snacks such as potato chips, cold cuts, high-fat cheese, cookies, chocolate, nuts, or ice cream
- small portions of low-fat or fat-free sweets for the regular versions (remember, they still have calories!)
- broth-based or vegetable-puree soups for cream-based soups
- high-fiber, low-fat breakfast cereals or a bagel with a light layer of reduced-fat cream cheese (or any other type of low-fat cheese) for high-fat muffins or scones; include a piece of fruit with your breakfast to add nutrients and replace fat
- thin-crust pizza topped with vegetables for pizza with sausage or pepperoni; blot any surface fat with a napkin

MAKE YOUR OWN VINAIGRETTES

Traditional vinaigrettes are made with a ratio of three parts oil to one part vinegar. To spare fat, combine equal parts of oil (preferably extra-virgin olive oil), a good-quality vinegar (balsamic, sherry, fruit-flavored, herb-infused, and rice wine vinegars work well), and water. For more flavor, substitute stock or fresh juice for water. A pinch of fresh herbs or mustard can also add flavor. Vegetable purees, such as red pepper, watercress, spinach, or roasted garlic, can contribute nutrients, color, a creamier texture, and flavor (an example is Roasted Red Pepper Vinaigrette; see Index).

Protein

Getting enough protein is rarely a health concern for most Americans: the average American under sixty-five years of age consumes one to two times more than the daily reference intake (DRI). Two-thirds of the protein intake is from meat, fish, poultry, or dairy; the remaining one-third is from plant sources, such as legumes, grains, cereals, and vegetables. Animal protein sources provide high-quality protein and vitamins B_6, B_{12}, and zinc (nutrients that are hard to get from a strict vegetarian diet) and contain a form of iron that is easily absorbed by the body. However, they also contain significant amounts of total fat, saturated fat, and cholesterol. Researchers have linked diets high in animal protein to increased risk of heart disease and certain types of cancer. People whose intake of protein is moderate and more predominantly from plant sources also consume less fat and more fiber, vitamins, minerals, and other substances such as phytochemicals. They are healthier in general and are less prone to these diseases.

Why are high-protein diets so popular? Every decade or so high-protein diets are repackaged as a "new" concept for weight loss. The most recent wave of these books blames the increase in obesity on excessive carbohydrate intake, which supposedly causes insulin resistance and thus weight gain in many people. In fact the relationship between insulin resistance and obesity is often just the opposite: insulin resistance is often the result of obesity, not the cause of it. Furthermore, many of the extreme variations of these diets "work" by limiting food choices and food groups and, in the final analysis, total calories. Most nutrition experts agree that weight control is a matter of "calories in = calories out." Whenever calorie intake exceeds calories burned, whatever the source of the calories—carbohydrate, protein, or fat—the excess will be stored as fat. The exceptions to this rule are rare medical conditions that cause irregular metabolism or interfere with the body's ability to digest and

To make yogurt cheese, drain nonfat plain or vanilla yogurt through a funnel lined with cheesecloth overnight in the refrigerator. This will remove the whey, which contains the distinctive tart flavor characteristic of yogurt. The "cheese" that remains is creamy and bland and can be seasoned with condiments or herbs or sweetened for cooking, baking, or spreading.

absorb nutrients. Limiting refined carbohydrates and sugar-laden foods and replacing them with low-fat protein sources can be an effective component of a weight-reducing or weight-maintaining eating plan. "Healthy" carbohydrates, such as fruits, vegetables, whole grains, and legumes, should not be eliminated from your diet to make room for more protein, especially animal protein, which can be high in saturated fat.

As for the safety of high-protein diets, studies are ongoing. To date there is no definite evidence that protein intake up to 50 percent greater than the DRI has detrimental health consequences, provided that intake of animal protein and fat is not excessive and the individual does not have any conditions or diseases that compromise kidney function. In the long run, however, these diets can be problematic if protein foods replace fruits, vegetables, and high-fiber whole grains and cereals. Some recent research does support the possibility, though, that high-protein diets increase the risk of developing osteoporosis, because the more protein is consumed, the more calcium is excreted.

How Much Protein Do You Need?

According to the latest report from the National Academies' Institute of Medicine, to meet the body's daily energy and nutritional needs while minimizing risk for chronic disease, adults should get 45 percent to 65 percent of their calories from carbohydrates, 20 percent to 35 percent from fat, and 10 percent to 35 percent from protein. The ranges are wide, and possibly the most important considerations should be to focus on healthy carbohydrates (fruits, vegetables, whole grains, and legumes), healthy fats (mono- and polyunsaturated sources), and healthy proteins (plant and lean animal sources).

The newly established DRIs for protein, which include RDAs, are 56 grams a day for adult men and 46 grams a day for adult women. The DRI during pregnancy or lactation is 71 grams a day.

When you consider that an 8-ounce steak (half the portion served in many restaurants) provides approximately 56 grams of protein, you realize how easy it is to get adequate protein and even more. By keeping animal protein at around 6 to 8 ounces per day (two 3- to 4-ounce servings or one large one), while increasing plant protein sources, you will meet key nutrient requirements (vitamin B_{12}, iron, and zinc) and at the same time be moderating your total fat, saturated fat, and cholesterol intake. With careful planning, a totally plant-based vegan diet can meet all of your body's nutrient requirements.

Until the long-term effectiveness and safety of very-high-protein diets are proven, it is prudent to keep your intake below the tolerable upper intake level (UL) of 35 percent of total calories and balance your intake with carbohydrate-rich foods—fruits, vegetables, whole grains, and legumes—that have known health benefits. The bottom line for protein: it's important to pay attention to what comes along with the protein in your food choices. If you're partial to beef, stick with the leanest cuts. Fish and poultry are excellent alternatives. Even better options are vegetable sources of protein, such as beans, nuts, and whole grains. The following list of lean high-protein foods will familiarize you with quality plant and animal protein sources that are low in total and saturated fats.

Lean Protein Sources

BEEF/PORK/POULTRY/GAME/FISH AND SHELLFISH (6 TO 8 GRAMS PROTEIN PER OUNCE)

BEEF
For lean cuts of beef, longer moist-heat cooking methods such as stewing and braising should be considered to help tenderize them. Keep in mind that even lean beef contains significant amounts of saturated fat and cholesterol, so if you eat beef, choose lean cuts on an occasional basis, not more than three to four times a month.

Sources

arm, chuck	flank
bottom round	tenderloin
calf's liver*	top loin
eye round	top round

PORK
Fresh pork tenderloin is a terrific alternative protein source for those who are all "chickened out." It is almost as lean as skinless chicken breast and is very tender. Pork tenderloin and loin chops cook quickly, so be careful not to overcook. Searing, grilling, roasting, and braising are cooking techniques to consider. For marinating ideas, refer to Marinated Pork Tenderloin with Mashed Orange-Scented Sweet Potatoes (see Index). Another form of pork, extra-lean ham, can be as low in fat as 1.5 grams per ounce; however, you should still limit consumption because even "fresh" hams often contain nitrites.

Sources

arm shoulder, lean, trimmed	loin chop, lean, trimmed
center loin, lean, trimmed	tenderloin, lean, trimmed
ham, extra-lean	

POULTRY

Poultry, particularly chicken, is one of the most popular protein sources. Without its skin, breast meat from turkey or chicken can contain less than 1 gram of fat per ounce. Recommended cooking methods include roasting, stewing, sautéing (with a minimal amount of fat in a nonstick or cast-iron skillet), grilling, braising, and poaching.

Sources (skin removed)

chicken breast	domestic turkey breast
chicken leg	domestic turkey, dark meat
chicken liver*	

GAME

As consumer demand for game has increased in recent years, different varieties have become more available in some supermarkets, at gourmet specialty shops, and from butchers. Many types of game can also be purchased through mail-order sources. Wild game tends to have even less fat than ranch-raised varieties but is typically stronger tasting and not quite as tender. Because game meat tends to be so lean, it will dry out quickly, particularly when roasted. Be careful not to overcook it. For nonpoultry game such as buffalo, elk, or venison, grill or sear quickly (medium-rare to medium) in a hot nonstick or cast-iron pan with a little oil. This will preserve juices and tenderness. Other cooking methods for boar, rabbit, or venison include careful roasting or braising in flavorful liquids such as stocks, fruit juices, wines, or combinations. Flavorings and seasoning that complement game include fresh herbs such as thyme, rosemary, sage (for stronger-flavored game), and tarragon; frozen, fresh, or dried berries (great additions to a sauce, and fresh and dried berries are nice garnishes); juniper berries; peppercorns; currant preserves; and roasted garlic.

Sources (skin removed)

buffalo	rabbit, wild and domestic
duck breast	rhea
elk	squab
ostrich	venison

pheasant

quail breast

wild boar

wild turkey, breast and dark meat

FISH AND SHELLFISH

Even some fattier fish, high in good omega-3 fatty acids, are low in total fat as compared with many other protein sources. For information about the protective type of fat found in wild and sea versions of fattier fish, see the "Unsaturated Fats" section earlier in this chapter. There are many varieties of fish with 3 or fewer grams of fat per serving. To keep the fat down in these already-low-fat protein choices, avoid breading and frying and heavy butter- and/or cream-laden sauces. Use simple cooking techniques such as grilling, roasting, pan searing, poaching, and steaming to keep the fat low and allow the full flavors of the fish to come through.

Sources (skin removed)

bluefish, Atlantic

catfish

cod, Atlantic†

crab†

flounder†

grouper†

haddock†

lobster, northern, spiny†

ocean perch

oysters†

pike†

pollack†

rockfish

salmon, king or chinook, coho, chum,
    sockeye, Atlantic

scallops†

sea bass

shrimp†

snapper

sole†

striped bass

swordfish

trout, sea trout, wild rainbow trout

tuna, bluefin, yellowfin, albacore
    (water packed)

---

*Though high in cholesterol (you get a day's worth in a 3-ounce serving), liver still has only 3 grams or less of fat per ounce and is an economical protein source rich in vitamins A, B_{12} and other B vitamins, zinc, copper, iron, and phosphorus. However, liver is the animal tissue most likely to contain pesticides as well as antibiotic or drug residues. Even though the USDA randomly checks liver and other meats for toxic levels of these substances, liver should be only an occasional source of protein. Some natural foods stores, supermarkets, and butchers sell meat from animals not treated with hormones or antibiotics, and these may provide a healthier source of liver.

†Very low in fat: contains 0.5 gram or less of fat per cooked ounce.

Low-Fat Dairy and Eggs

Skim or low-fat dairy products are convenient and are high-quality protein sources. Check the "Nutrition Facts" on the label. "Reduced-fat" cheeses typically have 25 percent or less fat than the regular versions, but the remaining amount can still be high. For example, a reduced-fat cheddar may still have 7 grams of fat per ounce. *Low-fat* means no more than 3 grams of fat per 1-ounce serving. Try to eat two to three servings per day of low-fat dairy and don't sweat the occasional indulgence of a full-fat cheese or ice cream.

Milk and Yogurt (portion sizes as indicated)
skim or 1 percent milk (all types): 8 grams protein per cup
evaporated skim milk: 8 grams protein per ½ cup
nonfat or fat-free yogurt: 13 grams protein per cup

Cheeses (labeled "low-fat"—7 to 10 grams protein per ounce; portion size is 1 ounce)
American
cheddar
cottage (½ cup)
Monterey Jack

mozzarella
Muenster
ricotta
Swiss

Eggs and Egg Substitutes
whole eggs: 6 grams protein, 5 grams fat each
egg whites: 7 grams protein, 0 gram fat (for two egg whites)
egg substitute: 7 grams protein, 0 gram fat per ¼ cup

Myth: People who exercise frequently require substantially more protein than the recommended dietary allowance (RDA).

Fact: High-protein powders, drinks, capsules, and bars are unnecessary for frequent exercisers. The RDA furnishes sufficient protein to build and repair muscle. Considering that most people, including vegetarians, exceed the RDA for protein, there is no need to supplement protein in the form of food or amino acids. Professional athletes and weight trainers may require slightly more protein than the RDA, but they also require higher calorie levels, which in itself often leads to higher protein intake. An extra 8 grams of protein a day can be added with one glass of milk (1 percent or nonfat, regular, or soy). A cup of nonfat or low-fat yogurt provides 13 grams of protein, so why buy expensive supplements?

PLANT PROTEIN SOURCES

After computing your daily protein requirement, note how easy it is to achieve it with plant sources alone. Plants that are good protein sources also tend to be rich in fiber, vitamins, minerals, and protective phytochemicals. The macronutrient profile of most plant foods is a mixture of carbohydrate and protein. Fat levels will vary from none to quite high, as in the case of the "healthy" fat found in avocados.

Sources
dried (cooked) or canned beans: 7 to 8 grams protein, 0 to 1 gram fat per ½ cup
other starches (rice, pasta, breads, and cereals): 3 grams protein per serving
   (serving sizes vary)
nuts and seeds*: 4 to 8 grams protein, 5 to 10 grams fat per ¼ cup
soybeans: 14 grams protein, 7 grams fat per ¼ cup boiled
vegetables: 2 grams protein, 0 gram fat per serving (½ cup cooked, 1 cup raw =
   1 serving)

Vegetarianism

People who consume a vegetarian diet may have a decreased risk of developing cancer. Almost 7 percent of Americans consider themselves vegetarian; approximately 2.5 percent *are* vegetarians according to the following definition: a person who does not eat meat, fish, fowl, or products containing these foods.

Eating patterns may vary considerably among vegetarians:

- Lacto-ovo vegetarians consume dairy foods and eggs but no meat, fish, or poultry.
- Lacto vegetarians eat dairy foods but no eggs or any other animal products.
- Vegans do not eat animal foods of any type.

Even within these classifications a great deal of variation may exist with respect to which animal products are avoided; therefore, a diet's adequacy should be evaluated on the basis of individual intake rather than classification. If a wide variety of foods is eaten each day, a vegetarian diet can be easy and healthy. The more food groups that are eliminated, however, the more attention is required to assure that nutrients are replaced by other foods.

---

*High in fat; limit portion sizes.

Here are the American Dietetic Association's recommendations for people who follow vegetarian diets:

- Consult a registered dietitian or other qualified nutrition professional, especially during periods of growth, pregnancy, breast-feeding, or recovery from illness.
- Minimize intake of less nutritious foods, such as sweets and fatty foods.
- Limit egg intake to three to four yolks per week.
- Choose whole or unrefined grain products instead of refined products.
- Choose a variety of nuts, seeds, legumes, fruits, and vegetables, including good sources of vitamin C to improve iron absorption.
- Choose low-fat or nonfat varieties of any dairy products included in the diet.
- For infants, children, and teenagers, ensure adequate intake of calories, vitamin D, calcium, iron, and zinc. (Intakes of vitamin D, calcium, iron, and zinc are usually adequate when a variety of foods and sufficient calories are consumed.)
- If exclusively breast-feeding premature infants or babies beyond four to six months of age, take vitamin D and iron supplements beginning from birth or at least by four to six months, as your doctor recommends.
- Take iron and folate (folic acid) supplements during pregnancy.
- Vegans should use properly fortified food sources of vitamin B_{12} such as fortified soy beverages or commercial breakfast cereals or take a cyanocobalamin supplement. If sunlight is inadequate, vegans should take a vitamin D supplement during pregnancy or while breast-feeding. You may not be getting enough sunlight if you either don't spend a lot of time outdoors or do spend a fair amount of time in the sun but wear sunscreen to block out ultraviolet rays. Also, if you live in a northern climate you may need to consider vitamin D supplementation during winter months, when the sun's ultraviolet rays are not strong, preventing the body from synthesizing vitamin D.

You don't have to give up animal products altogether to reap the health benefits of a vegetarian-style diet. Many self-described vegetarians are semivegetarians, or occasional meat eaters. Additionally, growing numbers of people are opting for a more plant-based diet, limiting rather than excluding animal products from their diet. Americans could greatly improve their diets—and decrease risk of both cancer and cardiovascular disease—by increasing consumption of fruits and vegetables and decreasing consumption of animal protein.

These four small changes are the starting point in making the transition to a more plant-based diet:

1. **Moderate portion sizes of meat, fish, and poultry.** Keep portion sizes to 3 to 4 cooked ounces, about the size and thickness of the palm of your hand. Be flexible: if you have eaten a meat-free breakfast and lunch, enjoy that 6- to 8-ounce fish portion served to you in a restaurant. In general, however, meat should not take up more than one-quarter of the space on your dinner plate, with the remaining area left for grains, legumes, and vegetables.

2. **Use meat as a side dish or condiment.** When meats are used in soups, stews, casseroles, or stir-fries, you can use a lot less (2 to 3 ounces per serving), with the remaining bulk of ingredients being grains, legumes, and vegetables.

3. **Eat more meatless meals.** Try eliminating meat from one meal per day and then move on to a couple of days per week. Replace meat with plant protein sources, especially soybeans and soy products. Cooking ideas include using ratatouille or beans with pasta; vegetable curries or chili with tofu; burritos with vegetables, rice, and beans; salads with grains, vegetables, and beans.

4. **Adapt a vegetarian plan that suits your lifestyle and preferences (lacto, lacto-ovo, vegan).** If you adopt a vegan plan, choose foods fortified with nutrients found in animal foods.

GOOD SOURCES OF NUTRIENTS IN A VEGETARIAN DIET

PROTEIN
grains

legumes

nuts and seeds

soybeans and soy products

vegetables

IRON*
dried fruit

green leafy vegetables: collard greens, kale, Swiss chard, spinach, turnip greens

iron-fortified breads and cereals

legumes

some tofu

ZINC
legumes

nuts and seeds

tofu

whole grains

CALCIUM
bok choy

broccoli

collard greens

kale

legumes: peas, red and white beans, soybeans

fortified cereals
fortified fruit juices
fortified soy and rice beverages

okra
tofu curded with calcium

VITAMIN D
fortified cereals

fortified soy and rice beverages

RIBOFLAVIN
asparagus
bananas
broccoli
enriched breads and cereals
figs
kale

legumes
lentils
seeds
tofu and tempeh
wheat germ

VITAMIN B$_{12}$
fortified cereals
fortified soy beverages

some brands of nutritional yeast

VITAMIN A/BETA-CAROTENE†
apricots
cantaloupe
deep yellow or orange vegetables

leafy dark green vegetables
mangoes
pumpkin

OMEGA-3 FATTY ACIDS
flaxseeds and flaxseed oil‡

Vegetarian diets can still be high in fat. Moderate your intake of avocados, oil, nuts, olives, cheese, mayonnaise, salad dressings, and high-fat processed foods.

---

*Eat these iron-rich plant foods with fruits, vegetables, or juices high in vitamin C to improve iron absorption.
†Consult "Carotene Food Sources" on page 68 for a more complete listing.
‡See suggestions for flaxseed uses on page 28.

Myth: Vegetarian diets require that different plant foods, such as whole grains, legumes, vegetables, seeds, and nuts, be combined at the same meal to assure all protein requirements are met.

Fact: It was previously thought that plant foods needed to be combined in such a manner that all essential and nonessential amino acids were available with each meal (protein complementing). We now know that this is unnecessary as long as a variety of foods is consumed throughout the day. Additionally, when consumed at the recommended level of protein intake, soy protein offers sufficient amounts of all essential amino acids, making it a "complete" plant protein source.

Myth: Macrobiotic diets can both prevent and cure many types of cancer.

Fact: There is no evidence that macrobiotic diets can stop cancer once the diagnosis has been made. In fact, they can lead to or advance malnutrition in some cancer patients who are unable to meet their calorie and protein requirements on such regimes. Inadequate nutrition can harm the immune system, which may further impair the body's ability to fight cancer. From a prevention standpoint, however, macrobiotic diets that do not advance to the restrictive Zen stage (consisting of only brown rice and water) are consistent with dietary recommendations for cancer prevention. They include foods such as whole grains, fruits, and vegetables and moderate amounts of tofu and fish.

Soy

The soya plant, the most widely eaten plant in the world, provides a quality source of protein to billions of people daily. The "fruits" of the soya plant are used mostly in Asian diets, but they are becoming a popular source of plant-based protein elsewhere.

Soy has been in the headlines since studies linked the intake of this bean to lower risk of heart disease and cancer, but recent research has not conclusively proven these associations. The evidence concerning soy's ability to lower cholesterol is fairly strong, but the mechanisms behind this relationship are not well understood. Soy is a very important alternative to red meat as a protein source and an important component in a healthy, more plant-based diet. As with so many elements of a healthy diet, moderation in the consumption of soy is key. Phytochemicals in soybeans may have beneficial health effects, but studies on this topic have not been conclusive. One group of these compounds, called *isoflavones*, are phytoestrogens, a plant form of estrogen. Isoflavones are much less potent than human estrogen but can still interfere with the action of human estrogen by mimicking its role in the body and causing less to be produced.

Soybeans also contain plant sterols, which may block estrogen and hinder cell division, possibly preventing cancer cells from multiplying. Protease inhibitors found in soybeans and other legumes may slow the rate of division in cancer cells, allowing time for genetic repair and interruption of the carcinogenic process. Again, though, it is important to note that epidemiological studies conducted to date have not confirmed these potential health effects.

Most people do not know how to incorporate soy into their diet to take the place of some of the animal-based protein sources with which they are more familiar. No longer is soy just about tofu. There are many convenience products available that are not only healthy but also very tasty. Soy products include soybeans, soy milk, soy-based yogurt, tofu (firm and silken), tempeh, miso, soy flour, textured soy protein, soy "meat products," soybean oil, soy cheese, and soy sauce.

Recent media attention to potential links between soy and health has led to "if some is good, hundreds of times more is better" thinking in some quarters. Many processed soy products on the supermarket and health food shelves offer isoflavones—such as genistein—at medicinal, not nutritional, levels. In high amounts isoflavones may have negative effects on hormones and may actually counteract potentially positive effects of the phytoestrogens. Additionally, soy contains variable amounts of chemicals known as *antinutrients* that interfere with the absorption of some nutrients such as calcium and zinc, which is not a concern at moderate levels of consumption but may become an issue at high levels. The best soy selections are those that are minimally processed (soybeans, tofu, tempeh, soy milk and its products, and miso).

The bottom line on soy products is that they should be used in moderation as part of a healthy plant-based diet, but they should not be consumed in supplement form. For subgroups of women at risk for estrogen-mediated diseases, such as breast and ovarian cancer, the decision to include soy in the diet should be discussed with their physicians.

SOYBEANS range in size from as small as a pea to as large as a grape. The beans can be any combination of yellow, black, red, green, or brown. Though their flavor is bland, their nutritive value is rich—they are high in protein, low in carbohydrates, and high in a desirable oil that is often extracted and sold as soybean oil.

A harvest bean, soybeans are generally available at Asian markets, some supermarkets, health or natural foods stores, and local producers during late summer to late fall. They are available dried all year long.

USES

- After presoaking, use in soups, stews, and casseroles.
- Buy sprouted soybeans (or sprout your own) and use in salads and stir-fries.
- Steam or boil for 10 to 15 minutes and eat plain or seasoned.

SOY MILK is a creamy beverage made from dried soybeans that have been soaked in water and then crushed and boiled. The remaining liquid, soy milk, is lactose free and can be used by those who are lactose intolerant or allergic to cow's milk. It is available plain and in a variety of flavors, such as vanilla, chocolate, almond, and mocha, and like regular cow's milk, its content ranges from fat free to full fat (unlike cow's milk, the fat in soy milk is predominantly unsaturated). Unfortified soy milk is high in protein, B vitamins, and some minerals; it does not, however, contain significant amounts of calcium or vitamins D and B_{12}, as does fortified cow's milk. More recently, though, soy milk producers have been fortifying their products with these important nutrients.

Soy milk is available at health and natural foods stores and most supermarkets.

USES

- Drink as a hot or cold beverage.
- Pour over hot or cold breakfast cereals.
- Use in cooking or baking as a substitute for milk or cream.
- Use soy milk for a milk shake (see Index for a recipe).

SOY YOGURT is made by adding bacterial culture to soy milk. The fat content and flavors vary like those of dairy yogurt.

Soy yogurt is available at health and natural foods stores.

USES

- Use as a part of breakfast or lunch.
- Try as a snack.
- Use in fruit smoothies or protein shakes.

TOFU is the curd remaining when soy milk is coagulated and the whey is discarded. Different coagulants are used in its production, including nigari, a natural compound of sea water, and calcium sulfate (tofu curded with calcium sulfate provides a substantial source of calcium). Low-fat or "lite" tofus are available and contain the beneficial properties of the soybean without all the fat.

Tofu is available at health and natural foods stores and many supermarkets. Commercially sealed packages of tofu have less bacteria than the kind sold in bulk containers floating in water. Cooking tofu until it reaches an internal temperature of 160°F kills all bacteria.

Firm tofu is a dense form of tofu that holds its shape nicely in cooking.

Uses

- Add to soups or stews to increase protein. Since tofu is bland in taste, it works better with well-seasoned foods like Indian, southwestern, and Asian dishes, rather than with subtle flavors.
- Marinate and grill, sear, or bake and then use as an animal protein replacement in a meal or inside a sandwich.
- Substitute for ground beef in spaghetti sauce, tacos, and burritos.
- Crumble and add bread crumbs and seasonings to make tofu burgers.
- Scramble with vegetables and seasonings.

Silken tofu is a soft variety that contains more water than firm tofu and becomes creamy when pureed or blended.

Uses

- Blend with fresh fruit and soy milk to make a protein-rich fruit smoothie.
- Puree and combine with seasonings to make a low-fat sandwich spread to replace mayonnaise. Seasoning suggestions include curry, saffron, tomato paste or pureed sun-dried tomatoes, olive paste, anchovies, cilantro, basil, and rosemary. Use in tuna or chicken salad.
- Use as a replacement for sour cream in cooking or in place of cream cheese in baking.
- Use as a base for a creamy salad dressing.

TEMPEH is a fermented soy patty made in combination with another grain, such as rice or barley. It has a nutty, mushroomy, meatlike flavor, and its texture makes it perfect for marinating, grilling, searing, or baking.

Tempeh is sold in blocks of various sizes (sometimes already marinated), often frozen, at health and natural foods stores and some supermarkets.

USES

- Grill or oven-roast with barbecue sauce and make a sandwich.
- Grate and use in veggie burgers with other grains and seasonings; use grated tempeh in soups, stews, chilies, and casseroles to add protein and a meaty texture.
- Use as a replacement for tuna or chicken in a salad.

MISO is a paste formed when water, salt, soybeans, rice, or barley and a fermenting agent are mixed. Miso comes in varieties distinguished by their colors and tastes. Miso is high in protein and low in fat but high in sodium. It should be used sparingly, and people who are salt sensitive or hypertensive should avoid miso as a soy protein source. Fortunately, after being aged in cedar vats for up to three years, the flavor is intense, and small amounts go a long way.

You'll find small and large plastic tubs of miso in the refrigerated section of health and natural foods stores and some supermarkets.

USES

- Use yellow miso (or light miso), which is less intense and less salty, to make a salad dressing.
- Enrich soups, sauces, or vegetable stocks with red miso (made with barley); it adds both color and flavor.
- Use dark miso, which has the most intense flavor, as a soup base.

SOY FLOUR is made from roasted soybeans that are rolled into flakes and then ground. Soy flour is loaded with soy protein (approximately 50 percent by weight) and adds color, texture, and moisture to baked goods. Since it contains no gluten, soy flour needs to be mixed with all-purpose or bread flour in a one-to-four ratio for yeast-raised products. In preparing quick breads, muffins, and cookies, up to 30 percent soy flour can be used. Full-fat soy flour can be very high in fat, so look for defatted "low-fat" soy flour, which is also a more concentrated source of protein.

Soy flour is available at health and natural foods stores.

USES

- Substitute for one-quarter to one-half of the wheat flour in baking. Unless you are using defatted soy flour, it contains more fat (in part, linolenic fatty acids— a "good" kind of fat) than wheat flour, so cut the fat in the recipe by up to one-quarter.

- Baked foods brown more quickly when using soy flour, so decrease the baking time or lower the cooking temperature.
- Because even defatted soy flour contains some oils, it is best to store it in the refrigerator or freezer to prevent spoilage.
- Soy flour is fine and gets compressed or packed easily, so sift it before using it in recipes.

- Replace one egg in baked goods with 1 tablespoon of soy flour and 1 tablespoon of water.
- Use in frying and sautéing. Because of its composition, soy flour absorbs less fat in cooking than does its wheat counterpart.
- Toasting the flour on a baking sheet in the oven or in a dry skillet (while stirring) on the stove until lightly browned produces a nutty aroma and flavor and helps with browning of baked goods.

ISOLATED SOY PROTEIN is made from defatted soy flour. Isolated soy protein is at least 90 percent protein: most of the carbohydrate and fat have been extracted. Because it is a fat-free source of high-quality protein, isolated soy protein is often found in weight-loss beverages, infant formulas, meal-replacement or "energy-boosting" bars, and "muscle-building" protein powders. It can be purchased generically or under a variety of labels. If you cannot locate a generic source of soy protein isolate, look for a protein powder in which soy protein isolate is listed as a first or second ingredient. Remember that studies do not support excessive soy protein intake, so take care not to overdo it.

Isolated soy protein is available at health and natural foods stores.

USES
- Blend with fruit and/or yogurt shakes.
- Add in baking (muffins, quick breads, or cookies) or cooking (puddings, soups, and casseroles) to increase protein content.

TEXTURED SOY PROTEIN is also made from defatted soy flour. The flour is compressed until the protein changes texture to a granular or chunky form. Textured soy protein is high in protein, isoflavones, calcium, and iron and is generally low in fat and calories. It is sold dry and can be rehydrated with stock or water before being used in recipes.

Textured soy protein is available at health and natural foods stores.

USES

- Use it rehydrated as an extender (or a medium to add both protein and bulk), replacing some or all of the ground beef, turkey, or chicken (and fat) in chili, meat loaf, hamburgers, tacos, sloppy joes, or casseroles.

SOY "MEAT PRODUCTS" are made to look, smell, and taste like the real thing. Products include soy-based vegetarian sausages, hot dogs, hamburgers, bacon, and cold cuts. One needs to read labels carefully when shopping for these products, because in some cases they are very high in fat and sodium and have been chemically preserved. Unless they have been fortified with vitamins and minerals, they are not an equivalent replacement for protein derived from animal products, and they are considerably lower in isoflavones than many other soy foods.

Soy "meat products" are available at health and natural foods stores.

USES

- Use as an occasional replacement for animal protein products.

SOYBEAN OIL is pressed from soy flakes and is a common ingredient in commercial baked goods. The flavor is subtle and is therefore good for cooking foods whose flavor you do not want influenced by the cooking oil. Due to its high smoking point, it is also good for sautéing or cooking in a wok, which requires high heat. Although soybean oil does not contain isoflavones, it does have other beneficial compounds. Unlike most other vegetable oils, it contains a significant amount of linolenic fatty acids, essential fatty acids that are not produced in the body. Linolenic fatty acids can be converted to omega-3 fatty acids in the body. As with all oils and fats, however, it should be used sparingly.

Soybean oil is available at health and natural foods stores and most supermarkets.

USES

- Use for sautéing or cooking in a wok.
- Use in baking.
- Try in salad dressings (in this case you may wish to use a rich-flavored vinegar and/or chopped herbs).

SOY CHEESE, made from the "milk" of soybeans, is an alternative to dairy cheese. Varieties include mozzarella, cheddar, Muenster, Monterey Jack (with or without jalapeño), and American. Most soy cheeses are not fat free, but they have about half the fat of the dairy equivalents and are very low in saturated fat. The fact that they do contain some fat makes them suitable for cooking, because they melt well. In a cooked dish such as lasagna it's difficult to tell the difference from dairy cheese.

Soy cheese is available at health and natural foods stores and most supermarkets.

Uses
- Grate and use in casseroles, lasagna, tacos, burritos, omelets, or any other recipe that calls for cheese.
- Use soy ricotta to replace dairy ricotta in baking and cooking.
- Try soy American cheese in a grilled cheese and tomato sandwich.
- Use in macaroni and cheese.

Soy sauce, shoyu, or tamari is made by adding mold to roasted soybeans and wheat. After a few days they are mixed with sea water and brewed in fermentation tanks for up to one year, after which the liquid is pasteurized. Soy sauce does not contain isoflavones; however, it is a great flavoring agent in cooking. Similar to miso, it is very high in sodium (even the low-sodium varieties), so it should be avoided by those with salt sensitivity or high blood pressure.

Soy sauce is available at health and natural foods stores and supermarkets.

Uses
- Chinese soy sauce is stronger in flavor and very salty, while Japanese soy sauce, such as tamari, is sweeter and less salty. Both can be used in stir-fries, sauces, marinades, and salad dressings.

Many soy products are also available from mail-order sources. For resource and reference information about soy and soy products, call (800) TALK-SOY [(800) 825-5769] or visit the Talk Soy website: talksoy.com. Talk Soy is sponsored by the United Soybean Board.

Carbohydrates

Carbohydrates are the major energy source in the human diet. Carbohydrate is an essential nutrient because it is necessary in the human body and is the only source of "fuel" for some organs. Foods rich in complex carbohydrates (starches or fiber) are generally rich in vitamins, minerals, and phytochemicals. The calories derived from fruit come almost exclusively from carbohydrates. Grains, cereals, legumes, and vegetables contain protein and in some cases fat, but they are composed of significantly more carbohydrate by weight. Carbohydrates come in the form of sugars, fibers, and starches and are found in a wide variety of foods. Potato chips, ice cream, oatmeal, apples, cookies, beans, bread, and pasta all contain carbohydrates, but they vary in the type of carbohydrate they contain. The traditional way to classify carbohydrates is as either simple or complex. Defining them nutritionally is a bit more complicated.

Carbohydrates are made solely of rings of carbon, oxygen, and hydrogen. The number and structure of the rings determine the type of carbohydrate. Simple carbohydrates contain one or two rings, and complex carbohydrates contain many. Complex carbohydrates are further differentiated as starches, which are digestible, and fiber, which is not digestible.

Simple carbohydrates include monosaccharides (fructose, glucose, and galactose) and disaccharides (sucrose, maltose, and lactose), which are split when digested. Common simple sugars include sucrose (fructose and glucose joined together), what we call *table sugar*; fructose, the main sugar in fruit (also used to make the high-fructose corn syrup used in many commercial products); and lactose (glucose and galactose), found in milk.

How Many and What Type of Carbohydrates Should You Eat?

According to the latest report from the National Academies' Institute of Medicine, to meet the body's daily energy and nutritional needs while minimizing risk for chronic disease adults should get 45 percent to 65 percent of their calories from carbohydrates, 20 percent to 35 percent from fat, and 10 percent to 35 percent from protein. The ranges are wide, and possibly the most important considerations should be to focus on healthy carbohydrates, healthy fats, and healthy proteins.

So What Are Healthy Carbohydrates?

Fruits, vegetables, legumes, and a type of complex carbohydrate called *whole grains* constitute healthy carbohydrates. Previous recommendations for complex carbohydrates were not as specific and lumped all complex carbohydrates—such as potatoes, rice, beans, and pasta—together as "healthy" and all simple carbohydrates—all forms of sweets and sugars—as "unhealthy" food to be limited. The very low-fat diets of the 1990s led to high consumption of low-fat, high-carbohydrate foods, including pasta, rice, and potatoes, as well as many "fat-free" and "low-fat" products comprised mainly of simple carbohydrates. In the end, the overindulgence in fat-free calories led to expanded waistlines, 8 pounds on the American average, and increased rates of heart disease and diabetes. While all complex carbohydrates provide nutrients, and none should be excluded from the diet, most of our carbohydrate intake should come from fruits, vegetables, legumes, and whole grains such as oats, barley, and whole-grain breads. These foods provide not only carbohydrates but also vitamins, minerals, phytochemicals, and fiber. Because of their high fiber content, these foods are generally digested slowly and can help play a significant role in maintaining a healthy body weight.

Many other words that appear in ingredients lists indicate that the product contains sugar. If you are trying to moderate your intake of empty calories from sugar, look for the following ingredients (the higher they appear in the ingredients lists, the greater the amount present):

Beet sugar	Honey
Brown sugar	Invert sugar
Cane sugar	Maltodextrin or dextrin
Confectioners' sugar (powdered)	Maple sugar
Crystallized cane sugar	Molasses
Dextrose	Raw sugar
Fructose	Sucrose
High-fructose corn syrup	Turbinado sugar

Starches from complex carbohydrates are chains of hundreds of glucose molecules. Starting with the digestive enzymes in the mouth, all the way to the small intestine, starches are broken down to form individual glucose molecules that are then absorbed for energy or storage in muscle or fat. The rate at which complex carbohydrates are digested and absorbed is significantly slower than that of simple carbohydrates. Complex carbohydrates are found predominantly in grains, cereals, legumes, fruits, and vegetables. They have much more nutritional value and typically less fat than foods high in simple carbohydrates.

Whole Grains

Whole grains, a subgroup of complex carbohydrates, are the nutritional powerhouse.

Whole (unprocessed) grains include all three parts of a grain kernel: the bran, germ, and endosperm. Whole-grain foods are made with all three of these grain components.

Myth: Simple carbohydrates, particularly refined white sugar, can cause cancer as well as other diseases.

Fact: Although sugar should not be a major component of your diet, especially if you are watching calories, researchers have not found a direct link between sugar and ill health. There are medical conditions, such as diabetes and elevated trigylcerides (a type of fat found in the bloodstream), that do warrant restrictions on sugar and other simple carbohydrates, but for most people sugar intake does not impose health dangers. Furthermore, all types of sugars (and complex carbohydrates) are broken down to the body's primary energy source, glucose. Whether refined or unrefined, sugar is not a source of any major nutrient except calories. For this reason you should limit your sugar intake to leave room for nutrient-packed complex carbohydrates.

Myth: Carbohydrates should be limited in the diet as they make you fat.

Fact: Moderating carbohydrate intake can be an effective strategy in weight reduction and maintenance; however, "healthy" carbohydrates should remain in the diet while low-nutrient, sugar-laden foods are limited. Carbohydrate-rich foods such as fruits, vegetables, whole grains, and legumes are foods that can lower risk for cancer, heart disease, and diabetes. None should be excluded from the diet. Refined complex carbohydrates, such as bread (not whole grain), white rice, and pasta, are best curbed to make room for the nutritious whole grains.

The individual components of whole grains—vitamins, minerals, fiber, and phytochemicals—may work together to help prevent chronic diseases such as heart disease, cancer, and diabetes.

In July 1999 the Food and Drug Administration (FDA) permitted the following health claim that allows qualifying products to promote the potential reduction in risk for heart disease and some cancers: "Diets rich in whole-grain foods and other plant foods and low in total fat, saturated fat, and cholesterol may reduce the risk of heart disease and some cancers."

Whole grains include:

Barley
Brown rice

Bulgur (cracked wheat)
Farro (spelt)
Oatmeal
Quinoa
Whole wheat couscous
Pasta made from whole wheat flour
Breads, cereals,* or other commercial products that list *whole* in front of the
    grain

A Sampling of Cereals Made from Whole Grains
(The following contain no trans fats and have little, if any, added sugar. Manufacturers change formulas, so be sure to still check labels.)

Cheerios (General Mills)
Chex, Wheat (General Mills)
Grape-Nuts (Post)
Just Right Fruit & Nut (Kellogg's)
Kashi (Kashi Company)
Mini-Wheats Raisin (Kellogg's)
Müesli (Familia)
Nutri-Grain, Almond-Raisin (Kellogg's)
Nutri-Grain, Golden Wheat (Kellogg's)
Oatmeal Crisp, Almond (General Mills)
Oatmeal Crisp, Apple Cinnamon (General Mills)
Oatmeal Crisp, Raisin (General Mills)
Organic Healthy Fiber Multigrain Flakes (Health Valley)
Puffed Wheat (Quaker)
Shredded Wheat (Post)
Shredded Wheat 'N Bran (Post)
Shredded Wheat, Spoon Size (Post)
Squares (oatmeal) (Quaker)
Uncle Sam (U.S. Mills)
Wheaties, Crispy 'n' Raisins (General Mills)

---

*Note: *bran, multigrain, 100% wheat, organic,* and *stone-ground* do not mean whole grain.

Fiber

That something indigestible could be good for you may seem odd. But such is the case with fiber, which is less an essential nutrient than an important element of internal maintenance. Fiber is a nonabsorbable complex carbohydrate that comes from the cell walls of plants. Most of the foods that are good sources of fiber—whole-grain breads, bran, oats, brown rice, vegetables, legumes, etc.—have endured little or no "processing."

There are two different types of fiber, each serving different dietary functions: those that are soluble in water and those that are not. Insoluble fiber, such as cellulose, hemicelluloses, and lignan, is found in wheat and rye bran, seeds, nuts, and vegetables. It passes intact through the intestinal tract, helping potential carcinogens exit rapidly. This laxative action may help prevent colon cancer and forestall other problems such as hemorrhoids or diverticulosis.

Soluble fiber, such as pectins, gums, and mucilages, is found in many fruits, some vegetables, oatmeal, oat bran, barley, and legumes. It is also used in commercial food products to provide fatlike consistency and texture without the fat. Soluble fiber absorbs water and nutrients in the stomach. This action slows food absorption, and the fiber's bulky texture creates a feeling of fullness that tends to reduce overall food intake (a nice benefit for people who are watching their weight). Soluble fiber may also be associated with prevention of heart disease and colon cancer. It binds with bile acids, which help to absorb cholesterol and other lipids (fats), and increases their excretion. The water-holding capacity of soluble fiber may also dilute the potential damaging effects of bile acids while positively modifying the bacterial flora (the resident bacterial growth) in the colon.

The average North American consumes 10 to 20 grams of dietary fiber a day. The U.S. National Cancer Institute recommends 25 to 35 grams per day. Too much fiber intake, however, can cause bloating and gas and produce loose stools. To meet these guidelines with minimal undesirable side effects, increase your fiber intake gradually.

There is no need to count the number of grams of fiber in every food you consume. Some basic concepts will help you work your way up to the recommended 25- to 35-gram range daily:

- Fruits and vegetables contain, on average, 2 grams of fiber per serving. Although some do contain higher or lower amounts, by eating a variety of fruits and vegetables, you should end up with an average intake at this level.

Reaching the minimum of your fruit and vegetable goal (five servings per day) will satisfy about 40 percent of your dietary fiber goal.

Fiber = 10 grams

- Start the day with a whole-grain cereal (hot or cold) that contains at least 5 grams of fiber. Top with wheat germ, dried fruit, bananas, or berries, all of which are good sources of fiber. Alternately, have an egg white and vegetable omelet with 2 slices of whole wheat toast.

Fiber = 5 grams

- Eat two slices of whole wheat or whole-grain bread (approximately 1½ to 2½ grams per slice).

Fiber = 4 grams

- Eat 1 cup brown, wild, or basmati rice or ¼ cup barley, whole wheat couscous, or bulgur (cooked).

Fiber = 3 grams

- When you're able to tolerate these additions to your diet, add ½ cup of any kind of beans or lentils (for example, black beans, chick-peas, pinto beans, white beans), which will provide about 5 to 8 grams of fiber.

Fiber = 5 grams

Grand total = 27 grams

Myth: Fiber supplements are an alternative to eating foods high in fiber.

Fact: Fiber supplements do not make up for dietary fiber. Fiber is a complex substance. Within the two major categories of fiber, soluble and insoluble, are many subcategories that may provide some of the beneficial effects associated with high-fiber diets. Fiber supplements usually contain only one type of fiber, such as psyllium or cellulose, and none of the nutrients found in high-fiber foods, although some can serve as laxatives and lower cholesterol. High-fiber foods like fruits and vegetables also contain other possibly beneficial phytochemicals.

When you consistently tolerate approximately 25 grams of dietary fiber per day, you can slowly bump it up, increasing portion sizes and varieties of whole grains and beans and fruit and vegetable servings (aim for nine servings per day).

Good Sources of Fiber

Grains	Grams of Fiber per Serving
amaranth, cooked (½ cup)	4
barley, cooked (½ cup)	3
basmati rice, cooked (1 cup)	2.5
bran muffin (medium, 2½ ounces)	4
brown rice, cooked (1 cup)	3.5
bulgur, cooked (½ cup)	4
couscous, cooked (1 cup)	2.5
General Mills Fiber One (½ cup)	13
hominy grits, yellow, regular, cooked (1 cup)	8
Kellogg's All-Bran (½ cup)	10
millet, cooked (1 cup)	3
Nabisco 100% Bran (½ cup)	12
oatmeal, cooked (1 cup)	4
pasta, cooked (1½ cups)	3.5
polenta, cooked (¾ cup)	3
pumpernickel bread (2 slices)	4
Wheatena, cooked (¾ cup)	5
whole wheat bread (2 slices)	3.5
whole wheat pita bread (1 each)	5
whole wheat tortilla	3
wild rice, cooked (1 cup)	3

Beans (½ cup, cooked)	Grams of Fiber per Serving
adzuki	6
black	8
chick-pea or garbanzo	5
fava	5
kidney, red	7
lentil	7
lima	7

mung	8
navy	7
pinto	7
soybean	5
white (Great Northern and cannellini)	6

Fruits (1 medium item = serving, unless indicated)	*Grams of Fiber per Serving*
apple, with skin	3
banana	2
blueberries (1 cup)	3
cantaloupe, cubed (1 cup)	1.5
cherries, pitted (20)	4
figs (2)	3
grapefruit (½)	1
grapes (1½ cups)	2
kiwifruit	2.5
mango, pitted (½)	2
nectarine	2
orange	2
peach	1.5
pear	4
pineapple (¾ cup)	1.5
plums (2)	2
prunes, uncooked (3)	1.5
raisins (¼ cup)	1.5
raspberries (1 cup)	6
strawberries (1¼ cups)	3
tomato, raw	1.5

Vegetables (½ cup cooked, unless indicated)	*Grams of Fiber per Serving*
asparagus	2
broccoli	2
brussels sprouts	3
butternut squash	3
cabbage	2
carrot	3

carrot, raw, shredded (1 cup)	3
cauliflower	1.5
corn	2
eggplant	1
green beans	1.5
iceberg lettuce, raw (1 cup)	0.5
kale	1.5
peas	3
potato, with skin (1 medium)	4
pumpkin, mashed	3
rutabaga	2
spinach	1.5
sweet potato, without skin	2
Swiss chard	2
turnip	1.5
zucchini	1

Bean Basics

Beans are a nearly perfect food. As a source of carbohydrate, they are complex and are therefore digested and absorbed more slowly, making them an ideal carbohydrate. They are a great source of protein, providing 7 to 9 grams per ½ cup, and most varieties contain only a trace of fat. Beans are loaded with fiber, ranging from 5 to 8 grams per ½ cup, depending on the variety. The B vitamins—thiamine, niacin, B6, and folate—and important minerals, such as iron, calcium, phosphorus, and potassium, are abundant in most types of beans. The iron in beans is absorbed more readily when beans are accompanied by vitamin C–rich foods, such as tomatoes, potatoes, peppers, broccoli, and citrus fruit or juices.

Beans contain insoluble fiber, the kind that promotes regularity and may lower risk of colon cancer, and soluble fiber, the type that is helpful for lowering blood cholesterol and controlling blood glucose. Many types of beans also contain the same possibly cancer-protective phytochemicals (isoflavones, plant sterols, and protease inhibitors) found in soybeans.

Like most high-fiber foods, beans are useful for weight control. They are absorbed slowly and have the capacity to draw and hold water in the stomach and the gut, producing a feeling of fullness and delaying the return of hunger. They also add weight and volume to food without adding many calories. By weight an ounce of cheese provides approximately 100 calories; an ounce of beans, 40 calories.

Some people avoid beans because they cause flatulence or gas, they take too long to cook, or they don't know what to do with them. All of these problems have solutions:

PREVENTING GAS FROM BEANS. The complex sugars in beans, oligosaccharides, cannot be digested by the human gut. In the lower intestine these molecules encounter the resident bacteria that eat the oligosaccharides and, as part of their own metabolic process, give off various gases. Flatulence is more often a problem with people who eat beans infrequently; it becomes less of a problem for those who eat beans regularly. If you do not tolerate beans well, start with small helpings, such as the amount you might sprinkle on a salad, and slowly work your way up. Soaking and attention to cooking methods may also decrease the likelihood of flatulence.

SOAKING AND COOKING BEANS. The process of soaking beans softens and rehydrates them and breaks down the indigestible oligosaccharides. Before beans are soaked, they should be rinsed and sorted to remove any grit, pebbles, or broken pieces. Changing the soaking water two or three times will help degrade the oligosaccharides. On average most beans need to soak for at least four hours (with two to three water changes). Exceptions are soybeans and fava, or broad, beans, which should be soaked overnight. Lentils, split peas, and black-eyed peas do not need soaking. Rinse the beans after they have been soaked and don't cook the beans with the soaking liquid. Adding baking soda or salt to beans when they soak or cook toughens the beans and, in the case of baking soda, destroys some nutrients. Cook beans thoroughly; uncooked starch is much harder to digest and can result in gas and bloating. See Table 2.2 on page 62 for recommended cooking times. Cooked beans should mash easily when pressed between two fingers. As dry beans get older, they also get harder, soak up less water, and fail to soften when cooked. Store beans in a well-sealed container in a cool, dark place.

In general beans double their volume in cooking. One cup of most dried beans will yield 2 to 2½ cups cooked (approximately four portions for a side dish). The exceptions are soybeans and chick-peas, which triple their volume.

CANNED BEANS. If soaking and cooking beans just does not fit into your schedule, try a good-quality canned bean. Avoid brands that list preservatives, added salt, and/or sugar in the ingredients. To minimize gas and reduce sodium when using canned beans, rinse after draining.

TABLE 2.2 COOKING TIMES FOR BEANS AFTER FOUR HOURS OF SOAKING

Type	Cooking	Pressure Cooking
adzuki	1 hour	15 minutes
black	1½ hours	15 minutes
black-eyed peas*	45 minutes	10 minutes
chick-peas (garbanzos)	2–2½ hours	25 minutes
fava beans†	3 hours	40 minutes
Great Northern	1 hour	20 minutes
kidney	1 hour	20 minutes
lentils, brown*	35 minutes	not appropriate
lentils, green*	40 minutes	not appropriate
lentils, red*	30 minutes	not appropriate
lima	1–1½ hours	20 minutes
mung	1 hour	not appropriate
navy	1½–2 hours	25 minutes
peas, split*	30 minutes	not appropriate
peas, whole	45 minutes	15 minutes
pink	1 hour	20 minutes
pinto	1–1½ hours	20 minutes
soybeans†	3–3½ hours	30 minutes
white (cannellini)	1 hour	20 minutes

*Do not require soaking.
†Require 12 hours of soaking.

USES FOR BEANS

- Sprinkle chick-peas, pinto beans, or black beans over a salad.
- Prepare bean puree soups using black beans or white beans. Other soups that include beans but are not typically pureed include minestrone, lentil, and pasta e fagioli.
- Use beans (canned are great too) to add texture, flavor, fiber, and protein to other soups, stews, chilies, and casseroles.
- Add beans to pasta or rice.
- Puree beans to replace high-fat sauces.
- Top bruschetta or toasted bread with bean salsas.
- Prepare or purchase lightly dressed bean salads.

- Make vegetarian terrines or pâtés.
- Prepare bean spreads to replace butter or high-fat dips. Some ideas include white bean spread, bean dips made with pinto beans, jalapeños, and spices, and hummus (for Healthy Hummus recipe, see Index).

Fluids

It's important to drink enough fluid with your fiber-rich diet. Unless you have a medical condition that limits fluid intake, a minimum of eight 8-ounce glasses daily is recommended. This should help move the fiber through your intestinal tract and prevent constipation, gas, and discomfort. Don't count caffeinated or alcoholic beverages toward your fluid goals. They are diuretics and will actually set you back. Limit high-calorie, nutrient-empty beverages, such as soda and "fruit drinks" that contain little or no fruit, and moderate your intake of caffeine-free diet sodas, sugar-free iced teas, lemonades, and fruit drinks that contain artificial sweeteners. Save room for more nutritious beverages. Some beverage ideas include:

- Water (spring, mineral, or sparkling)
- Milk (nonfat or 1 percent or soy milk)
- All-natural juices (if you don't squeeze your own juice or use a juicer, read labels to make sure you're actually buying 100 percent juice, not a "fruit drink" that may contain only 10 percent real juice). If you're watching your weight, go easy on fruit juices and instead try vegetable juices, which have fewer calories. Another option is to "spritz" or add fruit juice to a glass of seltzer or carbonated mineral water. Limit the amount of juices that you count as fruit and/or vegetable servings. Although nutritious, they contain slightly less vitamins, minerals, and phytochemicals and do not have nearly the amount of fiber that whole fruit and vegetables have.
- Decaffeinated coffees and teas

Green teas, and to a lesser extent black teas, contain flavonoids, catechins, and theaflavins, which may play a role in cancer prevention. Green tea is consumed mostly in Asian countries; Americans generally consume black tea. Lower rates of certain types of cancer in Asian populations are thought possibly to be partially a result of green tea consumption. Green tea is made by steaming or drying tea leaves and little other processing. The steaming process enhances flavor and inactivates the enzymes responsible for oxidation, leaving the polyphenol content intact. Polyphenols are phytochemicals that are potent antioxidants and may promote enzymes that rid the body of carcinogens. Black tea leaves are exposed to the air and allowed to ferment or oxidize for several hours, resulting in some loss of the beneficial polyphenols. When brewing tea, be sure to let it steep for at least 3½ minutes to get the full concentration. When shopping for tea, be sure the ingredients on the label list *tea* first. Iced, powdered, or bottled tea is OK, but these can be full of sugar.

Coffee consumption is not linked to an increased risk of cancer. In fact, coffee contains caffeic and ferulic acids (other types of plant polyphenols) that may have a role in cancer prevention. Still, moderate your coffee drinking, because excessive caffeine intake can lead to loss of calcium in urine.

The Importance of Fruits and Vegetables

Numerous studies have found a lower incidence of cancer among people who eat large amounts of fruits and vegetables. While it is not yet clear what nutrients or substances or what mechanisms may be responsible for this health-promoting effect, several theories are being studied. Nutrients such as vitamin C, vitamin A and related substances, and vitamin E may offer protection through their antioxidant properties. Other components like fiber or plant substances (phytochemicals) may have a beneficial effect. An important extra benefit of vitamin-rich foods is that they provide minerals, calcium, zinc, and iron, which may be associated with a decreased risk of cancer. These minerals are also vital for good health because they play a known role in the prevention of diseases such as anemia and osteoporosis.

It is likely that increasing consumption of fruits and vegetables will decrease the intake of fat-containing foods and thus have a favorable effect on obesity and coronary heart disease. A great deal of research is going on to determine how fruits and vegetables confer their health benefits. One thing is certain: a variety of fruits and vegetables (a total of five or more servings per day) will be beneficial to your health.

Most vegetables are excellent sources of vitamins A and C, yet dark green leafy vegetables like spinach, romaine, and kale and yellow, orange, and red vegetables are among the most valuable. Citrus fruits and juices and virtually all summer fruits are good sources of these vitamins.

Vegetables from the cabbage patch (cruciferous vegetables) also may reduce cancer risk. They are good sources of fiber as well as important vitamins and minerals. Several servings each week of this type of vegetable (brussels sprouts, cabbage, broccoli, cauliflower, rutabagas, and turnips) are part of a healthy diet.

Five to nine fruit and vegetable servings may sound like a lot, but it really is not difficult to get within this range. To determine whether you're close, you must first know what a serving is.

One Vegetable Serving Equals

- 1 cup of raw leafy vegetables such as spinach, lettuce varieties (dark in color), escarole, Swiss chard, collard greens, cabbage, or other leafy greens. For these vegetables, cooked, a serving equals ½ cup.
- ½ cup of other vegetables, raw or cooked, including broccoli, carrots, cauliflower, peppers, green beans, or squash
- ¾ cup vegetable juice (such as carrot or tomato)*
- 1 medium potato or sweet potato
- 5 to 6 asparagus spears
- 1 medium tomato

One Fruit Serving Equals

- 1 medium apple, orange, pear, or peach
- 1 small banana
- 2 medium plums, figs, or tangerines
- ⅓ cantaloupe
- ⅛ honeydew melon
- 15 small grapes or cherries
- ½ cup cut-up raw, cooked, or canned fruit
- ¾ cup raspberries or blueberries
- 8 large or 1¼ cups strawberries
- ¼ cup dried fruit
- ¾ cup (6 fluid ounces) fruit juice*

Your fruit and vegetable intake should include:
- One vitamin A–rich selection daily
- One vitamin C–rich selection daily
- At least one high-fiber (greater than 5 grams per serving) selection daily
- Several servings each week of cabbage family (cruciferous) vegetables

---

*Limit the number of servings counted from juices because they have much less fiber than whole fruits and vegetables. For diabetics, ½ cup is considered a fruit juice serving due to the high content of natural sugar.

TWENTY-FIVE TIPS TO HELP YOU MEET YOUR
DAILY FRUIT AND VEGETABLE GOAL

1. Add more vegetables and less meat to recipes for soups, stews, casseroles, stir-fries, burritos, or pastas, such as lasagna.
2. Make vegetables the entrée and meat and starches the side dishes.
3. Add more vegetables to store-bought sauces or soups.
4. Use grilled, roasted, or raw vegetable slices on sandwiches.
5. Puree cooked vegetables and use them as sauces or add them to risotto to increase flavor and creaminess.
6. Try vegetable puree soups.
7. Add fruit to breakfast cereals.
8. Have fruit juice with breakfast and a fruit snack each day.
9. Make fruits and vegetables visible. Leave fresh fruit out in bowls on tabletops. Place cut and washed vegetables, such as carrots, pepper slices or rings, broccoli, or cauliflower florets in airtight see-through containers in the refrigerator (add a little water to the bottom if you plan to keep them for more than one day).
10. Keep dried, frozen, and canned fruits and vegetables on hand for busy days.
11. If you eat convenience frozen foods, supplement the meal with a tossed green salad and a fruit dessert (choose dark green lettuce leaves when possible).
12. Expand your use of unfamiliar vegetables, such as broccoli rabe, collard greens, kale, and tropical fruits, such as mango, papaya, or kiwifruit.
13. If you do not like a particular vegetable, try a different cooking method. For example, if you don't like turnips, try oven-roasting turnips with other vegetables or mashing them with potatoes.
14. Add fruit to yogurt or blend them together to make fruit smoothies.
15. Try ethnic cuisines, such as Mediterranean, Middle Eastern, or Asian, that use lots of fruits and vegetables.
16. Shred vegetable scraps you might ordinarily throw away. Use them in casseroles, stir-fries, soups, or slaws or make a vegetable stock with them.
17. Add dried or grated fruits and vegetables to baked goods, such as muffins or quick breads.
18. Serve entrées with fruit or vegetable chutneys, compotes, or relishes.
19. Use fruit and vegetable salsas or relishes on sandwiches.
20. Add fruits and vegetables to salads (for Healthy Tuna Salad recipe, see Index).
21. Select or prepare desserts with fruit or fruit coulis (or sauces).
22. Top pizza with vegetable combinations and cut back on the cheese.
23. Top pancakes or French toast with fresh berries or fruit compote rather than butter and syrup.

24. Make omelets using one whole egg plus two egg whites per serving. Add fresh or leftover cooked vegetables, such as broccoli, spinach, asparagus, peppers, onions, and tomatoes.

25. Munch on fresh-cut vegetables while making dinner so you're not tempted to reach for chips.

Maximize Nutrient Retention in Cooking

After scrubbing well, leave edible skins on vegetables and fruits. If you do trim the skin, trim away as little as possible. Many vitamins and minerals are found in the skin or just underneath it. Avoid soaking fruits and vegetables as you wash them. Certain vitamins dissolve in water.

Cook fruits and vegetables in a minimum amount of water—or, better yet, use none at all. Steaming or microwaving vegetables and fruits is the best way to cook them. Steaming retains most of the nutrients because vegetables never come in contact with water. Cover vegetables while cooking. This speeds cooking time and preserves nutrients.

Save liquid from cooking vegetables; add it to soups, stews, and sauces. This is one way to recycle vitamins and minerals that otherwise may be lost when the cooking water is discarded.

Myth: Cooked fruits and vegetables are not as healthy as raw.

Fact: While cooking can diminish some vitamins and wash away some minerals, some phytochemicals become more available in the cooked food. Tomatoes are one example. They are one of the few (and best) sources of the protective antioxidant lycopene, which has been linked to lower rates of prostate cancer in several studies. Lycopene in the processed form (sauce and ketchup) seems to be more readily available to the body than raw and is particularly well absorbed in the presence of oil (think pizza!). Further research in the relatively new science of phytochemicals may provide insight into other fruits and vegetables. Until then we should enjoy some raw tomatoes, rich in vitamins A and C, on salads and sandwiches and others cooked as a sauce for pasta and pizza. Most important, cooked or raw, we should eat more fruits and vegetables.

Carotenoids in Fruits and Vegetables

Numerous foods contain carotenoids, including many plant species. A high intake of carotenoids has been linked to a decreased risk of many types of cancer. Of the more than six hundred identified carotenoids, the amounts found in foods are known for only a select few, such as beta-carotene, alpha-carotene, beta-cryptoxanthin, lycopene, and lutein. The others exist in foods, lending pigment and in some cases fragrance; however, their values have yet to be measured, and there is no recommended dietary allowance for the various carotenoids. Fortunately, numerical values are not necessary for the individual trying to include more carotenoids in his or her diet. Selecting from a variety of colorful fruits and vegetables and eating the recommended five to nine servings per day is all you need to do. The following list is not exhaustive but does give numerous examples of fruits and vegetables containing significant amounts of carotenoids.

CAROTENE FOOD SOURCES

apricots

arugula

basil, fresh

beets and beet greens

broccoli

broccoli rabe

cantaloupe

carrots

cherries

chicory greens

collard greens

coriander, fresh

corn

dandelion greens

dill, fresh

grapefruit, pink and red

guava

kale

lettuce, mâche

lettuce, red leaf

lettuce, romaine

mango

mint, fresh

mustard greens

nectarines

papaya

parsley, fresh

peaches

peas, green

peppers, all types

plums

rosemary, fresh

scallions

seaweed

spinach

squash, all winter varieties: acorn, butternut, delicata, golden nugget, Hubbard, pumpkin, spaghetti, and more

squash, summer

squash, zucchini

sweet potatoes

Swiss chard, red and green

turnip greens

The Balanced Plate

In trying to achieve the short-term (weight loss or maintenance) and long-term (disease prevention) benefits of healthy eating, balance and enjoyment of the foods we eat are an essential part of the plan. Up to this point we've provided formulas, percentages, and guidelines for a better understanding of individual nutritional needs. Once you're familiar with your goals, leave behind the calculations of calories, fat grams, and carbohydrates and take a look at your plate. A few simple changes can result in better weight management and overall health and disease prevention.

The sample plate in Figure 2.2 illustrates a healthy balance on the dinner plate. Notice that two-thirds of the plate is comprised of plant-based foods like vegetables, whole grains, and beans and only one-third animal protein. A fruit serving,

FIGURE 2.2 YOUR PLATE SHOULD LOOK LIKE THIS

Source: Reprinted with permission from the *American Institute for Cancer Research.*

TABLE 2.3 STANDARD SERVING SIZES

Food	Serving	Looks Like
Chopped vegetables	½ cup	½ baseball or rounded handful for average adult
Raw leafy vegetables (such as lettuce)	1 cup	1 baseball or fist of an average adult
Fresh fruit	1 medium piece	1 baseball
	½ cup chopped	½ baseball or rounded handful for average adult
Dried fruit	¼ cup	1 golf ball or scant handful for average adult
Pasta, rice, cooked cereal	½ cup	½ baseball or rounded handful for average adult
Ready-to-eat cereal	1 oz., which varies from ½ cup to 1¼ cups (check label)	
Meat, poultry, seafood	3 oz. (boneless cooked weight from 4 oz. raw)	Deck of cards
Dried beans	½ cup cooked	½ baseball or rounded handful for average adult
Nuts	⅓ cup	Level handful for average adult
Cheese	1½ oz. (2 oz. if processed cheese)	1 oz. looks like 4 dice

Source: U.S. Department of Agriculture

for dessert or as a snack, would only add to the overall balance and enjoyment of the meal.

Portion sizes are different from serving sizes. The USDA defines portion sizes as "the amount of food you choose to eat" and serving sizes as "a standard amount used to help give advice about how much to eat or to identify how many calories and nutrients are in a food." Familiarity with the USDA standard servings is key to making it all work. Depending on whether you need to lose weight, gain weight, or maintain your current weight, adjust your portions using standard serving sizes as a frame of reference. By taking a little time to measure and then remember what it looks like on the plate, you can quickly "eyeball" a balanced portion in the future.

Some easy "eyeball" guidelines are provided by the USDA (see Table 2.3). A few other comparisons to help you assess your serving sizes include:

- An open palm is roughly the size of 3 ounces of cooked meat or thick fish fillet.
- A checkbook is 3 ounces of cooked thin fish fillet.
- A 9-volt battery is 1½ ounces of cheese.
- A thumb tip (first knuckle to tip) is 1 teaspoon (think butter).

Vitamins and Minerals

The Food and Nutrition Board of the National Research Council, an arm of the National Academy of Sciences, has developed nutrition recommendations since 1943. They are revised approximately every five years to reflect the latest nutrition research. The Food and Nutrition Board sets the recommended dietary allowances (RDAs) for most vitamins and minerals based on the nutritional requirements of the majority (97 to 98 percent) of the healthy population.

The RDAs have sometimes been criticized because they are primarily set at levels to prevent deficiency of vitamins and minerals and do not address the levels needed for prevention of disease. In 1995 the Food and Nutrition Board indicated that the prevention of chronic disease should be considered in the formulation of future RDAs. New research was showing the importance of some nutrients in promoting health and preventing disease at levels considerably above the RDAs. Over an approximately seven-year period this board expanded and replaced the current RDAs with daily reference intakes (DRIs). DRIs are more complete reference values than RDAs because they include:

- Recommended dietary allowance (RDA)—the average daily intake level that meets the needs of almost all individuals by age and gender (almost no deficiencies should occur at these levels)
- Adequate intake (AI)—dietary intake levels that appear to sustain a nutritional state, such as growth, appropriate body levels of a nutrient, or some other measure of health. They are assumed to be adequate based on data available at this time, which is not sufficient to set an RDA.
- Tolerable upper intake level (UL)—the highest daily intake of a nutrient that is likely to pose no risk for toxicity for almost all individuals. The UL is not a recommended intake.

- Estimated average requirement (EAR)—the amount of a nutrient that is estimated to meet the requirement of half of all healthy individuals in the population.

Individuals should use RDAs and AIs as a goal for an average daily intake and ULs as an indicator of the highest safe amount. EARs are used predominantly by health professionals in food development, diet planning, and setting policies for food supplies for groups and populations.

Most healthy people can meet RDAs and AIs for their age and gender without supplementation. Vitamin and mineral supplementation *may* be required in some of these circumstances:

- Some vegetarians may not receive adequate calcium, iron, zinc, and/or B_{12}.
- People over sixty-five years old may require B_{12} supplementation, because production of stomach acid (needed to extract and absorb B_{12} from food) diminishes with age. Also, B_{12} supplementation may be indicated in older people who have difficulty meeting their caloric requirements and have lower intakes of protein food sources containing B_{12}.
- People with low caloric intake frequently consume diets that do not meet their nutritional needs for all nutrients. Intake of fewer than 1,200 calories per day should be supervised medically and generally requires a multivitamin and mineral supplement.
- Women who are pregnant or breast-feeding need more of certain nutrients, especially iron, folic acid, and calcium.
- Certain disorders and diseases and some medications may interfere with nutrient intake, digestion, absorption, metabolism, or excretion and thus change requirements and/or make supplementation necessary. Check with your doctor.
- Women with excessive menstrual bleeding may need to take iron supplements.
- People with limited milk intake and sunlight exposure may need vitamin D supplements.
- Calcium supplementation may be appropriate in some individuals, especially women.

Antioxidants such as vitamins C, E, and A, as well as many other substances in plants (phytochemicals), help to destroy or neutralize free radicals that have been implicated in cancer and heart disease, thereby protecting healthy cells. Although the evidence is not conclusive that vitamin and mineral supplements protect against cancer, the following supplements are considered safe for those people who occasionally do not have proper nutrition or who want a measure of added insurance.

Vitamin C

Vitamin C seems to protect against some types of cancer. The new RDA for vitamin C is 90 mg for men and 75 mg for women, up from 65 mg. The newly established tolerable upper intake level (UL) is 2,000 mg. The optimal level of vitamin C may exceed the current RDA; current research indicates that vitamin C levels of 200 to 300 mg per day may be beneficial to health. The UL indicates that it's safe (not optimal) to supplement at roughly twenty-five times the RDA. High doses of vitamin C can result in false negatives on some fecal occult blood tests for colon cancer screening; therefore vitamin C should not be taken for three days prior to occult blood testing. Eating five fruit and vegetable servings per day will meet (and likely exceed by at least double) the RDA. For most people there is no danger and potentially some benefit to supplementing vitamin C. Keep dosages under the UL of 2,000 mg.

Vitamin C Sources in Fruits and Vegetables

Best Sources	milligrams (mg)
artichoke, boiled, 1 medium	30
avocado, Florida, 1 medium	24
blackberries, raw, 1 cup	30
broccoli, boiled, ½ cup	58
brussels sprouts, boiled, ½ cup	48
cabbage, red, cooked, ½ cup	26
cauliflower, boiled, ½ cup	27
chicory greens, raw, chopped, ½ cup	22
currants, European, black, ½ cup	101
elderberries, raw, 1 cup	52
grapefruit, pink and red, ½ medium	42
grapefruit juice, fresh, 1 cup	44
guava, raw, 1 medium	165
kale, boiled, ½ cup	27
kiwifruit, raw, 1 medium	74
lemon, raw, 1 medium	31
lime, raw, 1 medium	19
mango, 1 medium	57
orange, raw, navel, 1 medium	75
orange juice, fresh, 1 cup	124
papaya, raw, 1 medium	188
parsley, raw, chopped, ½ cup	40

peppers, bell, green, raw, ½ cup chopped	45
peppers, bell, red, raw, ½ cup chopped	95
peppers, bell, yellow, ½ large	170
peppers, hot chile, raw, 1	109
pineapple, raw, 1 cup pieces	24
potato, baked with skin, 1	26
raspberries, raw, 1 cup	31
seaweed, laver (nori), raw, 3.5 oz.	39
strawberries, raw, 1 cup	84
sweet potato, baked with skin, 1	28
tomato, red, raw, 1	23
tomato juice, ¾ cup	33
turnip greens, boiled, ½ cup	20

Good Sources	*milligrams (mg)*
apricots, raw, 3 medium	11
asparagus, ½ cup (6 spears)	10
banana, peeled	10
blueberries, raw, 1 cup	19
chard, Swiss, boiled, ½ cup	16
collard greens, boiled, 1 cup	15
cranberries, whole, 1 cup	13
mustard greens, boiled, ½ cup	18
fennel bulb, raw, 1 cup slices	10
okra, boiled, ½ cup slices	10
peas, green, boiled, ½ cup	8
persimmon, Japanese, raw, 1 medium	18
rutabaga, boiled, ½ cup cubes	16
snowpeas, frozen, 3 oz.	15
soybeans, green, boiled, ½ cup	15
spinach, boiled, ½ cup	9
squash, butternut, baked, ½ cup	15

Vitamin E

Vitamin E is a fat-soluble vitamin found in nuts, oils, green leafy vegetables, and for-tified cereals. The RDA for vitamin E is 15 mg or 22 IU for healthy adults. Preliminary research led to a widely held belief that vitamin E may help prevent or delay coronary heart disease by reducing the oxidative damage caused by LDL (bad) cholesterol, but this association has still not been firmly established. Regarding a possible relationship between dietary vitamin E intake or supplementation and cancer, again the evidence is not convincing; however, vitamin E supplementation appears possibly protective against prostate cancer. Vitamin E may also help prevent Alzheimer's disease.

There are many forms of vitamin E with different biological activities. The natural form, d-alpha-tocopherol, is the basis for the RDA because it is the most active, or usable, form in the body. Most American adults get enough vitamin E from their normal diet to meet current recommendations. However, supplementation may be a consideration for individuals who consume low-fat diets, because vegetable oils are such a good dietary source of vitamin E. In general, vitamin E deficiency is rarely seen in healthy adults and is mostly a consideration for those with metabolic or malabsorptive fat diseases. Studies to establish levels of vitamin E intake to promote good health and prevent disease are ongoing.

The health risk of taking too much vitamin E is relatively low. The recently established tolerable upper intake level (UL) for vitamin E is 1,000 mg or 1,500 IU. The new RDAs list vitamin E in mg, while many food and supplement labels carry IU. For a quick conversion: 1 mg d-alpha-tocopherol = 1.5 IU.

For some people the effect of vitamin E on blood clotting might interfere with a medication's intended benefit. Vitamin E supplementation should be kept below the UL of 1,000 mg. It is prudent to discuss vitamin E supplementation with your physician.

VITAMIN E FOOD SOURCES*

Best Sources	milligrams (mg) d-alpha-tocopherol
almond oil, 1 tablespoon	5.5
almonds, dried, 1 oz.	6.7
breakfast cereals	†
cottonseed oil, 1 tablespoon	5.3
hazelnuts, 1 oz.	6.78
margarine, Mazola	8.0
mayonnaise, Best Foods/Hellmann's, 1 tablespoon	11.0
rice bran oil, 1 tablespoon	4.4
safflower oil, 1 tablespoon	6.03

*Nutrient values obtained from Pennington, J. A. T., *Bowes & Church's Food Values of Portions Commonly Used* (17th ed.), Lippincott, Williams & Wilkins, 1998.

sunflower seeds/kernels, dried, 1 oz.	14.2
wheat germ, toasted, ¼ cup	5.26
wheat germ oil, 1 tablespoon	25.94

Good Sources	*milligrams (mg) d-alpha-tocopherol*
avocado, raw, ½ medium	2.3
Brazil nuts, dried, 1 oz.	2.1
corn oil, 1 tablespoon	2.96
mango, 1 medium	2.3
olive oil, 1 tablespoon	1.7
peanut butter, 2 tablespoons	3.2
peanut oil, 1 tablespoon	1.81
peanuts, dry-roasted, 1 oz.	2.10
pistachios, dried, 1 oz.	1.48
rye flour, dark, 1 cup	3.30
soy mayonnaise, 1 tablespoon	1.65
soybean oil, 1 tablespoon	12.55

Note: *Green leafy vegetables, such as spinach, Swiss chard, kale, turnip greens, and kelp, are fair sources of vitamin E, providing 0.5 to 1 mg of d-alpha-tocopherol per 1-cup (raw) serving.*

Vitamin A

Vitamin A has many forms. Most of our vitamin A comes from plant sources. Carotenes are a group of pigments ranging from yellow to orange found in fruits and vegetables like carrots, cantaloupe, and spinach (in many deep green vegetables the chlorophyll masks the orange pigment). Beta-carotene is the most important carotene relative to vitamin A activity and is called *provitamin A*, a vitamin A precursor, because it is converted to the vitamin in the body. Preformed vitamin A, or retinol, is the natural, active form found in animal products, such as eggs, liver, and other organ meats. Vitamin A may be protective against certain types of cancer, possibly including breast cancer.

Vitamin A recommendations are in micrograms/day as retinol activity equivalents (RAEs). This takes into account the lesser activity of beta-carotene, as well as other carotenes, because it reflects the biological activity, the bioavailability or abil-

---

†Levels of fortification vary.

ity of the body to convert and use it, and the many forms of vitamin A. A man's RDA for vitamin A is 900 micrograms RAE (3,000 IU), and a woman's is 700 micrograms RAE (2,300 IU). The beta-carotene and other carotenoids in one sweet potato provide 1,139 micrograms RAE. Vitamin A deficiency is rarely seen in countries where food is abundant or foods have been fortified.

Active vitamin A or retinol is fat-soluble and can therefore be stored in the body. Two recent studies have demonstrated that vitamin A (retinol) toxicity can occur at levels lower than previously thought. In one study vitamin A levels of 25,000 IU over a period of time caused liver damage. Toxicity is particularly a concern for women of child-bearing age. In a large study pregnant women who were taking more than 10,000 IU (the amount found in some multivitamin formulas) of preformed (active retinol) vitamin A had a significantly higher risk of spontaneous abortions and birth defects in their infants.

Do not take single vitamin A supplements, particularly if you eat a lot of vitamin A–rich foods—listed below. If you take a multivitamin and mineral formula, be sure the vitamin A source is less than 10,000 IU (3,000 micrograms RAE) and preferably predominantly or completely in the form of precursor vitamin A (beta-carotene, alpha-carotene, or beta-cryptoxanthin).

1 RAE = 3.33 IU

1 RAE = 1 microgram retinol = 12 micrograms beta-carotene = 24 micrograms alpha-carotene or beta-cryptoxanthin

Vitamin A Sources in Fruits and Vegetables*

Best Sources	retinol activity equivalents (RAE)
apricots, raw, 3 medium	277
broccoli, boiled, ½ cup	108
brussels sprouts, boiled, ½ cup	56
cantaloupe, raw, 1 cup pieces	515
carrots, boiled, ½ cup	1,915
chard, Swiss, boiled, ½ cup	276
chicory greens, raw, ½ cup	360
collard greens, boiled, ½ cup chopped	349
guava, raw, 1 medium	71

*Nutrient values obtained from Pennington, J. A. T., *Bowes & Church's Food Values of Portions Commonly Used* (17th ed.), Lippincott, Williams & Wilkins, 1998.

kale, boiled, ½ cup	481
mango, raw, 1 medium	805
papaya, raw, 1 medium	85
parsley, raw, ½ cup chopped	156
persimmon, Japanese, 1 medium	365
pumpkin, boiled, ½ cup mashed	132
pumpkin, canned, ½ cup	2,691
seaweed, laver (nori), raw, 3.5 oz.	520
spinach, boiled, ½ cup	737
spinach, raw, 1 cup chopped	3,188
squash, acorn, baked, ½ cup cubes	44
squash, butternut, baked, ½ cup	714
squash, Hubbard, baked, ½ cup cubes	616
sweet potato, baked with skin, 1 medium	2,487
tomato, red, raw, 1 medium	76
turnip greens, boiled, ½ cup	396
watermelon, raw, 1 cup	54

Good Sources	*retinol activity equivalents (RAE)*
arugula, raw, 1 cup	24
asparagus, boiled, ½ cup (6 spears)	49
cherries, raw, 10	30
corn, yellow, boiled, ½ cup	18
grapefruit, pink and red, ½ medium	15
okra, boiled, ½ cup slices	41
plum, raw, 1	21
peppers, sweet, red, raw, ½ cup chopped	32
peppers, bell, yellow, ½ large	22
peppers, hot chile, raw, 1	35

Beta-Carotene

Beta-carotene is probably the most-well-known carotenoid. As mentioned previously, the body regulates the conversion of beta-carotene, as well as other carotenoids, such as alpha-carotene and beta-cryptoxanthin, to vitamin A. Only 10 percent of the more than six hundred carotenoids have the ability to be converted to active vitamin A. Unlike vitamin A (retinol), beta-carotene is nontoxic even in large amounts. Studies have linked diets high in beta-carotene and other carotenoid-containing foods to lower risk of certain types of cancer. The same may not be true for supplements. Numerous large and expensive studies have tried to link beta-carotene supplementation to lower risk of cancer. None has demonstrated such a relationship; in fact, an increased risk has been observed in smokers who take beta-carotene supplements. Considering these results, it is wise that smokers not take, or discontinue, beta-carotene supplements. For those who have not been able to quit smoking, the daily diet should contain an adequate amount of fruits and vegetables, because a diet high in fruits and vegetables has been linked to decreased risk of lung cancer.

The amount of beta-carotene found in most multivitamins is generally less than amounts found to be potentially harmful and is considered to be acceptable. It is not prudent to megadose with a single carotenoid like beta-carotene, because it may undermine the importance of the many other carotenoids. Carotenoids are abundant in many fruits and vegetables, and while only some of them can be converted to vitamin A, the remainder belong to an important group of food substances called *phytochemicals* (see Chapter 3) that appear to have cancer-fighting properties. It is possible that beta-carotene and other precursor carotenoids provide cancer protection only in the presence of other phytochemical substances in fruits and vegetables that are not found in pills. Beta-carotene is abundant in foods (for a list of such foods, see page 68). By eating at least five servings per day of a combination of vegetables and fruits, you will easily get enough dietary antioxidants, including beta-carotene.

Evidence does not support a cancer-protective effect of beta-carotene supplements. No RDA or tolerable upper intake level (UL) was set for beta-carotene or other carotenoids. Because the data on beta-carotene in pill form is inconsistent, keep supplement levels—both individually and as part of an antioxidant formula—at around 6 to 9 mg (10,000 to 15,000 IU or 3,000 to 4,500 RAE) daily. If you take a multivitamin and mineral formula, beta-carotene is the safest and preferred vitamin A source.

1 mg beta-carotene = 1,000 mcg = 1,666.7 IU vitamin A

Selenium

Selenium RDAs were established for the first time in 1989. Selenium is an antioxidant that can help prevent destruction of fat and cell membranes and may block the action of some cancer-causing substances. Over the last thirty years studies in laboratory animals have indicated that selenium may protect against many types of cancer, including cancers of the breast and esophagus. Some recent work suggests that selenium may reduce the risk of lung, colon, and prostate cancer, but these results must be confirmed.

The typical American diet provides the RDA for selenium (55 mcg). Selenium is found most abundantly in animal protein foods, such as fish, meats, and poultry. Various plant foods, such as some minimally processed grains, nuts, legumes, and fruits and vegetables, contain significant amounts. Brazil nuts sold in their shells are an extraordinary source of selenium: two nuts can provide more than the RDA. Toxicity is a real concern and has been seen with intakes as low as fifteen times the RDA, and a tolerable upper intake level (UL) of 400 micrograms has recently been established.

It's too early to make general recommendations for selenium supplementation, but don't worry about the 25 to 200 mcg that may be in a multivitamin supplement and be sure to include selenium-rich foods—listed below—in your diet. If you do supplement selenium, don't exceed 200 mcg daily (even though the UL is 400, this takes into consideration the amount likely to come from dietary sources).

SELENIUM FOOD SOURCES*

Best Sources

bass	molasses
beef	oysters
Brazil nuts	peanuts and peanut butter
cashews	red snapper
clams	salmon
cod	sunflower seeds
eggs	swordfish
haddock	tuna
lobster	turkey
mackerel	

*Selenium content of the growing soil is related directly to the amount found in plant foods. Levels of selenium in animal products depend on the quantity of these plants the animals consumed in their diet. The wide variation limits the information available in databases, so values are not provided for these foods.

Good Sources

barley	navy beans
breakfast cereals (some)	oat bran
broccoli	ocean perch
brown rice	organ meats: liver, kidney, etc.
chicken	pasta
coconut	pinto beans
crab	pork
flounder/sole	rye flour
garlic	scallops
halibut	shrimp
lamb	soybeans
lentils	veal
mushrooms	

Folic Acid

Folic acid or folate (the form of folic acid found in foods) is a B vitamin that may be linked to prevention of certain types of cancer (breast and colorectal) and heart disease. Adequate intake of folic acid may also offset the increase in cancer risk associated with drinking alcohol. Adequate folate intake during pregnancy can prevent birth defects related to the brain and spine. The relationship is so strong that the U.S. Public Health Service recommends that all women of child-bearing age consume 400 micrograms (mcg) of folic acid daily to reduce the incidence of spina bifida and other birth defects. The FDA has authorized use of health claims for food labels about the beneficial effects of folic acid and approved and guided the fortification of cereal and grain products with folate. It is preferable to meet folic acid requirements through diet rather than supplements because foods rich in folate also tend to be high in fiber and other possibly cancer-protective nutrients, such as vitamins A and C. National surveys, however, have indicated that the average intake of U.S. women is only about 230 mcg. Folate intakes of 400 mcg daily can be met easily with diets rich in fruits, vegetables, grains, and especially some types of beans; see the list below.

Because folic acid is a water-soluble vitamin that is not stored in the body, toxicity is not a major concern. For this reason people who doubt the consistent adequacy of their dietary intake should make efforts to consume fortified food products, such as some breakfast cereals, or supplement with folic acid in the form of a multivitamin. Almost all multivitamins now contain 400 mcg of folic acid.

Folic acid can mask B_{12} deficiencies, so be sure you consume B_{12}-rich foods (animal products, fortified cereals and beverages, and soy products). For animal products, a little goes a long way: 3½ ounces of cooked beef provides approximately 100 percent of the RDA for B_{12}.

FOLIC ACID FOOD SOURCES*

Best Sources	micrograms (mcg)
artichoke, boiled, 1 medium	153
asparagus, boiled, ½ cup (6 spears)	131
avocado, Florida, 1 medium	162
beef liver, braised, 3.5 oz.	217
black beans, boiled, 1 cup	256
breakfast cereals	†
chicken liver, simmered, 3.5 oz.	770
chick-peas, boiled, 1 cup	282
collard greens, frozen, boiled, ½ cup	65
cranberry beans, boiled, 1 cup	366
French beans (haricots verts), boiled, ½ cup	132
lentils, cooked, 1 cup	358
lima beans, boiled, 1 cup	156
pinto beans, boiled, 1 cup	294
red kidney beans, boiled, 1 cup	229
romaine lettuce, raw, 1 cup pieces	76
rye flour, dark, 1 cup	77
semolina flour, enriched, ½ cup	60
soy nuts, dry roasted, ½ cup	176
soybean flour, defatted, 1 cup	260
soybean flour, low-fat, 1 cup	361
spinach, boiled, ½ cup	131
split peas, cooked, 1 cup	127
sunflower seeds, oil roasted, 1 oz.	66
turnip greens, boiled, ½ cup	85
wheat germ, toasted, ¼ cup	102
white beans, boiled, 1 cup	144

*Nutrient values obtained from Pennington, J. A. T., *Bowes & Church's Food Values of Portions Commonly Used* (17th ed.), Lippincott, Williams & Wilkins, 1998.

Good Sources	micrograms (mcg)
beets, boiled, ½ cup slices	66
broccoli, boiled, ½ cup	39
brussels sprouts, boiled, ½ cup	47
corn, yellow, boiled, ½ cup	38
endive, raw, ½ cup chopped	36
okra, boiled, ½ cup slices	16
orange, navel, 1 medium	44
orange juice	†
parsley, raw, ½ cup	46
chopped parsnips, boiled, ½ cup slices	45
peas, green, boiled, ½ cup	57
pepper, bell, yellow, ½ large	48

Calcium

Although calcium is most often associated with maintenance of the skeletal structure for bones and teeth, a number of other vital bodily functions depend on this
important mineral, including blood clotting, muscle contraction and relaxation (particularly the heart), conduction of nerve impulses, and regulation of cell division. If
your diet does not supply the proper amount of calcium, your body will automati-
cally make up for the deficiency by drawing it from an emergency source—your
bones. If dietary calcium remains inadequate for a prolonged period of years, bone
deterioration may develop, which can lead to osteoporosis.

Osteoporosis, a reduction in bone mass or density, occurs more frequently in
women than in men and is particularly prevalent among postmenopausal women.
As much as one-third of bone calcium may be lost before the condition is detectable
through x-ray diagnosis. In fact it usually goes undetected until bone fracture occurs,
and by then it is usually too late to restore lost bone mass. Quite simply it is much
easier to prevent osteoporosis than it is to treat it, and a diet with the proper levels
of calcium—coupled with a regular exercise schedule—is your best protection.

Adequate calcium intake may also protect against salt-sensitive and pregnancy-
associated hypertension. High intakes of both dietary calcium and vitamin D (which
aids in the absorption of calcium) have been associated with reduced development

†Levels of fortification vary.

of precancerous changes in the colon. There is also some evidence that high levels of calcium intake may be associated with *increased* risk of prostate and ovarian cancer.

Magnesium, another mineral that plays a role in bone building, may be diminished with high calcium intake. It is for this reason that many calcium supplements include magnesium. Magnesium-rich foods include whole grains, legumes, and green leafy vegetables. Preliminary findings support a possible link between adequate magnesium intake and prevention of kidney cancers.

CALCIUM REQUIREMENTS. In August 1997 the Food and Nutrition Board of the National Research Council released a report on DRIs that began the process of expanding and updating the current RDAs. Because of their definitive role in maintaining bone health, calcium and vitamin D were among the first nutrients for which recommendations were adjusted; see Table 2.4.

Efforts should be made to meet your calcium requirements through dietary intake. In some cases it's difficult for people to reach their calcium requirements due to food preferences, intolerance to milk or milk products, and/or the high require-

---

TABLE 2.4 NEW DIETARY REFERENCE INTAKES FOR CALCIUM ISSUED BY THE NATIONAL RESEARCH COUNCIL, AUGUST 1997

Age	Adequate Intake (mg/day)
0–6 months	210
6–12 months	270
1–3 years	500
4–8 years	800
9–13 years	1,300
14–18 years	1,300
19–30 years	1,000
31–50 years	1,000
51–70 years	1,200
over 70 years	1,200
Pregnancy and Lactation	
under 19 years	1,300
19–50	1,000

Note: Calcium intake for women at menopause without estrogen replacement should increase toward 1,500 mg/day.

ments of some age groups. After checking your calcium requirements, refer to Table 2.5 on page 86 to see the amounts in the foods you eat.

Consider supplementing calcium if you are:

- an adolescent or a young adult (fourteen to eighteen years old) and do not regularly consume four to five milk equivalents per day
- a male or female between the ages of nineteen and fifty or a female fifty to sixty-five who is taking estrogen *and* you do not regularly consume three milk equivalents per day
- a female at menopause who is not undergoing estrogen replacement
- more than fifty-one years old and do not regularly consume four milk equivalents per day
- pregnant or lactating

Certain health conditions preclude calcium supplementation. Check with your physician before supplementing. Though calcium supplementation is safe for the majority of people, there is no need for most people to consume more than 1,500 mg per day.

Calcium carbonate provides the most calcium per tablet (often 500 to 600 mg) and has the least lead of any calcium supplement (bone meal has the most). For some people, such as the elderly, who produce less stomach acid, calcium carbonate is difficult to break down on an empty stomach and should be taken with meals. Calcium carbonate intake has been linked to constipation in some people. If increasing fiber and fluid intake does not help, try calcium citrate, which is as low in lead as calcium carbonate but contains significantly less calcium per tablet (usually 200 to 300 mg), so you will need to take more to reach your target.

For best absorption, spread your calcium supplementation into at least two doses. If you regularly tend to forget the second dose, take one large dose. Getting in the habit of taking supplements with meals is a good way to remember. Calcium carbonate is best absorbed if taken immediately after eating; calcium citrate is well absorbed whether taken between or with meals.

Table 2.5 on page 86 provides a list of select calcium-rich foods.

Vitamin D

Vitamin D plays a major role in calcium absorption and bone health. In the intestine vitamin D is the gatekeeper that allows calcium to enter the bloodstream. Vitamin D also works in the kidneys to help reabsorb calcium that would otherwise be

TABLE 2.5 CALCIUM-RICH FOODS

Food Item	Serving Size	Calcium Content (mg)	Calories
Milk			
Skim, lactose-reduced	1 cup	302	85
Calcium-fortified	1 cup	500	90
Soy milk plus	1 cup	300	150
Juice			
Orange juice, calcium-fortified	1 cup	330	110
Yogurt			
Fruit, low-fat	8 oz.	343	230
Plain, low-fat	8 oz.	415	145
Cheese			
Mozzarella, part skim	1 oz.	207	80
Ricotta, part skim	4 oz.	335	190
Cottage, low-fat (2%)	4 oz.	78	103
Ice milk, vanilla			
Hard (4%)	1 cup	176	185
Soft serve (3%)	1 cup	274	225
Fish and shellfish			
Oysters, raw (13–19 medium)	1 cup	226	160
Sardines, canned in oil, drained, including bones	3 oz.	372	175
Salmon, pink, canned, drained	3 oz.	167	120
Shrimp, canned, drained	3 oz.	98	100
Vegetables			
Bok choy, raw	1 cup	74	9
Broccoli, fresh, cooked, drained	1 cup	136	40
Broccoli, frozen, cooked, drained	1 cup	100	50
Soybeans, fresh, cooked, drained	1 cup	131	235
Collards, fresh, cooked, drained	1 cup	357	65
Turnips, fresh, cooked, drained, leaves and stems	1 cup	252	30
Tofu	4 oz.	108*	85

*The calcium content of tofu may vary depending on processing methods. Tofu processed with calcium salts can have as much as 300 mg per four ounces. Often the manufacturer's label can provide more specific information.

excreted. High intakes of both dietary calcium and vitamin D have been associated with reduced development of precancerous changes in the colon. The National Academy of Sciences report raised the recommendations for vitamin D to 400 IU a day for people between fifty-one and seventy years old and 600 IU for people seventy-one and older. Their guidelines for other adult age groups remain at 200 IU per day.

One cup of milk contains 100 to 125 IU. Other than fortified milk and cereals, not many food sources are rich in vitamin D. Luckily our body can make vitamin D. The skin contains a precursor of vitamin D, and, when exposed to the ultraviolet rays of the sun, the precursor turns into vitamin D. For older people the higher recommendations are difficult to achieve with diet alone, and they might consider a little bit of sunlight: a walk outside is good for older people because exercise will also help to maintain bone strength and muscle tone. Use of sunscreen is highly recommended for the prevention of skin cancer. Sunscreens, however, diminish the production of vitamin D in the skin, so if you don't consume 200 IU per day in your diet, you should consider supplementation. Vitamin D is fat-soluble (it can be stored in the body), so make sure you are not exceeding the tolerable upper intake level (UL), established at 2,000 IU per day for adults. Check the levels in milk, cereals, and all supplements (multivitamins, calcium, food and beverage supplements, etc.) and calculate your intake.

Some people may also need to consider supplements to reach their recommended requirements:

- adults under fifty years old who consume less than two milk servings per day
- men and women under fifty who have increased requirements and have less vitamin D precursor in their skin
- those who do not spend a lot of time outdoors, such as people who work at night and sleep during the day
- those who spend a fair amount of time in the sun but wear sunscreen to block out ultraviolet rays
- those who live in northern climates, where the sun is not strong enough to make vitamin D

Buying Supplements

If you take supplements, multivitamin and mineral formulas are probably the best and easiest way to balance your vitamin and mineral intake and are generally considered safe. Taking individual supplements has its risks. As many vitamins and minerals compete for absorption or need to work together, supplementing excessive amounts of one can disturb levels or diminish or enhance the action of another. For instance, calcium competes with copper, iron, phosphorus, and zinc for absorption. Taking too much of any one of these nutrients can affect the balance among all of them.

A standard vitamin and mineral supplement can be a nutritional safety net; however, it cannot make up for an unhealthy diet deficient in fruits, vegetables, whole grains, and legumes and their perfectly balanced array of vitamins, minerals, and phytochemicals. Most people get enough nutrients in their diet to prevent deficiencies, which are quite rare in healthy individuals. But a handful of nutrients that may be important in preventing chronic diseases are not consumed by everyone at optimal levels: calcium, vitamin D, folic acid, vitamin B_6, vitamin B_{12}, and vitamin E.

Sufficient amounts of the B vitamins folic acid, vitamin B_6, and vitamin B_{12} and in some cases vitamins D and E are available in standard multivitamin and mineral supplements, while calcium, if supplemented, needs to be taken individually. If you take a multivitamin and mineral supplement, be sure the vitamin A source is less than 10,000 IU (3,000 mcg RAE) and preferably predominantly or completely in the form of precursor vitamin A (beta-carotene, alpha-carotene, or beta-cryptoxanthin). Reading the Supplement Facts panel is essential in balancing your micronutrient intake.

Other things to look for on multivitamin labels include:

- Daily values. Under the Dietary Supplement Health and Education Act of 1994 (DSHEA), vitamin and mineral labels now must carry "Supplement Facts" similar to the Nutrition Facts label on commercial foods. They include percent daily values (% DV). Avoid supplements that provide more than 150 percent of the DVs of any one nutrient.
- Expiration date. Vitamins and minerals do lose their potency over time, so be sure to purchase with adequate time to use before they expire.
- Storage instructions. Heat, humidity, and light can destroy some nutrients.
- The vitamin should meet the U.S. Pharmacopeia (USP) standards for disintegration and dissolution of supplements. If vitamins and minerals are not dissolved by the time they reach the small intestine (thirty to forty-five minutes), absorption is unlikely. Look for a claim like *release assured* on the label.
- "Natural" vitamins are often combined with synthetic ones, and they are chemically the same. The exception is vitamin E. Natural vitamin E is absorbed more efficiently by the body, but many vitamins that call themselves natural may not have d-alpha-tocopherol, the natural form of vitamin E. Look for this term as the source of vitamin E.

- Balance of minerals. Many multivitamin and mineral formulas are complete in the spectrum of vitamins but lack key minerals such as calcium, chromium, copper, magnesium, and zinc. You will not find the DV for calcium in a multivitamin (it takes up too much room). Some calcium supplements provide magnesium and vitamin D. If you take supplemental calcium, read the labels and balance the amounts of all minerals with your multivitamin.
- Too much iron. Although the supplemental iron in multivitamin formulas may benefit some people, adult men and postmenopausal women are unlikely to need or benefit from additional iron. Supplemental iron can cause more harm than good; a substantial portion of the population has a genetic predisposition to store iron (hemochromatosis). For these people increased iron stores may result in an increased risk of cardiovascular disease or cancer.
- Buy vitamins sold by reputable stores, but keep in mind that the highest-priced supplement is not necessarily the best. Look at the sources of vitamins A and E and the overall completeness and balance of the formula. This is easier to assess with the new Supplement Facts labels.
- Source of dietary ingredient. Supplement labels now reveal from what source and in what quantity dietary supplements are derived: "Vitamin A (40 percent as beta-carotene)." Labeling of products containing herbal and botanical ingredients must also state the part of the plant from which the ingredient is derived.
- "Specialized Formulas" (for men and women). There is no regulation for these claims, and labels should be reviewed with the considerations listed previously.

The importance of reading labels cannot be overstated. Many foods are fortified with nutrients, and it's easy to megadose unknowingly simply by eating a breakfast cereal that provides nutrients at 100 percent of the daily values, taking a multivitamin and/or antioxidant formula, eating an energy bar at the gym (many are fortified with nutrients at the level of multivitamin supplements), and/or drinking a supplement beverage. If you take various supplements, add up the DV of all sources to be sure you're not taking too much.

Nutrition Facts Labels

Nutrition Facts labels help consumers make good food choices. With the great variety of food products available, we have an excellent opportunity to exercise discretion when choosing the foods we eat. In addition, food manufacturers have responded to contemporary dietary concerns by providing many healthy choices. Making informed decisions in today's supermarket aisles has been made easier with the implementation of the Nutrition Labeling and Education Act (NLEA) in May 1994. These changes include a more comprehensive and understandable Nutrition Facts label to help consumers make knowledgeable food choices and understand how a particular food fits into the daily diet.

For good health and cancer prevention, the Strang Cancer Prevention Center recommends limiting the percent of daily calories from fat to approximately 30 percent with the predominant sources being "healthy" fats from mono- and polyunsaturated sources. Nutrition labels include "calories from fat." It is just one of the many items of diet-related information manufacturers are required to provide on their food products. There is also information on saturated fat, cholesterol, dietary fiber, and other nutrients that relate to today's health concerns. In 2003 the FDA announced regulations adding a new line to the nutrition labels found on commercial foods to show the amount of trans fat in every serving. A sample of this label can be viewed in Figure 2.3. Food companies need not comply until January 1, 2006.

Nutrition Facts labels include daily values (DV) based on current nutritional content. The daily value was developed to make labels more "user friendly." Daily values reflect the amount of total fat, saturated fat, total carbohydrate, dietary fiber, and protein recommended based on a specified number of calories (most food labels provide daily values for 2,000- and 2,500-calorie diets). Daily values for sodium, potassium, vitamins, and minerals stay the same no matter what the caloric level. You may require more or fewer calories and nutrients than those featured on the food label because factors such as height, weight, activity level, and gender influence your true caloric needs. In this situation the daily values would need to be adjusted. Use the formula presented on page 21 to estimate your calorie requirements.

The changes reflected on the Nutrition Facts label are extremely helpful, but there are still some pitfalls to watch for:

1. Don't confuse percent daily values with percentage of a total nutrient. A pizza may have a daily value for fat of 25 percent; do not confuse this with 25 percent calories as fat. Rather, this is one-quarter of the fat allowance for the entire day. If you eat fewer than 2,000 calories per day (not uncommon for women), this daily value percent would be more than 25 percent. The daily value requirements (except those for cholesterol, sodium, and fiber) must be adjusted downward for people who consume fewer than 2,000 calories daily. For most men, large women, and athletes, however, the daily values should be adjusted upward to compensate for their increased

calorie needs. In general, a daily value of 20 percent should alert you that the food is high in that particular nutrient, and a daily value of 5 percent or less indicates that it is low.

2. A nutrient claim on a package like "90% fat-free" may sound good, but it does not mean that the product is low in fat, that it's healthy, or that only 10 percent of calories come from fat. This percentage refers to the *total weight* of the product. In this case, if the product is 90 percent fat-free by weight, the rest is made up of fat.

FIGURE 2.3 HOW TO UNDERSTAND AND USE THE NUTRITION FACTS PANEL ON FOOD LABELS

Start here →

Nutrition Facts

Serving Size 1 cup (228g)
Serving Per Container 2

Amount Per Serving

Calories 250   Calories from Fat 110

% Daily Value*

Quick guide to % DV:

5% or less is low
20% or more is high

Total Fat 12g	**18%**
Saturated Fat 3g	**15%**
Cholesterol 30mg	**10%**
Sodium 470mg	**20%**
Total Carbohydrate 31g	**10%**
Dietary Fiber 0g	**0%**
Sugars 5g	
Protein 5g	

Limit these nutrients

Vitamin A	4%
Vitamin C	2%
Calcium	20%
Iron	4%

Get enough of these nutrients

* Percent Daily Values are based on a 2,000 calorie diet. Your Daily Values may be higher or lower depending on your calorie needs:

	Calories:	2,000	2,500
Total Fat	Less than	65g	80g
Sat Fat	Less than	20g	25g
Cholesterol	Less than	300mg	300mg
Sodium	Less than	2,400mg	2,400mg
Total Carbohydrate		300g	375g
Dietary Fiber		25g	30g

Footnote

Because fat tends to weigh less than other ingredients, this could mean that 40, 50, or 60 percent of the total calories are from fat. It is always best to assess your fat gram allowance per day (or have it calculated by a registered dietitian) and then compare your daily fat gram "maximum" to the amount in the selected product.

3. What's in a serving? Although serving sizes on labels are now standardized, they may not reflect how much you're eating. If you eat more or less than the standard amount, you'll need to adjust the Nutrition Facts accordingly.

4. Trans fatty acids may be hidden in foods. Most current food labels do not tell you if trans fatty acids are present (food companies have until 2006 to comply). Why is this important? Trans fats, introduced earlier in this chapter, are formed when vegetable oils are hydrogenated to increase their shelf life and improve their texture for baking. Research suggests that they increase low-density lipoprotein (LDL) (bad) cholesterol just as saturated fats do, and worse, they decrease protective HDL cholesterol. When reading ingredient lists, search for *partially hydrogenated oil* or *vegetable shortening.* In the first case this term indicates that trans fats are present; in the second that they are likely to be present. Remember: foods that are listed as *cholesterol-free, low-cholesterol, low in saturated fat,* or *made with vegetable oil* are not necessarily trans fat–free.

5. Restaurants using Nutrition Facts to support health or nutrition claims on their menus will base claims on comparisons to standardized recipes or portion sizes. For example, if a traditional slice of cheesecake has 32 grams of fat and a restaurant calls their version "lite," it must have at least 50 percent less (16 grams or less) per serving. Nutrition Facts from restaurants can be confusing because it may be unclear what the "standard" is based on.

Nutrient Claims

Other changes in nutrition labeling include regulation of health and nutrient claims that food manufacturers can print on product labels. By law the terms *low-fat, light,* and *cholesterol-free* now have standard definitions that mean the same thing for all foods. The new label terms can help you choose foods that are lower in calories, fat, cholesterol, and sodium and higher in fiber, vitamins, and minerals.

You may find the following common food label terms helpful in selecting the foods that contribute to good health.

DEFINITIONS OF NUTRIENT CONTENT CLAIMS

Below are notes and comments on the terms *free*, *low*, and *reduced/less*, followed by the definitions of these terms for specific nutrients.

FREE

- Synonyms for *free*: *zero, no, without, trivial source of, negligible source of, dietarily insignificant source of*
- Definitions of *free* for meals and main dishes are the stated values per labeled serving

LOW

- Synonyms for *low*: *little* (*few* for calories), *contains a small amount of, low source of*

REDUCED/LESS

- Synonyms for *reduced/less*: *lower* (*fewer* for calories)
- *Modified* may be used in statement of identity
- Definitions for meals and main dishes are the same as for individual foods on a per-100-g basis

COMMENTS

- For *free*, *very low*, or *low*, must indicate if food meets a definition without benefit of special processing, alteration, formulation, or reformulation; e.g., *broccoli, a fat-free food* or *celery, a low-calorie food*

Calories

FREE

- Fewer than 5 calories per reference amount and per labeled serving

LOW

- 40 calories or less per reference amount (and per 50 g if reference amount is small)
- Meals and main dishes: 120 calories or less per 100 g

REDUCED/LESS

- At least 25% fewer calories per reference amount than an appropriate reference food
- Reference food may not be *low calorie*
- Uses term *fewer* rather than *less*

COMMENTS

- *Light* or *lite*: if 50% or more of the calories are from fat, fat must be reduced by at least 50% per reference amount. If less than 50% of calories are from fat, fat must be reduced at least 50% or calories reduced at least ⅓ per reference amount

continued →

DEFINITIONS OF NUTRIENT CONTENT CLAIMS (CONTINUED)

- *Light* or *lite* meal or main dish product meets definition of *low-calorie* or *low-fat* meal and is labeled to indicate which definition is met
- For dietary supplements: calorie claims can be made only when the reference product has more than 40 calories per serving

Total Fat

FREE

- Less than 0.5 g per reference amount and per labeled serving (or for meals and main dishes, less than 0.5 g per labeled serving)

LOW

- 3 g or less per reference amount (and per 50 g if reference amount is small)
- Meals and main dishes: 3 g or less per 100 g and not more than 30% of calories from fat

REDUCED/LESS

- At least 25% less fat per reference amount than an appropriate reference food
- Reference food may not be *low fat*

COMMENTS

- ___% *Fat Free*: OK if meets the requirements for "Low Fat"
- *100% Fat Free*: food must be "Fat Free"
- *Light* or *lite* meal or main dish product meets definition of *low-calorie* or *low-fat* meal and is labeled to indicate which definition is met
- For dietary supplements: calorie claims cannot be made for products that have 40 or fewer calories per serving

Saturated Fat

FREE

- Less than 0.5 g saturated fat and less than 0.5 g trans fatty acids per reference amount and per labeled serving (or for meals and main dishes, less than 0.5 g saturated fat and less than 0.5 g trans fatty acids per labeled serving)
- No ingredient that is understood to contain saturated fat except as noted below*

LOW

- 1 g or less per reference amount and 15% or less of calories from saturated fat
- Meals and main dishes: 1 g or less per 100 g and less than 10% of calories from saturated fat

REDUCED/LESS

- At least 25% less saturated fat per reference amount than an appropriate reference food
- Reference food may not be *low saturated fat*

COMMENTS

- Next to all saturated fat claims, the amount of cholesterol must be declared if 2 mg or more per reference amount; also the amount of total fat if more than 3 g per reference amount (or 0.5 g or more of total fat for *saturated fat free*)
- For dietary supplements: saturated fat claims cannot be made for products that have 40 or fewer calories per serving

Cholesterol

FREE

- Less than 2 mg per reference amount and per labeled serving (or for meals and main dishes, less than 2 mg per labeled serving)
- No ingredient that contains cholesterol except as noted below*
- If less than 2 mg per reference amount by special processing and total fat exceeds 13 g per reference amount and labeled serving, the amount of cholesterol must be *substantially less* (25%) than in a reference food with significant market share (5% of market)

LOW

- 20 mg or less per reference amount (and per 50 g of food if reference amount is small)
- If qualifies by special processing and total fat exceeds 13 g per reference and labeled serving, the amount of cholesterol must be *substantially less* (25%) than in a reference food with significant market share (5% of market)
- Meals and main dishes: 20 mg or less per 100 g

REDUCED/LESS

- At least 25% less cholesterol per reference amount than an appropriate reference food
- Reference food may not be *low cholesterol*

COMMENTS

- Cholesterol claims allowed only when food contains 2 g or less saturated fat per reference amount; or for meals and main dish products—per labeled serving size for *free* claims or per 100 g for *low* and *reduced/less* claims
- Must declare the amount of total fat next to cholesterol claim when fat exceeds 13 g per reference amount and labeled serving (or per 50 g of food if reference amount is small), or when the fat exceeds 19.5 g per labeled serving for main dishes or 26 g for meal products
- For dietary supplements: cholesterol claims cannot be made for products that have 40 or fewer calories per serving

continued →

DEFINITIONS OF NUTRIENT CONTENT CLAIMS (CONTINUED)

Sodium

FREE

- Less than 5 mg per reference amount and per labeled serving (or for meals and main dishes, less than 5 mg per labeled serving)
- No ingredient that is sodium chloride or generally understood to contain sodium except as noted below*

Low

- 140 mg or less per reference amount (and per 50 g if reference amount is small)
- Meals and main dishes: 140 mg or less per 100 g

REDUCED/LESS

- At least 25% less sodium per reference amount than an appropriate reference food
- Reference food may not be *low sodium*

COMMENTS

- *Light* (for sodium-reduced products): if food is *low calorie* and *low fat* and sodium is reduced by at least 50%
- *Light in sodium*: if sodium is reduced by at least 50% per reference amount. Entire term *light in sodium* must be used in same type, size, color, and prominence. *Light in sodium* for meals = *low in sodium*
- *Very low sodium*: 35 mg or less per reference amount (and per 50 g if reference amount is small). For meals and main dishes: 35 mg or less per 100 g
- *Salt free* must meet criteria for *sodium free*
- *No salt added* and *unsalted* must declare *This is not a sodium-free food* on information panel if food is not *sodium free*
- *Lightly salted*: 50% less sodium than normally added to reference food, and if not *low sodium*, so labeled on information panel

Sugars

FREE

- "Sugar Free": less than 0.5 g sugars per reference amount and per labeled serving (or for meals and main dishes, less than 0.5 g per labeled serving)
- No ingredient that is a sugar or generally understood to contain sugars except as noted below*
- Disclose calorie profile (e.g., "Low Calorie")

Low

- Not defined. No basis for recommended intake.

REDUCED/LESS

- At least 25% less sugars per reference amount than an appropriate reference food
- May not use this claim on dietary supplements of vitamins and minerals

COMMENTS

- *No added sugars* and *without added sugars* are allowed if no sugar or sugar-containing ingredient is added during processing. State if food is not *low* or *reduced calorie*
- The terms *unsweetened* and *no added sweeteners* remain as factual statements
- Claims about reducing dental caries are implied health claims
- Does not include sugar alcohols

Notes

- "Reference Amount" = reference amount customarily consumed.
- "Small Reference Amount" = reference amount of 30 g or less or 2 tablespoons or less (for dehydrated foods that are typically consumed when rehydrated with water or a diluent containing an insignificant amount, as defined in 21 CFR 101.9(f)(1), of all nutrients per reference amount, the per-50-g criterion refers to the prepared form of the food).
- When levels exceed 13 g fat, 4 g saturated fat, 60 mg cholesterol, and 480 mg sodium per reference amount, per labeled serving or, for foods with small reference amounts, per 50 g, a disclosure statement is required as part of claim (e.g., "See nutrition information for ___ content" with the blank filled in with nutrient(s) that exceed the prescribed levels).

*Except if the ingredient listed in the ingredient statement has an asterisk that refers to footnote (e.g., "*adds a trivial amount of fat").

Source: U.S. Food and Drug Administration, Center for Food Safety and Applied Nutrition, A Food Labeling Guide, September, 1994 (editorial revisions June 1999)

Health Claims

The following shows the relationships between nutrients (in foods and supplements) and disease that may be described in authorized health claims.

HEALTH CLAIMS

Calcium and Osteoporosis

FOOD REQUIREMENTS

- High in calcium
- Assimilable (bioavailable)

continued →

HEALTH CLAIMS (CONTINUED)

- Supplements must disintegrate and dissolve
- Phosphorus content cannot exceed calcium content

CLAIM REQUIREMENTS

- Indicates disease depends on many factors by listing risk factors for the disease: gender—female; race—Caucasian and Asian; age—growing older
- Primary target population: females, Caucasian and Asian races, and teens and young adults in their bone-forming years
- Additional factors necessary to reduce risk: eating healthful meals, regular exercise
- Mechanism relating calcium to osteoporosis: optimizes peak bone mass
- Foods or supplements containing more than 400 mg calcium must state that total intakes of greater than 2,000 mg calcium provide no added benefit to bone health.

MODEL CLAIM, STATEMENTS

Regular exercise and a healthy diet with enough calcium help teens and young adult white and Asian women maintain good bone health and may reduce their high risk of osteoporosis later in life.

Sodium and Hypertension

FOOD REQUIREMENTS

- Low sodium

CLAIM REQUIREMENTS

- Required terms: *sodium, high blood pressure*
- Includes physician statement (*Individuals with high blood pressure should consult their physicians*) if claim defines high or normal blood pressure

MODEL CLAIM, STATEMENTS

Diets low in sodium may reduce the risk of high blood pressure, a disease associated with many factors.

Dietary Fat and Cancer

FOOD REQUIREMENTS

- Low fat (fish and game meats: *extra lean*)

CLAIM REQUIREMENTS

- Required terms: *total fat* or *fat*; *some types of cancers* or *some cancers*
- Does not specify types of fats or fatty acids that may be related to risk of cancer

MODEL CLAIM, STATEMENTS

Development of cancer depends on many factors. A diet low in total fat may reduce the risk of some cancers.

Dietary Saturated Fat and Cholesterol and Risk of Coronary Heart Disease

FOOD REQUIREMENTS

- Low saturated fat
- Low cholesterol
- Low fat (fish and game meats: *extra lean*)

CLAIM REQUIREMENTS

- Required terms: *saturated fat and cholesterol*; *coronary heart disease* or *heart disease*
- Includes physician statement (*Individuals with elevated blood total—or LDL—cholesterol should consult their physicians*) if claim defines high or normal blood total—and LDL—cholesterol

MODEL CLAIM, STATEMENTS

While many factors affect heart disease, diets low in saturated fat and cholesterol may reduce the risk of this disease.

Fiber-Containing Grain Products, Fruits, and Vegetables and Cancer

FOOD REQUIREMENTS

- A grain product, fruit, or vegetable that contains dietary fiber
- Low fat
- Good source of dietary fiber (without fortification)

CLAIM REQUIREMENTS

- Required terms: *fiber, dietary fiber*, or *total dietary fiber*; *some types of cancer* or *some cancers*
- Does not specify types of dietary fiber that may be related to risk of cancer

MODEL CLAIM, STATEMENTS

Low-fat diets rich in fiber-containing grain products, fruits, and vegetables may reduce the risk of some types of cancer, a disease associated with many factors.

Fruits, Vegetables, and Grain Products That Contain Fiber, Particularly Soluble Fiber, and Risk of Coronary Heart Disease

FOOD REQUIREMENTS

- A fruit, vegetable, or grain product that contains fiber
- Low saturated fat
- Low cholesterol
- Low fat
- At least 0.6 g soluble fiber per RA (without fortification)
- Soluble fiber content provided on label

continued →

HEALTH CLAIMS (CONTINUED)

CLAIM REQUIREMENTS

- Required terms: *fiber, dietary fiber, some types of dietary fiber, some dietary fibers*, or *some fibers*; *saturated fat* and *cholesterol*; *heart disease* or *coronary heart disease*
- Includes physician statement (*Individuals with elevated blood total—or LDL—cholesterol should consult their physicians*) if claim defines high or normal blood total—and LDL—cholesterol

MODEL CLAIM, STATEMENTS

Diets low in saturated fat and cholesterol and rich in fruits, vegetables, and grain products that contain some types of dietary fiber, particularly soluble fiber, may reduce the risk of heart disease, a disease associated with many factors.

Fruits and Vegetables and Cancer

FOOD REQUIREMENTS

- A fruit or vegetable
- Low fat
- Good source (without fortification) of at least one of the following:
  - vitamin A
  - vitamin C
  - dietary fiber

CLAIM REQUIREMENTS

- Required terms: *fiber, dietary fiber*, or *total dietary fiber*; *total fat* or *fat*; *some types of cancer* or *some cancers*
- Characterizes fruits and vegetables as *foods that are low in fat and may contain vitamin A, vitamin C, and dietary fiber*
- Characterizes specific food as a *good source* of one or more of the following: dietary fiber, vitamin A, or vitamin C
- Does not specify types of fats or fatty acids or types of dietary fiber that may be related to risk of cancer

MODEL CLAIM, STATEMENTS

Low-fat diets rich in fruits and vegetables (foods that are low in fat and may contain dietary fiber, vitamin A, or vitamin C) may reduce the risk of some types of cancer, a disease associated with many factors. Broccoli is high in vitamins A and C, and it is a good source of dietary fiber.

Folate and Neural Tube Defects

FOOD REQUIREMENTS

- *Good source* of folate (at least 40 mcg folate per serving)
- Dietary supplements or foods in conventional food form that are naturally good sources of folate (i.e., only nonfortified food in conventional food form)

- The claim shall not be made on products that contain more than 100% of the DRI for vitamin A as retinol or preformed vitamin A or vitamin D
- Dietary supplements shall meet USP standards for disintegration and dissolution or be otherwise bioavailable
- Amount of folate required in nutrition label

CLAIM REQUIREMENTS
- Required terms:
  - Terms that specify the relationship (e.g., women who are capable of becoming pregnant and who consume adequate amounts of folate)
  - *Folate*; *folic acid*; *folacin*; *folate, a B vitamin*; *folic acid, a B vitamin*; *folacin, a B vitamin*; *neural tube defects*; *birth defects, spinal bifida, or anencephaly*; *birth defects of the brain or spinal cord—anencephaly or spinal bifida*; *spinal bifida or anencephaly, birth defects of the brain or spinal cord*
- Must also include information on the multifactorial nature of neural tube defects, and the tolerable upper intake level (UL)

MODEL CLAIM, STATEMENTS
Healthful diets with adequate folate may reduce a woman's risk of having a child with a brain or spinal cord defect.

Dietary Sugar Alcohol and Dental Caries

FOOD REQUIREMENTS
- Sugar free
- The sugar alcohol must be xylitol, sorbitol, mannitol, maltitol, isomalt, lactitol, hydrogenated starch hydrolysates, hydrogenated glucose syrups, erythritol, or a combination
- When a fermentable carbohydrate is present, the food must not lower plaque pH below 5.7

CLAIM REQUIREMENTS
- Required terms: *does not promote, may reduce the risk of, useful* [or *is useful*] *in not promoting* or *expressly* [or *is expressly*] *for not promoting dental caries*; *sugar alcohol* or *sugar alcohols* or the name or names of the sugar alcohols (e.g., *sorbitol*); *dental caries* or *tooth decay*
- Includes statement that frequent between-meal consumption of foods high in sugars and starches can promote tooth decay
- Packages with less than 15 square inches of surface area available for labeling may use a shortened claim.

MODEL CLAIM, STATEMENTS
Full claim: Frequent between-meal consumption of foods high in sugars and starches promotes tooth decay. The sugar alcohols in [name of food] do not promote tooth decay.

continued →

HEALTH CLAIMS (CONTINUED)

Shortened claim (on small packages only): Does not promote tooth decay.

Soluble Fiber from Certain Foods and Risk of Coronary Heart Disease (CHD)

FOOD REQUIREMENTS

- Low saturated fat
- Low cholesterol
- Low fat
- Include either (1) one or more eligible sources of whole oats, containing at least 0.75 g whole-oat soluble fiber per RA; or (2) psyllium seed husk containing at least 1.7 g of psyllium husk soluble fiber per RA
- Amount of soluble fiber per RA declared in nutrition label

Eligible source of soluble fiber (see updated information): Beta glucan soluble fiber from oat bran, rolled oats (or oatmeal), and whole-oat flour. Oat bran must provide at least 5.5% beta glucan soluble fiber, rolled oats must provide at least 4% beta glucan soluble fiber, and whole-oat flour must provide at least 4% beta glucan soluble fiber or psyllium husk wih purity of no less than 95%.

CLAIM REQUIREMENTS

- Required terms: *heart disease* or *coronary heart disease*; *soluble fiber* qualified by either *psyllium seed husk* or the name of the eligible source of whole-oat soluble fiber; *saturated fat* and *cholesterol*
- Daily dietary intake of the soluble fiber source necessary to reduce the risk of CHD and the contribution one serving of the product makes to this level of intake

Additional required label statement: Foods bearing a psyllium seed husk health claim must also bear a label statement concerning the need to consume them with adequate amounts of fluids; e.g., *NOTICE: This food should be eaten with at least a full glass of liquid. Eating this product without enough liquid may cause choking. Do not eat this product if you have difficulty in swallowing.* (21 CFR 101.17(f))

MODEL CLAIM, STATEMENTS

Soluble fiber from foods such as [name of soluble fiber source, and, if desired, name of food product], as part of a diet low in saturated fat and cholesterol, may reduce the risk of heart disease. A serving of [name of food product] supplies __ grams of the [necessary daily dietary intake for the benefit] soluble fiber from [name of soluble fiber source] necessary per day to have this effect.

Soy Protein and Risk of Coronary Heart Disease

FOOD REQUIREMENTS
- At least 6.25 g soy protein per RA
- Low saturated fat
- Low cholesterol
- Low fat (except that foods made from whole soybeans that contain no fat in addition to that inherent in the whole soybean are exempt from the low-fat requirement)

CLAIM REQUIREMENTS
- Required terms: *heart disease* or *coronary heart disease*; *soy protein*; *saturated fat* and *cholesterol*
- Claim specifies daily dietary intake levels of soy protein associated with reduced risk
- Claim specifies amount of soy protein in a serving of food

MODEL CLAIM, STATEMENTS
- Twenty-five grams of soy protein a day, as part of a diet low in saturated fat and cholesterol, may reduce the risk of heart disease. A serving of [name of food] supplies __ grams of soy protein.
- Diets low in saturated fat and cholesterol that include 25 grams of soy protein a day may reduce the risk of heart disease. One serving of [name of food] provides __ grams of soy protein.

Plant Sterol/Stanol Esters and Risk of Coronary Heart Disease

FOOD REQUIREMENTS
- At least 0.65 g plant sterol esters per RA of spreads and salad dressings *or* at least 1.7 g plant stanol esters per RA of spreads, salad dressings, snack bars, and dietary supplements
- Low saturated fat
- Low cholesterol
- Spreads and salad dressings that exceed 13 g fat per 50 g must bear the statement *See nutrition information for fat content*

Salad dressings are exempted from the minimum 10% DV nutrient requirement (see General Criteria below)

CLAIM REQUIREMENTS
- Required terms: *may* or *might* reduce the risk of CHD; *heart disease* or *coronary heart disease*; *plant sterol esters* or *plant stanol esters*, except *vegetable oil* may replace the term *plant* if vegetable oil is the sole source of the sterol/stanol ester

continued →

HEALTH CLAIMS (CONTINUED)

- Claim specifies plant sterol/stanol esters are part of a diet low in saturated fat and cholesterol.
- Claim does not attribute any degree of CHD risk reduction.
- Claim specifies the daily dietary intake of plant sterol or stanol esters necessary to reduce CHD risk and the amount provided per serving.
- Claim specifies that plant sterol or stanol esters should be consumed with two different meals each day.

MODEL CLAIM, STATEMENTS

- Foods containing at least 0.65 gram per serving of vegetable oil sterol esters, eaten twice a day with meals for a daily total intake of at least 1.3 grams, as part of a diet low in saturated fat and cholesterol, may reduce the risk of heart disease. A serving of [name of food] supplies __ grams of vegetable oil sterol esters.
- Diets low in saturated fat and cholesterol that include two servings of foods that provide a daily total of at least 3.4 grams of plant stanol esters in two meals may reduce the risk of heart disease. A serving of [name of food] supplies __ grams of plant stanol esters.

Whole-Grain Foods and Risk of Heart Disease and Certain Cancers

FOOD REQUIREMENTS

- Contains 51 percent or more whole-grain ingredients by weight per RA
- Dietary fiber content at least:
  - 3.0 g per RA of 55 g
  - 2.8 g per RA of 50 g
  - 2.5 g per RA of 45 g
  - 1.7 g per RA of 35 g
- Low fat

CLAIM REQUIREMENTS

Required wording of the claim: *Diets rich in whole-grain foods and other plant foods and low in total fat, saturated fat, and cholesterol may reduce the risk of heart disease and some cancers.*

MODEL CLAIM, STATEMENTS

NA

Potassium and the Risk of High Blood Pressure and Stroke

FOOD REQUIREMENTS

- Good source of potassium
- Low sodium

- Low total fat
- Low saturated fat
- Low cholesterol

CLAIM REQUIREMENTS

Required wording for the claim: *Diets containing foods that are a good source of potassium and that are low in sodium may reduce the risk of high blood pressure and stroke.*

MODEL CLAIM, STATEMENTS

NA

General Criteria All Claims Must Meet

- All information in one place without intervening material (reference statement permitted).
- Only information on the value that intake or reduced intake, as part of a total dietary pattern, may have on a disease or health-related condition.
- Enables public to understand information provided and significance of information in the context of a total daily diet.
- Complete, truthful, and not misleading.
- Food contains, without fortification, 10% or more of the daily value for one of six nutrients (dietary supplements excepted):

Vitamin A	500 IU	Calcium	100 mg
Vitamin C	6 mg	Protein	5 g
Iron	1.8 mg	Fiber	2.5 g

- Not represented for infants or toddlers less than 2 years of age.
- Uses *may* or *might* to express relationship between substance and disease.
- Does not quantify any degree of risk reduction.
- Indicates disease depends on many factors.
- Food contains less than the specified levels of four disqualifying nutrients:

Disqualifying Nutrients	Foods	Main Dishes	Meal Products
Fat	13 g	19.5 g	26 g
Saturated Fat	4 g	6 g	8 g
Cholesterol	60 mg	90 mg	120 mg
Sodium	480 mg	720 mg	960 mg

Abbreviations: RA = reference amount, IU = International Units

Source: U.S. Food and Drug Administration, Center for Food Safety and Applied Nutrition, A Food Labeling Guide, September, 1994 (editorial revisions June, 1999)

For further information on the Nutrition Facts food label and how to use it, visit The U.S. FDA Center for Food Safety and Applied Nutrition: Food Labeling and Nutrition at http://vm.cfsan.fda.gov/label.html.

3

Phytochemicals

The New Functional Foods

PHYTOCHEMICALS (*phyto* = "plant") are sometimes referred to as *functional foods* (because they are thought to prevent disease). These compounds originate from plants and are responsible for the color, odor, and flavor of certain foods. They are not nutrients, having no calories or known nutritional value. A particular fruit or vegetable may contain hundreds of different phytochemicals. We don't have the ability to make phytochemicals in our body, but we can absorb them through the foods we eat.

There is still much to be learned about these functional foods and their potential to fight disease, especially cancer. Phytochemicals are now actively being studied, and the National Cancer Institute (part of the National Institutes of Health) has focused research efforts on the anticancer constituents in these plant foods. Emphasis is on identifying and isolating new phytochemicals and studying their effects on cancer and other diseases.

We don't know exactly how phytochemicals work in the body, but it is thought that they may have antioxidant capabilities, as well as the potential to block and suppress carcinogens. Blocking agents increase enzymes that detoxify carcinogens and/or interfere with their activation. Suppressing agents oppose the carcinogenic changes in malignant cells by retarding or reversing the process, directly interfering with the promotion phase of carcinogenesis. In laboratory studies many phytochemicals have been shown to inhibit tumor development and growth in animals. Little research has been done on the long-term effects in people, but evidence is accumulating that phytochemicals may have the ability to decrease cancer and cardiovascular disease. Studies have shown that eating a diet high in plant-rich foods like fruits, vegetables, and whole grains decreases the risk of developing many cancers. These foods contain many phytochemicals in addition to other nutrients and nonnutrients, such as fiber, vitamins, minerals, and carbohydrates.

Phytochemicals are a complex group of food substances that includes many classes and subclasses. Although it's generally thought that phytochemicals might aid in preventing or treating cancer, each group appears to have unique and specific actions. Here is what we know about the different types of phytochemicals and how they may act to fight cancer.

MAJOR CLASSES OF PHYTOCHEMICALS

Allium Compounds

Glucosinolates

dithiolthiones
isothiocyanates

sulforaphane
indoles

Plant Polyphenols

Phenolic Acids

chlorogenic, caffeic, and ferulic acids
curcumin

ellagic acid

Flavonoids

catechins and theaflavins
anthocyanins
coumarin
kaempferol
quercetin (rutin)

tangeretin and nobiletin
phytoestrogens
    isoflavones (daidzein, genistein)
    coumestrans
    lignans

Capsaicin

Terpenes

Monoterpenes
d-limonene

myrcene

Diterpenes

carnosol   rosmarinic acid

Triterpenes

glycyrrhizin   zingiberene
6-gingerol

Carotenoids

carotenes (tetraterpenes)   xanthophylls (non–vitamin A)
  vitamin A precursors   zeaxanthin
    alpha-carotene   cryptoxanthin
    beta-carotene
    epsilon-carotene
  non–vitamin A precursors
    lutein
    lycopene
    gamma-carotene

Protease Inhibitors

Inositol (Phytic Acid)

Fatty Acids

linolenic acid (omega-3 fatty acid)

Plant Sterols

sterols   saponins

Allium Compounds

Allium is found in plants of the genus *Allium*: chives, garlic, leeks, onions, and shallots. Studies have shown a decreased risk of stomach and possibly colon cancer in people who consume foods rich in allium. Studies of laboratory animals have also produced some evidence of a beneficial effect on prostate, skin, and esophageal cancer. The sulfur-containing compounds, called *allicin* and *diallyl sulfide*, may be the active ingredients that help to reduce cancer risk.

Garlic, a significant food source of allium, has received considerable attention. Manufacturers of garlic supplements have made many claims about its cancer-fighting ability. It's important to remember that although some studies support an anticancer effect of garlic, research is in the preliminary stages and no definitive conclusion can be made at this time. We do know that most of the research done to date has looked at garlic from fresh foods; supplements may not confer the same benefit. Because garlic is rich in vitamins and minerals, it's prudent to incorporate it into your diet even though ongoing scientific studies have not proven that garlic protects against cancer.

SIGNIFICANT SOURCES OF ALLIUM COMPOUNDS

chives	onions, all types
garlic	shallots
leeks	

ALLIUM COMPOUNDS

Proposed anticancer functions: as blocking agents, stimulate production of detoxification enzymes, which help excrete carcinogens; decrease proliferation of tumor cells; antibacterial activity inhibits formation of N-nitroso compounds, which are associated with stomach cancer; may stimulate tumor-fighting immune cells

Other functions: lower low-density lipoprotein (LDL) blood cholesterol and blood pressure; inhibit blood clotting that can lead to stroke

---

Glucosinolates and Indoles

Many studies have looked at the effect of vegetables containing high amounts of glucosinolates (cruciferous vegetables, such as cabbage, kale, broccoli, and cauliflower) on cancer risk. These phytochemicals have shown a beneficial effect on cancer. People who consume large amounts of vegetables from this family appear at decreased risk of developing cancers of the lung, stomach, colon, and rectum. Also, there appears to be a positive effect for prostate, endometrial, and ovarian cancer, but the findings are not conclusive. Indoles are a breakdown product of glucosinolates and also seem to protect against cancers, especially those dependent on estrogen, like breast and endometrial cancer. A high intake of indoles has been reported to reduce recurrent laryngeal tumors.

SIGNIFICANT SOURCES OF GLUCOSINOLATES

Dithiolthiones, Isothiocyanates, and Sulforaphane

broccoli	kale
brussels sprouts	mustard greens
cabbage	radishes
cauliflower	turnips
horseradish	

Indoles

bok choy	kale
broccoli	kohlrabi
brussels sprouts	mustard greens
cabbage	rutabaga
cauliflower	turnips
collards	

GLUCOSINOLATES

Dithiolthiones, Isothiocyanates, Sulforaphane
Proposed anticancer functions: antioxidants; promote production of protective detoxifying enzymes that block carcinogens; decrease activity of enzymes that promote carcinogenesis; may inhibit tumor growth

Indoles
Proposed anticancer functions: promote production of enzymes that inactivate cancer-promoting estrogens and androgens; boost ability to detoxify carcinogens; increase immune activity

Plant Polyphenols

The plant polyphenols are a large class of phytochemicals that are potent antioxidants. They are thought to induce detoxification enzymes, prevent cancer at the initiation stage, and inhibit activity of enzymes involved in cancer progression. Results from animal studies have shown that polyphenols have anticarcinogenic effects. This class of polyphenols may have a beneficial effect on cholesterol, triglyceride fat, blood pressure levels, and cardiovascular disease. Antibacterial, antiviral, and anti-inflammatory properties have also been proposed.

Phenolic Acids

The phenolic acids, a subgroup of the plant polyphenols, are found in various foods, including fruits and vegetables as well as some spices. The phenolic acids include chlorogenic, caffeic, and ferulic acids; curcumin; and ellagic acid. These substances are believed to act as cancer protectors by neutralizing or blocking carcinogens.

PHENOLIC ACIDS

Chlorogenic, Caffeic, and Ferulic Acids; Curcumin; Ellagic Acid
Proposed anticancer functions: antioxidants; blocking agents; tumor suppressors; neutralize and reduce genetic damage caused by carcinogens like tobacco; anti-inflammatories

---

Flavonoids

The flavonoids, another subclass of the plant polyphenols, are found in fruits, vegetables, and soy products. Flavonoids may reduce cancer by acting as antioxidants. Subclasses of the flavonoids include the catechins and theaflavins, quercetin, and coumarin. Another subclass of flavonoids, called phytoestrogens, may inhibit hormones thought to be involved in cancer promotion and development.

CATECHINS AND THEAFLAVINS. Tea contains catechins (in green tea) and theaflavins (in black tea), which are part of the plant polyphenol family. Laboratory experiments have shown both green and black teas to be anticarcinogenic. Green tea has received most of the attention, and preliminary studies suggest it may decrease the risk for certain cancers and protect against heart disease. Specifically, decreased tumors of the skin, lung, esophagus, stomach, colon, liver, pancreas, and breast have been observed. Scientists believe polyphenols contained in both green and black teas are responsible for this anticancer activity. Green tea has higher levels of polyphenols than black tea. Decaffeinated teas appear to offer some of the same benefits. (Herbal teas are made using a different process from black or green tea and do not contain polyphenols.)

Relatively few studies have been conducted examining the link between tea and cancer. High tea consumption may explain why the lung cancer rates in Japan are only half those in the United States, even though the rate of cigarette smoking is nearly twice that of the United States. Not all studies have shown a beneficial effect, though; in fact, some have shown an increased risk of esophageal cancer in tea drinkers. This has been attributed specifically to drinking tea at burning temperatures, which causes injury to the esophagus.

At this time we can't definitively "prove" that tea drinking decreases the risk for cancer, but it's reasonable to conclude that tea is possibly beneficial for esophageal and stomach cancers. This remains a promising area of research.

FLAVONOIDS

Catechins and Theaflavins
Proposed anticancer functions: powerful antioxidants; promote production of detoxifying enzymes; inhibit tumor growth; may aid immune system and help rid body of potential carcinogens; anti-inflammatories
Other functions: may protect against atherosclerosis; cholesterol-lowering effect

Anthocyanins, Coumarin, Kaempferol, Quercetin, Tangeretin, Nobiletin
Proposed anticancer functions: antioxidants; blocking agents; promote production of detoxifying enzymes; tumor suppressors

---

PHYTOESTROGENS. Phytoestrogens are a subclass of flavonoids that have anticancer properties. They function as antioxidants, blocking enzymes that activate carcinogens, and suppressors of cell growth and division. Isoflavone-containing plants have a structure similar to human estrogen and contain hormones called *phytoestrogens*. More than three hundred plants have been identified with this estrogen activity, but the best sources are soybeans, soy products, and other legumes.

These phytoestrogens are believed to act like human estrogens or sex hormones to help regulate female reproductive cycles. Having much less potency than naturally occurring estrogens in the body, however, they act like weak estrogens. They reduce the level of the "stronger" estrogens by competing with them, furthering their excretion from the body as well as their promoting effects, which can convert normal cells to cancer cells. Cancers of the breast, ovary, and uterus (endometrium) depend on hormones for growth and proliferation. Tamoxifen, a synthetic drug used to treat cancer, has a structure similar to that of the phytoestrogens.

Studies have shown a five to eight times lower incidence of breast cancer in Asian women than American women. Asian women from countries such as Japan, China, and Korea traditionally eat a diet high in soy foods and have lower circulating levels of estrogen compared to women who eat a Western diet. Some scientists believe the differences in soy intake may explain this variation in breast cancer rates; however, we cannot definitely say that consumption of soy products reduces the risk of breast cancer. Additionally, some studies have raised the concern that these compounds could actually promote the growth of breast cancer. Other factors related to lifestyle differences between Asian and American women may also be affecting relative risk of breast cancer.

Soy may increase the length of the menstrual cycle, which would decrease the total exposure of a woman's body to estrogens. Asian women have a menstrual cycle that is two to three days longer than that of American women, and most of them do not experience menopausal symptoms. Phytoestrogens may function as hormone replacement for women during menopause, reducing hot flashes and mood swings. Because traditional hormone replacement therapy has been associated with an increased risk for some cancers, the potential of these substances to provide estrogen without raising cancer risk is being investigated as an alternative to estrogen replacement therapy for menopausal women.

Phytoestrogens may also have an effect on prostate cancer (a hormone-dependent cancer that occurs only in men) by blocking or reducing testosterone, which can foster growth of cancer. This theory is supported by the fact that estrogen has been shown to slow the growth of prostate cancer by affecting testosterone. Epidemiologic and laboratory experiments suggest that phytoestrogens, particularly quercetin (which has phytoestrogen and antioxidant properties), may lower the risk of prostate cancer. There is up to a thirtyfold variation in prostate cancer rates between Asian and American men. Men from Asian countries traditionally eat diets high in phytoestrogen-containing foods. These men do get prostate cancer, but their tumors seem to progress at a much slower rate, and mortality from this cancer is low. Complicating this picture, however, is the fact that Asian men tend to eat far less red meat and dairy products than American men do, and both of these food types are now suspected to be factors possibly increasing risk of prostate cancer.

PHYTOESTROGENS

Isoflavones (Daidzein and Genistein)
Proposed anticancer functions: may block growth of new vessels essential for some tumors to grow and spread by inactivating cancer enzymes; antiestrogen effects; stimulate differentiation of malignant cells
Other functions: lower serum cholesterol and may prevent heart disease and osteoporosis

Coumestrans and Lignans
Proposed anticancer functions: antioxidant; may block or suppress carcinogenic changes

Capsaicin

Another subclass of the plant polyphenols, capsaicin is present in hot chile peppers and produces the pungent characteristic burning sensation. Capsaicin appears to block carcinogenesis by neutralizing stomach carcinogens but in large quantities may actually increase the risk of stomach cancer. Little is known about the effects of capsaicin, and at this time hypotheses are preliminary.

CAPSAICIN
Proposed anticancer functions: blocks carcinogenesis; neutralizes carcinogens, but consumption of large quantities may be linked to stomach cancer
Other functions: anticoagulant; may help to prevent heart attack or stroke

SIGNIFICANT SOURCES OF PLANT POLYPHENOLS

Phenolic Acids

Chlorogenic, Caffeic, and Ferulic Acids

apples	peaches
citrus fruits: grapefruits, lemons, limes, oranges, tangerines	pears
	potatoes
coffee	strawberries
green peppers	tomatoes
lettuce	

Curcumin

curry	turmeric
mustard	

Ellagic Acid

cranberries	raspberries
grapes	strawberries
loganberries	walnuts

Flavonoids

Catechins and Theaflavins

berries, all types	green and black teas

Anthocyanins

apples	grapes
artichokes	licorice
berries	wine, varying amounts

Coumarin

broccoli	fenugreek, component of some
cabbage	herbal teas
carrots	squash
citrus fruits: grapefruits, lemons, limes, oranges	yams

Kaempferol

horseradish	radishes

Quercetin and Its Glycosides (e.g., Rutin)

bell peppers	onions
berries	pea pods
broad beans or fava beans	potatoes
citrus fruits and juices	rosemary
eggplant	shallots
flaxseed	tomatoes
green and black teas	

Tangeretin and Nobiletin

tangerines

Phytoestrogens

Isoflavones (Genistein and Daidzein)
soy products
soybeans

Coumestrans
bean sprouts
red clover
sunflower seeds

Lignans*
flaxseed
rye
sesame seeds
soybeans
soy products
wheat

Terpenes

Terpenes are one of the largest classes of phytochemicals, and their subclasses number in the thousands. They exist in different forms, including monoterpenes, diterpenes, triterpenes, and carotenoids (tetraterpenes), and are found in most fruits and vegetables. The terpenes function predominantly as antioxidants; however, some terpenes, particularly those found in citrus fruits, stimulate enzymes to block carcinogens. They may also inhibit cholesterol production and enhance immune function. Taxol is a member of the terpene family and is used to treat breast and ovarian cancers. Taxol is not found in food but was first derived from the Pacific yew tree and is now made semisynthetically.

SIGNIFICANT SOURCES OF TERPENES

Monoterpenes (Including D-Limonene)

basil	fennel seeds and bulb
broccoli	mint
cabbage	nutmeg
caraway seeds	parsley
cardamom	peppers
carrots	spearmint
celery seed	squash
citrus fruits: grapefruits, lemons, limes, oranges (especially their peels)	star anise
	thyme
	tomatoes
cucumbers	yams
eggplant	

*Lignans are a type of fiber; for grains, the less processing, the more lignans.

Myrcene
lemongrass

Diterpenes

oregano (rosmarinic acid)   rosemary (carnosol)

Triterpenes

citrus fruits   soybeans and soy products
licorice

6-Gingerol, Glycyrrhizin, and Zingiberene
ginger   licorice root

TERPENES

Monoterpenes (D-Limonene and Myrcene)
Proposed anticancer functions: antioxidants; blocking agents that increase protective enzymes that may interfere with carcinogens; may help differentiation of cells to nonmalignant state
Other functions: inhibit cholesterol production

Diterpenes (Carnosol, Rosmarinic Acid)
Proposed anticancer functions: potent antioxidants; increase detoxification enzymes; anti-inflammatories
Other functions: may have antiviral properties

Triterpenes (Glycyrrhizin,* 6-Gingerol, Zingiberene)
Proposed anticancer functions: may slow rate of growth of cancer cells; suppress enzymes and hormones related to cancer; enhance immune function

---

*Glycyrrhizin is one subclass of triterpenes and is contained in true licorice root (found at health food stores and in certain herbal teas). In excessive amounts glycyrrhizin can be toxic, so moderate your consumption of both licorice root and licorice-containing products.

Carotenoids

The carotenoids are a major subclass of the broad terpene group. Carotenoids are what give fruits and vegetables their yellow, orange, and red colors (dark green vegetables and herbs also contain carotenoids; however, their colors are masked by the green pigment chlorophyll). The six hundred or more different carotenoids can be divided into two distinct subgroups: carotenes and xanthophylls. Although carotenes are known to be precursors of vitamin A, only 10 percent of all carotenes can be converted to vitamin A. Carotenes include beta-carotene, lycopene, and lutein. All are known for their anticancer properties. Carotenes have varying degrees of antioxidant properties, and some enhance immune response and protect skin cells against ultraviolet radiation. The second group of carotenoids, xanthophylls, functions as antioxidants and include zeaxanthin and cryptoxanthin.

For food sources, see page 68.

CAROTENOIDS
Proposed anticancer functions: antioxidants; metabolized to vitamin A, which helps cell differentiation (lack of differentiation is a characteristic of cancer cells); may inhibit cell proliferation
Other functions: may reduce heart disease, stroke, and anti-inflammatory disorders; improve immune response; lower cholesterol levels; may reduce cataracts

---

Protease Inhibitors

Protease inhibitors are another major subclass of phytochemicals that act to limit the action of enzymes that break down protein. They are found predominantly in beans, seeds, and soy products. It has been suggested that these inhibitors act to slow the rate of cell division in cancer cells, allowing time for genetic repair. To date, there is little research on the effects of protease inhibitors in human cancer, but studies have shown a reduction of tumors in animals.

SIGNIFICANT SOURCES OF PROTEASE INHIBITORS*
grains: barley, oats, wheat, rye   soy
legumes   soy products
seeds

---

*Levels are more significant if food is not cooked extensively.

PROTEASE INHIBITORS
Proposed anticancer functions: prevent normal cells from being transformed to cancer cells; inhibit tumor promotion and cell proliferation; increase genetic repair of enzymes

Inositol (Phytic Acid)

Inositol is of plant origin and is found in legumes, cereals, and soybeans. An anticancer effect has been observed in laboratory experiments. In studies diets high in fiber, which are also high in this phytochemical, have been linked to decreased cancers of the breast, colon, and pancreas, but epidemiological studies on this topic have not been conclusive.

SIGNIFICANT SOURCES OF INOSITOL (PHYTIC ACID)

all types of bran (rice, rye, wheat, sesame seeds
   oat, corn, soy)* soybeans
lima beans soy products
nuts

INOSITOL (PHYTIC ACID)
Proposed anticancer functions: reduces cell proliferation; increases differentiation of cells; may bind with dietary minerals to decrease production of free radicals

Fatty Acids

Linolenic acid is a fatty acid found in plant sources (linseed oils, walnuts, green leafy vegetables) that can be converted to omega-3 fatty acid.

For food sources, see pages 29–30.

---

*The less processed the bran, the more inositol.

FATTY ACIDS

Linolenic Acid (Omega-3 Fatty Acid)
Proposed anticancer functions: regulates prostaglandin production that reduces inflammation and may stimulate the immune system

Plant Sterols

Plant sterols are a type of fat that is similar to cholesterol. Vegetables contain significant amounts of plant sterols. No research has been done in humans so far, but a decreased rate of colon tumors in animals fed plant sterols has been shown. Saponins are a subclass of the sterol group.

SIGNIFICANT SOURCES OF PLANT STEROLS*

Best Sources	milligrams (mg)
almonds, dried, 1 oz.	40
amaranth, 1 cup	47
cashews, dried, 1 oz.	45
corn oil, 1 tablespoon	136
mayonnaise (safflower), 1 tablespoon	40
mayonnaise (soybean), 1 tablespoon	49
peanuts, raw, 1 oz.	62
pine nuts, 1 oz.	40
rice bran oil, 1 tablespoon	167
sesame oil, 1 tablespoon	121
sesame seeds, whole dried, 1 tablespoon	64
soybeans, green, boiled, ½ cup	45
sunflower seeds/kernels, dried, 1 oz.	150
wheat germ oil, 1 tablespoon	77

*Nutrient values obtained from Pennington, J. A. T., *Bowes & Church's Food Values of Portions Commonly Used* (17th ed.), Lippincott, Williams & Wilkins, 1998.

Good Sources	milligrams (mg)
apple, raw, with skin, 1 medium	17
apricots, raw, 3 medium	19
asparagus, boiled, ½ cup	22
bamboo shoots, raw, ½ cup	14
banana, raw, 1 medium	18
cantaloupe, raw, 1 cup	16
cherries, sweet, raw, 10 each	8
cucumber, raw, ½ cup slices	7
figs, raw, 2 medium	32
grapefruit, raw, white, ½ medium	20
olive oil, 1 tablespoon	31
onion, raw, ½ cup	12
orange, navel, 1 medium	31
peach, raw, 1 medium	9
pear, raw, 1 medium	13
pecans, dried, 1 oz.	31
pomegranate, Japanese, raw, 1 medium	26
soybean oil, 1 tablespoon	35
tomato, red, raw, 1 medium	9
walnut oil, 1 tablespoon	25
walnuts, English/Persian, dried, 1 oz.	31

PLANT STEROLS

Sterols
Proposed anticancer functions: block estrogen promotion of breast cancer activity and act as differentiation agents of cancer cells during replication; suppress cancer growth
Other functions: cholesterol-lowering properties

Saponins
Proposed anticancer functions: influence genetic material in cancer cells not to multiply; reduce proliferation and decrease growth of various tumor cells
Other functions: cholesterol-lowering properties

Supplementation of Phytochemicals

Even though new phytochemicals are being discovered each day, we still have much to learn about the potential beneficial effect on disease. Many health food manufacturers have begun to market phytochemicals in supplement form: examples include garlic and broccoli pills, as well as supplements that contain polyphenols and isoflavones. It is premature at this time to be selling synthetically made phytochemicals, because we know so little about their beneficial and possibly harmful effects. Many questions are still unanswered.

It's unclear whether these substances protect against disease once extracted from plants and incorporated into pill form. Often the pill forms of these substances contain very little or none of the proposed active ingredient. The amount that is beneficial is not known; neither is the effect of megadoses (more is not always better). It may be dangerous for people to "treat" themselves with these substances. Furthermore, thousands of other unidentified substances in plants may work in conjunction with the phytochemical of interest that a supplement would not provide.

Given the current lack of knowledge about the effects of phytochemicals, it's better to get these substances from the foods we eat than to take a pill. Eating a variety of foods, including fruits, vegetables, grains, and legumes, each day will ensure this.

4

Cooking for Cancer Prevention

NOW THAT YOU KNOW WHY AND HOW to make improvements in your diet, let's get cooking! While the recipes in Chapter 5 aim to follow the guidelines we've given you, keep in mind two words that you've heard so often relative to diet: *balance* and *moderation*. This means your diet can include a dish, a meal, or even a full day of indulgence that can be balanced out by improvements in the next meal or on the following day. For example, some nutritious low-calorie dishes, such as Antoine Bouterin's Spinach Cake (see Index), with 57 percent of its calories derived from fat, is almost double our recommended 25 to 30 percent range. When you look more closely, however, the recipe contains only 104 calories and just 7 grams of fat per serving (just over a teaspoon), and when combined with a whole balanced meal (dishes that have a much lower fat percentage) the percentage of calories from fat will fall within the suggested range. Table 4.1 on page 126 illustrates how to balance the fat in a meal.

The range of enormously talented chefs who have provided recipes for this book proves that healthy eating and great taste are not mutually exclusive. Some chefs have provided recipes from their restaurants (encouraging news for those who try to maintain a healthy diet when dining out). If you visit Chef Daniel Boulud at one of his restaurants (Daniel, DB, or Café Boulud in New York) or Chef Michael Chiarello at Tra Vigne or next-door Tomatina during the summer months, you are likely to see their Summer Vegetable Casserole with Basil and Black Olives (see Index) and Lentil

TABLE 4.1 BALANCING THE FAT

Food Item	Calories	Fat (g)	% Calories from Fat
Spinach Cake*	104	7	57
Full-Flavor Roasted Chicken*	240	10	37
Juice (8 fl. oz.) or Sweetened Iced Tea (4 fl. oz.)	120	0	0
Strawberry Soup*	124	<1	3
Totals	588	18	28

*See Index for page numbers for recipes.

and Shelling Bean Stew (see Index), respectively, on the menu. Many chefs have also provided us with the inside scoop—a recipe from a rare day of cooking at home.

If you are unsure about putting all of the information together and making it work, consider this: the chefs who have successfully submitted recipes that are low in fat and high in cancer-protective nutrients were provided with the following guidelines:

1. Remember ease of preparation—skill level, time, and equipment—for the home cook.
2. Use colorful fruits and/or vegetables.
3. Choose "healthy" fats such as olive, vegetable, and nut oils and limit added fat to approximately ½ to 1 teaspoon per serving for appetizers, side dishes, or accompaniments and 1 teaspoon per serving for entrées and desserts.
4. Choose from all types of whole grains and legumes.
5. If your recipe includes meat, select leaner cuts, game, or poultry.
6. Select from all types of fish and shellfish.
7. Use fresh herbs and seasonings whenever possible.

Using this limited amount of information, the chefs almost unanimously met the specifications. In all cases the recipes have been tested and in some instances *slightly* modified for nutrient profile or ease of preparation in the home kitchen. With all of this information at your fingertips, you can do it too!

The nutritional analyses and commentary on recipes will add to your knowledge of the composition of foods—important for decision making when shopping, cooking, and dining out. The phytochemical lists include some technical terms that you will likely be hearing a lot more about in the future and that we have already introduced in this book, mainly in Chapter 3. Our goal in including them with recipes is not to overwhelm you but to demonstrate that a lot of these protective compounds are probably already in your diet, and we invite you to review the chapter on phytochemicals for more information about these potentially health-promoting substances.

Successful cooks, whether professional or in the home, have a few things in common. They read recipes in their entirety first, have all ingredients on hand and prepped before starting to cook, and make minor adaptations when necessary with regard to cooking facilities, equipment, and ingredient availability. The shopping and equipment lists will help you get your kitchen organized for healthy and tasty cooking. So, there you have it! You are on your way to making delicious meals for optimal health.

Ingredients for Healthy Cooking

It's much easier to prepare a healthy meal on a busy day when you already have the basic ingredients on hand. Here's a shopping list to work from: not every food is absolutely necessary; this is a sample of balance and variety in food choices.

DAIRY
"lite" 1 percent soy milk (or 1 percent or skim cow's milk)
low-fat cheese (soy cheese or any other type with less than 3 grams of fat per
   ounce)
low-fat or fat-free sour cream
low-fat or nonfat yogurt (also soy-based yogurts)

FRESH PRODUCE
citrus fruits: grapefruits, lemons, limes, oranges
cruciferous vegetables: broccoli, brussels sprouts, cabbage, cauliflower,
   kohlrabi, rutabagas, turnips
green leafy vegetables: collard, dandelion, turnip, and mustard greens; kale;
   mesclun; spinach; Swiss chard; watercress

fresh herbs: basil, cilantro, oregano, parsley, rosemary, sage, tarragon, thyme

onion family: chives, garlic, leeks, onions, shallots

other deep green, orange, red, and yellow produce (rich in vitamins A and/or C, carotenes, and other phytochemicals): apricots; seasonal berries; carrots; cherries; chiles; melons (all types); peaches; peppers (all types); potatoes (sweet and white); tomatoes; tropical fruit such as mangos, kiwi, and papaya; winter and summer squash

BEEF/PORK/POULTRY/GAME/FISH
(FOR LEAN PROTEIN LISTS, SEE PAGES 36–38)

beef: flank steak; choice or select top, bottom, or eye round (trimmed); chuck

pork: trimmed center loin or tenderloin, extra-lean ham

chicken: skinless breast, skinless boneless thigh meat, ground chicken (ask your butcher to grind skinless breast meat to help keep fat low)

turkey: skinless breast meat

game: skinless duck or quail breast, rabbit, venison, elk, ostrich

lamb: trimmed leg

fish: any fish, particularly those rich in omega-3 fatty acids (see pages 20–30)

FATS AND OILS

butter (store frozen to keep fresh for its limited uses)

canola oil

extra-virgin olive oil

nut, flavored, or spice- or herb-infused oils (walnut, chile, rosemary, etc.)— a little bit goes a long way

sesame oil (dark or light)

CANNED GOODS

beans: an assortment such as chick-peas, black beans, Great Northern, kidney, and pinto

broths, low-sodium (vegetable, chicken, and/or beef broths help you make a quick and tasty soup, stew, or braised dish)

soups, low-fat, low-sodium (bean, vegetable, or other broth-based soups that can be enriched further with fresh vegetables)

tomato paste*

tomatoes, stewed*

tomatoes, whole*

---

*Processed or cooked tomatoes have more of the phytochemical lycopene—a powerful antioxidant—than fresh uncooked tomatoes.

DRIED FRUIT
apricots
cranberries
currants
raisins

GRAINS, CEREALS, DRIED LEGUMES
barley (a good way to add texture and fiber to soup; a rice substitute for risotto)
beans, dried: black beans, chick-peas, red beans, white beans
bread: rye, multigrain, whole wheat, flaxseed, pita, walnut raisin
breakfast cereals, hot and cold (look for one with more than 3 grams of fiber per serving and less than 2 to 3 grams of fat)
bulgur (finely ground bulgur cooks quickly and is a good source of fiber)
couscous, whole wheat: quick cooking and easy to prepare; a great base to top with any type of lean stewed meat or vegetables
cracked wheat (great for high-fiber salads such as tabbouleh)
crackers (low-fat, whole-grain)
flaxseed: whole or ground (a tasty way to increase nutrients and fiber in baked goods)
flour: all-purpose, low-fat soy, whole wheat
lentils: red and green
pasta, dry: any shape (although not a whole grain, pasta cooks quickly and makes a great "bed" for vegetables and low-fat protein sources such as shell-fish and chicken)
polenta (finely ground cornmeal cooks quickly and makes a nice change from the usual starch)
rice, brown and long-grain (other good selections to have around include Arborio, an Italian short-grain rice; wild; and basmati rices)
tortillas (whole wheat, fat-free)

DRIED SPICES AND HERBS*

bay leaves	nutmeg
cayenne	oregano
chili powder	paprika
cloves	peppercorns (white and black)
coriander seed	rosemary (dried)
cumin, ground	tarragon

*Dried herbs and spices lose their potency and flavor over time, so buy small containers when possible.

curry powder
fennel seed
ginger

thyme (dried)
turmeric

BAKING BASICS

baking powder
baking soda
cornstarch
kosher or coarse salt

sea salt
sugar (brown, white, granulated,
    and powdered)
vanilla extract

CONDIMENTS, MISCELLANEOUS

capers
Dijon or other flavored mustards
dried mushrooms, such as porcini
    or morels
honey
ketchup*
maple syrup

olives
tahini (sesame paste)
tamari or soy sauce
vinegars (an assortment of types
    and flavors is useful)
Worcestershire sauce

FROZEN FOODS

all-natural, low-fat soy products (frozen soy burgers, sausages, bacon, and hot
    dogs can provide a quick and healthy protein source; soy burgers can be
    ground and substituted for ground beef in recipes; soy sausages can be eaten
    plain or added to soups, stews, or casseroles)
fruit: berries (great for savory or dessert sauces or sorbets)
low-fat pizzas that can be topped later with more vegetables
vegetables: broccoli, corn, brussels sprouts, spinach, winter squash, or vegetable
    combinations (plain vegetables, not in the form of soufflés or with sauces)

HOMEMADE GOODS

defatted stocks or broths such as beef, chicken, mushroom, or vegetable, stored
    frozen in 2- to 4-cup portions to make healthy cooking easier
sauces and soups (when preparing healthy sauces or soups, double or triple the
    recipe and freeze in small containers—a low-fat tomato sauce, for instance,
    can be used in a variety of recipes)

---

*Processed or cooked tomatoes have more of the phytochemical lycopene—a powerful antioxi-
dant—than fresh uncooked tomatoes.

OTHER SHOPPING TIPS

- Try not to shop on an empty stomach. This encourages "impulse shopping" and can lead to selection of all the wrong foods.
- Learn to read Nutrition Facts food labels (see pages 89–92). This is an empowering component of healthy food selection.
- Go straight to the fruits and vegetables. Here is where you should direct most of the energy you expend filling your cart. Having them around will be helpful in meal planning, cooking, and snacking.
- Fruits and vegetables bought in season not only taste better but are also cheaper. (For an extensive list, see page 132.)
- Though fresh vegetables taste terrific, don't hesitate to buy frozen vegetables; in many cases they are nutritionally equivalent.
- Buy bags of frozen fruits and vegetables instead of boxes—it's easier to store leftovers for another use.
- When buying canned goods, like fruit or beans, save some calories by seeking out fruits canned in juice, not syrup, or plain beans, canned in their cooking liquid, not sauces.
- Try bulk shopping; depending on your family size, you can buy larger portions of your favorite grains, cereals, beans, or dried fruits.
- Try a new fruit, vegetable, grain, or legume frequently. This will add variety and enjoyment to eating as well as different nutrients and phytochemicals.
- Consider keeping a cooler in your car. This will provide some protection for perishable purchases, allowing you to stop and run a few errands on a very hot (or cold) day.

Seasonal Ingredients

Growing season should be among your first thoughts in selecting quality fruits and vegetables. Simply telling people to eat more fruits and vegetables because "they're good for you" has a small impact. Have you ever had a peach in January? Most likely it was mealy and flavorless. Now, if this were your first taste, your natural reaction might be "I don't like peaches." Whereas had this delicious fruit been tasted in the height of its season, its unique character just might have sparked your sense of taste and a desire to include it in your diet more often. Eating fruits and vegetables when their flavor peaks is the key to improving *and* enjoying our diets. It is also part of eating economically; the price of the awful peach far exceeds that of the succulent, juicy, sweet summer variety. You shouldn't compromise on the quality of your ingredients—selecting superior ingredients is one of the easiest ways to improve your cooking abilities.

Let the following lists be your insight into the seasons.

WINTER

avocados	dates	parsnips
broccoli rabe	endive	radicchio
carrots	fennel	rutabagas
citrus	kale	sprouts (year-round)
collards	leeks	turnips

SPRING

artichokes	mâche	radishes
asparagus	morels	rhubarb
baby carrots	new potatoes	sorrel
baby greens	peas	watercress
baby turnips		

SUMMER

apricots	garlic	plums (stone fruit)
berries	herbs	shell beans
cherries (stone fruit)	melons	strawberries
corn	nectarines (stone fruit)	summer squash
cucumbers	onions and scallions	tomatoes
eggplant	peaches (stone fruit)	

FALL

apples	chard	persimmons
arugula	cranberries	pomegranates
beets and beet greens	grapes	potatoes
bell peppers and chiles	lettuce/mixed greens	prunes
broccoli	mushrooms	quince
brussels sprouts	mustard greens	spinach
cauliflower	nuts	sweet potatoes
celery root	pears	winter squash

Snacking

Snacking can help or hurt a healthful diet. The difference lies in what you choose and how much you eat. You can make snacking work for you, satisfying between-meals hunger *and* adding protective nutrients to your diet. It just takes a little planning so that you have the desired food on hand when you need it. You don't want to be forced to choose from limited, and usually unhealthy, selections from a deli, vending machine, or inadequately stocked pantry or refrigerator. Make snacking a conscious activity instead of eating in front of the TV or while reading. This can help prevent inadvertent overeating. Finally, choose healthier snacks, such as those from the following lists.

GRAB-AND-GO SNACKS
- Mini rice cakes
- Breadsticks
- Baked chips
- Fresh fruits
- Dried fruits (apricots, raisins, etc.)
- Nuts and trail mixes
- Applesauce or other fruit cups
- Low-fat ready-to-serve pudding cups
- Light popcorn
- Low-fat graham crackers
- Gingersnaps
- Pretzels
- Granola bars
- Fruit bars, such as Fig Newtons or Apple Newtons
- Fruit smoothies
- Frozen fruit bars
- Fudgsicles
- Frozen fruit, such as bananas, grapes, or berries
- Pretzels and whole wheat pretzels
- Plain, vanilla, and fruited low-fat yogurts
- Frozen yogurt (soft serve and pops)

EASY MAKE-AHEAD SNACKS

- Raw vegetable sticks dipped in peanut butter, low-fat or fat-free salad dressing, or low-fat sour cream dip
- Low-fat tortillas with bean dip and salsa
- Rice cakes with peanut butter or fruit butters
- Rice cake stackers: rice cakes sandwiched with peanut butter or fruit butters and sliced fruit such as bananas
- Whole-grain crackers with peanut butter or fruit butters
- Low-fat graham crackers
- Low-fat vanilla yogurt mixed with granola and/or dried fruit
- Homemade trail mix: pretzels mixed with nuts and low-fat cereals such as Cheerios, corn flakes, or Chex
- Quick grilled cheese—melt on low-fat tortilla, fold in half, and dip in salsa
- Instant low-fat pudding mixes: blend any flavor with low-fat milk and let sit 5 minutes.
- Fruit smoothies
- Pizza bagel or English muffin halves: top with tomato sauce, cheese, and vegetables
- Apple sandwiches: Core apple and slice into rings. Place slice of cheese between rings.

Kitchen Equipment for Healthy Cooking

ESSENTIAL

2 nonstick skillets (small and large), preferably with a metal handle that allows
    transfer from stove to oven*

nonstick sauté pan (12- or 14-inch) with a lid*

2-quart pot with a lid

6-quart pot with a lid

roasting pan, preferably nonstick

---

*Nonstick cookware and bakeware emit fumes called perfluorinated chemicals (PFCs). Research on PFCs is ongoing. To date, the Environmental Protection Agency (EPA) has said there is no reason for consumers to stop using nonstick products. Nonstick cookware and bakeware can be helpful in creating flavorful dishes while moderating fat. Low or medium heat should be used for cookware and bakeware with nonstick surfaces. The coatings can withstand temperatures up to 500°F, which is well above what is recommended for frying or baking.

one or two 9- × 12-inch nonstick cookie sheets

bottle opener

can opener

colander

blender (whipping air into sauces and vinaigrettes produces a smooth texture
without added fat; also great for fruit smoothies)

food processor

grater (grating cheese allows you to spread it out more evenly and therefore use
less; also good for zesting citrus or shredding vegetables)

1 large fork

chef's knife (8-, 10-, or 12-inch)

paring knife

serrated knife (for bread, tomatoes, vegetable terrines)

2 wooden spoons

kitchen tongs

slotted and solid kitchen spoons

2 ladles (2-oz. and 4-oz.)

2 spatulas (metal and for nonstick cookware)

rubber spatula

measuring cups and measuring spoons

plastic containers with lids (useful for storing and freezing batches of soups,
sauces, stews, and leftovers)

pot holders

2 strainers (medium- and fine-mesh, for straining sauces, soups, fruit purees,
and coulis)

salad spinner (useful for salad greens, herbs, and other washed vegetables)

stainless-steel mixing bowls

steamer basket

wire rack

wire whisk

wooden and/or plastic cutting board

vegetable peeler

Helpful

4-quart pot with a lid

12-quart stockpot

mandoline (Used for chopping, mandolines can save a lot of time when a large
amount of slicing is required. They make vegetables more attractive, and the

thinner slices shorten cooking time, preserving nutrients. Mandolines are usually sold with a variety of blades for thin slicing and julienne and french-fry cutting. Inexpensive, good-quality plastic mandolines are available at most culinary stores.)

kitchen scale

electric mixer

hand blender

4-, 6-, and/or 8-oz. ramekins (an individual baking dish usually made of porcelain or earthenware; perfect for low-fat puddings, soufflés, and molds)

terrine mold (great for making vegetable terrines; the possible vegetable, herb, and seasoning combinations are limitless)

nonstick loaf pan for low-fat fruit and vegetable quick breads, meat, poultry, or fish loafs

nonstick muffin pans

cast-iron pan* (Once well seasoned, there is usually no need to add more fat, even when sautéing a delicate meat. A properly seasoned pan has been treated with enough oil to permeate the relatively porous metal. After a pan has been seasoned, it should be wiped clean rather than washed to maintain its protective seal.)

pastry rings (great for making low-fat tarts using fresh fruits with phyllo dough crust)

slicing and boning knives

zesting plane (for quick and easy removal of the flavorful and nutritious peels from fruits)

Pans with heavy bottoms (usually from a copper core that conducts and distributes heat well) allow you to sauté vegetables for long periods without browning (unless desired) or burning. This technique is called *sweating* and is important for concentrating and extracting maximum flavor.

---

*To season a cast-iron pan: rinse a new cast-iron pan in warm sudsy water. Dry thoroughly, then pour a small amount of oil into the pan. Using a paper towel or a kitchen towel, spread the oil evenly on the bottom and sides of the pan. Place the pan in an oven preheated to 350°F for one to two hours. Let cool. Repeat the process. After use, do not wash a cast-iron pan with dish soap. Instead, scrub with an abrasive sponge, dry, rub with a small amount of oil, then dry over heat on the stove.

General Tips for Healthy Cooking

How much should you worry about cancer risk from pesticide residues, food additives, or even natural carcinogens in food? In 1996 a twenty-member panel of the National Research Council confirmed that cancer-causing substances, both natural and synthetic, exist in foods, but their potential to cause cancer is minimal when compared with overconsumption of calories and fat. Obesity and diets high in saturated fat are linked much more strongly to cancer. Many fruits and vegetables have natural carcinogens that do not pose a risk of cancer unless eaten in enormous amounts. In addition, any cancer risk from fruits and vegetables is far outweighed by their anticarcinogenic compounds—vitamins, minerals, and phytochemicals. Still, there are steps you can take to further minimize the amounts of cancer-causing compounds in food and from cooking.

To prevent or limit formation of carcinogenic compounds during cooking, take some of the following steps:

- Trim all excess fat from meat and remove the skin from poultry. This limits the amount of fat that drips during grilling, reducing, or charring.
- Marinate meat, fish, poultry, or vegetables, but wipe them off before grilling.
- Precook (microwave, poach, or roast) chicken or pork before placing on the grill, limiting high-heat contact and charring. (This will also help to ensure that bacteria that can cause food-borne illnesses is killed.)
- Do not use juices that are released from the cooked meat once it has been taken off the grill.
- When grilling, cook food at least 6 inches above the heat source.
- If charring occurs, do not eat the burned portions.
- Don't use mesquite; it produces very high heat that can cause charring.
- If drippings from fat create a lot of smoke, remove food from the grill or reduce the heat.
- Serve grilled foods with vitamin C–rich foods. Try tomato salads, fruit or vegetable salsas, chutneys or relishes, or orange and red onion salad.
- Steam foods sealed in foil wrap over the grill.
- Brush vegetables with a little oil to prevent sticking to the grill and burning.
- Slice vegetables less than 2 inches thick to reduce cooking time on the grill or precook slightly by roasting.
- Limit fried foods.
- Think about how often you grill, what foods you grill, how well done the meat is, and what other foods you eat.

MINIMIZING PESTICIDE RESIDUES

- Rinse all fruits and vegetables thoroughly to remove dirt, bacteria, and any surface residues from pesticides. If you use a small amount of mild detergent to help remove pesticides, be sure to rinse thoroughly; otherwise chemicals not meant for consumption will be left behind.
- Peel vegetables with wax-coated skins, such as apples, cucumbers, and eggplant, but do not peel all vegetables, because fiber and other nutrients are concentrated in or near the skin. Also, seasonal produce is less likely to be coated with wax.
- Use a scrub brush for potatoes, sweet potatoes, carrots, zucchini, or summer squash when you plan to eat the skin.
- Chop or tear vegetables with nonuniform shapes and curvatures, such as broccoli, cauliflower, spinach, or lettuce leaves, before rinsing to help ensure that the water reaches all areas.
- Discard outer leaves of the head of salad vegetables like cabbage or lettuce.
- Root vegetables (grown under the ground) accumulate more pesticides than those grown aboveground, so consider buying organic root vegetables.
- Eat a variety of foods to minimize your exposure to pesticides.
- Try to eat locally grown produce when in season and ask the farm if pesticides are used. Becoming a "certified organic" farm is a lengthy and expensive process. Many farmers use organic methods but cannot promote their products as "organic." In that case they often advertise that their produce is grown "without pesticides" or "pesticide-free."
- Buy some or all organic produce. Look for food with the USDA Organic label (for a sample, see Figure 4.1).

MINIMIZING FOOD ADDITIVES

- Food additives are put in during processing, so eat minimally processed foods that have more fiber, vitamins, minerals, and phytochemicals.
- Limit use of "instant" and quick-cooking products.
- Limit convenience products or meals with seasoning packs, such as rices and other packages that say "just add . . .".
- Limit commercial sweets and snack foods. Select fruit or some other form of whole food instead.
- Buy some or all organic meats and poultry. Look for food with the USDA Organic label (for a sample, see Figure 4.1).

Organic Foods

The Organic Foods Production Act passed in 1990 promised national certification and a standardized definition of organic foods. In 2000 the USDA announced the final national standards for the production, handling, and processing of organically grown agricultural products. *Organic* now has a national definition rather than multiple state and private standards. This helps consumers know exactly what they are buying.

The National Organic Program defines organic food as:

> Organic food is produced by farmers who emphasize the use of renewable resources and the conservation of soil and water to enhance environmental quality for future generations. Organic meat, poultry, eggs, and dairy products come from animals that are given no antibiotics or growth hormones. Organic food is produced without using most conventional pesticides; fertilizers made with synthetic ingredients or sewage sludge; bioengineering; or ionizing radiation. Before a product can be labeled "organic," a government-approved certifier inspects the farm where the food is grown to make sure the farmer is following all the rules necessary to meet USDA organic standards. Companies that handle or process organic food before it gets to your local supermarket or restaurant must be certified, too.

FIGURE 4.1 USDA ORGANIC FOODS LABEL

Source: ams.usda.gov/nop/Consumers/brochure.html

Using the now-uniform definition of *organic*, the National Organic Program has created a nationwide system to certify producers.

To date, no studies have clearly demonstrated detrimental effects of pesticides and drug residues present in livestock and poultry. Still, many people choose to buy meat and poultry from producers who do not expose their animals to hormones or antibiotics and who feed their animals organic grains. These products are available at many supermarkets, butcher shops, specialty markets, and through mail order.

The USDA definition for *free range* is that this poultry has been allowed access to the outside. Many free-range poultry farmers complain that this leaves a lot of wiggle room: a larger producer can provide *access* to an outdoor poultry yard, and whether or not the chickens actually use it, they can be labeled *free range*. It is easier to assess the quality and cleanliness of the yards of local producers, who often gladly provide tours of their facilities. Although *free range* does not assure that the animal is fed grains devoid of antibiotics, pesticides, or other chemicals, their relative freedom of movement makes them better exercised than their commercial counterparts, and therefore free-range products generally contain less fat. Because free-range animals spend more time outside and have liberty to forage, they can be more prone to salmonella. As with all poultry, be sure to cook meat completely (165°F internal temperature).

The USDA does not endorse organic foods as being more nutritious than those produced by conventional methods. To date, studies comparing nutrient and phytochemical levels are inconclusive. Some show higher levels of nutrients, especially vitamin C, minerals, and some polyphenols, while others demonstrate no significant difference between organic and conventionally grown foods. Research to determine the varying nutrient levels is ongoing throughout the world; however, variations in the quality of research, soils, and organic practices make conclusive findings difficult to obtain.

Even though scientific evidence does not support the idea that pesticide residues are highly causative factors associated with incidence of cancer, nor that nutrient values are higher in organic produce, there are still some very good reasons to buy organic foods:

- Reduction in intake of pesticides and fertilizers. Even though under the best of circumstances organic food is not completely free of pesticides, the amounts that can be detected are generally trace.
- Many people think organic foods taste better.
- This type of farming replenishes the soil and helps to protect the water supply.

When not to buy organic:

- Buying exclusively organic foods limits the variety of fruits and vegetables in your diet.
- The expense may limit your consumption of fruits and vegetables.

The USDA Organic label lets you know that a product is at least 95 percent organic. For more information about organic foods, visit the National Organic Program website: ams.usda.gov/nop/Consumers/brochure.html.

Cooking with Olive Oil

By increasing public awareness of the variety of uses and health benefits of olive oil, the International Olive Oil Council (IOOC), an intergovernmental agency, was largely responsible for the increase in consumption seen in the last two decades. Part of the IOOC's education campaign was informing consumers about the different classifications of olive oil. Having an understanding of the different types of olive oil will help you in selecting and using this flavorful and healthful type of fat.

1. "Extra-Virgin Olive Oil" and "Virgin Olive Oil." Virgin olive oil is obtained from the fruit of the olive tree solely by mechanical or other physical means under conditions that do not lead to deterioration of the oil. This oil does not undergo any treatment other than washing, decantation, centrifugation, and filtration.

The two kinds of virgin olive oil sold in the United States are "extra-virgin olive oil" and "virgin olive oil," the latter being a very small part of the market. These oils differ in terms of flavor, aroma, color, and acidity level. Extra-virgin olive oil is described as having the perfect balance of these characteristics. To be labeled *extra-virgin olive oil*, its acidity must not exceed 1 percent (1 gram per 100 grams). Virgin olive oil can contain up to 3.3 percent acidity, but industry practice in the producing countries is to keep levels under 2 percent.

Extra-virgin olive oils share many of the same characteristics; however, they do vary in taste. Many nuances contribute to the diversity of flavors, color, and aromas found in olive oil. Connoisseurs generally categorize olive oil flavors as mild (delicate, light, or buttery), semifruity (stronger, with more taste of the olive), and fruity (oil with a full-blown olive flavor). The best way to become familiar with the wide range of olive oil flavors is to taste as many of them as possible. One very cost-effective way is to split up a number of large bottles of different oils with friends.

2. What is now called *olive oil* is defined as the blend of refined olive oil with virgin olive oil. The blend of refined olive oil and virgin olive oil may bear on the label, beneath its designation, the term *pure* or *100% pure*. The addition of virgin olive oil adds "fruitiness," color, aroma, and certain basic elements, especially d-alpha-tocopherol (vitamin E). The amount of virgin olive oil added varies from one producer to another and depends on the desired flavor the producer is trying to create.

For heavy-duty, high-heat cooking, it's probably best to use olive oil, as it is less rich in volatile compounds that disappear with heat and may "perfume" your kitchen. It has the same fatty acid content as virgin olive oil, and this is what gives it such good resistance to high temperatures. It is also less expensive than virgin olive oils.

3. "Olive Pomace Oil." Pomace is the portion of the olive that remains after pressing or centrifuge operations remove the oil and water. Additional oil can be extracted from the olive pomace with the use of solvents. This oil is then refined to produce a product that has no specific taste or color. To produce a product that is acceptable to consumers, this oil is then blended with virgin olive oil. As with olive oil, the relative proportions of virgin olive oil and oil extracted from the pomace are determined by the individual manufacturer. The percentage of virgin olive oil is usually quite low. The final product is called *olive pomace oil*. It is produced at a lower cost than olive oil because pomace, the starting material, does not have nearly the value of olives that are used for pressing into oil. Olive pomace oil, like olive oil, can be used for high-heat cooking.

Studies indicate that a Mediterranean diet low in saturated fats such as butter, lard, and animal fats, but rich in monounsaturated fats such as olive oil, in addition to whole grains, fruits, and vegetables, helps keep the artery-clogging LDL ("bad cholesterol") low while maintaining healthful levels of HDL ("good cholesterol"). HDL has a preventive effect on cardiovascular illness because it may help to eliminate the LDL from the blood by carrying it to the liver. In addition, many medical researchers and nutritionists agree that olive oil is a good source of vitamin E, which may protect against cancer and heart disease. Olive oil also contains other compounds that are being investigated for their potential to lower risk of cancer.

An important study on this topic reported recently in the *New England Journal of Medicine* found that adherence to a Mediterranean diet in a Greek population substantially reduced risk of death from cancer as well as risk of death from heart disease and total mortality risk. The traditional diet assessed includes lots of olive oil, an abundance of vegetables and fruits, legumes, nuts, cereals, and a moderate intake of fish and alcohol (mostly wine). No one ingredient in this diet was associated with the health-protective effects; rather it appears to be the whole diet that confers these benefits.

Cooking Tips

When a recipe just calls for olive oil, how do you know what kind to use? Let your own taste preferences be your guide, but temper it by the end result you want. Light or extra-light olive oil is light in color and mild in flavor. It is a good choice for baking and for recipes in which you don't want the oil to impart its flavor to the dish. For salad dressings and other recipes in which you do want to taste the oil's characteristic flavor, use the more pungent extra-virgin olive oil. As a general rule, cook with olive oil and season or drizzle with extra-virgin after food is cooked.

Light and delicate dishes like poached or sautéed fish, chicken, or veal, or perhaps mild-flavored soups, may be better served by a milder, less fruity olive oil. Often Italian oils from Liguria, Lake Garda, or Tuscany work well. Full-flavored robust dishes such as hearty stews, soups, or tomato-based sauces welcome a more fruity, flavorful olive oil, as do steamed vegetables and salads. In these cases, consider Sicilian (or other southern Italian), Greek, or Spanish oils.

For roasted, barbecued, and braised dishes that require high-temperature or prolonged cooking, it is probably best to use olive oil (or even olive pomace oil), because it is less rich in the volatile compounds that evaporate with heat. Equally important, it has the same health benefits as virgin olive oils and is less expensive.

Olive Oil and Frying

Because olive oil is stable at high temperature, you can fry, sauté, stir-fry, and deep-fry in olive oil. You can even filter olive oil after frying and use it again. Standard olive oil is the best for these forms of high-heat cooking.

Olive Oil and Baking

Olive oil, a monounsaturated fat, has a small fat crystal that yields even, fine-textured baked goods. Using olive oil in baking dramatically cuts the saturated fat in baked goods.

Baking with olive oil produces lighter, tastier baked goods than butter and allows the flavor of the other ingredients to come through with more clarity.

Olive oil contains tocopherols (vitamin E) that act as emulsifiers, producing a smooth, homogenous batter that results in baked goods with a moist and tender crumb.

Tocopherols also have antioxidant properties that retard staling and result in a fresher product.

Olive oil is particularly suited to the baking of carrot, chocolate, spice, and fruit cakes; cookie bars; brownies; graham cracker, nut, or cookie crusts; corn bread or sticks and other quick breads, muffins, and biscuits; pancakes, blinis, and crepes; and flat breads and pizzas.

Baking Conversions

Using olive oil in baked goods often allows for use of less fat. Here are some conversions for recipes:

Butter/Margarine	Olive Oil
1 teaspoon	¾ teaspoon
1 tablespoon	2¼ teaspoons
2 tablespoons	1½ tablespoons
¼ cup	2 tablespoons
⅓ cup	¼ cup
½ cup	¼ cup plus 2 tablespoons
⅔ cup	½ cup
¾ cup	½ cup plus 1 tablespoon
1 cup	¾ cup

5

Recipes

&ô H ERE ARE MORE THAN A HUNDRED RECIPES that will make delicious, healthful eating a day-to-day reality. Included is everything from savory vegetables and side dishes to appetizers and main dishes, breads and desserts. The recipes focus on everyday favorites from hearty stews, light summer salads, Crispy Oven-Roasted Vegetables, and a homey Apple Cake (*Gâteau aux Pommes*) to a very special Traditional Christmas Roll (*Bûche de Noël*). Developed by the top chefs in America, these recipes will start the most basic cook on the road to preparing fresh, easy, and healthful meals.

Nutritional analysis for each recipe was performed using a widely accepted software application. Sources of nutrition information are believed to be reliable and accurate, including but not limited to the original manufacturers and the U.S. Department of Agriculture. Although computerized nutritional analysis provides an accurate approximation of nutrients, the values are just that—an approximation.

Within each recipe reference is made to the amount of nutrients provided compared to the daily values (DVs).* For instance, if a serving provides 30 percent of the DV for vitamin C, this has been calculated based on the reference value of 60 mg

---

*Daily values (DVs) comprise daily reference intakes (DRIs) and daily reference values (DRVs). DRIs apply to essential vitamins and minerals and protein; DRVs apply to fat, saturated fat, cholesterol, carbohydrates, protein, fiber, sodium, and potassium.

for vitamin C. The following are the bases for the daily reference intakes (DRIs) and daily reference values (DRVs) for the nutrients highlighted in the recipes:

Vitamin A	5,000 IU
Vitamin C	60 mg
Calcium	1,000 mg
Vitamin D	400 IU
Vitamin E	30 IU
Folate	400 mcg
Dietary fiber	25 g

- Nutrient levels are rounded to the nearest whole number.
- When total fat is less than 0.5 gram, it is considered a trace amount and represented by 0. If you try to calculate the percentage of calories from fat, carbohydrate, or protein using the rounded numbers, your results will not always match ours.
- Comments about the levels of selenium and omega-3 fatty acids are expressed as *potentially good* or *potentially very good* sources of these nutrients because these values are dependent on other factors and nutritional database information is incomplete.

In circumstances in which total fat seems high as a percentage of calories, keep the following in mind:

- You should view the fat in a single recipe or dish within the context of your goal for the day—or even the week—as discussed in Chapter 4. The percentage of calories from fat for a low-calorie, low-fat vinaigrette, for example, may be 60 percent, which sounds very high, but a serving contains only 30 calories and 2 grams of fat (much less than a classic vinaigrette), meaning this dressing is not going to contribute much to your overall fat intake for the day.
- The type of fat is important. In many cases the fat source in the recipes is predominantly monounsaturated fatty acids, which may play a protective role in the prevention of cancer.
- The total nutrient profile of the menu item is more important than the fat content alone. Rather than focus on the goal of keeping everything you eat at less than 30 percent of calories from fat, put more emphasis on getting a wide variety of the nutrients and phytochemicals that play a significant role in promoting good health.

Appetizers

Healthy Hummus with Toasted Pita Chips

Laura Pensiero, R.D., co-owner, Gigi Trattoria, Rhinebeck, New York; nutritionist, Strang Cancer Prevention Center

Use hummus instead of mayonnaise as a sandwich spread to lower your fat intake or serve it with crackers or crusty bread as an alternative to the pita chips.

8 servings

Hummus

1½ cups cooked or rinsed and drained canned chick-peas (see Notes)

2 garlic cloves, peeled, or 1 head roasted garlic (see Index)

1 small potato (about ¼ pound), baked or microwaved and peeled

½ cup 1% cottage cheese or 2 ounces lite silken tofu

¼ cup water

¼ cup tahini (toasted sesame seed paste)

1 tablespoon extra-virgin olive oil

1 teaspoon toasted sesame oil

2 teaspoons lemon juice

¼ teaspoon ground cumin

⅛ teaspoon cayenne pepper

salt

Pita Chips

6 whole wheat pitas, halved horizontally and cut into quarters

olive oil cooking spray or oil mister filled with extra-virgin olive oil

salt

dash cayenne pepper

To prepare the hummus, combine all the ingredients in the bowl of a food processor and puree until smooth.

147

To prepare the toasted pita chips, preheat the oven to 375°F. Spread the pita wedges in a single layer on a large baking sheet (use two if necessary) and lightly mist with the cooking spray or the oil mister. Sprinkle with salt and lightly dust with the cayenne. Bake for 6 to 8 minutes, until golden brown and crisp; be careful not to burn. Serve on a platter with a bowl of hummus in the center.

NOTES: To cook dried chick-peas, soak them in water to cover for 4 hours, changing the water 2 or 3 times. Drain and place in a saucepan, cover with water, and add a bay leaf (along with 1 to 2 celery ribs, a carrot, and ½ large onion for more flavor if you like). Bring to a boil and then reduce to a gentle simmer. Cook uncovered until the beans are tender but firm, 2 to 2½ hours, adding more water as necessary to keep the beans covered. Drain and use in a recipe or as an addition to soups and salads.

- Roasted garlic not only adds flavor and creaminess but also provides cancer-protective allium compounds.
- Sesame seeds (toasted and ground for tahini) are a good source of the following cancer-protective compounds: inositol or phytic acid, protease inhibitors, plant sterols, and isoflavones.
- The addition of baked potato provides a fat-free creaminess to this recipe and also bolsters the potassium and vitamin C content.
- A good source of fiber

PER SERVING OF HEALTHY HUMMUS (⅓ CUP)

calories	protein	carbohydrates	fat	cholesterol	dietary fiber	saturated fat
141	7 g	11 g	7.5 g	0 mg	3 g	1 g

PER SERVING OF TOASTED PITA CHIPS (6 CHIPS)

calories	protein	carbohydrates	fat	cholesterol	dietary fiber	saturated fat
142	5 g	25 g	3 g	0 mg	4 g	0 g

PER SERVING OF HEALTHY HUMMUS WITH TOASTED PITA CHIPS

calories	protein	carbohydrates	fat	cholesterol	dietary fiber	saturated fat
283	12 g	36 g	10.5 g	0 mg	7 g	1 g

% OF CALORIES: 50% carbohydrate, 17% protein, 33% fat

MAJOR SOURCES OF POTENTIAL CANCER FIGHTERS

Phytochemicals: capsaicin, phytic acids, plant polyphenols (flavonoids, isoflavones, phenolic acids), plant sterols, protease inhibitors, terpenes (monoterpenes)

⚘ Roasted Eggplant Dip

Laura Pensiero, R.D., co-owner, Gigi Trattoria, Rhinebeck, New York; nutritionist, Strang Cancer Prevention Center

---

This low-fat, phytochemical-rich spread is terrific with toasted pita chips (see Healthy Hummus, preceding recipe) or can replace mayonnaise as a zesty sandwich spread.

---

8 servings

1 medium eggplant (about 1¼ pounds), halved lengthwise
1 tablespoon olive oil
1 head roasted garlic (see Index) or 2 garlic cloves, peeled
1 medium potato (about 6 ounces), baked or microwaved and peeled
½ cup 1% cottage cheese or 2 ounces lite silken tofu

2 tablespoons tahini (toasted sesame seed paste)
1 teaspoon lemon juice
⅛ teaspoon cayenne pepper
2 teaspoons toasted sesame oil
salt

Preheat the oven to 350°F.

Brush the flesh of the halved eggplant with 1 teaspoon of the olive oil. Place on a nonstick baking pan, cut side down, and roast for 20 to 30 minutes. Turn over and continue roasting for approximately 20 minutes. Remove from the oven and let cool.

Scoop the pulp from the skin of the eggplant and place in the bowl of a food processor. Add the roasted garlic and potato and puree. Then add the cottage cheese, tahini, lemon juice, and cayenne and puree again until smooth. With the motor running, drizzle in the sesame oil and remaining 2 teaspoons olive oil. Season to taste with salt and transfer to an attractive serving bowl.

▪ The addition of potato not only adds a fat-free creaminess to this dip but also enriches it with vitamin C.

▪ Although not particularly rich in vitamins, eggplant contains flavonoids such as quercetin that act as antioxidants and help to boost cancer-fighting enzymes.

PER SERVING

calories	protein	carbohydrates	fat	cholesterol	dietary fiber	saturated fat
110	4 g	15 g	4 g	1 mg	2 g	1 g

% OF CALORIES: 50% carbohydrate, 15% protein, 35% fat

MAJOR SOURCES OF POTENTIAL CANCER FIGHTERS

Phytochemicals: allium compounds, plant polyphenols (flavonoids, phenolic acids), phytic acids, plant sterols, terpenes (monoterpenes)

Pastina Risotto with White Beans and Baby Clams

Nick Morfogen, 32 east, Delray Beach, Florida

The perfect warm appetizer for lunch or a brunch buffet. Or serve in the center of the table for a family-style meal. Toasted bread rounds rubbed with garlic make a delicious accompaniment.

Pastina means "tiny dough" and refers to any very small pasta shape. Both pastina and clam juice, bottled or canned, are available at most supermarkets. Pastina cooks quickly, so have all ingredients on hand once you begin preparation.

8 servings

PASTINA

1 cup clam juice or Vegetable Stock
  (see Index)
¼ cup water
½ medium onion (about 2 ounces),
  diced fine
2 teaspoons minced garlic
2 tablespoons olive oil

1 cup pastina
½ cup dry white wine
1½ cups well-drained cooked or
  canned white beans
salt and freshly ground black pepper
¼ cup unseasoned bread crumbs

CLAMS

1 tablespoon olive oil	¼ cup clam juice
1 tablespoon minced garlic	¼ cup dry vermouth
1 tablespoon chopped fresh basil	salt and freshly ground black pepper
1 tablespoon chopped fresh oregano	½ cup chopped tomatoes
2 pounds littleneck or Manila clams, rinsed	(about 1 medium)

To make the pastina, in a small saucepan, combine the clam juice and water, bring to a boil, then reduce the heat to low.

In a heavy ovenproof medium saucepan, sauté the onion and garlic in the olive oil over medium heat for 2 to 3 minutes, until tender. Add the pastina and stir with a wooden spoon to coat evenly with oil. Add the white wine and cook, stirring, until the wine is mostly absorbed or cooked off, less than 1 minute. Add one-third of the clam juice–water mixture to the saucepan and reserve the remaining two-thirds. Maintain a low simmer over medium-low heat and stir frequently.

To cook the clams, in a large nonstick sauté pan, heat the olive oil over high heat. Add the garlic and cook until it just turns golden, then reduce the heat to medium, stir in the herbs, and continue to cook for another minute. Do not burn the garlic. Add the clams, clam juice, and vermouth, season with salt and pepper, and bring to a boil. Cover and, after less than 1 minute, begin to transfer the opened clams to a clean bowl. Add the tomatoes to the clam juice–vermouth mixture left in the sauté pan and reduce the liquid over high heat until the volume is halved.

Preheat the oven to 425°F.

Add the cooking liquid from the clams, the white beans, and another one-third of the clam juice–water mixture to the saucepan with the pastina. Continue stirring until all the liquid is absorbed, about 5 minutes, then add the remaining one-third of the clam juice–water mixture. It should be somewhat soupy at this point, and the pasta should be al dente. Season to taste with salt and pepper.

Place the clams, open edges up, over the pastina. Sprinkle with the bread crumbs, transfer to the oven, and bake until the mixture is bubbly and lightly browned, 8 to 10 minutes. Place the pan on a pot holder or a heavy kitchen towel in the middle of the table. Have oyster forks and spoons available.

- Clams are a potentially good source of selenium.
- Each serving provides 15 percent of the DV for vitamin C.
- White beans provide fiber (17 percent of the DV per serving), as well as many of the same protective phytochemicals found in soybeans.

PER SERVING

calories	protein	carbohydrates	fat	cholesterol	dietary fiber	saturated fat
234	10 g	29 g	6 g	7 mg	3 g	1 g

% OF CALORIES: 51% carbohydrate, 16% protein, 23% fat, 10% alcohol

MAJOR SOURCES OF POTENTIAL CANCER FIGHTERS

Phytochemicals: allium compounds, phytic acids, plant polyphenols (flavonoids, phenolic acids), protease inhibitors, terpenes (carotenoids, monoterpenes)

PORTOBELLO MUSHROOM–STUFFED CHILES RELLENOS

Miles Angelo, Caribou Club, Aspen, Colorado

6 servings

CHILES RELLENOS

3 large ears corn or 1½ cups
  (6 ounces) frozen corn kernels,
  thawed and drained
6 medium poblano chiles (about
  5 ounces)
juice of 1 lemon
1 tablespoon olive oil

1½ pounds portobello mushrooms,
  brushed with a moist cloth, stems
  and gills removed
salt and freshly ground white pepper
¼ pound queso blanco, grated
  (1 cup; see Notes)
½ bunch fresh cilantro, chopped

CHIMAYO CHILE SAUCE

6 dried chimayo, New Mexican, or
  ancho chiles, seeded and stemmed
1 small yellow onion
  (about 2 ounces), sliced

2 garlic cloves, peeled
2 cups water
1 bay leaf
salt

To cook the corn, heat 1 gallon of water in a large pot. Bring to a boil, place the ears of corn in the pot, and cook for 6 to 8 minutes. Drain and let cool.

Preheat the broiler. Rub or, using a mister, mist the chile peppers with a small amount of olive oil and place on a cookie sheet lined with foil about 5 to 6 inches from the heat in the broiler. Broil the chiles until charred on all sides, using tongs to turn them so they char evenly. Remove the chiles from the oven, place in a bowl, and cover with foil or plastic wrap so that steam helps to loosen the skins. When cool, carefully remove the skins, seeds, and stems, leaving the chiles whole. Set aside.

To prepare the filling, in a medium bowl, combine the lemon juice and olive oil. Add the mushrooms, season with salt and pepper, and turn to coat evenly. Marinate for at least 20 minutes.

Meanwhile, cut the corn kernels from the cobs and place them in a medium bowl with the queso blanco.

Grill the mushrooms over medium heat until tender (or roast at 400°F on a non-stick baking pan for 7 to 8 minutes); remove from the grill and cool. Cut the mushrooms into medium cubes and add to the corn-queso mixture. Season with the cilantro and salt and white pepper. Mix to combine and set aside.

To prepare the sauce, combine all the ingredients except the salt in a saucepan and bring to a boil. Reduce the heat and simmer for 10 minutes. Turn off the heat, remove the bay leaf, and let cool slightly. Transfer to the bowl of a food processor or blender and puree until very smooth; add a little water if necessary to thin to a sauce consistency. Strain through a fine-mesh strainer into a small bowl and season to taste with salt.

To stuff the chiles, bring some water to a boil in a pot with a steamer insert. Lightly season the inside and outside of each poblano. Fill each with the mushroom mixture and then wrap individually in plastic wrap, twisting the ends to form a seal. Place the chiles in the steamer insert and steam, covered, for 8 to 10 minutes. Carefully remove the chiles and set aside to cool slightly. When they are cool enough to handle, gently unwrap the plastic. Spoon the chimayo chile sauce on serving plates and place the chiles on top. Drizzle a little more sauce over the chiles.

NOTES: You can use low-fat white cheddar, Monterey Jack, or soy versions of either instead of queso blanco.

- Capsaicin, found in chile peppers, may help to neutralize carcinogens.
- Chile peppers are very good sources of vitamin C; each serving provides more than 25 percent of the DV.
- Although corn does not contain substantial amounts of vitamins, it derives its color from the carotenoid lutein, a potent antioxidant.
- Mushrooms are a potentially good source of selenium.

PER SERVING

calories	protein	carbohydrates	fat	cholesterol	dietary fiber	saturated fat
123	11 g	10 g	4 g	7 mg	5 g	1 g

% of Calories: 32% carbohydrate, 36% protein, 32% fat

MAJOR SOURCES OF POTENTIAL CANCER FIGHTERS

Phytochemicals: allium compounds, capsaicin, plant polyphenols (flavonoids, phenolic acids), terpenes (carotenoids, monoterpenes)

Roasted Tomato and Mint Salsa

Jerry Traunfeld, The Herbfarm, Woodinville, Washington

Jerry suggests using this high-flavor, nutrient-rich condiment for grilled or roasted meat, fish, or poultry.

4 servings

10 plum or medium tomatoes
  (1½ pounds), halved
1 tablespoon olive oil
2 tablespoons minced red onion
½ jalapeño pepper, seeded and
  minced

¼ cup shredded fresh mint leaves
1½ tablespoons red wine vinegar
salt to taste

Preheat the oven to 450°F.

In a large bowl, toss the tomatoes in the olive oil. Arrange them on a wire rack, cut side down, and place the rack on a baking pan. Roast the tomatoes for 10 to 15 minutes or until they start to brown. Remove from the oven and let cool. Coarsely dice the tomatoes. Toss them in a bowl with the remaining ingredients. Let the salsa sit for at least 1 hour to blend the flavors.

- Tomatoes and tomato products are a great source of the carotenoid lycopene, a powerful cancer fighter.
- Mint contains monoterpenes, phytochemicals of the terpene class, which may help bolster cancer-fighting enzymes.
- One serving provides 60 percent of the DV for vitamin C.

PER SERVING

calories	protein	carbohydrates	fat	cholesterol	dietary fiber	saturated fat
72	1 g	9g	4 g	0 mg	2 g	1 g

% OF CALORIES: 50% carbohydrate, 6% protein, 44% fat

MAJOR SOURCES OF POTENTIAL CANCER FIGHTERS

Phytochemicals: allium compounds, plant polyphenols (flavonoids, phenolic acids), plant sterols, terpenes (carotenoids, monoterpenes)

🐝 Tomato-Basil Sauce

Laura Pensiero, R.D., co-owner, Gigi Trattoria, Rhinebeck, New York; nutritionist, Strang Cancer Prevention Center

The best way to extend the enjoyment of the flavorful summer tomato is to double or triple this recipe, put the sauce in small containers, and freeze. You will have a quick and healthy tomato sauce for a busy day.

4 servings

2 pounds plum tomatoes (10 to 12)
1 tablespoon olive oil
2 garlic cloves, crushed
1 small onion (about ¼ pound), chopped

½ cup fresh basil leaves cut into long strips
salt and freshly ground black pepper

Core the tomatoes and drop them into boiling water for 20 to 30 seconds. Slip off the skins and slice the tomatoes in half horizontally. Gently squeeze the halves over a bowl to force out the seeds. Use your fingers to remove any remaining seeds. Discard the seeds, chop the tomatoes, and reserve.

Heat the olive oil in a medium nonstick skillet over high heat. Add the crushed garlic and cook until lightly browned, then remove and discard. Add the onion to the skillet and cook over medium heat until soft, about 5 minutes, stirring often.

Add the reserved tomatoes and bring to a simmer. Cook, uncovered, over medium heat, stirring occasionally, for 30 minutes, until the sauce thickens.

Stir in the basil, season with salt and pepper, and simmer for 2 to 3 minutes.

- Contains the carotenoids lycopene and beta-carotene; both are powerful antioxidants.
- One serving provides 60 percent of the DV for vitamin C and more than 10 percent for vitamin A.
- A good source of fiber

PER SERVING (½ CUP)

calories	protein	carbohydrates	fat	cholesterol	dietary fiber	saturated fat
93	3 g	14 g	4 g	0 mg	3 g	1 g

PER SERVING WITH 1½ CUPS COOKED PASTA

calories	protein	carbohydrates	fat	cholesterol	dietary fiber	saturated fat
422	13 g	79 g	6 g	0 mg	5 g	1 g

% OF CALORIES: 75% carbohydrate, 12% protein, 13% fat

MAJOR SOURCES OF POTENTIAL CANCER FIGHTERS

Phytochemicals: allium compounds, plant polyphenols (flavonoids, phenolic acids), plant sterols, phytic acids, terpenes (carotenoids, monoterpenes)

❧ VENETIAN PEPERONATA

Francesco Antonucci, co-owner/executive chef, Remi, Le Zie, Le Zoccole, New York City ▪ Adapted with permission from *Venetian Taste*, Abbeville Press, 1995.

Francesco recommends serving this tasty Venetian peperonata as a sauce for pasta, an accompaniment for fish, or a topping for polenta.

---

4 servings

1 large eggplant (about 18 ounces)
2 tablespoons extra-virgin olive oil
1 large red onion (about ½ pound),
   sliced ¼ inch thick
2 garlic cloves, peeled
2 large red bell peppers
   (about 1 pound), seeded and
   cut into julienne strips

1 medium zucchini (about 6 ounces),
   sliced ¼ inch thick
1 cup canned plum tomatoes,
   drained and crushed
salt and freshly ground black pepper
handful of fresh basil leaves, slivered

Quarter the eggplant and cut away the flesh to within ½ inch of the skin. Save the center of the eggplant for another use and cut the skin crosswise into slivers about ¼ inch wide. Set aside. Heat the olive oil in a large heavy skillet. Add the onion and garlic and sauté over medium heat, stirring, until the onion is golden, about 15 minutes. Add the peppers and sauté for another 10 to 15 minutes. Add the eggplant and zucchini. Continue to sauté for another 15 to 20 minutes, adjusting the heat if necessary and stirring often to prevent browning or burning.

Stir in the tomatoes and cook for another few minutes, then season with salt and pepper, stir in the basil, and serve.

■ One serving provides 100 percent of the DV for vitamin C. By weight, peppers have 2 to 3 times more vitamin C than citrus fruit. Green, yellow, and red bell peppers and chile peppers are also great sources of beta-carotene as well as other carotenoids.

■ High in fiber—24 percent of the DV per serving

PER SERVING

calories	protein	carbohydrates	fat	cholesterol	dietary fiber	saturated fat
150	4 g	20 g	7 g	0 mg	6 g	1 g

PER SERVING WITH 1½ CUPS COOKED PASTA

calories	protein	carbohydrates	fat	cholesterol	dietary fiber	saturated fat
469	14 g	84 g	9 g	0 mg	9 g	1 g

% OF CALORIES: 71% carbohydrate, 12% protein, 17% fat

MAJOR SOURCES OF POTENTIAL CANCER FIGHTERS

Phytochemicals: allium compounds, plant polyphenols (flavonoids, phenolic acids), plant sterols, terpenes (carotenoids, monoterpenes)

Soups and Stocks

🐸 Black Bean Soup

Jimmy Sneed, The Frog and the Redneck, Richmond, Virginia

Garnish with grilled or seared shrimp or scallops and serve with a tossed green salad for lunch or dinner. To have quick, high-fiber meals on hand for busy days, double the recipe and freeze the soup in small containers.

6 servings

1 pound dried black beans
2 tablespoons olive oil
2 medium carrots (about 6 ounces), peeled and diced
2 medium celery ribs (about ¼ pound), diced
1 medium onion (about 5 ounces), diced
1 large red bell pepper (about 7 ounces), diced

3 garlic cloves, minced
1 bay leaf
6 cups White Chicken Stock, Brown Chicken Stock, or Vegetable Stock (see Index), or low-sodium canned broth
salt and freshly ground black pepper
3 scallions, chopped
6 tablespoons low-fat sour cream

In a medium bowl, soak the black beans in water to cover for 4 to 6 hours, changing the water 2 or 3 times. Drain and set aside.

In a large heavy saucepan, heat the olive oil. Add the carrots, celery, onion, and red pepper and sauté over medium-high heat, without browning, until tender, about 10 minutes. Add the garlic and cook for 2 to 3 minutes, then add the drained beans, bay leaf, and stock. Simmer, covered, until the beans are tender enough to be crushed easily between two fingers, about 45 minutes. Remove the bay leaf and puree in a blender or food processor until smooth or, for a chunkier texture, puree only half of the beans and vegetables and return them to the saucepan. Season to taste with salt and pepper. Serve in soup bowls, garnished with the chopped scallions and low-fat sour cream.

- Black beans contain isoflavones, which may lower the risk of breast and other types of cancer. They are also high in fiber and folate: this dish provides 50 percent of the DV for both.
- One serving provides 85 percent of the DV for vitamin A and more than 50 percent for vitamin C.

PER SERVING

calories	protein	carbohydrates	fat	cholesterol	dietary fiber	saturated fat
345	18 g	47 g	6 g	7 mg	13 g	1 g

% OF CALORIES: 64% carbohydrate, 20% protein, 16% fat

MAJOR SOURCES OF POTENTIAL CANCER FIGHTERS

Phytochemicals: allium compounds, phytic acids, plant polyphenols (flavonoids, isoflavones), protease inhibitors, terpenes (carotenoids, monoterpenes)

CAULIFLOWER SOUP

Francesco Antonucci, co-owner/executive chef, Remi, Le Zie, Le Zoccole, New York City ▪ Adapted with permission from *Venetian Taste*, Abbeville Press, 1995.

"In Venice we have big soups, simple soups," says Francesco. "This is a good example." *Serve hot or at room temperature.*

4 servings

1 tablespoon olive oil
1 small onion (about ¼ pound), chopped
1 leek, white part only, chopped (about 2 ounces)
1 medium baking potato (about 6 ounces), peeled and chopped coarse

1 small head cauliflower (about 1¼ pounds), cored and chopped coarse
2 anchovy fillets, rinsed and chopped
2 quarts cold water
salt and freshly ground white pepper
3-inch rounds of Italian country bread
1 garlic clove, crushed

Heat the olive oil in a medium saucepan, preferably nonstick. Add the onion and leek and sauté over medium heat, stirring often, until tender but not brown, about 10 minutes. Adjust the heat, if necessary, to prevent browning.

Add the potato, cauliflower, anchovy, and water. Bring to a gentle simmer and cook, uncovered, for 1 hour. Allow the soup to cool briefly, then puree it, in batches if necessary, in a blender or food processor. Return the soup to the saucepan, bring it to a simmer, and season with salt and white pepper.

Five minutes before serving, rub the bread rounds with the garlic and toast them until golden. Serve them alongside the soup.

- Cauliflower, a member of the cruciferous vegetable family, contains cancer-fighting phytochemicals and is rich in vitamin C: one serving of this soup provides more than 100 percent of the DV.
- Anchovy adds omega-3 fatty acids and a subtle dimension to the flavor of this soup.
- A good source of fiber

PER SERVING

calories	protein	carbohydrates	fat	cholesterol	dietary fiber	saturated fat
152	5 g	24 g	4 g	0 mg	3 g	<1 g

% OF CALORIES: 63% carbohydrate, 12% protein, 25% fat

MAJOR SOURCES OF POTENTIAL CANCER FIGHTERS

Phytochemicals: allium compounds, glucosinolates, omega-3 fatty acids, plant polyphenols (flavonoids, phenolic acids)

Gazpacho

Martin Saylor, executive chef, Butterfield 9, Washington, D.C.

This soup is ideal for a summer lunch or first course. Best of all, it's easy to prepare (under 30 minutes) and full of flavor and helps keep those vegetable servings high.

8 servings

2 medium yellow bell peppers
  (about ¾ pound)
2 medium red bell peppers (about
  14 ounces)
5 medium tomatoes (about 1 pound)
2 cups low-sodium tomato juice
1 tablespoon olive oil
2 medium cucumbers (about
  1½ pounds), peeled, seeded,
  and diced

1 jalapeño pepper, seeded and diced
1 shallot, minced
1 garlic clove, minced
juice of 1 lime
3 scallions, sliced thin
3 tablespoons chopped fresh cilantro
3 tablespoons chopped fresh basil
salt and freshly ground black
  pepper to taste

Preheat the broiler. Rub or, using a mister, mist the peppers with a small amount of olive oil and place on a cookie sheet lined with foil about 5 to 6 inches from the heat in the broiler. Broil until charred on all sides, using tongs to rotate the peppers to assure even charring. Remove the peppers from the oven, place in a bowl, and cover with foil or plastic wrap so that steam helps to loosen the skins. When cool, remove the skins, seeds, and stems. Dice the peppers and set aside.

To peel and seed the tomatoes, cut the core from the tomatoes with a paring knife and plunge them into boiling water for 30 seconds. Slip off the skins, slice the tomatoes in half, and squeeze gently to force out the seeds. Use your fingers to remove any remaining seeds. Discard the seeds, chop the tomatoes, and set aside.

In a large bowl, combine all the ingredients. Serve chilled.

- One serving provides more than 250 percent of the DV for vitamin C.
- Tomatoes and tomato products contain the carotenoid lycopene, a potent antioxidant. Peppers and tomatoes contain plant polyphenols that may act as blocking agents against cancer.
- A good source of fiber

PER SERVING

calories	protein	carbohydrates	fat	cholesterol	dietary fiber	saturated fat
86	3 g	14 g	2 g	0 mg	3 g	0 g

% OF CALORIES: 65% carbohydrate, 14% protein, 21% fat

MAJOR SOURCES OF POTENTIAL CANCER FIGHTERS

Phytochemicals: allium compounds, plant polyphenols (flavonoids, phenolic acids), plant sterols, protease inhibitors, terpenes (carotenoids, monoterpenes)

❧ Ratatouille Soup

Michael Romano, Union Square Cafe, New York City ▪ Adapted with permission from *Union Square Cafe Cookbook*, HarperCollins Publishers, 1994.

Serve this delicious year-round soup hot or cold. If you're trying to use up all of those summer garden vegetables, prepare a large batch and can or freeze in small containers.

---

4 servings

2 pounds ripe tomatoes (about 6 medium or 10 to 12 plum tomatoes)
2 tablespoons olive oil
⅓ cup chopped red onion (1 small)
1 teaspoon minced garlic
¾ cup chopped zucchini (¼ pound)
¾ cup peeled and chopped eggplant (3 ounces)
¾ cup chopped red bell pepper (¼ pound)
2 tablespoons sliced fresh basil leaves, plus 4 to 6 sprigs for garnish

1 teaspoon minced fresh thyme leaves
2 cups Vegetable Stock, White Chicken Stock, or Brown Chicken Stock (see Index), or low-sodium canned broth
pinch of cayenne pepper
1 teaspoon kosher salt
⅛ teaspoon freshly ground black pepper

Core the tomatoes and plunge them into boiling water for 30 seconds. Remove with a slotted spoon and slip off the skins. Cut the tomatoes in half crosswise and squeeze them gently over a strainer set in a bowl to separate the seeds from the juice. Reserve the juice. Gently flatten the tomato halves on a cutting board and coarsely chop into 1-inch pieces. Place the chopped tomatoes and the reserved juice in a bowl and set aside.

Heat the olive oil in a 3-quart saucepan over medium heat. Add the onion and garlic and cook for 1 minute. Stir in the zucchini, eggplant, and red pepper, sautéing until softened but not browned, about 5 minutes.

Add the tomatoes and their juice, the basil, thyme, stock, cayenne, salt, and black pepper. Bring to a boil, lower the heat to a simmer, cover, and cook until soft, about 15 minutes.

Carefully pour the hot soup into a blender or food processor and puree until smooth. Serve hot or chilled with a sprig of fresh basil as a garnish.

- One serving provides 3 times the DV for vitamin C and enough carotenoids to supply 20 percent of the DV for vitamin A.
- A good source of fiber

PER SERVING

calories	protein	carbohydrates	fat	cholesterol	dietary fiber	saturated fat
130	3 g	19 g	5 g	0 mg	4 g	1 g

% OF CALORIES: 60% carbohydrate, 10% protein, 30% fat

MAJOR SOURCES OF POTENTIAL CANCER FIGHTERS

Phytochemicals: allium compounds, capsaicin, plant polyphenols (flavonoids, phenolic acids), plant sterols, terpenes (carotenoids, monoterpenes)

❧ ROASTED PUMPKIN SOUP

RoxSand Scocos, chef/owner, RoxSand's Restaurant & Bar, Phoenix, Arizona

Roasting vegetables before adding them to a soup creates a unique concentrated flavor. Use this technique with other vegetables to replace the pumpkin, such as butternut squash, turnips, or celery root.

4 servings

1 small pumpkin (about 1½ pounds), peeled, seeded, and cut into large pieces (about 3 cups)
2 large onions (about 14 ounces), cut into large pieces
6 garlic cloves, peeled and crushed
2 large baking or Yukon Gold potatoes (about 1 pound), peeled and cut into medium chunks

2 tablespoons olive oil
4 fresh rosemary sprigs
3 fresh thyme sprigs
6 cups Vegetable Stock, White Chicken Stock, or Brown Chicken Stock (see Index), or low-sodium canned broth or water
salt and freshly ground black pepper

Preheat the oven to 375°F.

In a large bowl, combine the pumpkin, onions, garlic, and potatoes. Toss with the olive oil and fresh herbs and then spread out in a single layer on a nonstick baking pan. Roast for 50 minutes, stirring halfway through the cooking time, until all the vegetables are tender and lightly browned. Transfer to a saucepan and cover with the stock. Stir and bring to a boil. Lower the temperature and simmer until the flavors meld, about 15 minutes. Turn off the heat and let cool slightly. Remove the stems of fresh herbs and carefully puree the soup in a food processor or blender. Return the puree to the saucepan and season to taste with salt and pepper. Heat to a simmer and adjust the seasoning. For a thinner consistency, add more stock or water.

- Winter squash such as pumpkin provides substantial amounts of beta-carotene.
- Rich in vitamins A and C, this soup provides 65 percent and 50 percent of the DV, respectively.
- Rosemary contains carnosol, a cancer-fighting phytochemical.
- A good source of fiber

PER SERVING

calories	protein	carbohydrates	fat	cholesterol	dietary fiber	saturated fat
258	8 g	43 g	9 g	0 mg	4 g	1 g

% OF CALORIES: 61% carbohydrate, 12% protein, 27% fat

MAJOR SOURCES OF POTENTIAL CANCER FIGHTERS

Phytochemicals: allium compounds, plant polyphenols (flavonoids), plant sterols, terpenes (carotenoids, carnosol, monoterpenes)

❧ LEEK AND POTATO SOUP

Laura Pensiero, R.D., co-owner, Gigi Trattoria, Rhinebeck, New York; nutritionist, Strang Cancer Prevention Center

Serve this broth-based soup chunky or pureed, hot or chilled. Add ½ cup of milk to the puree to lighten the color and add creaminess.

4 servings

4 medium leeks, white part only
(about 10 ounces)

2 teaspoons canola oil

1 teaspoon unsalted butter

1 garlic clove, minced

5 cups White Chicken Stock, Brown
Chicken Stock, or Vegetable Stock
(see Index), or low-sodium
canned broth or water

2 medium potatoes (about ¾ pound),
peeled and cubed

salt and freshly ground white pepper

To clean the leeks, slice them in half lengthwise, leaving the root end intact, and place under running water. Run your fingers through the leaves to remove all dirt. Place the leeks, flat side down, on a cutting board and slice thin.

Heat the canola oil and butter in a medium saucepan. Sauté the leeks over moderate heat for at least 15 minutes, stirring frequently; do not brown. (This step is essential to concentrate the flavor and bring out the natural sweetness of the leeks, so be patient.) Add the garlic and cook for another minute, then add the stock and potatoes. Bring the mixture to a boil, reduce the heat, and simmer for 20 minutes or until the potato chunks are tender when pierced with a knife. Season to taste with salt and white pepper and serve.

- Leeks are rich in allium compounds, vitamin C, and folate (if the green part is used). They are generally considered a good source of selenium; however, amounts depend on the soil in which they are grown.
- Potatoes are also high in vitamin C; combined with leeks, they provide more than 25 percent of the DV per serving.

PER SERVING

calories	protein	carbohydrates	fat	cholesterol	dietary fiber	saturated fat
209	9 g	32 g	5 g	3 mg	2 g	1 g

% OF CALORIES: 61% carbohydrate, 17% protein, 22% fat

MAJOR SOURCES OF POTENTIAL CANCER FIGHTERS

Phytochemicals: allium compounds, plant polyphenols (flavonoids, phenolic acids)

🐝 WINTER VEGETABLE SOUP (*RIBOLLITA*)

Gianni Scappin, chef/co-owner, Finch Tavern, Croton Falls, New York

---

This traditional Tuscan "reboiled" soup is flavorful and hearty, making a nutrient-rich winter meal by itself. To cook dried chick-peas, consult the Notes with Healthy Hummus (see Index).

---

8 servings

3 medium celery ribs (about 7 ounces), chopped
3 medium carrots (about 9 ounces), peeled and chopped
2 garlic cloves, peeled and crushed
1 large red onion (about ½ pound), peeled and chopped
2 tablespoons olive oil
2 bunches Swiss chard (about 2 pounds), cleaned
½ head napa or savoy cabbage (about 20 ounces)

¼ cup chopped flat-leaf parsley
2 fresh rosemary sprigs
1 14½-ounce can plum tomatoes, drained
3 cups cooked or drained canned chick-peas
7 cups water, White Chicken Stock or Brown Chicken Stock (see Index), or low-sodium canned broth
5 ounces stale bread, such as semolina or baguette, sliced (about ¾ loaf)
salt and freshly ground black pepper

In a large saucepan over medium-low heat, cook the celery, carrots, garlic, and onion in the olive oil, stirring often, until the vegetables are soft and fragrant but not browned, about 20 minutes.

Cut out the tough, triangular inner core of the Swiss chard leaves and slice into ¼- to ½-inch slices. Add to the vegetables in the saucepan. Tear the Swiss chard leaves and set aside.

Cut out and discard the triangular core of the cabbage head. Place the cabbage cut side down on a cutting board and slice thinly with a large chef's knife to make long shreds. Set aside with the Swiss chard leaves.

Add the parsley, rosemary sprigs, and tomatoes to the saucepan and cook at a low simmer for 15 minutes. Add the cabbage and Swiss chard leaves, half of the chick-peas, and 6 cups of the water or stock. Simmer for 20 minutes.

Puree the remaining chick-peas in a food processor with the remaining cup of water or stock. Add to the saucepan and stir to combine. Remove the rosemary sprigs and stir in the bread slices. Add more liquid if necessary, but keep in mind that the soup should have a very thick stewlike consistency. Season with salt and pepper to taste.

- Chick-peas add fiber, flavor, and a creamy consistency with minimal fat. They also contain phytoestrogens.
- Rich in cancer-protective vitamins A, C, and folate: one serving provides more than 120 percent, 100 percent, and 40 percent of the DV, respectively.
- Cabbage, a member of the cruciferous family of vegetables, contains glucosinolates, powerful inducers of protective enzymes.
- High in fiber; each serving provides 25 percent of the DV.

PER SERVING

calories	protein	carbohydrates	fat	cholesterol	dietary fiber	saturated fat
250	11 g	41 g	5 g	0 mg	6 g	1 g

% OF CALORIES: 65% carbohydrate, 17% protein, 18% fat

MAJOR SOURCES OF POTENTIAL CANCER FIGHTERS

Phytochemicals: allium compounds, glucosinolates, plant polyphenols (flavonoids, phenolic acids), plant sterols, protease inhibitors, terpenes (carotenoids, carnosol, monoterpenes)

🌿 TOMATO BREAD SOUP

Michael Otsuka, co–executive chef/owner, Verbena, New York City

A perfect soup for any time, especially when you're trying to use up all of those perfectly ripe tomatoes at the end of the summer. Serve hot or at room temperature.

6 servings

3 pounds ripe tomatoes (about
   12 medium)
2 tablespoons olive oil
3 garlic cloves, peeled and crushed
2 large leeks, white part plus a little
   green (about 10 ounces), rinsed
   thoroughly and chopped rough
2 medium celery ribs (about
   ¼ pound), chopped
2 large carrots (about ¼ pound),
   chopped
1 medium onion (about 6 ounces),
   sliced
½ cup dry white wine

3 bay leaves
2 to 3 fresh thyme sprigs
1 quart White Chicken Stock, Brown
   Chicken Stock, or Vegetable Stock
   (see Index), or low-sodium canned
   broth or water
¼ pound bread, cut into small cubes
   (about ⅓ Italian semolina loaf or
   ½ medium French baguette)
1 bunch fresh basil (about 3 ounces),
   leaves only, cut into long strips
salt and freshly ground black pepper
⅓ cup freshly grated Parmesan cheese

Core the tomatoes and plunge them into boiling water for 30 seconds. Remove with a slotted spoon and slip off the skins. Slice the tomatoes in half and squeeze gently to force out the seeds. Use your fingers to remove any remaining seeds. Discard the seeds, chop the tomatoes, and set aside.

In a large, heavy saucepan, heat the olive oil and add the garlic, leeks, celery, carrot, and onion. Cook over medium heat, stirring often, until the vegetables are tender and slightly wilted but not browned, about 15 minutes.

Add the tomatoes, white wine, bay leaves, and thyme. Cook over medium-high heat until most of the wine evaporates, about 2 minutes. Add the stock and bring to a boil, then reduce the heat and simmer for 25 minutes.

Remove the bay leaves and thyme sprigs, then carefully puree the soup in small batches in a food processor. Return to the saucepan and bring to simmer. (The soup may be prepared to this point up to 2 days in advance.)

Meanwhile, preheat the oven to 375°F.

Place the bread cubes in a single layer on a baking sheet and place in the oven until they are toasted and dried out, 12 to 15 minutes.

Toss the croutons with the basil leaves and divide them among 6 soup bowls. Season the soup with salt and pepper if necessary and ladle into the bowls. Sprinkle Parmesan over the top of each bowl and serve.

- Tomatoes and tomato products are made red by the carotenoid lycopene, a potent antioxidant.
- The combination of carrots, leeks, and tomatoes provides more than 65 percent of the DV for vitamin A, 90 percent of the DV for vitamin C, and more than 20 percent of the DV for folate per serving.
- High in fiber—20 percent of the DV per serving

PER SERVING

calories	protein	carbohydrates	fat	cholesterol	dietary fiber	saturated fat
261	11 g	34 g	9 g	4 mg	5 g	2 g

% OF CALORIES: 52% carbohydrate, 17% protein, 31% fat

MAJOR SOURCES OF POTENTIAL CANCER FIGHTERS

Phytochemicals: allium compounds, plant polyphenols (flavonoids, phenolic acids), plant sterols, terpenes (carotenoids, monoterpenes)

Miso Soup

Laura Pensiero, R.D., co-owner, Gigi Trattoria, Rhinebeck, New York; nutritionist, Strang Cancer Prevention Center

There are many different types of miso, all with different intensities of flavor (see page 48). For soup, dark miso can be combined with water to make a broth or "tea" or enriched with vegetables.

This healthy recipe freezes well; make a large batch and store in small containers for easy defrosting and reheating.

4 to 6 servings

3 tablespoons dark miso paste

1 tablespoon canola oil

1 celery rib (about 2 ounces), sliced thin

1 medium red onion (about 5 ounces), sliced thin

1 garlic clove, peeled and crushed

1 medium carrot (about 3 ounces), peeled and sliced thin

2 cups shredded white, savoy, or Chinese cabbage

1 cup sliced mushrooms

½ teaspoon grated fresh ginger

2 teaspoons rice wine vinegar or sherry vinegar

1 tablespoon tamari (a Japanese soy sauce)

salt and freshly ground black pepper

2 teaspoons brown sugar

½ pound extra-firm low-fat ("lite") tofu, cut into small cubes

2 scallions, sliced thin, for garnish

In a large bowl, dissolve the miso paste in 6 cups boiling water or whatever the package instructions call for—usually 1 tablespoon miso for 2 cups water. Stir to combine well. Set aside.

Heat the canola oil in a large nonstick saucepan over medium-high heat. Add the celery, onion, and garlic and cook, stirring often, for 5 minutes. Add the carrot, cabbage, and mushrooms. Continue cooking for 15 more minutes; lower the heat if necessary and stir often to prevent browning. Add the ginger and miso-water mixture, bring to a boil, then reduce the heat so the mixture simmers. Cook for 15 to 20 minutes, then season with the rice wine vinegar, tamari, salt and pepper to taste, and brown sugar. Add tofu 1 to 2 minutes before serving. Garnish with scallions.

- This recipe contains three sources of soy: tofu, miso paste, and tamari. All can be found at most natural foods stores as well as some supermarkets.
- By adding cooked adzuki beans, you can add texture and further increase the fiber and nutrient content.
- Each serving provides 110 percent of the DV for vitamin A and more than 25 percent for vitamin C.

PER SERVING (BASED ON 4 SERVINGS)

calories	protein	carbohydrates	fat	cholesterol	dietary fiber	saturated fat
135	8 g	15 g	5 g	0 mg	4 g	0 g

% OF CALORIES: 43% carbohydrate, 24% protein, 33% fat

MAJOR SOURCES OF POTENTIAL CANCER FIGHTERS

Phytochemicals: allium compounds, glucosinolates, phytic acids, plant polyphenols (flavonoids, isoflavones), plant sterols, protease inhibitors, terpenes (carotenoids, monoterpenes, triterpenes)

VEGETABLE STOCK

Diane Forley, co–executive chef/owner, Verbena, New York City

Use this stock as a low-calorie, low-fat base for sauces, soups, and stews. Freeze it in 1-pint containers so that you have a healthful stock available whenever a recipe calls for it.

About 2 quarts

3 medium celery ribs (about 6 ounces), cut into thirds

2 large leeks, white part and a little green (about 5 ounces), halved, washed, and sliced thin

2 medium parsnips (about 5 ounces), peeled and sliced into 3 to 4 segments each

2 large carrots (about 6 ounces), peeled and sliced into 3 to 4 segments each

1 large fennel bulb (about ½ pound), cut into 8 segments

1 tablespoon olive oil

1 gallon water

2 medium onions (about 10 ounces), halved

1 large plum tomato (about 3 ounces), quartered

In a large saucepan, preferably nonstick, over medium-high heat, cook the celery, leeks, parsnips, carrots, and fennel in the olive oil, stirring often, until soft and translucent, about 15 minutes. Add the water and bring to a boil, then reduce the heat and simmer.

Rub or, using a mister, mist the cut sides of the onions with olive oil. Place the onions, cut side down, on a heated cast-iron pan or griddle and "burn" them over medium-high heat until they are a deep brown color, about 3 minutes. Add the onions and the tomato to the rest of the vegetables and simmer for 1½ hours. Carefully strain through a cheesecloth-lined colander or fine-mesh strainer into a large bowl.

Place the stock in a sink filled with ice water to cool quickly. Cover and refrigerate for at least 12 hours. Keep refrigerated for 3 to 4 days or freeze.

PER SERVING (1 CUP)

calories	protein	carbohydrates	fat	cholesterol	dietary fiber	saturated fat
33	1 g	4 g	1.5 g	0 mg	0 g	0 g

% OF CALORIES: 47% carbohydrate, 12% protein, 41% fat

🌿 WHITE CHICKEN STOCK

Laura Pensiero, R.D., co-owner, Gigi Trattoria, Rhinebeck, New York; nutritionist, Strang Cancer Prevention Center

This stock can be used as a flavorful low-calorie, low-fat base for soups, stews, and sauces. Freeze it in small portions to have on hand when needed.

2 quarts

5 pounds chicken bones, as much
   skin and fat removed as possible
6 quarts cold water
3 medium celery ribs (about
   5 ounces), cut into large pieces
2 medium onions (about ½ pound),
   chopped

1 large carrot (about ¼ pound),
   washed and cut into large pieces
1 bay leaf
1 fresh thyme sprig or 1 teaspoon
   dried thyme
4 to 5 black peppercorns

Rinse the chicken bones and place them in a large stockpot with the water. Bring to a full boil, uncovered, and boil for 5 minutes, then reduce the heat and simmer for 1 hour. Using a skimmer, remove any particles, foam, or fat that rise to the surface.

Add the celery, onions, carrot, bay leaf, thyme, and peppercorns. Maintain a low boil, uncovered, for 3 to 4 more hours. Carefully strain the stock through a cheesecloth-lined colander or fine-mesh strainer into a large container or bowl.

Place the stock in a sink filled with ice water to cool quickly. Cover and refrigerate for at least 12 hours. Skim off and discard any fat that has solidified on the surface. Keep refrigerated for 3 to 4 days or freeze.

■ Almost all fat can be removed by chilling the stock overnight and removing the hardened fat the next day.

PER SERVING (1 CUP)

calories	protein	carbohydrates	fat	cholesterol	dietary fiber	saturated fat
33	4 g	2 g	1 g	0 mg	0 g	0 g

% OF CALORIES: 24% carbohydrate, 49% protein, 27% fat

Brown Chicken Stock

Laura Pensiero, R.D., co-owner, Gigi Trattoria, Rhinebeck, New York; nutritionist, Strang Cancer Prevention Center

---

It is always good to have brown chicken stock on hand (frozen in pint containers) for whenever a recipe calls for it. Use it as a low-calorie, low-fat base for sauces.

---

2 quarts

5 pounds chicken bones, as much
    skin and fat removed as possible
2 large carrots (about ½ pound),
    washed and cut into large pieces
2 medium onions (about ½ pound),
    quartered
1 cup dry white wine

2 gallons cold water
3 medium celery ribs (about
    5 ounces), cut into large pieces
2 fresh thyme sprigs or 1 teaspoon
    dried thyme
1 bay leaf
1½ teaspoons tomato paste

Preheat the oven to 425°F.

Spread out the bones in a single layer on a large roasting pan and roast for 40 minutes, stirring occasionally so that they do not burn. During the last 20 minutes of roasting, mix in the carrots and onions. The bones and vegetables should be well browned.

Transfer the bones and vegetables to a large stockpot; use tongs or a slotted spoon to minimize the amount of fat transferred. Discard any fat in the roasting pan, then pour the wine into the pan. Bring to a boil on the stovetop and stir with a wooden spoon to dissolve the particles on the bottom of the roasting pan. Add these juices to the stockpot along with the water.

Bring the mixture to a boil, then reduce the heat and boil gently for 1 hour. Using a fine-mesh skimmer, remove any particles, foam, or fat that rise to the surface.

Add the celery, thyme, bay leaf, and tomato paste. Keep the stock at a low boil, uncovered, for 4 to 5 more hours.

Strain the stock through a cheesecloth-lined colander or fine-mesh strainer into a large container or bowl. You should have about 2 quarts of stock. If you have substantially more, boil until it reduces to about 2 quarts; if you have less, add water to bring the total volume to 3 quarts, then boil and reduce to 2 quarts.

Place the stock in a sink filled with ice water to cool quickly. Cover and refrigerate for at least 12 hours. Skim off and discard any fat that has solidified on the surface. Keep refrigerated for 3 to 4 days or store in small containers in the freezer.

PER SERVING (1 CUP)

calories	protein	carbohydrates	fat	cholesterol	dietary fiber	saturated fat
33	5 g	1 g	1 g	0 mg	0 g	0 g

% OF CALORIES: 13% carbohydrate, 60% protein, 27% fat

🐟 FISH STOCK

Laura Pensiero, R.D., co-owner, Gigi Trattoria, Rhinebeck, New York; nutritionist, Strang Cancer Prevention Center

---

Fish stock can be used to make sauces, soups, bisques, risottos, and other dishes that include seafood or shellfish. Fish stock is also a flavorful liquid for poaching fish.

---

2 quarts

1 gallon cold water
4 pounds fish bones (snapper,
   striped bass, grouper, or halibut)
1 cup dry white wine
2 strips lemon zest
1 bay leaf

3 to 4 parsley stems
1 cup mushrooms (about
   2½ ounces), chopped
1 fresh thyme sprig or ½ teaspoon
   dried thyme

Combine all the ingredients in a large stockpot and bring slowly to a simmer. Using a fine-mesh skimmer or spoon, remove any particles or foam that rise to the surface.

Simmer, uncovered, for 30 to 40 minutes, then strain the stock through a cheesecloth-lined colander or fine-mesh strainer into a large bowl.

Place the stock in a sink filled with ice water to cool quickly. Keep refrigerated for up to 2 days or store in small containers in the freezer.

PER SERVING (½ CUP)

calories	protein	carbohydrates	fat	cholesterol	dietary fiber	saturated fat
16	2 g	1 g	<1 g	0 mg	0 g	0 g

% OF CALORIES: 25% carbohydrate, 50% protein, 25% fat

❦ Root Vegetable Broth (*Potage Maigre aux Racines*)

André Soltner, master chef and senior lecturer, the French Culinary Institute, New York City

---

André suggests cooking julienned or finely diced vegetables, rice, pastina, or risotto in this flavorful broth.

About 1 quart

1 cup dried lentils
2 quarts water
salt and freshly ground black pepper
1 tablespoon olive oil
2 to 3 medium carrots, peeled and
    diced (1 to 1½ cups)
1 medium leek, white part only
    (about 1½ ounces), diced

1 medium onion (about 5 ounces),
    diced
1 large celery rib (about 2 ounces),
    diced
1 bunch flat-leaf parsley sprigs
    (about 1 ounce)

Thoroughly wash the lentils under cold running water. In a medium saucepan, combine the lentils and water and season with salt and pepper to taste. Bring to boil, then reduce the heat and simmer, stirring occasionally, until the lentils are very soft, about 45 minutes. Let them stand in the cooking liquid for at least 5 minutes.

Pour the cooking liquid through a cheesecloth-lined colander into a large bowl. Do not press the lentils against the cloth—the liquid will become cloudy. Reserve the lentils for another use, perhaps a salad, and set the cooking liquid aside.

Heat the olive oil in a medium saucepan over medium heat. Add the carrots, leek, onion, and celery and cook, stirring often, until golden brown, about 10 minutes. Add the reserved liquid and the parsley and bring to a boil. Reduce the heat to simmer, uncovered, for 1 hour. Adjust the seasoning with more salt and pepper if necessary.

Line a colander with a moistened cloth napkin (not cheesecloth) and pour the broth through it into a medium container or bowl. Set aside to cool. Keep refrigerated for up to 2 days or store in small containers in the freezer.

PER SERVING (¾ CUP)

calories	protein	carbohydrates	fat	cholesterol	dietary fiber	saturated fat
38	1 g	4 g	2 g	11 mg	0 g	<1 g

% OF CALORIES: 42% carbohydrate, 11% protein, 47% fat

CARROT SOUP WITH CHIVES

Alain Sailhac, executive vice president and senior dean of studies, the French Culinary Institute, New York City

---

For creamy texture without the fat, Alain Sailhac recommends vegetable puree soups and sauces. After vegetables soften with cooking, they can be pureed and strained to make them velvety smooth. The small amount of rice in this recipe acts as a thickening agent. In many recipes a starch, such as rice or potato, can replace a high-fat roux (equal proportions of butter and flour).

For a nice presentation, garnish each serving with a large butterflied shrimp that has been sautéed until lightly browned.

---

8 servings

1 tablespoon canola oil
1 teaspoon unsalted butter
2 pounds carrots, peeled
   and chopped
2 large leeks, white part only
   (about 5 ounces), washed
   and sliced
1 medium onion (about 5 ounces),
   chopped

2 quarts White Chicken Stock or
   Brown Chicken Stock (see Index),
   or low-sodium canned broth
   or water
¼ cup uncooked long-grain
   white rice
1½ cups 2% milk
salt and freshly ground black pepper
¼ cup snipped fresh chives

In a large saucepan over medium heat, heat the oil and butter. When the butter melts and is foamy, add the carrots, leeks, and onion. Cook, stirring often, until the leeks and onion are soft but not browned, about 10 minutes. Add the chicken stock and rice and bring to a boil. Reduce the heat so that the mixture simmers; cover the pot and cook until the rice is soft and the carrots are tender enough to be crushed easily between your fingers, about 45 minutes. Stir from time to time to make sure the vegetables do not stick to the bottom of the saucepan and burn.

Puree the soup in batches in a blender or food processor. If the soup is too thick, add a little more stock or water (don't thin the soup too much—milk will be added). Using a rubber spatula, push as much liquid as possible through a medium-mesh strainer into a clean saucepan. Add the milk and bring the soup to a low simmer. Add salt and pepper to taste.

Ladle into warm soup bowls and sprinkle chives in the center of each serving for garnish.

- Carrots provide the majority of beta-carotene: per serving this recipe provides more than 300 percent of the DV for vitamin A.
- A good source of fiber

PER SERVING

calories	protein	carbohydrates	fat	cholesterol	dietary fiber	saturated fat
192	9 g	26 g	6 g	6 mg	4 g	2 g

% OF CALORIES: 53% carbohydrate, 19% protein, 28% fat

MAJOR SOURCES OF POTENTIAL CANCER FIGHTERS

Phytochemicals: allium compounds, plant polyphenols (flavonoids, phenolic acids), terpenes (carotenoids, monoterpenes)

Salads

RED ONION, GRAPEFRUIT, AND TOMATO SALAD

Jacques Pépin, PBS-TV cooking series host and dean of special programs, the French Culinary Institute, New York City ▪ Adapted with permission from *Jacques Pépin's Simple and Healthy Cooking* (Rodale, 1994).

A refreshing salad for any season. The classic sherry vinaigrette serves well for many other salads.

6 servings

RED ONION, GRAPEFRUIT, AND TOMATO SALAD

3 medium tomatoes (about 1 pound)
1 large Ruby Red grapefruit (about 1 pound)
1 medium red onion (6 ounces), peeled and cut into ¼-inch dice
½ cup fresh basil leaves, sliced into long, thin strips
1 bunch watercress (about 2 ounces)

SHERRY VINAIGRETTE *(about ¼ cup)*

2 tablespoons extra-virgin olive oil
1 tablespoon sherry vinegar
½ teaspoon salt
¼ teaspoon freshly ground black pepper

Core the tomatoes and plunge them into boiling water for 30 seconds. Remove with a slotted spoon and slip off the skins. Slice the tomatoes in half and squeeze gently to force out the seeds. Use your fingers to remove any remaining seeds. Discard the seeds and cut the tomatoes into 1-inch pieces. Set aside.

Using a sharp knife, peel the grapefruit, removing all the skin and the underlying white pith so the flesh of the fruit is totally exposed. Then cut between the membranes on each side of every segment and remove the flesh in wedgelike pieces. Cut each grapefruit wedge in half and place the pieces in a large bowl. Then, holding the membranes over the bowl, squeeze them over the grapefruit flesh to extract any remaining juice before discarding them. (You should have about 1 cup of grapefruit flesh and 3 tablespoons of juice.) Add the tomatoes, onion, and basil to the bowl. Mix well.

To make the sherry vinaigrette, mix the oil, vinegar, salt, and pepper in a small bowl. Toss with the grapefruit mixture.

Cut the bottom 2 inches of stems from the watercress and discard. Wash and thoroughly dry the rest of the bunch. Arrange the watercress attractively around the periphery of a platter and mound the salad in the center.

- Ruby Red grapefruit and tomatoes are made red by the carotenoid lycopene, a potent antioxidant. Together with watercress, they provide 65 percent of the DV for vitamin C per serving.
- Red onions are a good source of the flavonoids quercetin and rutin, which act as blocking agents against cancer.

PER SERVING

calories	protein	carbohydrates	fat	cholesterol	dietary fiber	saturated fat
106	2 g	11 g	6 g	0 mg	2 g	0 g

% OF CALORIES: 42% carbohydrate, 8% protein, 50% fat

MAJOR SOURCES OF POTENTIAL CANCER FIGHTERS

Phytochemicals: allium compounds, plant polyphenols (flavonoids, phenolic acids), plant sterols, terpenes (carotenoids, monoterpenes, triterpenes)

❧ BROCCOLI, POTATO, AND TOMATO SALAD

Laura Pensiero, R.D., co-owner, Gigi Trattoria, Rhinebeck, New York; nutritionist, Strang Cancer Prevention Center

Serve warm or at room temperature; this is a portable vegetable salad you can take to work, a picnic, or a party.

6 to 8 servings

1 gallon water
salt
2 medium potatoes (about ¾ pound), peeled and cut into 1-inch cubes
1 large head broccoli (about 2 pounds)
2 shallots (about 2 ounces), peeled and sliced very thin

2 medium tomatoes (about 10 ounces), diced
1 tablespoon rice wine vinegar or white wine vinegar
2½ tablespoons extra-virgin olive oil
freshly ground black pepper

Add the water and salt to taste to a large pot, preferably with an insert so that the same water can be used for both the potatoes and the broccoli. Bring to a boil and add the potatoes. Cook until they are tender and can easily be pierced with a sharp paring knife, about 10 minutes. Remove the insert and transfer the potatoes to a large mixing bowl. Keep the water at a boil.

Trim and blanch the broccoli. Separate the florets from the stems; break the florets into bite-size pieces and, using a vegetable peeler, peel the tough outer skin from the stems until you reach the tender green part. Slice the stems into ¼-inch coins.

Add the coins to the boiling water and cook until slightly tender but still firm, about 4 minutes; add the florets. Check for doneness after 2 to 3 minutes: it should be easy to pierce both stem pieces and florets with a knife. Drain and transfer to a bowl of ice water. When cool, drain again and transfer to the bowl with the potatoes.

Add the shallots, tomatoes, vinegar, and olive oil to the serving bowl and toss to combine with the broccoli. Season with salt and pepper to taste and serve.

■ Broccoli is a near-perfect vegetable; it is rich in beta-carotene, vitamin A, vitamin C, folate, and calcium. It is also a member of the cruciferous vegetable family and contains cancer-fighting phytochemicals.
■ Broccoli is a potentially good source of selenium.
■ Tomatoes and tomato products are also rich in vitamin C and contain the carotenoid lycopene, a potent antioxidant.
■ High in fiber—20 percent of the DV per serving

PER SERVING (BASED ON 6 SERVINGS)

calories	protein	carbohydrates	fat	cholesterol	dietary fiber	saturated fat
135	6 g	19 g	5 g	0 mg	6 g	1 g

% OF CALORIES: 51% carbohydrate, 17% protein, 32% fat

MAJOR SOURCES OF POTENTIAL CANCER FIGHTERS

Phytochemicals: allium compounds, glucosinolates, plant polyphenols (flavonoids, phenolic acids), plant sterols, terpenes (carotenoids, monoterpenes)

ASPARAGUS SALAD WITH BLACK TRUFFLES

Roberto Donna, Galileo, Washington, D.C.

This flavorful spring or summer salad is perfect for entertaining. Double or triple the recipe and serve on a decorative platter. It also makes an elegant first course, which can be followed by a simply prepared grilled fish, such as sea bass, tuna, salmon, or swordfish.

4 servings

¼ pound Vidalia onions or shallots
1 tablespoon plus 1 teaspoon
    olive oil
1 ounce black truffles,* cut into
    thin matchsticks
2 tablespoons balsamic vinegar

2 tablespoons White Chicken Stock
    or Brown Chicken Stock
    (see Index), or water
salt and freshly ground black pepper
20 fresh asparagus stalks (about
    1¼ pounds)

Preheat the oven to 375°F.

To roast the onions, toss the unpeeled onions with 1 teaspoon of the olive oil and place them in a single layer in a small baking dish. Add a little water or broth to the bottom of the pan and bake until tender when pierced with a knife, about 30 minutes. Let cool slightly, cut in half, and remove the skins.

Slice the roasted onions lengthwise as thinly as possible and place in a bowl with the truffles. Add the balsamic vinegar, stock, and remaining tablespoon of olive oil. Stir with a fork to combine. Season with salt and pepper to taste. Cover and let rest

---

*Sold in gourmet stores fresh, frozen, and oil preserved.

for at least 4 hours (refrigerate if stock is used). The black truffles will release their flavor into the vinaigrette.

Rinse the asparagus. If their stems are tough, peel them with a vegetable peeler. In a steaming basket or in a skillet with a little water, steam the asparagus until just tender, 2 to 4 minutes, depending on thickness. Place them on an attractive serving platter and top with the vinaigrette. They are best when still warm.

- Low in calories, asparagus is a great source of folate, providing 35 percent of the DV per serving in this recipe, and a good source of vitamin C and carotenoids.
- Truffles, grown under the earth, are a potentially good source of selenium.
- A good source of fiber

PER SERVING

calories	protein	carbohydrates	fat	cholesterol	dietary fiber	saturated fat
88	5 g	8 g	4 g	0 mg	3 g	1 g

% OF CALORIES: 37% carbohydrate, 21% protein, 42% fat

MAJOR SOURCES OF POTENTIAL CANCER FIGHTERS

Phytochemicals: allium compounds, plant polyphenols (flavonoids), plant sterols, terpenes (carotenoids)

❧ BLACK-EYED PEA–TEXMATI RICE SALAD

Dean Fearing, The Mansion on Turtle Creek, Dallas, Texas

This salad can be made quickly and offers a variety of flavors, textures, and cancer-preventive nutrients and phytochemicals.

6 servings

2 cups cooked or rinsed and drained
   canned black-eyed peas (see Notes)
2 cups cooked Texmati rice
   (see Notes)
1 cup diced tomato
¼ cup minced shallot
   (about 2 shallots)
2 tablespoons minced garlic
¼ cup thinly sliced white part of
   scallion (about 3 scallions)
2 teaspoons chopped fresh
   thyme leaves

2 tablespoons chopped fresh cilantro
2 tablespoons chopped fresh basil
2 canned chipotle chiles, chopped
   (see Notes)
2 tablespoons malt vinegar
   (see Notes)
1 tablespoon fresh lemon juice
¼ cup extra-virgin olive oil
salt
3 cups mesclun

In a medium bowl, combine all the ingredients except the mesclun and mix well. Allow to marinate for at least 2 hours. Place ½ cup of mesclun on each plate and top with the black-eyed pea–rice salad.

NOTES: To cook dried black-eyed peas, soak them in water to cover for 4 hours, changing the water 2 or 3 times. Drain and place in a saucepan with water to cover and cook for 45 minutes or until tender but still firm.

Texmati rice is a cross between American long-grain rice and basmati rice. Like basmati rice, it has a fragrant aroma and a slightly nutty taste. It can be found at most supermarkets.

Chipotle chiles are dried, smoked jalapeño peppers. They have a rich flavor, and their hotness is mellowed by the smoking process. They are available at some supermarkets and gourmet specialty stores.

Malt vinegar is made from sprouted fermented barley and has a slightly lemony salty flavor. It can be found at some supermarkets and most gourmet specialty stores.

■ Each serving provides more than 10 percent of the DV for vitamin A, 30 percent for vitamin C, and 20 percent for folate.
■ Texmati rice is a good source of fiber and a potentially good source of selenium.
■ High in fiber—20 percent of the DV per serving

PER SERVING

calories	protein	carbohydrates	fat	cholesterol	dietary fiber	saturated fat
233	8 g	44 g	3 g	5 mg	6 g	2 g

% OF CALORIES: 53% carbohydrate, 8% protein, 39% fat

MAJOR SOURCES OF POTENTIAL CANCER FIGHTERS

Phytochemicals: allium compounds, phytic acids, plant polyphenols (flavonoids, phenolic acids), protease inhibitors, terpenes (carotenoids, monoterpenes)

❧ Curried Whole Wheat Couscous Summer Salad

Charlie Trotter, Charlie Trotter's, Chicago, Illinois

Serve alone as a light summer salad or surrounded by seared shrimp or scallops.

4 servings

2 cups White Chicken Stock or Brown Chicken Stock (see Index)
1 teaspoon curry powder
½ teaspoon sweet paprika
¼ teaspoon cayenne pepper
1 cup whole wheat couscous (see Notes)
1 tablespoon unsalted butter
1 leek, white part only, washed and sliced thin
¼ cup cleaned and blanched fresh or thawed and drained frozen wax beans, cut diagonally into ¼-inch pieces
¼ cup cleaned and blanched fresh or thawed and drained frozen green beans, cut diagonally into ¼-inch pieces
¼ cup cleaned and blanched fresh or thawed and drained frozen peas
¼ cup cleaned and blanched fresh or thawed and drained frozen corn kernels
juice and grated zest of 1 lime
salt and freshly ground black pepper

Place the chicken stock in a saucepan and whisk in the spices. Bring to a boil, stir in the couscous, then reduce the heat and simmer for 1 minute. Remove from the heat and let sit, covered, for 10 to 15 minutes. Fluff with a fork. Let cool.

Heat the butter in a nonstick skillet over medium heat. When bubbly, add the leek and cook, stirring occasionally, until soft and golden, about 5 minutes. Add all other vegetables to the skillet and cook, tossing or stirring, for 2 to 3 minutes. Add the lime juice and zest and cook for 1 minute. Fold the vegetables into the couscous and season with salt and pepper.

NOTES: A staple of North African cuisine, couscous is granular semolina (very small pieces of pasta). Like pasta, it cooks very quickly and is a great starch choice for a busy day. It serves well as a bed for vegetables and/or a moderate portion of meat, fish, or poultry (usually stewed or braised); a last-minute addition to soups, stews, or porridge; or a dessert sweetened with milk and fruit. Couscous is available at most supermarkets.

- Whole wheat couscous is less processed than white couscous and contains more fiber, protein, B vitamins, and minerals, such as iron and magnesium. Whole wheat couscous is available in health food and gourmet stores and some supermarkets.
- Using the peel of citrus (or zest) in cooking is encouraged; not only does it lend aroma and flavor, but it also contains limonene, a phytochemical that may help your body dispose of carcinogens.
- Curry powder contains curcumin, a plant polyphenol that lends yellow color and acts as an antioxidant; it may also play a role as a cancer-blocking agent.
- High in fiber—25 percent of the DV per serving

PER SERVING

calories	protein	carbohydrates	fat	cholesterol	dietary fiber	saturated fat
233	8 g	44 g	3 g	5 mg	6 g	2 g

% OF CALORIES: 76% carbohydrate, 14% protein, 10% fat

MAJOR SOURCES OF POTENTIAL CANCER FIGHTERS

Phytochemicals: capsaicin, phytic acids, plant polyphenols (flavonoids, phenolic acids), plant sterols, terpenes (carotenoids, monoterpenes, limonene, triterpenes)

WARM PASTA VEGETABLE SALAD

Michael Chiarello, Tra Vigne and Tomatina, St. Helena, California; host of "NapaStyle" (Fine Living Network) and "Easy Entertaining with Michael Chiarello" (The Food Network)

Michael prefers the blended flavors of pasta salad when served warm. The "pan-made" vinaigrette and vegetables can be cooked ahead of time, but he recommends cooking the pasta at the last minute so that it is hot when mixed with the vinaigrette.

Use other vegetables, such as asparagus or fresh baby peas, in season. Roasted peppers are available year-round and are a perfect addition to this recipe.

8 servings

1 pound broccoli (1 small head)
3 tablespoons extra-virgin olive oil
2 tablespoons finely chopped garlic
1 tablespoon finely chopped fresh
   thyme leaves
¼ teaspoon New Mexican chile flakes
   or hot red pepper flakes
salt and freshly ground black pepper
2 cups White Chicken Stock or
   Brown Chicken Stock (see Index),
   or low-sodium canned
   chicken broth
3 small zucchini (about 1 pound),
   sliced into ¼-inch-thick rounds

3 tablespoons herb vinegar, preferably
   flavored with oregano (available at
   supermarkets and gourmet
   specialty stores)
2 medium tomatoes (about ½ pound),
   cut into large chunks
2 tablespoons finely chopped
   flat-leaf parsley
1 pound uncooked fusilli pasta
½ cup freshly grated
   Parmesan cheese

Bring a large pot of salted water to a boil.

Separate the broccoli stems and florets, breaking or cutting the florets into bite-size pieces. Using a vegetable peeler, peel the stems down to the tender light green core, then slice diagonally into thin rounds. Reserve the florets and stems separately.

Heat 1 tablespoon of the olive oil and the garlic in a large nonstick sauté pan over medium-high heat. Cook until the garlic is golden, being careful not to burn it. Add the thyme and red pepper flakes and cook for about 30 seconds. Add the broccoli florets, season with salt and pepper to taste, and cook, tossing or stirring, for about 1 minute.

Add the chicken stock to the pan and bring to a boil. Cook until the broccoli is half cooked, about 3 minutes. Add the broccoli stems and zucchini and cook until tender but still firm, about another 3 minutes. Using a handheld strainer or a slotted spoon, skim the vegetables from the pan and transfer to a baking sheet or shallow pan to cool quickly.

Bring the cooking liquid to a boil and boil until it thickens and reduces to about ½ to ¼ cup. Stir in the vinegar and then add the tomatoes, allowing the tomatoes to warm for 1 minute. Remove the pan from the heat and season to taste with salt and pepper. Add the remaining olive oil and parsley. Mix well.

While the sauce is reducing, add the pasta to the boiling water and cook until al dente, 9 to 10 minutes. Drain well and transfer to a serving bowl. Immediately add the vinaigrette, vegetables, and half of the cheese and toss. Sprinkle with the remaining cheese and serve warm.

- Broccoli is a near-perfect vegetable; it is rich in protective vitamins and minerals. Combined with other vegetables in this dish, it provides more than 110 percent of the DV for vitamin C, 20 percent for vitamin A and folate, and more than 10 percent for calcium. Broccoli is also a member of the cruciferous vegetable family and contains cancer-fighting phytochemicals.
- Broccoli, zucchini, garlic, and pasta are all potentially good sources of selenium.
- A good source of fiber

PER SERVING

calories	protein	carbohydrates	fat	cholesterol	dietary fiber	saturated fat
320	13 g	50 g	8 g	7 mg	4 g	2 g

% OF CALORIES: 61% carbohydrate, 16% protein, 23% fat

MAJOR SOURCES OF POTENTIAL CANCER FIGHTERS

Phytochemicals: allium compounds, glucosinolates, phytic acids, plant polyphenols (flavonoids, phenolic acids), plant sterols, terpenes (carotenoids, monoterpenes)

❧ Healthy Tuna Salad

Laura Pensiero, R.D., co-owner, Gigi Trattoria, Rhinebeck, New York; nutritionist, Strang Cancer Prevention Center

Serve over mixed greens or fill a whole wheat pita or spread on slices of whole-grain bread, adding fresh tomato slices and a leaf or two of lettuce.

4 servings

1 7-ounce can white tuna packed
  in water

¾ cup shredded carrot (about
  2 medium carrots)

1 cup small broccoli florets
  (3 ounces), blanched if desired

½ small red onion (about 2 ounces),
  diced fine

1 medium celery rib
  (about 2 ounces), diced

2 teaspoons fresh lemon juice

1 teaspoon grated lemon zest

½ cup 1% cottage cheese, pureed in
  a food processor if desired,
  or low-fat sour cream

2 tablespoons low-fat mayonnaise

freshly ground black pepper to taste

Drain the tuna. In a medium bowl, mix it with the remaining ingredients.

- One serving provides more than 40 percent of the DV for vitamin C and enough carotenoids to supply 60 percent of the DV for vitamin A.
- Tuna is a lean protein source that is a potentially good source of selenium and protective omega-3 fatty acids.

PER SERVING

calories	protein	carbohydrates	fat	cholesterol	dietary fiber	saturated fat
120	17 g	6 g	3 g	16 mg	2 g	1 g

% OF CALORIES: 22% carbohydrate, 58% protein, 20% fat

MAJOR SOURCES OF POTENTIAL CANCER FIGHTERS

Phytochemicals: allium compounds, glucosinolates, omega-3 fatty acids, plant polyphenols (flavonoids), plant sterols, terpenes (carotenoids, monoterpenes, limonene, triterpenes)

❧ CHERIMOYA-AVOCADO SALAD WITH CRISPY CHINESE CHICKEN

Norman Van Aken, NORMAN'S, Coral Gables, Florida

A light dinner for any season. For a vegetarian first course, prepare only the Cherimoya-Avocado Salad with Passion Fruit Vinaigrette.

4 servings

CHICKEN AND MARINADE

3 tablespoons light soy sauce

1 teaspoon Chinese five-spice
  powder (see Notes)

2 garlic cloves, minced

1 inch fresh ginger, peeled
  and minced

1 Scotch bonnet chile or jalapeño
  pepper, seeded and minced

3 tablespoons honey

1 tablespoon toasted sesame oil

4 split chicken breasts (about
  1½ pounds), boneless but with skin

¼ cup cashews (optional)

salt and freshly ground black pepper

PASSION FRUIT VINAIGRETTE *(½ cup)*

¼ cup passion fruit juice, strained

1 teaspoon honey

1 teaspoon light soy sauce

salt and freshly cracked black pepper

¼ cup canola oil

SALAD

1 ripe cherimoya (about 18 ounces),
  peeled, seeded, and cut into
  bite-size cubes (1 cup; see Notes)

½ ripe avocado (about 10 ounces),
  peeled, pitted, and cut into
  bite-size pieces

4 cups mixed greens
  (about 3 ounces)

To prepare the marinade, in a medium bowl combine the soy sauce, five-spice powder, garlic, ginger, chile, honey, and sesame oil. Mix well and add the chicken breasts, rolling them in the marinade to coat evenly. Cover the bowl and refrigerate.

Toast the cashews in a skillet on the stovetop or spread them out on a baking sheet and toast them in a 400°F oven for 4 to 6 minutes, until fragrant and golden brown. Set aside.

To prepare the vinaigrette, in a small mixing bowl combine the passion fruit juice, honey, soy sauce, and salt and pepper to taste. Whisk in the canola oil. Set aside.

To prepare the salad, in a small bowl combine the cherimoya, avocado, and about 2 tablespoons of the vinaigrette. Toss together and chill, covered. (This can be done up to 1 hour in advance.)

Preheat the broiler or grill. When hot, remove the excess marinade from the chicken, season with salt and pepper, and cook, breast side down, for about 5 minutes or until it is nicely browned. Turn the chicken breasts and cook for another 5 minutes. Reduce the heat or move the chicken to a cooler portion of the grill and cook until the juices run clear when the meat is pierced with a fork and the internal temperature reaches 165°F, another 5 to 7 minutes.

Toss the greens in a bowl with the remaining dressing. Mound the greens at the top of a large plate and top with the avocado and cherimoya salad. Remove and discard the chicken skin, then thinly slice the chicken and fan it out next to the salad. Garnish with toasted cashews.

NOTES: Chinese five-spice powder is a combination of cinnamon, cloves, fennel seed, star anise, and Szechuan peppercorns. Available at Asian markets and most supermarkets.

Cherimoya is also called a *custard apple*. It is grown in California from November to May. This tropical fruit tastes like a delicate combination of apple, pineapple, papaya, and banana. If you cannot find cherimoyas, substitute an equal proportion of these fruits.

- Cherimoya, passion fruit, chile peppers, and salad greens all contain substantial amounts of vitamin C: combined, they provide 65 percent of the DV.
- This recipe is also rich in carotenoids, providing 25 percent of the DV of vitamin A.
- Mixed greens and avocado provide substantial amounts of folate: more than 25 percent of the DV per serving.
- High in fiber—more than 25 percent of the DV per serving

PER SERVING

calories	protein	carbohydrates	fat	cholesterol	dietary fiber	saturated fat
500	32 g	48 g	20 g	73 mg	7 g	3 g

% OF CALORIES: 39% carbohydrate, 25% protein, 36% fat

MAJOR SOURCES OF POTENTIAL CANCER FIGHTERS

Phytochemicals: capsaicin, plant polyphenols (flavonoids, phenolic acids), plant sterols, terpenes (carotenoids, triterpenes)

SEARED SCALLOPS WITH LIMA BEANS

Lidia Bastianich, Felidia and Becco, New York City; Lidia's in Pittsburgh and Kansas City

This salad is easy to prepare and makes a perfect light lunch or first course.

4 servings

¾ pound large sea scallops (approximately 8), sliced in half horizontally
salt and freshly ground black pepper
1 tablespoon plus 2 teaspoons extra-virgin olive oil
1 garlic clove, peeled and crushed

⅛ to ¼ teaspoon hot red pepper flakes
2 cups cooked dried or drained and thawed frozen lima beans (see Notes)
2 teaspoons fresh lemon juice
2 tablespoons chopped fresh flat-leaf parsley

Spread out the scallop slices in a single layer on a plate and season with salt and pepper to taste.

In a nonstick skillet over medium-high heat, heat 2 teaspoons of the olive oil and sauté the garlic until golden. Remove the garlic, turn up the heat, and add the scallops and hot red pepper flakes, to taste. Sauté until browned lightly around the edges, about 1 to 2 minutes, turn over, and cook for 1 minute more.

Add the lima beans. Drizzle with the remaining tablespoon of olive oil and the lemon juice and season with salt and pepper. Sprinkle with the parsley and serve.

NOTES: To cook dried lima beans, soak 1¼ cups beans in water to cover for 4 to 6 hours, changing the water 2 or 3 times. Drain and place in a saucepan with water to cover and bring to a boil. Simmer for 1 to 1½ hours, until tender.

- With a total fat content of less than 0.3 g per ounce, scallops are almost a fat-free, high-quality protein source. In this salad, fat and flavor are added through extra-virgin olive oil. The total fat content is still very low compared to total calories and the other nutritional merits of this entrée.
- Lima beans not only lend a nice texture contrast to this salad, but also are high in protein, fiber, folate and other B vitamins, phosphorus, calcium, iron, and potassium.

PER SERVING

calories	protein	carbohydrates	fat	cholesterol	dietary fiber	saturated fat
248	25 g	24 g	6 g	20 mg	7 g	1 g

% OF CALORIES: 38% carbohydrate, 40% protein, 22% fat

MAJOR SOURCES OF POTENTIAL CANCER FIGHTERS

Phytochemicals: capsaicin, phytic acids, plant polyphenols (flavonoids, isoflavones), protease inhibitors, terpenes (monoterpenes)

Warm Shrimp and Barley Salad

Barbara Lynch, No. 9 Park, Boston, Massachusetts

The perfect all-season lunch or light dinner. Use extra shrimp oil to sauté shrimp, adding infused flavor.

4 servings

Shrimp Salad
8 large tiger shrimp (about ¾ pound)
1 small eggplant (about ¾ pound)
2 tablespoons olive oil
1 tablespoon chopped fresh basil
1 tablespoon chopped fresh mint
1 tablespoon chopped fresh
    flat-leaf parsley
salt

8 ripe plum tomatoes
    (about 1 pound)
½ cup pearl barley
2½ cups water
freshly ground black pepper
1 tablespoon fresh lemon juice
4 handfuls arugula

Shrimp Oil *(½ cup)*
reserved shrimp shells
½ cup olive oil

salt and freshly ground black pepper

Preheat the oven to 400°F.

Peel and devein the shrimp, leaving the tail end intact. Reserve the shrimp shells and shrimp separately.

To prepare the shrimp oil, place the shrimp shells and olive oil in a small baking pan. Season with salt and pepper and bake for about 20 minutes. Strain through a fine-mesh strainer. Set the oil aside and discard the shells.

Cut the eggplant into ¼-inch dice and marinate with 1 tablespoon of the olive oil and half of the basil, mint, and parsley. Season the eggplant with salt and roast on a nonstick cookie sheet for 10 to 12 minutes, until golden. Transfer to a bowl and set aside.

Slice the tomatoes in half lengthwise, remove the seeds and pulp, and discard. Cut the tomato halves into ¼-inch dice. Set aside.

Place the barley in a saucepan with the water, season with salt to taste, and bring to a boil. Reduce to a simmer and cook, covered, for 30 to 35 minutes, until almost all of the liquid has been absorbed. Let stand, covered, for 5 minutes.

In a large nonstick skillet, heat the remaining tablespoon of olive oil. Season the shrimp with salt and pepper to taste and place in the very hot pan, searing for 2 minutes on each side. Turn off the heat and add the lemon juice while stirring with a wooden spoon.

Toss the shrimp, tomatoes, barley, eggplant, remaining herbs, remaining pan juices, and 2 tablespoons of the shrimp oil together in a bowl. Add salt and pepper to taste. Divide the arugula among 4 salad plates and arrange the shrimp-barley salad over the top.

- Tomatoes and arugula contribute vitamin C (almost 50 percent of the DV per serving) and carotenoids, such as the antioxidant lycopene and beta-carotene (more than 15 percent of the DV for vitamin A per serving).
- Shrimp and barley are potentially good sources of selenium.
- Like most minimally processed grains, barley provides inositol (phytic acid), which may have a variety of anticancer functions. Barley also contributes substantial fiber—this recipe provides 28 percent of the DV per serving.

PER SERVING

calories	protein	carbohydrates	fat	cholesterol	dietary fiber	saturated fat
291	22 g	32 g	9 g	122 mg	7 g	1 g

% OF CALORIES: 43% carbohydrate, 29% protein, 28% fat

MAJOR SOURCES OF POTENTIAL CANCER FIGHTERS

Phytochemicals: phytic acids, plant polyphenols (flavonoids, phenolic acids), plant sterols, protease inhibitors, terpenes (carotenoids, monoterpenes)

VEGETABLES AND SIDE DISHES

❧ CRISPY OVEN-ROASTED VEGETABLES

Gianni Scappin, chef/co-owner, Finch Tavern, Croton Falls, New York

Who said healthy cooking is only poaching and steaming? High-temperature roasting caramelizes the natural sugar in vegetables and concentrates flavor. The vegetable combinations are limitless—just be sure to cut vegetables according to their cooking times (small cubes for those that take a longer time to cook).

Gianni recommends serving these vegetables warm with roasted or grilled meat or fish or at room temperature on a buffet table for lunch or brunch.

4 servings

1 large bell pepper (about ½ pound), seeded and cut into large pieces

2 medium sweet potatoes (about ¾ pound), peeled and cut into medium cubes

2 medium turnips (about 10 ounces), peeled and cut into small to medium cubes

2 medium potatoes, preferably Yukon Gold (about 9 ounces), peeled and cut into medium cubes

2 large carrots (about 7 ounces), peeled and sliced ½ inch thick

1 large red onion (about ½ pound), peeled and cut into large pieces

3 garlic cloves, peeled and crushed

3 fresh rosemary sprigs

1½ tablespoons olive oil

salt and freshly ground black pepper

Preheat the oven to 450°F.

Place the vegetables in a large mixing bowl with the garlic and rosemary sprigs. Drizzle with the olive oil and toss the vegetables so that they are evenly coated. Spread in one even layer on a large nonstick baking pan. Sprinkle with salt and pepper to taste and place in the oven. Roast for 20 minutes or until the vegetables are golden brown, then turn them using a spatula safe for nonstick cookware. Lower the heat to 375°F and continue roasting until the vegetables are crispy, browned, and tender when pierced with a knife, about 15 minutes. Remove the rosemary sprigs and serve.

- One serving provides enough carotenoids to supply almost 200 percent of the DV for vitamin A and 100 percent of the DV for vitamin C, as well as significant amounts of folate and protective phytochemicals from the allium compounds and cruciferous family of vegetables.
- High in fiber—20 percent of the DV per serving

PER SERVING

calories	protein	carbohydrates	fat	cholesterol	dietary fiber	saturated fat
240	4 g	40 g	7 g	0 mg	5 g	1 g

% OF CALORIES: 67% carbohydrate, 7% protein, 26% fat

MAJOR SOURCES OF POTENTIAL CANCER FIGHTERS

Phytochemicals: allium compounds, carnosol, glucosinolates, plant polyphenols (flavonoids, phenolic acids), plant sterols, terpenes (carotenoids, monoterpenes, triterpenes)

GRILLED VEGETABLES WITH ROASTED RED PEPPER VINAIGRETTE

Laura Pensiero, R.D., co-owner, Gigi Trattoria, Rhinebeck, New York; nutritionist, Strang Cancer Prevention Center

Serve with crusty multigrain bread to make a tasty summer lunch or a light and healthy first course for an evening menu. Use the Roasted Red Pepper Vinaigrette to dress other salads.

4 servings

ROASTED RED PEPPER VINAIGRETTE *(1½ cups)*

2 medium red bell peppers
  (about ¾ pound)
1 tablespoon olive oil plus about
  another ½ teaspoon to rub
  the peppers

2 tablespoons sherry vinegar
1 garlic clove, peeled and crushed
⅓ cup water
salt and freshly ground black pepper

GRILLED VEGETABLES

1 small fennel bulb (about 1 pound),
  long stems removed, feathery
  leaves reserved for garnish, and
  bulb quartered with root left intact
2 medium carrots (about 7 ounces),
  sliced diagonally ¼ inch thick
2 large yellow bell peppers (about
  ¾ pound), quartered lengthwise,
  stemmed, and seeded

1 large red onion (about 7 ounces),
  quartered with root left intact to
  hold the slices together
  when grilling
2 medium red potatoes (about
  9 ounces), boiled until just slightly
  undercooked, sliced ¼ inch thick
1 tablespoon olive oil
salt and freshly ground black pepper

To prepare the vinaigrette, first roast the peppers. Preheat the broiler. Rub or, using a mister, mist the peppers with a small amount of olive oil, place on a sheet pan lined with foil, and broil about 6 inches from the heat source until charred on all sides, using tongs to turn the peppers so they char evenly. Remove the peppers from the oven, place in a bowl, and cover with foil or plastic wrap so that steam helps to loosen the skins. When cool, remove the skins, seeds, and stems.

Place the peppers, vinegar, garlic, and water in the bowl of a food processor or blender and puree until very smooth. With the machine running, drizzle in the tablespoon of olive oil. Season with salt and pepper to taste. Thin with a little more water if necessary; the dressing should be thick enough to coat the roasted vegetables.

Bring a medium saucepan of water to a boil. Season with salt and add the fennel. Cook until tender but still quite firm, about 2 minutes. Using a skimmer, transfer to a cookie sheet with a rim. Add the carrots to the water and blanch for 3 to 4 minutes, until tender but still quite firm. Transfer to the pan with fennel. Add the remaining vegetables to the pan, keeping them separated, lightly brush with the olive oil, and season with salt and pepper.

To grill the vegetables, heat a grill to medium temperature. Place the vegetables on the grill and cook until they are at the desired tenderness and lightly brown. *Do not char!* If the vegetables begin to brown faster than they are cooking, raise the grill higher above the heat, move the vegetables to a cooler area of the grill, or, if necessary, transfer the vegetables to a platter until the grill temperature lowers.

Spoon a pool of red pepper vinaigrette on the bottom of 4 salad plates. Arrange the vegetables decoratively on top, then drizzle with a little more vinaigrette. Garnish with reserved feathery fennel leaves.

■ One serving provides more than 80 percent of the DV for vitamin A and 250 percent of the DV for vitamin C, as well as many protective phytochemicals.

PER SERVING OF ROASTED RED PEPPER VINAIGRETTE (¼ CUP)

calories	protein	carbohydrates	fat	cholesterol	dietary fiber	saturated fat
25	0 g	1 g	2 g	0 mg	0 g	0 g

PER SERVING OF GRILLED VEGETABLES WITH ROASTED RED PEPPER VINAIGRETTE

calories	protein	carbohydrates	fat	cholesterol	dietary fiber	saturated fat
135	2 g	19 g	6 g	0 mg	2 g	1 g

% OF CALORIES: 55% carbohydrate, 6% protein, 39% fat

MAJOR SOURCES OF POTENTIAL CANCER FIGHTERS

Phytochemicals: allium compounds, plant polyphenols (flavonoids, phenolic acids), plant sterols, terpenes (carotenoids, monoterpenes)

❧ SUMMER VEGETABLE CASSEROLE WITH BASIL AND BLACK OLIVES

Daniel Boulud, Daniel, Café Boulud, and DB, New York City ■ Adapted with permission from *Cooking with Daniel Boulud*, Random House, 1993.

4 servings

2 tablespoons olive oil

salt and freshly ground black pepper

1 large red bell pepper (about
7 ounces), quartered lengthwise,
stems and seeds discarded

1 small zucchini (about 5 ounces),
ends trimmed and cut lengthwise
into thin slices

1 small eggplant (about 14 ounces),
ends trimmed, peeled, and cut
horizontally into thin slices

3 quarts water

16 to 20 wax beans, ends trimmed
and cut into ½-inch segments

3 ears fresh corn, husks and
silk removed

¼ cup small black olives (Niçoise)

1 celery heart (about 1 ounce), cut
into ¼-inch slices (reserve the
small yellow leaves for garnish)

2 medium tomatoes (about
½ pound), cored, seeded, and
cut into ⅛-inch dice

3 scallions, white part only,
sliced fine

1 small cucumber (about ¼ pound),
preferably European hothouse,
peeled, halved lengthwise, seeded,
and cut into ¼-inch dice

1 bunch watercress (about
2 ounces), leaves only

3 fresh basil sprigs, leaves only,
chopped coarse

juice of 2 lemons

6 to 8 drops Tabasco sauce

1 bunch arugula (about 3 ounces),
leaves only

6 radishes (about 3 ounces),
trimmed and sliced very thin

Preheat the broiler.

Brush a nonstick baking sheet or shallow roasting pan large enough to hold each of the vegetables in a single layer with ½ teaspoon of the olive oil and sprinkle with salt and pepper. Place the red pepper cut side down in the pan and broil about 6 inches from the heat source until the skin turns black, 8 to 10 minutes. Transfer the red pepper to a plate and cool. When cool, rub off the burned skin with a paper towel and set the pepper pieces aside.

Wipe off the baking sheet with a paper towel. Brush it with another ½ teaspoon of the olive oil and sprinkle with salt and pepper. Place the zucchini and eggplant slices tightly side by side in the pan. Brush the top of the slices with 2 teaspoons of the remaining olive oil and season with a pinch each of salt and pepper. Broil about 6 inches from the heat source for 7 to 8 minutes or until lightly browned. Turn the slices over and broil for another 5 to 7 minutes. When done, remove from the pan and set aside to cool.

Bring the water and 1½ teaspoons salt to a boil in a large pot over medium heat. Add the wax beans and boil for 8 to 10 minutes or until very tender. Transfer the beans with a slotted spoon to a colander and cool.

Add the corn on the cob to the same boiling water used for the beans and boil for 4 to 5 minutes. Drain and set aside to cool. When cool, remove the kernels from the cob and set aside, discarding the cobs.

Place the black olives in a resealable plastic bag and seal. Lightly pound with a mallet or rolling pin. Remove the olives and pit them. Cut the pitted olives into small pieces and set aside.

When ready to serve, in a large bowl, combine the wax beans, corn kernels, celery heart, tomatoes, scallions, cucumber, half of the olives, the watercress, basil, juice of 1 lemon, remaining tablespoon olive oil, salt to taste, and Tabasco. Toss well and taste for seasoning.

Form a ring around the edge of a round casserole by alternating the zucchini and eggplant slices. Fill the center of the ring with the corn mixture. Place a tight bunch of arugula leaves in the center of the corn mixture. Arrange the red pepper pieces around the arugula on top of the corn mixture and place the radish slices over and around the arugula on top of the corn mixture. Sprinkle the whole dish with the remaining chopped black olives, celery leaves, and a pinch of salt and pepper. Drizzle the remaining lemon juice over the top and serve at room temperature.

- Peppers, tomatoes, and watercress are all rich in vitamin C—each serving of this delicious casserole provides 95 percent of the DV.
- Contains more than 15 percent of the DVs for vitamin A and folate
- A good source of fiber—16 percent of the DV per serving

PER SERVING

calories	protein	carbohydrates	fat	cholesterol	dietary fiber	saturated fat
224	4 g	22 g	15 g	0 mg	4 g	2 g

% OF CALORIES: 37% carbohydrate, 7% protein, 56% fat

MAJOR SOURCES OF POTENTIAL CANCER FIGHTERS

Phytochemicals: allium compounds, glucosinolates, plant polyphenols (flavonoids, phenolic acids), plant sterols, terpenes (carotenoids, monoterpenes, triterpenes)

🌺 Spicy Sweet Potato and Chestnut Gratin

Charles Wiley, executive chef, Elements Restaurant at the Sanctuary at Camelback Mountain, Paradise Valley, Arizona

This side dish is colorful and creamy. The sweet potatoes and maple syrup lend a sweetness that is balanced by the smokiness and slight spiciness of the ancho chiles.

6 servings

1 teaspoon olive oil
1⅓ cups whole milk
¼ cup maple syrup
3 garlic cloves, chopped
2 ancho chiles, stemmed, seeded, and torn into ½-inch pieces (see Notes)
2 large sweet potatoes (about 1¼ pounds), peeled
salt and freshly ground black pepper
3 medium leeks, white part only, washed and sliced thin
¾ cup roasted chestnuts, coarsely chopped (see Notes)
¾ cup grated aged Monterey Jack cheese
2 tablespoons snipped fresh chives

Preheat the oven to 350°F.

Evenly rub a 9- × 12-inch ovenproof casserole dish with the olive oil. Set aside.

In a small saucepan, heat the milk and maple syrup until steaming; do not boil. Remove from the heat, add the garlic and chiles, and let steep for 30 minutes. Puree in a blender. Set aside.

Slice the peeled sweet potatoes thinly. (A mandoline is best for this. Inexpensive, good-quality plastic mandolines are available at most kitchenware stores.) Lay about one-third of the potato slices in a single layer in the casserole dish, overlapping them slightly. Season with salt and pepper. Ladle one-third of the milk mixture over the potatoes. Sprinkle with one-third of the leeks and one-third of the chestnuts, then top with one-third of the cheese. Repeat this process two more times to form a 3-layer gratin.

Cover with foil and bake for 40 minutes. Uncover and bake for another 15 minutes or until brown and bubbly. Let sit for 20 minutes. To serve, cut the gratin into squares or circles or spoon out of the casserole. Sprinkle with snipped chives before serving.

NOTES: Ancho chiles are dried poblano peppers available at some supermarkets and most gourmet specialty stores. When soaked or steeped, they lend a rich smoky flavor to sauces and broths without too much heat.

Chestnuts are available fresh from September to February. To roast them, use the tip of a knife to cut a small × in the flat side of their outer shell, then spread them out on a baking pan. Roast at 400°F for 25 to 30 minutes, then let them cool slightly. The shells should then be easy to remove. Frozen chestnuts are another option all year long. Thaw, lightly mist with olive or vegetable oil, and then roast them at 425°F until they are lightly browned, about 15 to 20 minutes.

- Sweet potatoes are phenomenal sources of beta-carotene. This recipe contains enough to supply 130 percent of the DV for vitamin A.
- Sweet potatoes, leeks, chestnuts, and chiles combined contribute 40 percent of the DV for vitamin C per serving.
- The chiles provide capsaicin, which may block or neutralize carcinogens.
- Leeks, members of the allium compound family, provide allyl sulfides, which may boost cancer-fighting enzymes.
- Each serving provides 20 percent of the DV for calcium.

PER SERVING

calories	protein	carbohydrates	fat	cholesterol	dietary fiber	saturated fat
233	7 g	38 g	6 g	17 mg	1 g	3 g

% OF CALORIES: 65% carbohydrate, 12% protein, 23% fat

MAJOR SOURCES OF POTENTIAL CANCER FIGHTERS

Phytochemicals: allium compounds, capsaicin, plant polyphenols (flavonoids), plant sterols, terpenes (carotenoids, monoterpenes)

🌿 No-Fuss Broccoli Soufflé

Laura Pensiero, R.D., co-owner, Gigi Trattoria, Rhinebeck, New York; nutritionist, Strang Cancer Prevention Center

Great for broccoli lovers, this untraditional soufflé is a good alternative for those who don't like broccoli straight up. It provides 2 vegetable servings and a significant amount

of protein without the fat. The recipe also works equally well with cauliflower, spinach, or brussels sprouts: simply substitute the same amount of any of these vegetables for the broccoli.

The dish is just as flexible in size as in ingredients. Prepare a larger soufflé and cut into wedges for a nutritious and easy family-style or brunch side dish. Or, because this puree freezes well, you can double or triple the recipe and pack it in small containers. Defrost and microwave for a quick, delicious serving of vegetables.

---

4 servings

4 cups fresh broccoli florets or
   1¼ pounds frozen broccoli,
   thawed and drained
1 medium potato, peeled and cut
   into ½-inch cubes
2 large egg whites
1 large egg
⅓ cup freshly grated
   Parmesan cheese

⅛ to ¼ teaspoon cayenne
   pepper, to taste
⅓ teaspoon salt
freshly ground black pepper to taste
1 teaspoon olive oil or
   olive oil–based cooking spray

Cook the broccoli florets and potato in boiling salted water until very tender, 5 to 7 minutes. Drain.

Puree the broccoli and potato in a food processor until no large chunks remain. Add the remaining ingredients except the olive oil and puree until very smooth.

Evenly coat 4 4- to 6-ounce ramekins or small ceramic bowls with olive oil and fill with the broccoli mixture. Pat down and smooth out the surface with a rubber spatula so that it is flat and firmly packed.

Microwave individually for 5 to 8 minutes on high (time depends on the power of the oven), until the center is set and firm. Run a paring knife around the sides of the ramekins to loosen the soufflés for easy removal. Carefully invert each mold and serve hot or at room temperature.

Notes: For a lighter soufflé, whip the egg whites separately until soft peaks form. Fold the egg whites into the seasoned, pureed broccoli mixture and continue as directed.

- Broccoli is a near-perfect vegetable, rich in beta-carotene, vitamin A, vitamin C, folate, and calcium. It is also a member of the cruciferous vegetable family and contains cancer-fighting phytochemicals.
- Broccoli is a potentially good source of the cancer-protective mineral selenium.
- One serving provides almost 100 percent of the DV for vitamin C, 30 percent of the DV for vitamin A, and approximately 20 percent of the DV for calcium and folate.
- A good source of fiber

PER SERVING

calories	protein	carbohydrates	fat	cholesterol	dietary fiber	saturated fat
126	12 g	14 g	4 g	59 mg	5 g	2 g

% OF CALORIES: 40% carbohydrate, 34% protein, 26% fat

MAJOR SOURCES OF POTENTIAL CANCER FIGHTERS

Phytochemicals: capsaicin, glucosinolates, plant polyphenols (flavonoids), plant sterols, terpenes (carotenoids, monoterpenes)

ROASTED GARLIC

Laura Pensiero, R.D., co-owner, Gigi Trattoria, Rhinebeck, New York; nutritionist, Strang Cancer Prevention Center

The process of roasting mellows the flavor of garlic, allowing one to eat much greater amounts of this nutrient-rich allium vegetable.

Squeeze the roasted garlic directly onto crusty bread or use in recipes for dips, sauces, and spreads to add flavor and creaminess.

8 servings

4 large heads garlic
½ cup water or defatted White
   Chicken Stock or Brown Chicken
   Stock (see Index) or canned broth

1 tablespoon olive oil
salt

Preheat the oven to 325°F.

Remove any loose papery skin from the garlic, but leave the heads intact. Using a large knife, slice off the top tips of all of the cloves, leaving the root end uncut.

Arrange the heads in a single layer in a small baking pan. Pour the water or chicken stock into the dish to come up the sides of the garlic heads. Drizzle the garlic with olive oil and season with salt. Cover tightly with aluminum foil and oven-roast for 50 minutes. Uncover and bake for 15 minutes longer, adding more liquid if necessary. When the garlic heads are cool enough to handle, squeeze the creamy roasted garlic paste out of the skins.

■ Garlic contains protective allium compounds and substantial amounts of vitamin C. This recipe supplies more than 10 percent of the DV per serving.

PER SERVING

calories	protein	carbohydrates	fat	cholesterol	dietary fiber	saturated fat
49	2 g	7 g	2 g	0 mg	0 g	0 g

% OF CALORIES: 57% carbohydrate, 12% protein, 31% fat

MAJOR SOURCES OF POTENTIAL CANCER FIGHTERS

Phytochemicals: allium compounds

❧ Sautéed Spinach with Garlic

Laura Pensiero, R.D., co-owner, Gigi Trattoria, Rhinebeck, New York; nutritionist, Strang Cancer Prevention Center

---

This cooking method produces a quick and tasty spinach side dish. It can be applied to other leafy greens, such as Swiss chard, escarole, broccoli rabe, and beet or turnip greens.

---

4 servings

1¼ pounds fresh spinach

1 tablespoon extra-virgin olive oil

4 large garlic cloves, peeled, lightly crushed, and quartered lengthwise

pinch of hot red pepper flakes (optional)

salt and freshly ground black pepper

Remove the stems from the spinach and tear any large leaves into bite-size pieces. Rinse thoroughly and drain.

Heat the olive oil in a large skillet. Add the garlic and red pepper flakes, if using, and cook over medium heat until the garlic is light gold; don't let the garlic get too brown or it will be bitter. Remove the garlic and set aside. Reserve the oil in the skillet and increase the heat to medium-high.

Add the spinach and season with salt and pepper to taste. Sauté, turning the spinach with tongs to cook evenly. When the spinach is just wilted and tender, 2 to 3 minutes, remove the skillet from the heat. Using a slotted spoon or tongs, lift the spinach from the skillet, leaving behind excess liquid. Transfer to plates or a platter. Top with the garlic and serve.

- Spinach is exceptionally high in beta-carotene (110 percent of the DV for vitamin A per serving of this recipe) as well as other carotenoids, folate (more than 80 percent of the DV), vitamin C (more than 80 percent of the DV), and minerals such as calcium, iron, magnesium, and potassium. It is also high in protein when compared to other vegetables.
- A good source of fiber

PER SERVING

calories	protein	carbohydrates	fat	cholesterol	dietary fiber	saturated fat
82	5 g	7 g	4 g	0 mg	4 g	1 g

% OF CALORIES: 33% carbohydrate, 24% protein, 43% fat

MAJOR SOURCES OF POTENTIAL CANCER FIGHTERS

Phytochemicals: allium compounds, terpenes (carotenoids)

Sicilian-Style Cauliflower

Laura Pensiero, R.D., co-owner, Gigi Trattoria, Rhinebeck, New York; nutritionist, Strang Cancer Prevention Center

Serve hot or at room temperature as a vegetable side dish for everyday lunch or dinner or as a delicious addition to the buffet table when entertaining. Toss with pasta for a quick and healthy meal.

4 servings

2 tablespoons olive oil

2 celery ribs, sliced

2 garlic cloves, peeled, lightly crushed, and sliced

1 medium onion, halved and sliced

½ jalapeño pepper or ¼ teaspoon hot red pepper flakes

3 anchovy fillets, chopped

1 bay leaf

1 large head cauliflower (2 pounds), cored, outer leaves removed, and florets broken into small pieces

2 tablespoons rinsed and drained capers

1 medium potato, peeled and cubed

⅓ cup dry white wine

5 cups White Chicken Stock or Brown Chicken Stock (see Index), low-sodium canned broth, or water

salt

Heat the olive oil in a large saucepan, preferably nonstick, set over medium-high heat. Add the celery, garlic, onion, and jalapeño and cook, stirring often, until soft, about 5 minutes. Add the anchovies and bay leaf, cook for another minute, then add the cauliflower, capers, and potato. Cook, stirring, for 2 to 3 minutes. Add the wine and cook until almost completely evaporated, 1 to 2 minutes. Add the stock and bring to a boil. Reduce the heat and simmer until the vegetables are very tender. Add ½ cup of water here and there, if necessary, during cooking; the vegetables should be breaking apart, and the mixture will be stewlike in consistency. Adjust the seasoning with salt, if necessary.

Serve warm or at room temperature.

- The cruciferous family, including cauliflower, is a significant source of cancer-fighting phytochemicals, such as indoles and isothiocyanates.
- Each serving provides more than 45 percent of the DV for vitamin C.
- A good source of fiber

PER SERVING

calories	protein	carbohydrates	fat	cholesterol	dietary fiber	saturated fat
96	4 g	12 g	4 g	1 mg	3 g	1 g

% OF CALORIES: 49% carbohydrate, 18% protein, 33% fat

MAJOR SOURCES OF POTENTIAL CANCER FIGHTERS

Phytochemicals: allium compounds, glucosinolates, phytic acids, plant polyphenols (flavonoids), terpenes (carotenoids, monoterpenes)

Sweet and Sour Cabbage

Laura Pensiero, R.D., co-owner, Gigi Trattoria, Rhinebeck, New York; nutritionist, Strang Cancer Prevention Center

This dish makes a nutritious, colorful bed for fanned-out slices of Gianni Scappin's Marinated Pork Tenderloin (see Index) or slices of roasted chicken breast. Vegetarian ideas include mashed potatoes or couscous served in a center well of the cabbage.

6 servings

1 tablespoon olive oil
2 medium red onions (about
 ½ pound), sliced
2 garlic cloves, peeled and crushed
2 tablespoons sugar
⅓ cup rice wine vinegar
1 small red cabbage, cored and
 shredded (1½ pounds
 shredded cabbage)

2 apples (about 10 ounces), peeled,
 cored, and cut into cubes
½ cup raisins
salt

Heat the olive oil in a nonstick 4-quart saucepan or large nonstick sauté pan. Add the onions and garlic and cook over low heat until limp, about 20 minutes. Add the sugar and turn up the heat, caramelizing the onions, about 2 to 3 minutes. Stir constantly with a wooden spoon to prevent overbrowning, sticking, and burning.

Stir in the rice wine vinegar. After most of the liquid has cooked off, add the cabbage and stir to combine thoroughly. Turn down the heat to low and cook, covered, for 1 hour. Stir occasionally and add water, 1 or 2 tablespoons at a time, if more liquid is needed. During the last 5 minutes of cooking, add the apples and raisins. Season with salt to taste.

- Cabbage, like other members of the cruciferous vegetable family, contains glucosinolates, which act as antioxidants, promote protective enzymes, and inhibit the activity of other enzymes and hormones that may promote cancer.
- Contains protective enzyme-boosting allium compound vegetables: onion and garlic
- One serving provides more than 70 percent of the DV for vitamin C and 15 percent of the DV for folate.
- High in fiber—20 percent of the DV per serving

PER SERVING

calories	protein	carbohydrates	fat	cholesterol	dietary fiber	saturated fat
162	3 g	31 g	3 g	0 mg	5 g	0 g

% OF CALORIES: 77% carbohydrate, 7% protein, 16% fat

MAJOR SOURCES OF POTENTIAL CANCER FIGHTERS

Phytochemicals: allium compounds, glucosinolates, indoles, plant polyphenols (flavonoids, isoflavones, phenolic acids), plant sterols, terpenes (carotenoids, monoterpenes)

✺ Tuscan-Style Cannellini Beans

Lidia Bastianich, Felidia and Becco, New York City; Lidia's in Pittsburgh and Kansas City

These beans can be served as a simple side dish (warm or at room temperature) with grilled meat or fish or as an appetizer, topping small toasted bread slices.

6 servings

1 tablespoon olive oil

2 garlic cloves, peeled and crushed

3 cups cooked or drained canned
cannellini beans (see Notes)

1 bay leaf

3 fresh sage leaves

pinch of hot red pepper flakes

2 medium tomatoes (½ pound),
peeled, seeded, and diced

salt and freshly ground black pepper

In a large nonstick skillet, heat the olive oil and add the garlic. When the garlic turns golden brown, add the beans, bay leaf, sage leaves, and hot red pepper flakes to the skillet. Stir and sauté for 2 to 3 minutes, then add the tomatoes and season with salt and pepper. Cover and simmer over medium-low heat for about 20 minutes to blend the flavors. Discard the bay leaf, sage leaves, and crushed garlic before serving.

NOTES: To cook dried beans, soak them in water to cover for 4 hours, changing the water 2 or 3 times. Drain and place in a medium saucepan with water to cover, add a bay leaf, and cook until tender, about 1 hour.

- Tomatoes and tomato products are rich in vitamin C and contain the carotenoid lycopene, a potent antioxidant.
- Sage also contains phytochemicals that act as antioxidants.
- High in fiber—20% of the DV per serving

PER SERVING

calories	protein	carbohydrates	fat	cholesterol	dietary fiber	saturated fat
132	7 g	21 g	3 g	0 mg	5 g	1 g

% OF CALORIES: 61% carbohydrate, 22% protein, 17% fat

MAJOR SOURCES OF POTENTIAL CANCER FIGHTERS

Phytochemicals: allium compounds, phytic acids, plant polyphenols (flavonoids, isoflavones, phenolic acids), plant sterols, protease inhibitors, terpenes (carotenoids, monoterpenes)

❧ Barley Stuffing with Dried Fruit and Sage

Laura Pensiero, R.D., co-owner, Gigi Trattoria, Rhinebeck, New York; nutritionist, Strang Cancer Prevention Center

---

A great blend of flavors, textures, and colors, this version of Thanksgiving stuffing has much less fat and much more fiber, nutrients, and protective phytochemicals than traditional bread stuffing. Prepare throughout the fall and winter.

---

10 servings

2 cups dried pearl barley

1 quart White Chicken Stock, Brown Chicken Stock, or Vegetable Stock (see Index), or low-sodium canned broth

2 bay leaves

1 tablespoon olive oil

2 shallots (about 3½ ounces), minced

4 small carrots (about ½ pound), peeled and diced

3 celery ribs (about 6 ounces), diced

4 fresh sage leaves, chopped

1 cup mixed dried fruit (any combination of apricots, raisins, currants, cranberries, or prunes cut into small pieces)

salt and freshly ground black pepper

Rinse the barley and place in a saucepan with the stock and bay leaves; bring to a boil. Reduce the heat to simmer and cook, covered, for 25 to 30 minutes, until the barley is tender and the stock has been absorbed.

In a medium nonstick skillet, heat the olive oil over medium heat. Add the shallots and cook, stirring, for 1 minute, and then add the carrots and celery. Cook, tossing or stirring often, until the vegetables are soft and aromatic, about 10 minutes. Add the sage and cook for 2 to 3 more minutes. Set aside.

Transfer the barley to a very large bowl and discard the bay leaves. Add the sautéed vegetables and dried fruit to the barley and toss to combine. Season with salt and pepper to taste.

- Each serving provides more than 30 percent of the DV for vitamin C and enough carotenoids to supply almost 200 percent of the DV for vitamin A.
- Barley is a potentially good source of selenium.
- High in fiber—almost 50 percent of the DV per serving

PER SERVING

calories	protein	carbohydrates	fat	cholesterol	dietary fiber	saturated fat
309	9 g	52 g	7 g	0 mg	12 g	1 g

% OF CALORIES: 68% carbohydrate, 12% protein, 20% fat

MAJOR SOURCES OF POTENTIAL CANCER FIGHTERS

Phytochemicals: allium compounds, plant polyphenols (flavonoids, phenolic acids), plant sterols, protease inhibitors, terpenes (carotenoids, monoterpenes)

Citrus Cranberry Sauce

Laura Pensiero, R.D., co-owner, Gigi Trattoria, Rhinebeck, New York; nutritionist, Strang Cancer Prevention Center

This easy-to-prepare relish has just the right contrast of sweet and tart flavors. It is the perfect accompaniment to all poultry entrées and can replace the mayonnaise on turkey or chicken breast sandwiches.

10 servings

¾ pound fresh cranberries
½ cup packed brown sugar
1 cup fresh orange juice

grated zest of 1 orange
grated zest of 1 lime

In a medium saucepan, combine all the ingredients. Bring to a boil, then lower the heat to simmer, cover, and cook until the cranberries burst open, about 10 minutes. Let the sauce cool and refrigerate.

- Cranberries contain ellagic acid, a phytochemical that may help boost enzymes that rid the body of cancer-causing substances.
- Cranberries also have a substantial amount of vitamin C—30 percent of the DV per serving (canned has about 75 percent less than fresh).
- The peel or zest of citrus fruit contains limonene, a phytochemical that may help increase the production of cancer-fighting enzymes that get rid of carcinogens.

PER SERVING

calories	protein	carbohydrates	fat	cholesterol	dietary fiber	saturated fat
70	1 g	17 g	0 g	0 mg	2 g	1 g

% OF CALORIES: 97% carbohydrate, 3% protein, 0% fat

MAJOR SOURCES OF POTENTIAL CANCER FIGHTERS

Phytochemicals: plant polyphenols (flavonoids, phenolic acids), plant sterols, terpenes (carotenoids, limonene)

Root Vegetable Mashed Potatoes

Laura Pensiero, R.D., co-owner, Gigi Trattoria, Rhinebeck, New York; nutritionist, Strang Cancer Prevention Center

This blend of autumn root vegetables is nutrient rich and contains only half the fat and calories of traditional mashed potatoes.

10 servings

1 medium rutabaga (about 1½ pounds), peeled and cut into 1-inch chunks
3 medium turnips (about 1 pound), peeled and cut into 1½-inch chunks
⅓ teaspoon salt
4 large white potatoes (about 2½ pounds), peeled and cut into 1½-inch chunks
1½ cups warm 2% milk
2 tablespoons unsalted butter
salt and freshly ground black pepper

Place the rutabaga and turnips in a large saucepan, cover with cold water, and add the salt. Bring to a boil, then reduce the heat and simmer for 30 minutes. Add the potatoes and cook until the vegetables are tender when pierced with a knife, 10 to 15 minutes.

Drain the boiled vegetables and transfer them to a large bowl.

Heat the milk in a small saucepan on the stove or in the microwave. Using an electric mixer, begin creaming the rutabaga, turnips, and potatoes while slowly pouring the warm milk into the bowl (use only as much milk as is needed to make the puree creamy and light). Beat in the butter and season with salt and pepper to taste. Serve hot.

- Potatoes and rutabagas are both rich in vitamin C; this recipe provides more than 60 percent of the DV per serving.
- Rutabagas and turnips belong to the cancer-protective cruciferous family of vegetables.
- A good source of fiber—13 percent of the DV

PER SERVING

calories	protein	carbohydrates	fat	cholesterol	dietary fiber	saturated fat
174	5 g	30 g	4 g	10 mg	3 g	1 g

% OF CALORIES: 68% carbohydrate, 11% protein, 21% fat

MAJOR SOURCES OF POTENTIAL CANCER FIGHTERS

Phytochemicals: allium compounds, glucosinolates, plant polyphenols (flavonoids, phenolic acids)

Spinach Cake

Antoine Bouterin, chef/owner, Bouterin, New York City

Antoine provides us with a quick and delicious new option for spinach, one of nature's nutrient powerhouses. Serve this on its own or with roasted or grilled chicken or lean pork. Top with chopped fresh tomatoes before serving.

4 to 6 servings

2 tablespoons corn or peanut oil

2 pounds fresh spinach, well washed and tough stems removed to yield 1 to 1¼ pounds

2 garlic cloves, crushed and peeled

2 tablespoons minced fresh flat-leaf parsley

1 tablespoon minced shallot

pinch of grated lemon zest

pinch of freshly grated nutmeg

salt and freshly ground black pepper

¼ cup all-purpose flour

2 large eggs

¼ cup whole milk

1 teaspoon unsalted butter, softened

Lightly spray or oil a 10-inch round cake pan. Preheat the oven to 400°F.

Cut the spinach leaves into chiffonade (long thin ribbons). In a large skillet over medium-high heat, heat the oil until very hot but not smoking. Add the spinach leaves, garlic, parsley, shallot, lemon zest, and nutmeg and season with salt and pepper. Cook, stirring often, until the spinach has wilted, 1 or 2 minutes. Sprinkle the flour over the spinach and mix well; there should be no lumps.

In a small bowl, whisk together the eggs and the milk. Add the mixture to the saucepan with the spinach and stir to combine. Remove the pan from the heat and stir in the butter. Pour into the prepared pan and press down to an even layer using a wooden spoon or rubber spatula. Bake until firm and lightly browned, 12 to 15 minutes.

- Spinach is an excellent source of vitamins A and C; this recipe provides 157 percent and 61 percent of these nutrients, respectively.
- Spinach is also a good source of calcium; 1 serving adds 15 percent of the DV.
- An excellent source of fiber

PER SERVING (BASED ON 4 SERVINGS)

calories	protein	carbohydrates	fat	cholesterol	dietary fiber	saturated fat
104	8 g	3 g	7 g	111 mg	8 g	2 g

% OF CALORIES: 12% carbohydrate, 31% protein, 57% fat

MAJOR SOURCES OF POTENTIAL CANCER FIGHTERS

Phytochemicals: plant polyphenols (flavonoids, phenolic acids), terpenes (carotenoids, monoterpenes)

Vegetarian Entrées

❧ Toasted Angel Hair Pasta with Mushroom Broth

Diane Forley, co–executive chef/owner, Verbena, New York City

Toasting pasta gives it an earthy, nutty flavor that marries well with mushrooms. Use this mushroom broth in other recipes—as a soup base or as the broth for a risotto, for example.

4 servings

Mushroom Broth

1 pound white button mushrooms
   (about 6 cups), cleaned and halved
   or quartered if large
½ head garlic, unpeeled and
   sliced crosswise

6 shallots, peeled
2 fresh thyme sprigs
1 tablespoon olive oil
salt and freshly ground black pepper
10 cups water

Toasted Pasta

1 pound angel hair pasta,
   broken in half
2 tablespoons olive oil
1 garlic clove, minced
¼ cup sliced shallot (2 medium)

1½ cups sliced oyster mushrooms
salt and freshly ground black pepper
¼ cup fresh flat-leaf parsley leaves
1 tablespoon snipped fresh chives

Preheat the oven to 375°F.

To prepare the mushroom broth, in a bowl, toss the mushrooms, garlic, shallots, and thyme with the olive oil and spread out evenly on a nonstick baking pan.

Season with salt and pepper. Roast in the oven for 20 to 25 minutes, until the juice runs out and the mushrooms are well caramelized. Place the contents in a medium saucepan and cover with the water. Bring to a boil, reduce the heat, and cook at a low boil for 30 minutes or until reduced by about half. Pour through a strainer into a medium bowl. Set aside.

While the mushrooms are baking, prepare the toasted pasta. Place the uncooked pasta on a large baking sheet, spreading it out as evenly as possible. Drizzle with 1 tablespoon of the olive oil and, using your hands, toss to coat evenly. Bake in the oven until golden, 6 to 8 minutes (turn the pan around halfway through baking and periodically shake for even browning). Remove from the oven and set aside.

Heat the remaining tablespoon of olive oil in a medium saucepan (preferably nonstick) over medium-high heat. Add the garlic and shallot and cook until the garlic just starts to brown, about 1 minute. Then add the oyster mushrooms and cook for 3 to 4 minutes, stirring often. Turn up the heat and add the mushroom broth (make sure you have about 4 cups; add a little water if you are short); when it boils, add the toasted pasta, cooking until al dente, 4 to 5 minutes. Turn off the heat; season with salt and pepper, and add the parsley leaves and chives. Immediately transfer the pasta to shallow bowls and spoon about ½ cup of broth over the top.

- Mushrooms contain significant amounts of B vitamins as well as copper and other minerals. They are also a potentially very good source of selenium.
- Mushrooms and parsley both contribute vitamin C, providing more than 15 percent of the DV per serving.
- A good source of fiber

PER SERVING OF MUSHROOM BROTH (1 CUP)

calories	protein	carbohydrates	fat	cholesterol	dietary fiber	saturated fat
39	1 g	2 g	3 g	0 mg	0 g	0 g

PER SERVING OF TOASTED ANGEL HAIR PASTA WITH MUSHROOM BROTH (BASED ON 4 SERVINGS)

calories	protein	carbohydrates	fat	cholesterol	dietary fiber	saturated fat
359	11 g	60 g	8 g	0 mg	3 g	1 g

% OF CALORIES: 68% carbohydrate, 12% protein, 20% fat

MAJOR SOURCES OF POTENTIAL CANCER FIGHTERS

Phytochemicals: allium compounds, phytic acids, plant polyphenols (flavonoids), terpenes (carotenoids, monoterpenes)

❧ Summer Vegetables in a Creamy Chile Cheese Sauce (*Calabacitas con Queso*)

Zarela Martínez, Zarela Restaurant, New York City ▪ Adapted with permission from *Food from My Heart* (Macmillan, 1992).

Serve as an appetizer with Toasted Pita Chips (see Index)—the recipe will serve 8—or as a vegetarian main course over rice or baked potatoes or a filling for steamed tortillas.

---

4 servings

2 fresh or canned poblano chiles

1½ pounds zucchini (5 small zucchini), cut into ¼-inch dice

1 cup water

salt and freshly ground black pepper

1 tablespoon olive oil

1 medium onion (about 5 ounces), chopped fine (about 1 cup)

1 large garlic clove, minced

1 large ripe red tomato (about 7 ounces), chopped

2 cups fresh corn kernels, 1 10-ounce package frozen corn, or 1 16-ounce can corn kernels, drained

1 5-ounce can evaporated skim milk

½ pound low-fat (not fat-free) white cheddar cheese, diced

If using fresh chiles, preheat the broiler. Rub or, using a mister, mist the peppers with a small amount of olive oil, place on a baking sheet lined with foil, and broil about 6 inches from the heat source until charred on all sides, using tongs to turn the chiles so they char evenly. Remove the chiles from the oven, place in a bowl, and cover with foil or plastic wrap so that steam helps to loosen the skins. When cool, remove the skins, seeds, and stems. Finely chop the peeled chiles and set aside.

Place the zucchini in a medium saucepan with the water; season lightly with salt and pepper. Bring to a boil, then lower the heat and simmer, covered, over medium heat for 2 minutes. Set aside without draining.

Heat the oil in a large nonstick skillet over high heat until hot but not smoking. Reduce the heat slightly and add the onion and garlic. Cook, stirring, until the onion is translucent, about 2 minutes. Stir in the tomato and cook until its liquid is partly evaporated, about 5 minutes. Stir in the corn and poblanos and simmer for 5 minutes more. Add the zucchini and its cooking liquid along with the evaporated milk and bring to a boil. Reduce the heat to low, stir in the cheddar, and cook just until it melts. Serve immediately.

- One serving contains 75 percent of the DV for calcium.
- Zucchini, tomato, and chiles all contribute substantial amounts of vitamin C: more than 40 percent of the DV per serving. This recipe also contains 25 percent of the DV for vitamin A per serving.
- Moderate consumption of capsaicin, found in chile peppers, may help the body neutralize carcinogens.
- High in fiber—20 percent of the DV per serving

PER SERVING

calories	protein	carbohydrates	fat	cholesterol	dietary fiber	saturated fat
270	18 g	31 g	8 g	0 mg	5 g	1 g

% OF CALORIES: 46% carbohydrate, 27% protein, 27% fat

MAJOR SOURCES OF POTENTIAL CANCER FIGHTERS

Phytochemicals: allium compounds, capsaicin, plant polyphenols (flavonoids, phenolic acids), plant sterols, protease inhibitors

Fusilli with Cherry Tomatoes

Lidia Bastianich, Felidia and Becco, New York City; Lidia's in Pittsburgh and Kansas City

A quick, easy entrée, first course, or side dish—6 servings if not a main course—perfect with grilled or roasted chicken or fish.

4 servings

3 cups cherry tomatoes (about
   1 pound), halved
2 tablespoons extra-virgin olive oil
½ teaspoon hot red pepper flakes
¼ teaspoon salt

1 pound dried fusilli
10 fresh basil leaves
½ cup pecorino cheese,
   grated (optional)

In a large serving bowl, toss the tomatoes with the oil, red pepper flakes, and salt. Marinate at room temperature for 20 minutes.

Cook the fusilli in a large pot of boiling salted water until al dente, 8 to 12 minutes, depending on brand. Drain the pasta, reserving ⅓ cup of the cooking water.

Stir the pasta water into the tomatoes and add the basil. Add the pasta and toss. Add the pecorino and toss again. Serve immediately.

- Pasta is a potentially good source of selenium.
- Tomatoes are rich in vitamins A and C, providing more than 10 percent and 50 percent of the DV, respectively. They also contain the carotenoid lycopene, a powerful antioxidant.
- High in fiber

PER SERVING

calories	protein	carbohydrates	fat	cholesterol	dietary fiber	saturated fat
579	21 g	94 g	12 g	10 mg	5 g	3 g

% OF CALORIES: 66% carbohydrate, 14% protein, 20% fat

MAJOR SOURCES OF POTENTIAL CANCER FIGHTERS

Phytochemicals: capsaicin, phytic acids, plant polyphenols (flavonoids, phenolic acids), plant sterols, terpenes (carotenoids, monoterpenes)

🌿 FARFALLE WITH ASPARAGUS AND PEAS

Marta Pulini, corporate chef, Toscorp., New York City

Serve this light spring vegetable sauce with other pasta shapes, such as fusilli, penne, or cheese-stuffed tortellini or ravioli.

---

4 servings

1½ cups fresh or frozen peas

5 quarts water

salt

½ pound asparagus (1 small bunch), stem ends trimmed

2 medium shallots (about 2 ounces), chopped fine

2 tablespoons plus 1½ teaspoons olive oil

1 teaspoon sugar

1 cup Vegetable Stock (see Index) or low-sodium canned broth

¼ teaspoon freshly ground black pepper

3 tablespoons chopped flat-leaf parsley

¾ pound dried farfalle (bow ties)

¾ cup freshly grated Parmesan cheese (about 3 ounces)

If using fresh peas, remove them from their shells. In a large saucepan, bring the water to a boil, add salt to taste, and cook the asparagus until tender but still firm. Using tongs, transfer the asparagus to an ice bath to cool them down quickly and maintain their bright color. Place fresh peas in a steamer insert and drop them into the boiling water for 2 to 3 minutes, then transfer to a small bowl of ice water (separate from the asparagus). Reserve the cooking water at a low simmer to cook the pasta, adding more water if necessary. If using frozen peas, place them in a small strainer over a bowl to thaw.

Drain the vegetables and slice the asparagus stems diagonally into slices about ¼ inch thick; reserve the tips separately. In a medium nonstick sauté pan over medium-high heat, sauté half of the shallots in 1½ teaspoons of the olive oil for 2 minutes, stirring. Add the peas and cook, tossing or stirring, for 2 more minutes. Add the sugar and ½ cup of the stock and season with ½ teaspoon salt and the pepper. Bring to a boil, reduce the heat, and simmer for about 1 minute. Remove half of this mixture and puree in a food processor or blender with 2 tablespoons of the parsley, 1 tablespoon of the remaining olive oil, and a little more stock if the sauce needs to be thinned slightly—it should be creamy and rather thick. In a medium bowl, combine the whole peas with the puree. Taste and add salt if necessary; reserve in a small bowl.

In a medium heavy saucepan (preferably nonstick) over medium-high heat, cook the remaining shallots in the remaining tablespoon of olive oil until soft, about 2 minutes. Add the asparagus stems, season with salt and pepper, and continue to cook. After 1 to 2 minutes, add the remaining ½ cup stock and bring to a simmer. When the asparagus are tender but not overcooked, add the asparagus tips and continue to simmer until tender, about 2 minutes.

Meanwhile, bring the water to a rolling boil and add the pasta. Cook until al dente, 10 to 12 minutes, drain the pasta, and add to the saucepan along with the reserved pea sauce. Toss with the Parmesan and remaining chopped parsley.

- Peas, asparagus, and parsley all contribute folate, vitamin C, and carotenoids. This recipe provides more than 20 percent of the DV for folate, 30 percent of the DV for vitamin C, and enough carotenoids to supply more than 15 percent of the DV for vitamin A per serving.
- Asparagus contains plant sterols, which may suppress cancer growth.
- Pasta is a potentially good source of selenium.
- High in fiber—20 percent of the DV per serving

PER SERVING

calories	protein	carbohydrates	fat	cholesterol	dietary fiber	saturated fat
526	22 g	78 g	14 g	10 mg	6 g	4 g

% OF CALORIES: 60% carbohydrate, 16% protein, 24% fat

MAJOR SOURCES OF POTENTIAL CANCER FIGHTERS

Phytochemicals: allium compounds, plant polyphenols (flavonoids), protease inhibitors, terpenes (carotenoids, monoterpenes)

CANNELLONI WITH ROASTED EGGPLANT AND RICOTTA

Roberto Donna, Galileo, Washington, D.C.

Roberto has created delicious cannelloni with more vegetables and less than half of the fat of traditional versions. To save time, you can substitute a good-quality low-fat commercial tomato-basil sauce for the sauce made with the recipe.

Pasta sheets can be purchased in gourmet and pasta stores as well as through many online businesses.

4 servings

1 large eggplant (about 1¼ pounds)
1 tablespoon olive oil
pinch of cayenne pepper
4 medium very ripe tomatoes
  (about 1 pound)
2 garlic cloves, minced
¼ cup fresh chopped basil

¾ cup low-fat sour cream
salt and freshly ground black pepper
5 quarts water
8 6-inch pasta squares
2 cups low-fat ricotta cheese
2 teaspoons chopped fresh
  marjoram leaves

Preheat the oven to 375°F.

Halve the eggplant lengthwise, brush the flesh with olive oil, and sprinkle with cayenne. Place on a nonstick baking sheet, flat side down, and roast for 20 to 30 minutes. Turn over and continue roasting for approximately 20 more minutes. Remove from the oven and let cool. Scoop the pulp from the skin of the eggplant, place in a large bowl, and mash.

To prepare the sauce, core the tomatoes and plunge them into boiling water for 30 seconds. Slip off the skins. Slice the tomatoes in half and gently squeeze to force out the seeds. Use your fingers to remove any remaining seeds. Discard the seeds and chop the tomatoes.

In a food processor or blender, puree the tomato. Transfer to a medium saucepan and add the garlic and basil. Bring to a boil, reduce the heat, and simmer for about 5 minutes. Turn off the heat and side aside to cool slightly. Stir in ¼ cup of the sour cream and season with salt and pepper to taste.

Bring the water to a boil, add salt to taste, and cook the pasta until al dente, 6 to 8 minutes. Drain and transfer to lightly oiled baking pans in a single layer to prevent sticking.

Add the ricotta, the remaining ½ cup sour cream, and the marjoram to the mashed eggplant. Season with salt and pepper and mix well. Divide the mixture among the pasta squares and roll them up. Place in a small nonstick rectangular baking dish and bake for 15 minutes, until crisp.

Spoon some sauce onto 4 plates and place the cannelloni on top. Top the cannelloni with a little more sauce.

- Each serving provides more than 40 percent of the DV for vitamin C and 20 percent for vitamin A.
- High in fiber—22 percent of the DV per serving

PER SERVING

calories	protein	carbohydrates	fat	cholesterol	dietary fiber	saturated fat
418	28 g	54 g	11 g	22 mg	6 g	3 g

% OF CALORIES: 49% carbohydrate, 27% protein, 24% fat

MAJOR SOURCES OF POTENTIAL CANCER FIGHTERS

Phytochemicals: allium compounds, plant polyphenols (flavonoids, phenolic acids), plant sterols, terpenes (carotenoids, monoterpenes)

Curry Roasted Summer Vegetables over Basmati Rice

Nick Morfogen, 32 east, Delray Beach, Florida

Nick serves these aromatic and delicious vegetables as a side dish or over grains such as basmati or brown rice, barley, couscous, or polenta.

6 servings

RICE
2½ cups basmati rice
3½ cups water
½ teaspoon salt

1 teaspoon unsalted butter
2 cardamom pods

VEGETABLES

12 pearl onions (about ¼ pound),
    ends cut off

2 tablespoons plus 1 teaspoon
    olive oil

2 medium carrots (about 5 ounces),
    peeled and sliced diagonally

2 medium potatoes (about
    10 ounces), peeled and quartered

½ pound green beans, split in half
    lengthwise and cut into
    2-inch pieces

12 asparagus spears (about ½ pound),
    cut into 2-inch pieces

1 medium eggplant (about 14 ounces),
    cut into large dice

1 medium zucchini (about ½ pound),
    cut into large dice

1 tablespoon curry powder

kosher salt and freshly ground
    white pepper

2 teaspoons minced garlic

2 medium tomatoes (about 10 ounces),
    quartered

1 cup Vegetable Stock (see Index) or
    low-sodium canned broth

12 fresh basil leaves, sliced

In a medium bowl, soak the rice in warm water for 30 minutes; drain.

Preheat the oven to 400°F. In a small bowl, toss the pearl onions with 1 teaspoon of the olive oil and spread out in a small roasting pan. Place the pan in the oven and roast until tender, about 15 minutes. Allow to cool and then peel. Set aside.

In a saucepan, combine the soaked rice, water, salt, butter, and cardamom. Bring to a boil over high heat, reduce the heat to low, and simmer gently, covered, for 15 minutes or until the rice is light and fluffy and the water has been absorbed.

While the onions roast, place the carrots in a medium saucepan filled with cold salted water. Bring to a boil, then reduce the heat. When the carrots are almost cooked but still firm, after about 7 minutes, add the potatoes. Cook for 4 more minutes and add the green beans. After 2 minutes, drain the water from the vegetables and reserve in a large stainless-steel bowl.

Add the asparagus, eggplant, and zucchini to the bowl, sprinkle with curry powder, and season with salt and white pepper. In a Dutch oven or ovenproof saucepan over medium-high heat, heat the remaining 2 tablespoons of olive oil. When it is almost smoking, carefully add the seasoned vegetables. Shake the pan once or twice after 30 seconds, then place the pan in the oven. Cook for 10 minutes, then remove the pan from the oven and place it on the stove.

Stir in the garlic, tomatoes, stock, and basil. Bring to a boil, reduce the heat, and simmer for 2 to 3 minutes.

Spread out the rice on a serving platter and spoon the vegetables over the top. Pour the curry broth over the vegetables.

- One serving provides more than 100 percent of the DV for vitamin C, 85 percent for vitamin A, and 25 percent for folate.
- Curry powder contains curcumin, a plant polyphenol that lends yellow color and acts as an antioxidant; it may also play a role in blocking cancer at the initiation stage.
- High in fiber—more than one-third of the DV per serving

PER SERVING

calories	protein	carbohydrates	fat	cholesterol	dietary fiber	saturated fat
416	9 g	80 g	7 g	2 mg	7 g	1 g

% OF CALORIES: 76% carbohydrate, 9% protein, 15% fat

MAJOR SOURCES OF POTENTIAL CANCER FIGHTERS

Phytochemicals: allium compounds, phytic acids, plant polyphenols (flavonoids, phenolic acids), plant sterols, terpenes (carotenoids, monoterpenes)

ᨃ Apple and Acorn Squash Risotto

RoxSand Scocos, chef/owner, RoxSand's Restaurant & Bar, Phoenix, Arizona

This combination of apple and squash is both delicious and nutritious. To cut cooking time on a busy day, peel the squash, remove the seeds, cut into small cubes, and add directly to the risotto rather than roasting first.

4 main-course servings or 6 first-course servings

Apple-Leek Broth

2 small leeks, white part only (about 5 ounces), washed and sliced thin

2 teaspoons olive oil

3 fresh thyme sprigs

salt and freshly ground black pepper

3 cups fresh apple juice or cider

RISOTTO

1 acorn squash (about 1½ pounds)	3 fresh thyme sprigs
½ cup water	2 Granny Smith apples (about
3 cups Vegetable Stock (see Index),	10 ounces), peeled, cored, and
low-sodium canned broth, or	cut into small cubes
water, boiling	3 tablespoons freshly grated
1 tablespoon olive oil	Parmesan cheese
1 medium onion (about 6 ounces),	1 tablespoon unsalted butter
chopped fine	salt
1½ cups Italian Arborio rice	

Preheat the oven to 375°F.

To prepare the apple-leek broth, in a small saucepan, cook the leeks in the olive oil over medium heat, stirring often, until soft but not browned, about 5 minutes. Add the thyme sprigs and season with salt and pepper to taste. Cook for another minute, then add the apple juice. Heat just until it simmers, then remove from the heat and set aside.

To roast the squash, split the acorn squash in half, remove the seeds, and place in a small roasting pan. Add ½ cup water to the bottom of the pan and seal with aluminum foil. Roast for about 50 minutes, until very tender. Let cool slightly. Remove the pulp from the skin and set aside.

Combine the apple-leek broth and the stock in a medium saucepan, bring to a boil, and reduce the heat.

In a medium heavy saucepan, heat the oil over medium heat. Add the onion and cook, stirring, until soft, about 3 minutes. Add the rice, squash, and thyme sprigs and cook, stirring often, for 2 to 3 minutes. Add 1 cup of the hot broth. Cook at an aggressive boil, stirring often, adding 1 cup of broth at a time, as necessary; the rice should almost completely absorb the broth between additions. Add the apples after 10 minutes and cook the rice until al dente and the mixture is moist but not watery, a total of 17 to 18 minutes. Remove the pan from the heat. Stir in the Parmesan cheese and butter, whipping with a wooden spoon to incorporate fully, and add salt if necessary. Divide the rice among serving plates and serve immediately.

- This recipe provides more than 25 percent of the DV for vitamins A and C per serving.
- Apples provide not only flavor and fiber but also plant polyphenols that act as antioxidants, blocking agents against carcinogens.
- A good source of fiber

PER SERVING (BASED ON 4 SERVINGS)

calories	protein	carbohydrates	fat	cholesterol	dietary fiber	saturated fat
445	9 g	81 g	11 g	11 mg	7 g	3 g

% OF CALORIES: 71% carbohydrate, 8% protein, 21% fat

MAJOR SOURCES OF POTENTIAL CANCER FIGHTERS

Phytochemicals: allium compounds, plant polyphenols (flavonoids), plant sterols, terpenes (carotenoids, monoterpenes)

❧ GREEN CHILE STEW

Robert McGrath, chef/owner, Roaring Fork restaurants, Scottsdale, Arizona, and Austin, Texas

Serve as a vegetarian entrée or with pan-seared or roasted game or spicy roasted chicken. You'll find poblanos particularly plentiful at supermarkets and Latin groceries in summer and fall. Cooking times and amount of liquid needed for the hominy will vary depending on the product and how coarse the grain is.

4 servings

8 poblano chiles
1 tablespoon extra-virgin olive oil
¾ cup peeled carrots in ¼-inch dice
½ cup chopped yellow onion
3 garlic cloves, minced
2 cups hot Vegetable Stock (see Index),
   low-sodium canned broth, or water

½ cup yellow hominy
¼ cup white hominy
salt and freshly cracked black pepper
¼ cup toasted pumpkin seeds

Preheat the broiler, rub or, using a mister, mist the peppers with a small amount of olive oil, and place on a baking sheet lined with foil about 6 inches under the broiler. Broil the peppers until charred, using tongs to rotate them so they char evenly. Remove the peppers from the oven, place in a bowl, and cover with foil or plastic wrap so that the steam helps to loosen the skins. When cool, remove the skins, seeds, and stems. Puree in a food processor or blender.

Heat the olive oil in a 2-quart saucepan (preferably nonstick) over medium heat and cook the carrots and onion, stirring often, until the onion is soft, about 10 minutes. Add the garlic and cook for another minute, being careful not to burn it. Add the poblano puree, 1½ cups of the stock, and the hominy, stir, and bring to a boil. Reduce the heat and simmer, stirring constantly, until the liquid has been absorbed and the hominy is cooked, about 15 minutes. (Add more liquid while cooking, if necessary.) Season with salt and pepper to taste, top with the toasted pumpkin seeds, and serve.

- Capsaicin, found in chile peppers, may help the body neutralize carcinogens.
- Chile peppers are a very good source of vitamin C, providing more than 40 percent of the DV per serving.
- Each serving provides 110 percent of the DV for vitamin A.
- A good source of fiber

PER SERVING

calories	protein	carbohydrates	fat	cholesterol	dietary fiber	saturated fat
256	9 g	36 g	10 g	0 mg	4 g	2 g

% OF CALORIES: 53% carbohydrate, 13% protein, 34% fat

MAJOR SOURCES OF POTENTIAL CANCER FIGHTERS

Phytochemicals: allium compounds, capsaicin, phytic acids, plant polyphenols (flavonoids, phenolic acids), protease inhibitors, terpenes (carotenoids, monoterpenes)

🌿 LENTIL AND SHELLING BEAN STEW

Michael Chiarello, Tra Vigne and Tomatina, St. Helena, California; host of "NapaStyle" (Fine Living Network) and "Easy Entertaining with Michael Chiarello" (The Food Network)

Michael Chiarello comments that the meaty flavor of lentils (particularly when smoked) makes a stew such as this a perfect vegetarian entrée. He originally created this recipe to pair with the beautiful medium-bodied red wines produced near his restaurant.

　　Serve alone or as a bed for sausages or roasted fish, such as cod or halibut. (Soy sausages, browned, sliced, and added to the stew, provide all of the protective benefits of soy protein as well as a spicy flavor kick, without the fat. Also, try chicken or turkey sausages.) Roasted or grilled chicken also goes well with this lentil stew.

4 servings

2 tablespoons extra-virgin olive oil
1 tablespoon finely chopped garlic
2 medium carrots (about 6 ounces),
   cut into ¼-inch dice
1 large onion (about 7 ounces),
   cut into ¼-inch dice
1 medium celery rib (about 2 ounces),
   cut into ¼-inch dice
1 tablespoon finely diced fresh
   thyme leaves
1 bay leaf

1 quart White Chicken Stock or
   Brown Chicken Stock (see Index)
   or low-sodium canned broth
½ pound dried green lentils (1¼ cups)
1 cup shelling beans (such as
   cranberry beans), removed from
   the pods and cooked (see Notes)
salt and freshly ground black pepper
2 tablespoons sherry vinegar
2 tablespoons chopped fresh
   flat-leaf parsley

Heat the oil and garlic in a large saucepan over medium heat until the garlic just starts to brown, a minute or two. Add the carrots, onion, and celery and cook, stirring, until the vegetables are soft, about 10 to 12 minutes. Add the thyme and bay leaf and stir to combine. Add 2½ cups of the stock, bring to a boil, and add the lentils. Lower the heat to a simmer, cover, and cook until the lentils are about half cooked, about 20 minutes, adding more stock if necessary to continue cooking.

Stir the cooked shelling beans into the lentils and season with salt and pepper to taste. Add another ¾ to 1 cup stock to produce a stewlike consistency. Bring to a boil and simmer until the lentils are tender, about 10 minutes. Remove and discard the bay leaf. Add the vinegar. Season to taste with salt, pepper, and more vinegar if necessary. Ladle into 4 soup bowls and garnish with parsley.

NOTES: Fresh shelling beans (or cranberry beans) must be removed from their large beige and red pods before cooking. The beans inside are pearl colored with red streaks and have a subtle nutty flavor. They are available fresh during the summer months and dried all year long. To cook fresh shelling beans, cover them with water, bring to a boil, reduce the heat, and simmer until tender, about 20 minutes. To cook dried shelling beans, soak the dried beans for 4 hours, changing the water 2 or 3 times. Drain, place in a saucepan, and cover with fresh water. Simmer for 1 hour or until tender.

Fresh fava beans (removed from their pods and outer shells), frozen lima beans, or canned chick-peas (rinsed and drained) can be substituted for shelling beans (add during the last 5 minutes of cooking to prevent overcooking). Frozen peas may be added during the last 2 to 3 minutes of cooking.

Other fruit and vegetable additions could include diced roasted red peppers, chopped tomatoes, sautéed or roasted mushrooms, and even peeled and diced apples or pears.

- Each serving provides 100 percent of the DV for vitamin A and more than 20 percent for vitamin C.
- Beans, particularly lentils, are very good sources of folate—more than 80 percent of the DV is provided per serving of this recipe.
- Lentils are a potentially good source of selenium.
- High in fiber—35 percent of the DV per serving

PER SERVING

calories	protein	carbohydrates	fat	cholesterol	dietary fiber	saturated fat
256	9 g	36 g	10 g	0 mg	4 g	2 g

% OF CALORIES: 51% carbohydrate, 24% protein, 25% fat

MAJOR SOURCES OF POTENTIAL CANCER FIGHTERS

Phytochemicals: allium compounds, glucosinolates, phytic acids, plant polyphenols (flavonoids, isoflavones), plant sterols, protease inhibitors, terpenes (carotenoids, monoterpenes)

INDIAN SPICED VEGETABLE STEW

Laura Pensiero, R.D., co-owner, Gigi Trattoria, Rhinebeck, New York; nutritionist, Strang Cancer Prevention Center

This is a nice vegetable side dish served with grilled or seared fish, such as tuna, swordfish, salmon, or snapper. To make this into a protein-rich one-pot meal, try adding chicken breast (cut into 2-inch-long strips and add during the last 10 minutes of cooking) or firm tofu cut into cubes (add 2 to 3 minutes before serving).

If you don't like Indian seasonings, omit them and use fresh herbs, such as thyme or basil.

4 servings

2 teaspoons olive oil
1 medium red onion (about
    5 ounces), peeled and sliced
4 small carrots (about 7 ounces),
    peeled and sliced ¼ inch thick
½ small jalapeño pepper,
    seeded and diced
1 garlic clove, peeled and crushed
¼ teaspoon cumin seeds
1 teaspoon curry powder
1 teaspoon turmeric
1 medium head cauliflower, washed,
    core removed, and broken into
    medium-size florets, or 18 ounces
    frozen cauliflower florets,
    thawed and drained

2 medium white potatoes, preferably
    Yukon Gold (about 11 ounces),
    peeled and cut into 1½-inch cubes
1 medium sweet potato (about
    6 ounces), peeled and cut
    into 2-inch cubes
1 14½-ounce can stewed tomatoes
¾ cup water
salt
1 cup drained canned or
    dried cooked chick-peas
1 cup frozen peas

Heat the olive oil in a heavy 4-quart saucepan (preferably nonstick) over medium-high heat. Add the onion, carrots, jalapeño, and garlic. Cook, stirring often, until the onion slices are limp, about 10 minutes. Add the cumin seeds and ground spices, stirring for about 1 minute to combine and release their flavors. Add the cauliflower, white and sweet potatoes, stewed tomatoes, and water. Season with salt to taste and stir to combine all ingredients. Bring to a boil, then reduce the heat and simmer for 20 minutes, covered, until all the vegetables are tender but firm. Add the chick-peas and peas 2 to 3 minutes before serving and adjust the seasoning with salt if necessary.

- One serving provides more than 100 percent of the DVs for vitamins C and A.
- Cauliflower belongs to the cruciferous family of vegetables and has protective phytochemicals.
- Curry and turmeric contain curcumin, a plant polyphenol that may provide many protective benefits.
- High in fiber—40 percent of the DV per serving

PER SERVING

calories	protein	carbohydrates	fat	cholesterol	dietary fiber	saturated fat
262	10 g	47 g	4 g	0 mg	10 g	0 g

% OF CALORIES: 72% carbohydrate, 15% protein, 13% fat

MAJOR SOURCES OF POTENTIAL CANCER FIGHTERS

Phytochemicals: allium compounds, capsaicin, glucosinolates, indoles, plant polyphenols (flavonoids, phenolic acids), plant sterols, terpenes (carotenoids, monoterpenes)

HERBED VEGETABLE AND PARMESAN FRITTATA

Maria Helm, cookbook author and culinary instructor, Napa Valley, California

Makes a great vegetarian entrée, brunch dish, or first course for dinner.

4 to 6 servings

1 tablespoon plus 2 teaspoons
    olive oil
3 garlic cloves, peeled and
    sliced thin
1 small red onion (about ¼ pound),
    sliced thin
1 large leek, white part only (about
    2 ounces), washed thoroughly,
    halved, and sliced thin
1 large bunch Swiss chard (about
    1 pound), leaves sliced thin
    (stems reserved for another use)
2 cups sliced shiitake mushrooms
    (about 10 ounces)
1 large red bell pepper (about
    7 ounces), diced

pinch of hot red pepper flakes
salt and freshly ground black pepper
1 medium zucchini (about
    7 ounces), halved and sliced thin
½ teaspoon dried rosemary
½ teaspoon dried thyme leaves
¼ cup julienned fresh basil leaves
1 cup unseasoned bread crumbs
4 large egg whites plus 2 whole eggs,
    lightly beaten, or 2 cups egg whites,
    nonfat egg product, or egg substitute
2 medium tomatoes (about
    ¾ pound), sliced
⅓ cup freshly grated
    Parmesan cheese

Preheat the oven to 375°F.

In an ovenproof nonstick skillet over medium heat, heat 2 teaspoons of the olive oil. Add the garlic, onion, and leek and cook, stirring often, until soft, about 10 minutes. Transfer to a small bowl and set aside.

Meanwhile, blanch the Swiss chard in boiling salted water for 3 minutes. Drain and place in a large bowl filled with ice water until it is completely chilled (this refreshing process helps keep the color a vibrant green). Drain and squeeze out as much water as possible. Transfer to a bowl and set aside.

Heat 2 teaspoons of the remaining olive oil in a nonstick skillet over medium-high heat until almost smoking, then add the mushrooms. Do not stir. After the mushrooms begin to brown, add the red bell pepper and red pepper flakes and season with salt and pepper to taste. Cook, tossing or stirring here and there, for 2 to 3 minutes. Add the zucchini and cook until all water from the vegetables has evaporated and the vegetables are tender but slightly firm, about 5 minutes. Add the Swiss chard, cook for another minute, then add the leek mixture and herbs. Season with salt and pepper and toss or stir to combine. Mix in ¾ cup of the bread crumbs and the eggs and, using a rubber spatula, pat down firmly. Top with the sliced tomatoes in a single layer.

Combine the remaining 1 teaspoon olive oil, the Parmesan, and the remaining bread crumbs and sprinkle on top of the tomatoes.

Bake for 25 minutes or until the eggs are set.

- Swiss chard is a good source of vitamin C; this recipes provides more than 45 percent of the DV. The vegetable mix also provides carotenoids, folate (20 percent of the DV), and calcium (more than 10 percent of the DV).
- A good source of fiber

PER SERVING (BASED ON 4 SERVINGS)

calories	protein	carbohydrates	fat	cholesterol	dietary fiber	saturated fat
224	15 g	19 g	11* g	112* mg	3 g	3 g

% OF CALORIES: 33% carbohydrate, 25% protein, 42% fat

MAJOR SOURCES OF POTENTIAL CANCER FIGHTERS

Phytochemicals: allium compounds, capsaicin, plant polyphenols (flavonoids, phenolic acids), terpenes (carnosol, carotenoids, monoterpenes)

---

*Total fat = 9 g and cholesterol = 6 mg if nonfat egg substitute is used.

SCRAMBLED EGG BURRITO

Laura Pensiero, R.D., co-owner, Gigi Trattoria, Rhinebeck, New York; nutritionist, Strang Cancer Prevention Center

---

A quick, nutritious weekday dinner or weekend breakfast. Substitute whatever vegetables you have on hand if you like. You can use store-bought salsa or make your own.

---

1 serving

3 large egg whites
2 tablespoons skim milk
salt and freshly ground black pepper
2 teaspoons olive oil
½ small red onion (about
   1½ ounces), diced
⅓ cup diced green bell pepper
   (about 2 ounces)
⅓ cup diced red bell pepper
   (about 2 ounces)

2 cups torn spinach leaves
1 10-inch whole wheat tortilla
⅓ cup cooked or drained and rinsed
   canned black beans (see Notes)
¼ cup shredded jalapeño Monterey
   Jack cheese (about 1 ounce)
2 tablespoons tomato salsa

Whip the egg whites, skim milk, and salt and pepper to taste in a small bowl. Set aside.

Heat the olive oil in a small nonstick skillet over medium-high heat. Add the onion and peppers and cook, stirring often, until the vegetables are soft, about 7 minutes. Add the spinach leaves and cook until wilted and all the water has evaporated.

Heat the tortilla in the microwave or on a heated pan (cast iron works well) until just warmed. Place the tortilla, loosely covered, on a large plate.

Add the egg mixture to the vegetable mixture and cook, stirring frequently, until the eggs reach the desired firmness. Transfer the eggs to the center of the tortilla and add the black beans and shredded cheese. Wrap up the tortilla, folding in both ends, then rolling it into a tight log. Garnish with a tomato salsa.

NOTES: To cook dried black beans, soak them in enough water to cover for 4 hours, changing the water 2 to 3 times. Drain and place them in a saucepan with enough water to cover by 2 inches. A halved onion, a carrot, and a bay leaf or two can be added to the water for flavor. Bring to a boil and then reduce to a gentle simmer. Cook until the beans are tender but firm, about 2 hours.

If you don't have the time to soak the beans, boil them in water for 1 to 3 minutes, turn off the heat, cover the pot, and let them sit for 1 hour. Drain and proceed as per the recipe.

- One serving provides 190 percent of the DV for vitamin C and more than 85 percent of the DV for vitamin A.
- Black beans contain isoflavones that may lower the risk of breast and other types of cancer. They are also high in fiber and folate, providing 50 percent and 85 percent of the DV, respectively.

PER SERVING

calories	protein	carbohydrates	fat	cholesterol	dietary fiber	saturated fat
398	30 g	43 g	12 g	1 mg	13 g	1 g

% OF CALORIES: 43% carbohydrate, 30% protein, 27% fat

MAJOR SOURCES OF POTENTIAL CANCER FIGHTERS

Phytochemicals: allium compounds, phytic acids, plant polyphenols (flavonoids, isoflavones, phenolic acids), plant sterols, protease inhibitors, terpenes (carotenoids, monoterpenes, triterpenes)

🍇 Mexican Lasagna

Laura Pensiero, R.D., co-owner, Gigi Trattoria, Rhinebeck, New York; nutritionist, Strang Cancer Prevention Center

---

This tortilla lasagna is loaded with flavor and nutrients. Vegetables can be added or substituted using leftovers or trimmings that you have on hand.

If you think you don't like tofu, try it in a well-seasoned composition like this. If tofu is not for you, the same amount of chicken strips can be sautéed and seasoned with chili powder.

You can prepare this lasagna 1 or 2 days before serving. Or freeze and then thaw and bake to have a healthy meal at your fingertips on a busy day. Add twenty minutes to the cooking time if you bake from frozen.

---

6 servings

1 tablespoon olive oil

1 medium red onion (about
6 ounces), chopped

1 large red bell pepper (about
9 ounces), seeded and chopped

1 large green bell pepper (about
½ pound), seeded and chopped

1 small jalapeño pepper, seeded
and diced

1 pound extra-firm low-fat ("lite")
tofu, drained and cubed

1 teaspoon chili powder

2 cups salsa or picante sauce

8 8-inch flour, whole wheat, or
corn tortillas

½ cup fat-free sour cream, pureed
silken tofu, or soy sour cream

1½ cups cooked brown rice
(see Notes)

2 cups cooked black or pinto beans
or 1 16-ounce can, drained
and rinsed

1½ cups shredded Monterey Jack
cheese (about 6 ounces) or
soy cheese

Preheat the oven to 350°F. Lightly coat a 13- × 9- × 2-inch baking dish or rectangular casserole that holds at least 8 cups with a vegetable oil–based cooking spray. Set aside.

Heat the olive oil in a large nonstick skillet over medium-high heat. Add the onion and red, green, and jalapeño peppers and cook, stirring often, until soft, about 10 minutes. Transfer to a medium bowl and set aside.

Add the tofu to the skillet and cook, tossing or stirring here and there, for 2 to 3 minutes. Add the chili powder and stir to combine. Turn up the heat and cook until most of the liquid evaporates, 1 to 2 minutes. Transfer the tofu to the bowl with the onion and pepper mixture.

Arrange the tofu-pepper mixture and all the other ingredients on your work surface for easy assembly of the lasagna. Spread about ½ cup of the salsa on the bottom of the prepared baking dish. Place 2 tortillas in a single layer, slightly trimmed to fit the rectangular baking dish, on top. Lightly spread a third of the sour cream on top of the tortillas, then layer with a third of the rice, followed by a third of the tofu-pepper mixture, a third of the beans, and another ½ cup of salsa. Set aside ⅓ cup of the cheese and then add a third of the remaining shredded cheese to the pan. Add another 2 tortillas and continue layering as above 2 more times, ending with the last 2 tortillas.

Cover the baking dish with aluminum foil and bake for 50 minutes. Remove the foil and cover the top tortilla layer evenly with the reserved cheese. Bake for 10 minutes more. Remove from the oven and let cool for 10 minutes before serving.

Notes: If you do not have leftover brown rice, start it before cooking the tofu and peppers. Simply measure out 1 cup long-grain brown rice and add to 2½ cups boiling water. Stir in ⅓ teaspoon salt, reduce the heat to simmer, and cook, covered, for 25 to 30 minutes.

- With only 10 percent of calories from fat, this entrée can help keep you below the goal of 30 percent of calories from fat in a day.
- Eighteen of the 23 grams of protein per serving are derived from soy and other legume sources.
- Black beans are high in fiber and, like soy, contain isoflavones and other phytochemicals that may lower the risk of breast and other types of cancer. They are also rich in folate; one serving of Mexican Lasagna provides 35 percent of the DV.
- Each serving provides more than 175 percent of the DV for vitamin C and more than 10 percent of the DV for vitamin A.
- Brown rice is a potentially good source of selenium and is a good source of fiber. One slice of lasagna provides more than half of the DV for fiber.

PER SERVING

calories	protein	carbohydrates	fat	cholesterol	dietary fiber	saturated fat
434	23 g	55 g	14 g	25 mg	15 g	5 g

% OF CALORIES: 50% carbohydrate, 22% protein, 28% fat

MAJOR SOURCES OF POTENTIAL CANCER FIGHTERS

Phytochemicals: capsaicin, phytic acids, plant polyphenols (flavonoids, isoflavones, phenolic acids), plant sterols, protease inhibitors, terpenes (carotenoids, monoterpenes, triterpenes)

⁂ Root Vegetable Lasagna

Laura Pensiero, R.D., co-owner, Gigi Trattoria, Rhinebeck, New York; nutritionist, Strang Cancer Prevention Center

Serve as a colorful, nutritious vegetarian entrée or a vegetable side dish with roasted chicken or pork. Use a mandoline (see page 135) to produce uniform thin slices of the root vegetables.

6 servings

2 ancho chiles
1½ cups Vegetable Stock (see Index)
    or low-sodium canned broth
1 teaspoon olive oil
2 large baking potatoes (about
    1 pound), peeled and sliced
    lengthwise ⅛ inch thick
2 medium sweet potatoes (about
    14 ounces), peeled and sliced
    lengthwise ⅛ inch thick
2 medium parsnips (about
    ½ pound), peeled and sliced
    lengthwise ⅛ inch thick

3 medium turnips (about ¾ pound),
    peeled and sliced ⅛ inch thick
salt
¾ cup diced roasted peppers,
    drained if jarred
2 cups shredded low-fat cheddar or
    Monterey Jack cheese
    (about ½ pound)

Preheat the oven to 375°F.

In a small saucepan, simmer the ancho chiles in the stock for 10 minutes. Turn off the heat and let steep while you prepare the lasagna.

Rub a casserole or baking pan (about 3-quart) with the olive oil. Arrange the root vegetable slices in the pan, starting with a layer of slightly overlapping potatoes, followed by sweet potato, parsnip, and turnip; repeat the sequence. Season each layer with salt to taste and sprinkle with diced roasted pepper and shredded cheese, reserving about ⅓ cup of shredded cheese.

Strain the stock, discarding the chiles, and pour evenly over the casserole. Cover with foil and bake for 50 minutes. Remove the foil, sprinkle with the reserved cheese, and bake for 15 more minutes. Let cool for 15 minutes before serving.

- One serving provides more than 100 percent of the DV for vitamin C and vitamin A and 20 percent of the DV for calcium.
- Turnips belong to the cruciferous family of vegetables and have protective phytochemicals.
- Moderate consumption of capsaicin, a phytochemical found in chile peppers, may help the body neutralize carcinogens.
- High in fiber—20 percent of the DV

PER SERVING

calories	protein	carbohydrates	fat	cholesterol	dietary fiber	saturated fat
285	13 g	41 g	8 g	0 mg	5 g	1 g

% OF CALORIES: 57% carbohydrate, 18% protein, 25% fat

MAJOR SOURCES OF POTENTIAL CANCER FIGHTERS

Phytochemicals: capsaicin, glucosinolates, phytic acids, plant polyphenols (flavonoids, isoflavones, phenolic acids), plant sterols, terpenes (carotenoids, triterpenes)

FISH

✣ TUNA WITH PROVENÇAL CRUST AND BABY GREENS WITH RED WINE VINAIGRETTE

Susan Weaver, former executive chef at Fifty Seven Fifty Seven, Four Seasons Hotel, New York City

The ingredients of Provence not only taste good but also contain cancer-fighting nutrients and phytochemicals.

Tuna with Provençal Crust can be served with almost any salad, such as a simple tomato salad with grilled or toasted bread, a Niçoise salad, or Francesco Antonucci's Venetian Peperonata (see Index), served at room temperature.

4 servings

TUNA

2 cups fine fresh bread crumbs (about 10 slices white bread, crusts removed) or commercial unseasoned bread crumbs

2 tablespoons finely chopped drained capers

2 tablespoons finely chopped anchovy

1 tablespoon finely chopped garlic

2 tablespoons each finely chopped fresh basil, tarragon, oregano, and parsley

4 6-ounce portions ahi tuna

1 cup flour seasoned with salt and freshly ground black pepper

2 large eggs, slightly beaten

1 tablespoon olive oil

VINAIGRETTE (⅓ *cup*)

2 tablespoons red wine vinegar

½ tablespoon finely chopped shallot

½ teaspoon finely chopped garlic

2 teaspoons each finely chopped
   fresh basil, tarragon, oregano,
   and parsley

salt and freshly ground black pepper

¼ cup extra-virgin olive oil

4 cups baby greens or mesclun

Preheat the oven to 400°F.

To make the tuna, combine the bread crumbs, capers, anchovy, garlic, and herbs. Roll each portion of tuna in the flour, shake off any excess, and coat with the egg. Drain off any excess egg and evenly cover with the bread crumb mixture; gently shake off any excess.

Heat the olive oil in a large ovenproof nonstick skillet. Place the tuna in the skillet, shake the pan gently, and cook over medium-high to high heat until a light brown crust forms on one side, about 2 minutes, then turn over and transfer to the oven. Cook until medium-rare, about 3 minutes.

To make the vinaigrette, in a medium bowl, combine the vinegar, shallot, garlic, and herbs and season with salt and pepper. Whisk in the olive oil and adjust the seasoning if necessary. Just before serving, toss the baby greens with ¼ cup of the vinaigrette.

With a sharp knife, slice each tuna steak into 3 diagonal slices. Pile the dressed baby greens in a neat mound at the top of the plate. Fan the tuna slices in front of the greens.

▪ The fat sources in this recipe are predominantly monounsaturated (more than 50 percent), including potentially protective omega-3 fatty acids.

▪ Tuna is a potentially good source of selenium.

▪ Rich in vitamins A, C, and folate, providing more than 20 percent of the DV for each

▪ A good source of fiber

PER SERVING OF TUNA WITH PROVENÇAL CRUST

calories	protein	carbohydrates	fat	cholesterol	dietary fiber	saturated fat
418	49 g	34 g	9 g	160 mg	2 g	1 g

PER SERVING OF RED WINE VINAIGRETTE (1 TABLESPOON)

calories	protein	carbohydrates	fat	cholesterol	dietary fiber	saturated fat
90	0 g	0 g	9 g	0 mg	0 g	1 g

PER SERVING OF TUNA WITH PROVENÇAL CRUST AND BABY GREENS WITH RED WINE VINAIGRETTE

calories	protein	carbohydrates	fat	cholesterol	dietary fiber	saturated fat
507	50 g	36 g	18 g	160 mg	3 g	2 g

% OF CALORIES: 28% carbohydrate, 39% protein, 33% fat

MAJOR SOURCES OF POTENTIAL CANCER FIGHTERS

Phytochemicals: allium compounds, plant polyphenols (flavonoids, phenolic acids), terpenes (carotenoids, monoterpenes)

⚘ HERB- AND SPICE-CRUSTED MAHIMAHI WITH WATERMELON SALSA

Erasmo "Razz" Kamnitzer, Razz's Restaurant and Bar, Scottsdale, Arizona

Use this herb and spice mixture to crust other fish, such as swordfish, tuna, or halibut.
Serve the watermelon salsa as a topping for grilled, seared, or roasted salmon, tuna, or swordfish. Try it over Coriander-, Fennel-, and Pepper-Crusted Tuna (see Index). It also helps cool down spicy chicken.

4 servings

WATERMELON SALSA

2 cups peeled, seeded, and
   diced watermelon
1 tablespoon sliced onion
1 tablespoon diced poblano chile or
   1 teaspoon diced jalapeño pepper
½ cup diced yellow bell pepper

3 tablespoons chopped fresh cilantro
1 teaspoon chopped garlic
1 teaspoon grated lime zest
juice of 2 limes
salt and freshly ground black
   pepper to taste

HERB- AND SPICE-CRUSTED MAHIMAHI

1 tablespoon each chopped fresh basil, tarragon, marjoram, thyme, rosemary, and parsley	½ teaspoon cayenne pepper
	1 tablespoon maple sugar (optional)
	½ teaspoon salt
1 tablespoon each cracked black pepper, ground cumin, curry powder, and ground coriander	1½ pounds mahimahi (4 6-ounce steaks)
	1 tablespoon olive oil

To prepare the salsa, in a mixing bowl, combine all the ingredients. Refrigerate, allowing the flavors to meld for at least 20 minutes.

To prepare the herb and spice mixture, combine the herbs, spices, maple sugar, and salt and spread the mixture out on a large plate. Place one side of the mahimahi steaks into the herb-spice blend, lift it up, and shake off any excess.

Heat 1½ teaspoons of the olive oil in a large nonstick skillet until almost smoking. Carefully place 2 of the mahimahi steaks, coated side down, in the skillet. A crust should form within 1 minute. Using tongs, turn over the fish, lower the heat, and cook for 3 to 4 minutes more, until the flesh is firm when touched. Transfer to a plate and loosely cover with foil to keep warm. Repeat the process with the remaining olive oil and mahimahi. Serve the steaks, crust side up, topped with watermelon salsa.

- Curry powder contains curcumin, a plant polyphenol that lends yellow color and acts as an antioxidant; it may also play a role in blocking cancer at the initiation stage.
- Though watermelon is not often thought of as a nutrient-rich fruit, its red color is provided by the carotenoid lycopene. It is also a good source of vitamin C and potassium.

PER SERVING OF WATERMELON SALSA (⅓ CUP)

calories	protein	carbohydrates	fat	cholesterol	dietary fiber	saturated fat
38	1 g	7 g	1 g	0 mg	1 g	0 g

PER SERVING OF HERB- AND SPICE-CRUSTED MAHIMAHI WITH WATERMELON SALSA

calories	protein	carbohydrates	fat	cholesterol	dietary fiber	saturated fat
335	39 g	15 g	13 g	86 mg	2 g	2 g

% OF CALORIES: 20% carbohydrate, 47% protein, 33% fat

MAJOR SOURCES OF POTENTIAL CANCER FIGHTERS

Phytochemicals: allium compounds, capsaicin, plant polyphenols (flavonoids), terpenes (carotenoids, monoterpenes, limonene, triterpenes)

❧ Tandoori Sea Bass with Minted Couscous, Banana Salsa, and Fresh Coconut-Mango Chutney

Adam Busby, chef instructor, the Culinary Institute of America at Greystone, St. Helena, California

---

This dish has great contrasts: hot and cold temperatures and sweet and savory flavors. All components are easy to prepare and are very versatile.

The Banana Salsa and Coconut-Mango Chutney also marry well with other well-spiced fish, such as snapper, tuna, and swordfish. Try it with Coriander-, Fennel-, and Pepper-Crusted Tuna (see Index).

The Minted Couscous is the perfect bed for braised or stewed meat or vegetables. Try it with Indian Spiced Vegetable Stew or Curry Roasted Summer Vegetables (see Index).

---

4 servings

Sea Bass
1 garlic clove, minced
1 shallot, chopped coarse
½ bunch fresh cilantro, chopped
1 ½-inch piece fresh ginger, peeled and minced
2 teaspoons ground cumin
2 tablespoons paprika

¾ cup low-fat or fat-free sour cream
1½ pounds sea bass, cut into 4 medallions
2 teaspoons unsalted butter, cut into small pieces
salt and freshly ground black pepper

Banana Salsa
1 large slightly underripe banana (about ¼ pound), peeled and diced fine
1 tablespoon fresh lime juice

½ shallot, chopped fine
1 tablespoon chopped fresh cilantro
salt and freshly ground black pepper

Coconut-Mango Chutney
½ cup fresh or commercial shredded coconut

¼ cup mango chutney, such as Major Grey's

MINTED COUSCOUS

2 cups White Chicken Stock, Brown
    Chicken Stock, or Vegetable Stock
    (see Index), or water
1 cup couscous

⅓ cup chopped fresh mint
1 teaspoon unsalted butter
salt

To prepare the marinade, in a food processor, puree the garlic, shallot, cilantro, ginger, cumin, and paprika. Transfer to a mixing bowl and stir in the sour cream. Place the sea bass medallions into this marinade, cover, and refrigerate for at least 2 hours and preferably overnight.

To prepare the salsa, in a mixing bowl, combine all the ingredients, being careful not to mash the banana. Cover and refrigerate until ready to use.

To prepare the chutney, toss the coconut and mango chutney together in a small mixing bowl. Cover and refrigerate.

To cook the sea bass, preheat the oven to 400°F. Wipe excess marinade off the sea bass, leaving an even thin coating on the top and sides. Place the medallions on a nonstick baking pan. Dot with pieces of butter and season with salt and pepper to taste. Bake until a little golden crust forms and the fish is just cooked, 10 to 12 minutes.

While the fish cooks, prepare the couscous. In a medium saucepan, bring the stock to a boil. Add the couscous in a steady stream, stirring constantly. When all of the couscous has been added, stop stirring, reduce the heat, and simmer for 2 minutes. Remove the pan from the heat, mix in the mint and butter, and season with salt to taste. Let sit, covered, for 5 minutes. Fluff with a fork before serving.

Put a portion of couscous into the center of each plate. Place a sea bass medallion on top and spoon the chutney and salsa over the fish.

- Sea bass is a potentially very good source of selenium and protective omega-3 fatty acids.
- Mint contains monoterpenes that act as antioxidants and blocking agents to interfere with carcinogens.
- Each serving provides more than a third of the DV for vitamin A.
- A good source of fiber

PER SERVING OF BANANA SALSA (¼ CUP)

calories	protein	carbohydrates	fat	cholesterol	dietary fiber	saturated fat
28	0 g	7 g	0 g	0 mg	1 g	0 g

PER SERVING OF COUSCOUS (¾ CUP)

calories	protein	carbohydrates	fat	cholesterol	dietary fiber	saturated fat
185	6 g	36 g	1 g	3 mg	2 g	1 g

PER SERVING OF COCONUT-MANGO CHUTNEY (2 TABLESPOONS)

calories	protein	carbohydrates	fat	cholesterol	dietary fiber	saturated fat
75	0 g	11 g	3 g	3 mg	1 g	3 g

PER SERVING OF TANDOORI SEA BASS WITH MINTED COUSCOUS, BANANA SALSA, AND FRESH COCONUT-MANGO CHUTNEY

calories	protein	carbohydrates	fat	cholesterol	dietary fiber	saturated fat
515	40 g	63 g	11 g	78 mg	4 g	6 g

% OF CALORIES: 50% carbohydrate, 31% protein, 19% fat

MAJOR SOURCES OF POTENTIAL CANCER FIGHTERS

Phytochemicals: allium compounds, plant polyphenols (flavonoids, phenolic acids), terpenes (carotenoids, monoterpenes, triterpenes, gingerol)

❧ SHRIMP WITH GARLIC AND CAPERS

Laura Pensiero, R.D., co-owner, Gigi Trattoria, Rhinebeck, New York; nutritionist, Strang Cancer Prevention Center

Serve as a first course along with some crusty bread or as a main course over rice.

4 servings

1½ pounds large shrimp, peeled and deveined

salt and freshly ground black pepper

1 tablespoon unflavored vegetable oil (canola, corn, or safflower)

3 teaspoons unsalted butter

1 tablespoon minced garlic

¼ cup dry white wine

2 tablespoons chopped fresh flat-leaf parsley

2 tablespoons fresh lemon juice

2 tablespoons drained capers

1 tablespoon water

Season the shrimp with salt and pepper to taste.

Heat 2 teaspoons of the oil and 1 teaspoon of the butter in a large nonstick skillet over medium-high heat. Roll the fat around the pan to distribute evenly. When the butter stops foaming, add the shrimp and cook until browned and just cooked, about 2 minutes per side. Transfer the shrimp to 4 plates and cover to keep warm.

Add the garlic and the remaining teaspoon of oil to the skillet and cook, stirring, until the garlic just starts to brown, less than 1 minute. Add the white wine and parsley and, using a wooden spoon, stir to dissolve the flavorful particles on the bottom of the pan. Simmer for just a few seconds, and then stir in the lemon juice, capers, and water. Cook for another minute, then remove the pan from the heat and whisk in the remaining 2 teaspoons of butter. Pour the pan sauce over the shrimp and serve immediately.

- With less than 2 grams of fat per 5-ounce serving, shrimp is a very lean protein source. It can quickly become a high-fat dish, however, if cooked in butter- or cream-based sauces or if served with high-fat condiments. For recipes that include shrimp and other low-fat shellfish, such as scallops, crab, or lobster, try sautéing in a nonstick pan heated with a minimal amount of olive or canola oil or cooking in a flavorful liquid medium, such as in soups, stews, risotto, and paellas.
- Shrimp is a potentially good source of selenium.

PER SERVING

calories	protein	carbohydrates	fat	cholesterol	dietary fiber	saturated fat
251	35 g	3 g	9 g	266 mg	0 g	3 g

% OF CALORIES: 4% carbohydrate, 57% protein, 35% fat, 4% alcohol

MAJOR SOURCES OF POTENTIAL CANCER FIGHTERS

Phytochemicals: allium compounds, plant polyphenols (flavonoids), terpenes (monoterpenes)

❧ CHILE-CRUSTED TUNA WITH SOBA NOODLE–CUCUMBER SALAD

Ming Tsai, Blue Ginger, Wellesley, Massachusetts

This Asian-southwestern salad is a terrific light meal or first course. It characterizes the type of modern East-West fusion cuisine created by Ming Tsai.

The Soba Noodle–Cucumber Salad with cilantro-honey vinaigrette can be served alone as a vegetarian course. Use the leftover chili oil to spice up other vinaigrettes and marinades, or drizzle over grilled shrimp or chicken.

---

4 servings

CHILI OIL *(1 cup)*
2 tablespoons chili powder
1 teaspoon ground cumin

1 cup canola oil

TUNA
⅓ cup chili powder (preferably
   chimayo or ancho)
⅓ cup freshly ground cumin seeds
⅓ cup freshly ground fennel seeds
¾ pound center-cut ahi tuna loin
   (ask your fishmonger to cut it into
   a rectangular block shape)

salt
1 tablespoon canola oil

CILANTRO-HONEY VINAIGRETTE *(1¼ cups)*
2 small serrano chiles, seeded
   and minced
1½ tablespoons honey
1 tablespoon Dijon mustard

½ cup fresh cilantro leaves
¼ cup ice water
¾ cup canola oil
salt and freshly ground black pepper

SOBA NOODLE–CUCUMBER SALAD

5 quarts water

salt

½ pound dried buckwheat
   soba noodles

1 seedless cucumber (about
   8 ounces), peeled and julienned

2 scallions, green part only,
   sliced thin

freshly ground black pepper

1 cup daikon sprouts (optional)

To prepare the chili oil, heat the chili powder and cumin together in a small sauté pan or saucepan over medium heat until almost smoking. Whisk in the oil. Carefully transfer to a glass jar and let stand overnight so the oil separates from the spices and is fully flavored.

To prepare the tuna, grind the spices in a spice grinder or small food processor. Spread the spice mixture out evenly on a large flat plate. Season the tuna with salt to taste and roll in the spice mixture. Heat the oil in a nonstick skillet; add the tuna and sear for 10 seconds on each side. (It is best to keep high-quality tuna very rare, but if you prefer it more cooked, you can place the skillet with the seared tuna in an oven preheated to 400°F for 2 to 5 minutes, depending on desired doneness.) Let cool slightly, and then refrigerate to chill completely for easy slicing.

To prepare the vinaigrette, in a blender or food processor, combine the serrano chiles, honey, mustard, cilantro, and ice water and puree until smooth. With the motor running, slowly drizzle in the oil. Season to taste with salt and pepper. Store excess vinaigrette in a sealed container in the refrigerator for up to 1 week.

To cook the soba noodles, bring the water to a boil and add salt to taste. Cook the noodles according to the package instructions, drain, rinse thoroughly under cold water, and drain again.

Toss the soba noodles, cucumber, and scallions with ⅓ cup of the vinaigrette. Add salt and pepper if necessary. Place a mound of salad in the center of 4 plates. Surround with thin slices of the tuna. Drizzle with 1 tablespoon of vinaigrette and a teaspoon or two of the chili oil. Garnish with daikon sprouts if desired.

- The types of fatty acids in this recipe are predominantly cancer-protective monounsaturated fatty acids and linolenic fatty acids. Use a little less vinaigrette and/or chili oil if you wish to reduce fat further.
- Chiles contain capsaicin, which may help to neutralize carcinogens.

PER SERVING OF CHILE-CRUSTED TUNA WITH CHILI OIL

calories	protein	carbohydrates	fat	cholesterol	dietary fiber	saturated fat
276	40 g	0 g	12 g	38 mg	0 g	1 g

PER SERVING OF SOBA NOODLE–CUCUMBER SALAD WITH CILANTRO-HONEY VINAIGRETTE

calories	protein	carbohydrates	fat	cholesterol	dietary fiber	saturated fat
238	6 g	44 g	4 g	0 mg	4 g	1 g

PER SERVING OF CHILE-CRUSTED TUNA WITH SOBA NOODLE–CUCUMBER SALAD

calories	protein	carbohydrates	fat	cholesterol	dietary fiber	saturated fat
514	46 g	44 g	16 g	38 mg	4 g	2 g

% OF CALORIES: 35% carbohydrate, 37% protein, 28% fat

MAJOR SOURCES OF POTENTIAL CANCER FIGHTERS

Phytochemicals: allium compounds, capsaicin, plant polyphenols (flavonoids, phenolic acids)

Coriander-, Fennel-, and Pepper-Crusted Tuna

Laura Pensiero, R.D., co-owner, Gigi Trattoria, Rhinebeck, New York; nutritionist, Strang Cancer Prevention Center

The spice blend lends this recipe some heat. A nice cool fruit salsa such as Razz Kamnitzer's Watermelon Salsa (see Index) helps put out the fire and balance the flavors.

With a salad and Minted Couscous (see Index), preparation time is less than 30 minutes—a quick weekday meal.

4 servings

Spice Blend
1 tablespoon coriander seeds
1 tablespoon fennel seeds

2 teaspoons black peppercorns

TUNA

1½ pounds tuna (4 pieces about   1 tablespoon olive oil
    1½ inches thick)

To prepare the spice blend, grind all the spices in a small food processor or spice grinder until they are powdery. Spread the spice mixture evenly on a large plate.

Rinse the tuna fillets and pat dry. Place one side of each piece of tuna into the spice mixture. Shake off any excess.

In a large nonstick skillet over medium-high heat, heat 2 teaspoons of the olive oil. Carefully place 2 tuna fillets, spiced side down, into the skillet. A spice crust should form within 1 minute. Using tongs, turn over the tuna, lower the heat to medium, and cook for 2 to 5 minutes, to desired doneness. Transfer to a plate and loosely cover with foil to keep warm. Repeat the process with the remaining tuna fillets, adding 1 more teaspoon of oil to the skillet.

■ Tuna is a potentially good source of omega-3 fatty acids.

PER SERVING

calories	protein	carbohydrates	fat	cholesterol	dietary fiber	saturated fat
207	40 g	0 g	5 g	74 mg	0 g	1 g

% OF CALORIES: 1% carbohydrate, 77% protein, 22% fat

MAJOR SOURCES OF POTENTIAL CANCER FIGHTERS

Phytochemicals: omega-3 fatty acids

🌿 SEARED SALMON WITH FRESH CORN RELISH

Jimmy Sneed, The Frog and the Redneck, Richmond, Virginia

This sweet and sour relish is also wonderful over other seared or grilled fish, such as tuna and swordfish.

---

4 servings

RELISH

¾ cup sherry vinegar
½ cup sugar
2 cups water
1½ teaspoons celery seeds
sea salt and freshly cracked
   black pepper
4 ears corn or 10 ounces frozen corn,
   thawed and drained

½ small red onion (about
   2½ ounces), diced
2 teaspoons olive oil
1 red bell pepper (about ½ pound),
   seeded and diced fine

SALMON

2 teaspoons olive oil
4 6-ounce center-cut salmon
   fillets with skin

sea salt and freshly ground
   black pepper

Prepare the relish 1 day in advance. In a small saucepan, bring the vinegar, sugar, water, celery seeds, 1 teaspoon sea salt, and 2 teaspoons cracked black pepper to a boil. Reduce the heat and simmer for 5 minutes. Set aside.

If you're using fresh corn, cook the ears in boiling salted water for 3 minutes. Remove and place in cold water for 5 minutes. Slice the kernels off the cob, being careful not to slice too deeply into the cob. Puree a quarter of the corn in a food processor or blender, using just enough water to liquefy (1 to 2 tablespoons). Season the puree with salt and pepper and refrigerate. Put the remaining corn in a large mixing bowl.

In a small skillet over medium heat, cook the onion in the olive oil until softened, about 5 minutes. Add the red pepper, season with salt and pepper, and cook, tossing or stirring often, until the red pepper is tender but still firm, 3 to 4 minutes. Transfer to the mixing bowl with the corn. Add the marinade and refrigerate for at least 12 hours.

Heat the olive oil in a large cast-iron pan or ovenproof nonstick skillet. Season both sides of the salmon fillets with sea salt and pepper. Place the fillets in the heated pan, skin side down, and cook until the skin is browned and crispy, about 5 minutes. Flip the fillets over and cook for 1 to 2 minutes more, until the fish just loses its interior translucency.

Strain the relish, discarding the liquid, and place the corn-vegetable mixture in a small bowl. Add the corn puree and mix well. Generously spoon the relish over the salmon fillets.

- Salmon is a potentially good source of protective omega-3 fatty acids.
- Although corn is not substantially high in vitamin A or beta-carotene, it does contain other carotenes, such as lutein, that may protect against certain types of cancer.
- This recipe provides more than 30 percent of the DV for vitamin C per serving.

PER SERVING OF FRESH CORN RELISH

calories	protein	carbohydrates	fat	cholesterol	dietary fiber	saturated fat
193	3 g	44 g	3 g	0 mg	2 g	0 g

PER SERVING OF SEARED SALMON WITH FRESH CORN RELISH

calories	protein	carbohydrates	fat	cholesterol	dietary fiber	saturated fat
453	36 g	44 g	15 g	93 mg	2 g	2 g

% OF CALORIES: 40% carbohydrate, 30% protein, 30% fat

MAJOR SOURCES OF POTENTIAL CANCER FIGHTERS

Phytochemicals: allium compounds, plant polyphenols (flavonoids), terpenes (carotenoids)

Fresh Rockfish with Mussel Tomato-Basil Sauce on Redneck Caviar

Jimmy Sneed, The Frog and the Redneck, Richmond, Virginia

This Mussel Tomato-Basil Sauce is also terrific over pasta.

4 servings

REDNECK CAVIAR

2 cups White Chicken Stock or Brown Chicken Stock (see Index), or low-sodium canned broth
¾ cup coarse stone-ground grits (see Notes)

salt and freshly ground black pepper
1 tablespoon squid ink (available at most fish markets and in gourmet specialty stores)

Mussel Tomato-Basil Sauce

½ cup chopped shallot

2 garlic cloves, chopped fine

2 teaspoons olive oil

½ cup dry white wine

20 mussels, scrubbed and
   beards removed

½ cup diced tomato

2 tablespoons chopped fresh basil

salt and freshly ground black pepper

Rockfish

4 6-ounce rockfish
   (striped bass) fillets

salt and freshly ground black pepper

⅓ cup flour

1 tablespoon extra-virgin olive oil

To make the Redneck Caviar, bring the chicken stock to a boil in a heavy 2-quart saucepan. While stirring with a wooden spoon, add the grits. Simmer over low heat, stirring frequently, for about 30 minutes, until the grits thicken. Season to taste with salt and pepper and add the squid ink.

Preheat the oven to 400°F.

While the grits cook, prepare the Mussel Tomato-Basil Sauce. In a large sauté pan over medium heat, cook the shallots and garlic in the olive oil until softened, 2 to 3 minutes; do not allow the garlic to burn. Turn up the heat to medium-high and add the white wine and the mussels. Cook, covered, shaking the pan occasionally, until the mussels open, 3 to 4 minutes. Discard any that do not open. Reserve the cooking liquid in the sauté pan and set aside. Pick the meat out of the shells, adding any mussel juice to the reserved cooking liquid. Bring the liquid in the sauté pan to a simmer and add the mussel meat, tomatoes, and basil. Season with salt and pepper. After 1 minute, remove from the heat. Set aside.

Season the rockfish fillets with salt and pepper. Dredge them in flour, shaking off any excess. Heat the olive oil in a large nonstick or well-seasoned cast-iron sauté pan over medium-high heat. Lay the rockfish fillets in the pan and brown on one side, 1 to 2 minutes. Turn the fillets over and transfer the pan to the oven. Roast for 4 to 6 minutes. Reheat the Mussel Tomato-Basil Sauce if necessary.

Divide the Redneck Caviar among 4 bowls. Place a rockfish fillet on top and spoon the sauce over the fillets. Serve immediately.

Notes: Grits or hominy grits are available at supermarkets and specialty stores in a choice of grinds: coarse, medium, and fine. The amount of cooking liquid and cooking time are related directly to the size of the grind—the coarser the grind, the more liquid and longer cooking required.

- Striped bass is a good source of protective omega-3 fatty acids.
- Both striped bass and mussels are potentially good sources of selenium.

PER SERVING OF MUSSEL TOMATO-BASIL SAUCE (⅓ CUP)

calories	protein	carbohydrates	fat	cholesterol	dietary fiber	saturated fat
88	7 g	4 g	3 g	24 mg	0 g	0 g

PER SERVING OF REDNECK CAVIAR

calories	protein	carbohydrates	fat	cholesterol	dietary fiber	saturated fat
128	5 g	24 g	1 g	0 mg	1 g	2 g

PER SERVING OF FRESH ROCKFISH WITH MUSSEL TOMATO-BASIL SAUCE ON REDNECK CAVIAR

calories	protein	carbohydrates	fat	cholesterol	dietary fiber	saturated fat
411	42 g	28 g	11 g	160 mg	1 g	3 g

% OF CALORIES: 28% carbohydrate, 42% protein, 25% fat, 5% alcohol

MAJOR SOURCES OF POTENTIAL CANCER FIGHTERS

Phytochemicals: allium compounds, plant polyphenols (flavonoids), terpenes (carotenoids)

Grilled Salmon with Yellow Pepper Coulis and Beet Vinaigrette

Anthony Bourdain, bestselling author (*Kitchen Confidential*, Ecco Press, 2001), executive chef, Les Halles, New York City

Serve as a light lunch or dinner entrée. Use the Beet Vinaigrette with other salads and the Yellow Pepper Coulis as a bed for other grilled or seared fish, such as tuna, swordfish, or snapper.

4 servings

Yellow Pepper Coulis *(1 cup)*

2 medium yellow bell peppers
   (about 14 ounces)
1 garlic clove
1 tablespoon rice wine vinegar
¼ cup cold water
1 tablespoon olive oil
salt and freshly ground black pepper

BEET VINAIGRETTE *(¾ cup)*

1 medium beet (about 6 ounces)	1 tablespoon olive oil
1 tablespoon rice wine vinegar	salt and freshly ground black pepper
½ cup cold water	4 cups mesclun

SALMON

1½ pounds salmon (4 6-ounce fillets)	1 teaspoon olive oil
salt and freshly ground black pepper	

Preheat the broiler.

To roast the peppers, rub or, using a mister, mist the peppers with a small amount of olive oil, place on a baking sheet lined with foil, and broil about 6 inches from the heat source until charred on all sides, using tongs to turn the peppers so they char evenly. Remove the peppers from the oven, place in a bowl, and cover with foil or plastic wrap so that steam helps to loosen the skins. When cool, remove the skins, seeds, and stems. Turn the oven down to 375°F.

Puree the peppers in a blender or food processor with the garlic, vinegar, and water until very smooth. With the motor running, drizzle in the olive oil. If necessary, slowly add a bit more water to achieve a thick liquid consistency. Season with salt and pepper to taste.

To prepare the Beet Vinaigrette, trim the beet, but leave the root stem and do not puncture the skin, to prevent "bleeding" when cooking. Place the beet on a sheet of aluminum foil and roast for approximately 1 hour and 15 minutes, until tender. Let cool. Peel, roughly chop, and puree in a blender with the vinegar and water. With the motor running, drizzle in the olive oil. Strain through a fine-mesh strainer. Season with salt and pepper to taste and set aside.

To cook the salmon, season with salt and pepper to taste, lightly brush with oil, and place on a preheated grill. Cook until medium-rare and moist in the center, about 3 to 4 minutes per side. If you don't have a grill, sear the salmon in a heated nonstick pan over medium-high heat with 1 to 2 teaspoons of olive oil. After one side is crispy golden brown, flip over the salmon fillets and transfer to the oven for 4 to 5 minutes, depending on thickness.

While the salmon cooks, mask the bottom of 4 plates with the Yellow Pepper Coulis. In a large bowl, toss the mesclun with ½ cup of the Beet Vinaigrette and then divide evenly onto the center of the 4 plates, leaving a border of Yellow Pepper Coulis. Place the cooked salmon fillets on top of the salad and serve.

- Salmon is a potentially good source of protective omega-3 fatty acids.
- Beets, yellow peppers, and mesclun add up to more than 200 percent of the DV for vitamin C per serving; they are a good source of vitamin A as well: 20 percent of the DV per serving.
- Both beets and mesclun are rich in folate, providing more than 50 percent of the DV per serving.

PER SERVING OF YELLOW PEPPER COULIS (¼ CUP)

calories	protein	carbohydrates	fat	cholesterol	dietary fiber	saturated fat
60	1 g	7 g	4 g	0 mg	1 g	0 g

PER SERVING OF BEET VINAIGRETTE (2 TABLESPOONS)

calories	protein	carbohydrates	fat	cholesterol	dietary fiber	saturated fat
33	1 g	4 g	2 g	0 mg	1 g	0 g

PER SERVING OF GRILLED SALMON WITH YELLOW PEPPER COULIS AND BEET VINAIGRETTE

calories	protein	carbohydrates	fat	cholesterol	dietary fiber	saturated fat
336	37 g	11 g	16 g	93 mg	2 g	1 g

% OF CALORIES: 13% carbohydrate, 44% protein, 43% fat

MAJOR SOURCES OF POTENTIAL CANCER FIGHTERS

Phytochemicals: allium compounds, plant polyphenols (flavonoids, phenolic acids), plant sterols, terpenes (carotenoids)

❧ LOBSTER AND SQUASH RISOTTO

Gianni Scappin, chef/co-owner, Finch Tavern, Croton Falls, New York

Gianni remarks that the combination of lobster, butternut squash, and sage with tortellini, ravioli, or, as in this case, risotto, is "al fine del mondo (the best in the world)."

4 main-course servings, 6 first-course servings

2 tablespoons plus 1½ teaspoons extra-virgin olive oil

½ small onion (3 ounces), diced fine

2 cups peeled, seeded, and chopped butternut squash (about 9 ounces)

3 fresh sage leaves

10 ounces Italian rice (1½ cups; preferably Carnaroli or Superfino Arborio or Semifino Vialone Nano)

7 cups hot Fish Stock (see Index), store-bought fish broth, or water

3 tablespoons canned pumpkin puree

salt

8 to 10 ounces lobster meat or shrimp, cooked

freshly ground black pepper

1 tablespoon chopped fresh flat-leaf parsley

In a medium heavy saucepan over medium heat, heat 1 tablespoon plus 1½ teaspoons of the oil. Add the onion and cook, stirring, until soft, 2 to 3 minutes; do not brown. Add the butternut squash and sage leaves and cook for another minute, then add the rice; cook, stirring, for 1 minute. Stir in 1 cup of the hot stock and the pumpkin puree. Season with salt to taste and bring to a boil.

Cook at an aggressive boil, stirring often and adding 1 cup of broth at a time as necessary; the rice should almost completely absorb the liquid between additions. After 10 minutes, add half of the lobster. Cook for another 7 to 8 minutes, now adding ½ cup of liquid at a time as the rice absorbs the liquid. The rice should be moist and have movement, but not be soupy or watery. Add the remaining lobster, remove from the heat, and add salt and pepper to taste. Stir in the parsley and the remaining tablespoon of olive oil and serve immediately.

- Butternut squash is among the richest sources of beta-carotene. It provides most of the vitamin A in this recipe—more than 80 percent of the DV per serving. It also provides the majority of the vitamin C—more than 20 percent of the DV per serving.
- The natural oils found in sage have potent antioxidant properties.
- Lobster is a potentially excellent source of selenium.

PER SERVING (BASED ON 4 SERVINGS)

calories	protein	carbohydrates	fat	cholesterol	dietary fiber	saturated fat
492	26 g	73 g	11 g	46 mg	2 g	2 g

% OF CALORIES: 59% carbohydrate, 21% protein, 20% fat

MAJOR SOURCES OF POTENTIAL CANCER FIGHTERS

Phytochemicals: allium compounds, plant polyphenols (flavonoids), plant sterols, terpenes (carotenoids, monoterpenes)

COD BRODETTO VENETIAN STYLE

Gianni Scappin, chef/co-owner, Finch Tavern, Croton Falls, New York

---

Substitute snapper, grouper, tilefish, halibut, or monkfish for the cod and add vegetables such as snow peas, haricots verts, asparagus tips, and/or thinly sliced carrots to make this a versatile one-pot meal. It's also quick—total preparation time is less than 30 minutes. Serve each portion with a grilled piece of crusty bread rubbed with crushed garlic.

---

4 servings

3 medium tomatoes (about 14 ounces)

1 tablespoon olive oil

8 small shallots (about 7 ounces), sliced thin, or 2 small onions, sliced thin

2 bay leaves

4 medium Yukon Gold potatoes (about 1 pound), sliced ¼ to ½ inch thick (use a mandoline if you have one; see page 135)

10 fresh basil leaves, sliced into long strips

2 tablespoons chopped fresh flat-leaf parsley

salt and freshly ground black pepper

¾ cup dry white wine

½ cup water

4 skinless cod fillets (about 6 ounces each), 1½ inches thick

Preheat the oven to 375°F.

Core the tomatoes and plunge them into boiling water for 30 seconds. Slip off the skins. Slice the tomatoes in half and squeeze gently to force out the seeds. Use your fingers to remove any remaining seeds. Discard the seeds, dice the tomatoes, and reserve.

In a large wide braising pan or large nonstick ovenproof sauté pan over medium heat, heat the oil. Add the shallots and bay leaves and cook, stirring often, until soft, about 5 minutes. Transfer to a small bowl.

Spread the potato slices in a single layer in the pan. Place half of the sautéed shallots with bay leaves and half of the basil and parsley on top. Season with salt and pepper to taste, add the wine and water, and bring to a boil. Reduce the heat to medium-low and simmer for 3 to 4 minutes.

Season the cod fillets with salt and pepper to taste and place on top of the potatoes in a single even layer. Sprinkle with the remaining basil, parsley, and shallot–bay leaf mixture and the tomatoes. Return the mixture to a low simmer, cover, and transfer to the oven for 7 minutes. (You can also leave the fish on the stovetop to cook at a low simmer.) Be sure that the pan is well sealed to keep in flavor and moisture.

Remove the cod carefully from the pan with a spatula. Remove the bay leaves. Using a slotted spoon, divide the potatoes among 4 large soup or pasta bowls. Place a cod fillet on top of the potatoes. Bring the remaining juices and vegetables to a boil. Season to taste with salt and pepper and pour on top of each cod fillet.

- Cod is a potentially very good source of selenium and omega-3 fatty acids.
- One serving provides more than 50 percent of the DV for vitamin C and 40 percent for vitamin A.
- A good source of fiber

PER SERVING

calories	protein	carbohydrates	fat	cholesterol	dietary fiber	saturated fat
345	30 g	35 g	5 g	65 mg	4 g	1 g

% OF CALORIES: 37% carbohydrate, 40% protein, 14% fat, 9% alcohol

MAJOR SOURCES OF POTENTIAL CANCER FIGHTERS

Phytochemicals: allium compounds, plant polyphenols (phenolic acids, flavonoids), plant sterols, terpenes (carotenoids, monoterpenes)

Poached Maine Halibut with Sweet Onions, Boiled Potatoes, and Carrot-Lemongrass Glaze

Scott Cohen, executive chef, Las Canarias at La Mansion del Rio, San Antonio, Texas

This beautiful and fragrant dish can be made in less than 30 minutes. Other fish, such as sea bass, red snapper, and salmon, can be substituted for halibut.

4 servings

CARROT-LEMONGRASS GLAZE

2 lemongrass stalks, sliced

2 medium carrots (about 5 ounces), juiced, or ½ cup bottled or canned carrot juice

1 tablespoon plus 1½ teaspoons sugar

HALIBUT

1 large carrot (about 3 ounces), peeled

1 medium parsnip (about 3 ounces), peeled

1 tablespoon olive oil

2 small Texas Sweet or Vidalia onions, sliced (about 2 ounces)

½ cup dry white wine

4 to 5 small red potatoes (about 1 pound), sliced ¼ inch thick

2 cups Fish Stock (see Index), store-bought fish broth, or water

salt and freshly ground black pepper

16 snow peas, cut diagonally in half

1½ pounds boneless halibut (4 6-ounce fillets)

½ bunch fresh cilantro, stems trimmed and whole leaves reserved

1 bunch sunflower sprouts (optional)

In a small saucepan, combine the lemongrass, carrot juice, and sugar. Bring the mixture to a boil, and then reduce the heat to low and simmer until it becomes syrupy, about 20 minutes. Strain and reserve.

While the carrot juice reduces, prepare the garnish. Using a vegetable channeler or the back of a fork, create lengthwise grooves down the carrot and parsnip (this will give a flower shape when sliced). Cut into even, very thin slices (preferably with a mandoline; see page 135) and set aside.

Heat the olive oil in a medium saucepan over medium heat. Add the onions and cook, stirring often, until soft, 3 to 4 minutes. Add the white wine and cook until it reduces to a couple of tablespoons, about 3 minutes. Add the potatoes and fish stock. Season with salt and pepper and simmer until the potatoes are cooked about halfway. Add the snow peas and carrot and parsnip slices and simmer for 5 minutes. Season the fish fillets with salt and pepper to taste and place them over the vegetables. Sprinkle with the cilantro leaves and simmer gently, covered, until the fish just begins to flake, 7 to 9 minutes, depending on thickness.

Using a slotted spoon, carefully transfer the fish fillets to serving bowls. Scatter the vegetable garnish around the fish and spoon the carrot syrup over the top. Top the fish with a small handful of sunflower sprouts if desired.

- Each serving provides more than 150 percent of the DV for vitamin A, 40 percent for vitamin C, and 15 percent for folate.
- Halibut is a potentially good source of selenium.
- A good source of fiber

PER SERVING

calories	protein	carbohydrates	fat	cholesterol	dietary fiber	saturated fat
377	40 g	30 g	8 g	53 mg	4 g	1 g

% OF CALORIES: 33% carbohydrates, 42% protein, 20% fat, 5% alcohol

MAJOR SOURCES OF POTENTIAL CANCER FIGHTERS

Phytochemicals: allium compounds, plant polyphenols (flavonoids, phenolic acids), terpenes (carotenoids, monoterpenes)

POULTRY AND MEAT

❧ FULL-FLAVOR ROASTED CHICKEN

Laura Pensiero, R.D., co-owner, Gigi Trattoria, Rhinebeck, New York; nutritionist, Strang Cancer Prevention Center

---

Roasting chicken creates a dilemma: if you remove the skin before roasting, the meat ends up unpalatably dry when cooked, but if you season and cook the chicken with the skin, it makes it difficult to remove and dispose of this crispy, seasoned part later. The ideal solution is to season the chicken underneath the skin so the meat has the flavor, not the skin. In this recipe the natural oils and essences from the garlic, rosemary, and lemon peel seep into the meat, providing nutrients and great flavor. Other possibilities include orange, lime, or grapefruit peel, herbes de Provence, fresh thyme or tarragon—the combinations are limitless.

Almost any vegetable is the perfect accompaniment to this dish. Try Robert McGrath's Garlic Mashed Potatoes, Gianni Scappin's Crispy Oven-Roasted Vegetables, and Sautéed Spinach with Garlic (see Index).

---

4 servings

1 4- to 5-pound roasting
   chicken, giblets removed
salt and freshly ground black pepper
8 strips of peel from 1 large lemon

4 fresh rosemary sprigs
4 garlic cloves, peeled and crushed
1 teaspoon olive oil

Preheat the oven to 400°F.

Rinse the whole chicken and pat dry with paper towels or a clean cloth. Trim off any excess skin. Running your fingers underneath the skin, separate the thin lining that holds the skin to the meat without removing or tearing the skin. Sprinkle some salt and pepper under the skin, and then place the strips of lemon peel, yellow side touching the meat, whole rosemary sprigs, and crushed garlic cloves underneath

267

the skin of the breasts and legs. Season the outside of the chicken with salt and pepper to taste.

In a well-seasoned cast-iron skillet or Dutch oven, heat the olive oil over medium-high heat. When almost smoking, add the chicken to the pan, breast side down, and cook until well browned, about 5 minutes. Turn the chicken and brown the other side of the breast. Turn the chicken on its back and transfer to the oven. Roast for 50 minutes or until the juices at the leg run clear.

Remove from the oven and let rest for 5 minutes before carving. Remove the breasts and legs from the carcass. Remove the skin, cut the breasts in half diagonally, and separate the thighs from the drumsticks. Dispose of the seasonings. Serve a piece of breast and leg meat on each plate.

- Limonene, found in citrus peels, and carnosol, a phytochemical in rosemary, are potent antioxidants and help increase cancer-fighting enzymes in the body.

PER SERVING (SKIN REMOVED)

calories	protein	carbohydrates	fat	cholesterol	dietary fiber	saturated fat
240	35 g	2 g	10 g	105 mg	0 g	2 g

% OF CALORIES: 5% carbohydrate, 64% protein, 31% fat

MAJOR SOURCES OF POTENTIAL CANCER FIGHTERS

Phytochemicals: allium compounds, terpenes (monoterpenes, limonene, carnosol)

Poached Chicken Breast with Ratatouille Orzo Ragout

David Burke, Park Avenue Cafés, New York City and Chicago ▪ Adapted from *Cooking with David Burke* (Alfred A. Knopf, 1995).

This chicken becomes very moist and flavorful when poached in the ratatouille. Ratatouille by itself is an excellent low-fat, high-nutrient topping for polenta or pasta.

Mascarpone cheese has about 13 grams of fat per ounce; Parmesan varieties average about 8 grams of fat per ounce. Due to the intense flavor of Parmesan, one can generally use less and still get the full effect.

4 servings

1½ cups White Chicken Stock or
  Brown Chicken Stock (see Index),
  or low-sodium canned broth
1½ cups tomato sauce, homemade
  or canned
1½ pounds boneless, skinless chicken
  breasts (4 6-ounce split breasts)
coarse or kosher salt and freshly
  ground black pepper
1 large red bell pepper (about
  ½ pound), seeded and diced
1 yellow bell pepper (about
  5 ounces), seeded and diced
1 medium zucchini (about
  ½ pound), seeded and diced

1 medium yellow summer squash
  (about 10 ounces), diced
1 small eggplant (14 ounces),
  unpeeled, pulp scooped out,
  leaving outer 1½ inches close to
  the skin, diced
½ small onion (about 2 ounces),
  diced
3 garlic cloves, minced
2 cups cooked orzo pasta
1 cup chopped fresh basil
¼ cup mascarpone or freshly
  grated Parmesan cheese
4 fresh basil or parsley leaves

Combine the chicken stock and tomato sauce in a large saucepan or soup pot. Bring to a simmer. Season the chicken with salt and pepper to taste and add to the pot. Cover and simmer for 10 minutes or until the chicken is cooked. Add the peppers, zucchini, yellow squash, eggplant, onion, and garlic. Stir to combine, simmer for 3 minutes, then transfer the chicken breasts to a plate, covering them loosely to keep them warm.

Continue to cook the vegetable mixture, covered, until the vegetables are tender and the mixture has thickened slightly, about 15 minutes. Stir in the orzo and the basil and add salt and pepper to taste. Spoon the ratatouille into 4 large bowls. Cut each chicken breast horizontally into 2 pieces and place over the ragout. Top with 1 tablespoon of mascarpone or Parmesan and garnish with the basil or parsley leaves.

■ One serving provides three times the DV for vitamin C, 25 percent of the DV for folate, and
  enough carotenoids to supply 20 percent of the DV for vitamin A.
■ A good source of dietary fiber

PER SERVING

calories	protein	carbohydrates	fat	cholesterol	dietary fiber	saturated fat
478	64 g	35 g	9 g	150 mg	4 g	3 g

% OF CALORIES: 29% carbohydrate, 53% protein, 18% fat

MAJOR SOURCES OF POTENTIAL CANCER FIGHTERS

Phytochemicals: allium compounds, plant polyphenols (flavonoids, phenolic acids), plant sterols, terpenes (carotenoids, monoterpenes)

Middle Eastern Chicken Breasts with Smoky Lentils

Katy Keck, New World Grill, New York City

Prepare the marinade for this great weeknight meal in under 10 minutes in the morning and let the chicken breasts marinate all day—they will become incredibly tender and flavorful and will need only to be transferred to the oven for less than 30 minutes of cooking. Serve the chicken with or without the lentils. Use Smoky Lentils as a bed for other well-seasoned meats or poultry.

4 servings

MIDDLE EASTERN CHICKEN BREASTS

⅔ cup plain yogurt

1 bunch scallions, white part and a
   little green, sliced thin

¼ cup chopped fresh flat-leaf parsley

2 garlic cloves, minced

juice of 1 lime

1 tablespoon olive oil

2 teaspoons paprika

1 teaspoon ground coriander

1 teaspoon ground cumin

½ teaspoon salt

½ teaspoon cayenne pepper

4 boneless, skinless chicken breasts
   (4 to 6 ounces each)

Smoky Lentils

1 tablespoon olive oil

½ small onion, minced

2 garlic cloves, minced

2 medium carrots (about 7 ounces), peeled and diced

2 celery ribs (about ¼ pound), chopped

1½ cups tiny lentils, such as massor dal or DePuy

1 quart White Chicken Stock, Brown Chicken Stock, or Vegetable Stock (see Index), or low-sodium canned broth

1 tablespoon plus 1 teaspoon pureed chipotle chile (available in specialty stores and some supermarkets; or puree canned chipotle chiles in adobo in a blender)

1 teaspoon ground coriander

½ teaspoon salt

¼ cup chopped fresh flat-leaf parsley

To prepare the chicken marinade, combine all ingredients except the chicken in a small mixing bowl and stir to mix well. Place the chicken in a small rectangular baking dish lightly rubbed with olive oil. Pour the marinade over the chicken, turning to coat both sides. Cover and refrigerate for 2 to 4 hours, or up to 24 hours.

One hour before cooking the chicken, begin to prepare the lentils. Heat the olive oil in a medium saucepan over medium heat. Add the onion and garlic and cook, stirring, for 2 to 3 minutes, taking care not to burn the garlic. Add the carrots and celery and cook until slightly softened, about 5 minutes.

Add the lentils and stir to coat with the oil, then add the stock, chipotle puree, coriander, and salt. Bring to a boil, then reduce the heat and simmer for 45 to 50 minutes or until the lentils are tender and most of the liquid has been absorbed. Add water if additional liquid is needed. Remove from the heat and stir in the parsley.

To cook the chicken breasts, preheat the oven to 350°F. Bake the chicken, uncovered, for 25 to 30 minutes or until the juices run clear. Remove from the oven and let rest for 5 minutes.

Divide the lentils among 4 dinner plates. Slice each chicken breast into 4 slices and fan out over the lentils.

- Chicken is potentially a very good source of selenium.
- Each serving provides more than 150 percent of the DV for vitamin A and 50 percent of the DV for vitamin C.

- Lentils are a very good source of folate, providing more than 90 percent of the DV per serving.
- Very high in fiber—each serving provides more than 80 percent of the DV.

PER SERVING OF MIDDLE EASTERN CHICKEN BREASTS

calories	protein	carbohydrates	fat	cholesterol	dietary fiber	saturated fat
344	55 g	6 g	10 g	143 mg	1 g	2 g

PER SERVING OF SMOKY LENTILS

calories	protein	carbohydrates	fat	cholesterol	dietary fiber	saturated fat
312	22 g	50 g	4 g	0 mg	20 g	0 g

PER SERVING OF MIDDLE EASTERN CHICKEN BREASTS WITH SMOKY LENTILS

calories	protein	carbohydrates	fat	cholesterol	dietary fiber	saturated fat
656	77 g	56 g	14 g	143 mg	21 g	2 g

% OF CALORIES: 34% carbohydrate, 47% protein, 19% fat

MAJOR SOURCES OF POTENTIAL CANCER FIGHTERS

Phytochemicals: allium compounds, capsaicin, phytic acids, plant polyphenols (flavonoids), protease inhibitors, terpenes (carotenoids, monoterpenes)

✿ CHICKEN CACCIATORE

Laura Pensiero, R.D., co-owner, Gigi Trattoria, Rhinebeck, New York; nutritionist, Strang Cancer Prevention Center

In this quick and healthful one-pot meal, the chicken becomes very tender when braised in the flavorful vegetable stew.

4 servings

4 split boneless chicken breasts
(1½ pounds), skin trimmed of
all visible fat

salt and freshly ground black pepper

1 tablespoon olive oil

1 medium onion (about 6 ounces),
halved and sliced

1 large green bell pepper (about
½ pound), seeded and cut into
long, thin strips

2 medium celery ribs (about
3 ounces), chopped

2 medium carrots (about 5 ounces),
peeled and sliced ¼ inch thick

1 garlic clove, minced

1 tablespoon flour

¼ cup dry white wine

1 14½-ounce can stewed tomatoes

1 cup domestic mushrooms (about
2½ ounces), sliced

1 teaspoon grated lemon zest

2 tablespoons chopped fresh
flat-leaf parsley

Season the chicken with salt and pepper to taste. Heat the olive oil in a medium non-stick saucepan or casserole over medium-high heat and sauté the chicken until golden brown on both sides, about 5 minutes. Transfer to a plate and set aside.

In the same pan, cook the onion, green pepper, celery, and carrots over medium heat, stirring often, until the onion and pepper are soft, about 10 minutes. Add the garlic and cook for another minute. Sprinkle the flour over the vegetables and stir to blend in evenly—there should be no lumps.

Add the white wine and stir to dissolve all flavorful particles on the bottom of the pan. Add the tomatoes, mushrooms, lemon zest, and salt and pepper to taste; stir the mixture well. Bring to a boil, and then reduce the heat so that the mixture simmers.

Return the chicken breasts to the pan and braise, covered, until the chicken is done, about 15 minutes.

Place the chicken breasts in large shallow soup bowls and spoon the sauce and vegetables over the top. Garnish with parsley.

- Both chicken and mushrooms are potentially good sources of selenium.
- Using grated citrus zest (or peel) in cooking is recommended. Limonene, a phytochemical that may help your body eliminate carcinogens, is found in the peel.
- One serving provides more than 110 percent of the DV for vitamin A, 100 percent of the DV for vitamin C, and 10 percent of the DV for folate.
- A good source of fiber

PER SERVING

calories	protein	carbohydrates	fat	cholesterol	dietary fiber	saturated fat
388	42 g	19 g	14 g	106 mg	5 g	3 g

% OF CALORIES: 20% carbohydrate, 44% protein, 32% fat, 4% alcohol

MAJOR SOURCES OF POTENTIAL CANCER FIGHTERS

Phytochemicals: allium compounds, plant polyphenols (flavonoids, phenolic acids), plant sterols, terpenes (carotenoids, monoterpenes, limonene)

❧ VEGGIE-PACKED CHICKEN POT PIE

Laura Pensiero, R.D., co-owner, Gigi Trattoria, Rhinebeck, New York; nutritionist, Strang Cancer Prevention Center

This version is rich and creamy but contains almost half the fat of traditional chicken pot pie. It's a great way to introduce new vegetables to kids. Use the Olive Oil Pastry for other savory recipes that call for a crust, maybe a tomato and onion tart.

4 servings

OLIVE OIL PASTRY
1 cup flour
¼ teaspoon salt
2 tablespoons olive oil

1 tablespoon water
1 large egg, beaten

FILLING

1 tablespoon olive oil

1 small onion (about ¼ pound), chopped

1 large celery rib (about 2 ounces), sliced

2 small carrots (about 5 ounces), peeled and cut into small cubes

3 cups White Chicken Stock or Brown Chicken Stock (see Index), or low-sodium canned broth

1 medium potato (about 6 ounces), peeled and cut into medium cubes

1 small sweet potato (about 6 ounces), peeled and cut into medium cubes

1 medium turnip (about 5 ounces), peeled and cut into small cubes

¾ pound boneless, skinless chicken breast, trimmed of all visible fat and cut into small strips

1 tablespoon plus 1 teaspoon cornstarch

½ cup plus 1 tablespoon evaporated skim milk

2 tablespoons chopped fresh flat-leaf parsley

¾ cup fresh or thawed frozen peas

salt and freshly ground black pepper

Preheat the oven to 400°F.

To make the pastry, in the bowl of a food processor, combine the flour and salt. Pulse quickly to combine evenly. Add the olive oil and pulse again for 2 to 3 seconds. Add the water and the egg and turn on the processor for about 7 seconds. At this point the pastry dough should be crumbly but moist. Remove the dough from the food processor bowl and compact it to form a disk (do not knead). Wrap in plastic wrap or wax paper and let the dough rest in the refrigerator for at least 30 minutes. (Resting is especially important for low-fat doughs; it relaxes the gluten that can make the dough tough and chewy.)

Cut the pastry dough into quarters. Place the quarters of pastry dough between 2 sheets of plastic wrap or parchment paper. Flatten the dough, and then, making circular motions with the palm of your hand, spread out the dough evenly to form ⅛- to ¼-inch-thick circles large enough to cover the tops of ramekins. Put the dough in the refrigerator for at least 5 minutes—this will make it easier to peel the plastic wrap from the dough.

To make the filling, heat the olive oil in a large nonstick (or heavy) saucepan over medium heat. Add the onion and cook, stirring often, until softened, about 5 minutes. Add the celery and carrots, cook for another 5 minutes, then pour the stock into the pan. Bring to a boil, and then reduce the heat so that the mixture simmers. Add the potato, sweet potato, and turnip and cook, covered, until the vegetables are just cooked but still slightly firm, about 15 minutes, depending on the size of the cut vegetables. Strain the broth from the vegetables, placing the broth back into the saucepan and dividing the vegetables among 4 8-ounce ramekins or ovenproof casseroles. Add the chicken to the broth and simmer until the chicken is just cooked through, 3 to 4 minutes. Dilute the cornstarch in ½ cup evaporated skim milk and stir until well combined; add to the saucepan. While stirring, bring to a full boil for 4 minutes to cook the starch and thicken the sauce. Remove from the heat; stir in the parsley and peas and season to taste with salt and pepper.

Divide the chicken and thickened broth among the ramekins. Place circles of dough over the filled ramekins and press to form a tight seal. Place the ramekins on a baking sheet and brush the surface of the dough with the remaining evaporated milk. Bake until the crust becomes golden brown, about 15 minutes.

- These pot pies are rich in cancer-protective vitamins; one serving provides more than 125 percent of the DV for vitamin A and 40 percent of the DV for vitamin C. They also contain cancer-protective cruciferous vegetables (turnips) and onions and are rich in beta-carotene and other carotenoids.
- Olive oil, rich in protective monounsaturated fatty acids, provides more than 75 percent of the fat in this recipe.
- A potentially good source of selenium
- High in fiber—21 percent of the DV per serving

PER SERVING

calories	protein	carbohydrates	fat	cholesterol	dietary fiber	saturated fat
508	38 g	53 g	16 g	128 mg	5 g	3 g

% OF CALORIES: 42% carbohydrate, 30% protein, 28% fat

MAJOR SOURCES OF POTENTIAL CANCER FIGHTERS

Phytochemicals: allium compounds, glucosinolates, plant polyphenols (flavonoids, phenolic acids), terpenes (carotenoids, monoterpenes)

❦ Turkey Steaks with Grape and Currant Sauce

Jacques Pépin, PBS-TV cooking series host and dean of special programs, the French Culinary Institute, New York City ▪ Adapted with permission from *Jacques Pépin's Simple and Healthy Cooking* (Rodale, 1994).

Jacques recommends serving this as a dinner party entrée. He suggests either buying a whole turkey breast and cutting it into ½-inch steaks or asking your butcher to do it for you.

---

6 servings

6 turkey breast steaks (6 ounces
    each and about ½ inch thick)
salt and freshly ground black pepper
2 tablespoons extra-virgin olive oil
1 small leek (3 to 4 ounces),
    washed and chopped
1 medium onion (¼ pound),
    chopped

¼ cup balsamic vinegar
¼ cup red wine vinegar
1½ cups Brown Chicken Stock
    (see Index), or low-sodium
    canned broth
2½ cups seedless grapes
¼ cup dried currants
2 tablespoons chopped fresh chives

Preheat the oven to 180°F.

Season the turkey steaks with salt and pepper. Heat the olive oil in a very large heavy skillet set over high heat. Add the turkey steaks and cook them for 2 to 3 minutes on each side. They will be slightly undercooked at this point; transfer them to a small roasting pan or gratin dish and place them in the oven while you make the sauce. (They can wait there up to 30 minutes.)

Add the leek and onion to the skillet and sauté them for 2 minutes. Add the balsamic vinegar and red wine vinegar; cook until they have almost evaporated.

Add the chicken stock, grapes, currants, ½ teaspoon salt, ¼ teaspoon pepper, and any juices that have accumulated around the turkey steaks in the oven. Boil for 2 to 3 minutes, until the sauce thickens slightly.

Arrange the turkey steaks on a platter, cover them with the sauce, and sprinkle the chives on top. Serve.

- Turkey breast is very low in fat and, with the flavorful Grape and Currant Sauce, very moist. Turkey is also a potentially very good source of selenium.
- The skins of currants and grapes contain flavonoids, which act as potent antioxidants and may boost enzymes that help rid the body of carcinogens.
- Each serving provides 10 percent of the DV for vitamin C.

PER SERVING

calories	protein	carbohydrates	fat	cholesterol	dietary fiber	saturated fat
288	44 g	18 g	4 g	108 mg	2 g	1 g

% OF CALORIES: 25% carbohydrate, 62% protein, 13% fat

MAJOR SOURCES OF POTENTIAL CANCER FIGHTERS

Phytochemicals: allium compounds, plant polyphenols (flavonoids, phenolic acids)

SMOTHERED BONELESS PORK CHOPS WITH LENTILS

Frank Brigtsen, Brigtsen's, New Orleans, Louisiana

Frank explains that the term smothered *is a method of cooking whereby food is braised with moist heat. This tenderizes lean meats, such as center-cut pork chops trimmed of fat, and develops flavor.*

4 servings

1 tablespoon plus 2 teaspoons
   olive oil

½ cup plus 2 tablespoons peeled
   carrots in ¼-inch dice

½ cup plus 2 tablespoons celery
   in ¼-inch dice

⅔ cup plus 2 tablespoons onion
   in ¼-inch dice

1½ teaspoons minced garlic

1 bay leaf

¼ teaspoon dried whole-leaf
   summer savory

⅛ teaspoon dried whole-leaf thyme

⅛ teaspoon dried whole-leaf
   oregano

½ teaspoon salt

⅛ teaspoon freshly ground
   white pepper

⅛ teaspoon freshly ground
   black pepper

3 cups White or Brown Chicken
   Stock (see Index), low-sodium
   canned broth, or water

½ cup dried lentils (3 ounces)

4 4-ounce lean center-cut pork chops,
   trimmed of all visible fat

salt and freshly ground black pepper

¼ teaspoon Tabasco sauce

Heat 1 tablespoon of the olive oil in a small saucepan over medium heat. Add ½ cup of the carrots, ½ cup of the celery, and ⅔ cup of the onion and cook, stirring often, until the vegetables begin to brown, 12 to 15 minutes. Add the garlic, bay leaf, savory, thyme, oregano, salt, and pepper. Continue cooking, stirring constantly, until the mixture is well browned but not burned, about 5 minutes.

Add the stock and bring the mixture to a boil. Add the lentils and simmer for 20 to 25 minutes. Add the remaining 2 tablespoons of carrot, celery, and onion and continue to cook.

Meanwhile, season the pork chops with salt and black pepper. Heat the remaining 2 teaspoons of olive oil in a large nonstick sauté pan or well-seasoned cast-iron skillet over medium-high heat. When hot, add the pork chops and brown on both sides. Reduce the heat to medium-low and add the lentils and Tabasco. Simmer, uncovered, for 10 to 15 minutes or until the pork is cooked and the lentils are tender.

Place 1 pork chop on each plate and top with the lentils.

- Lean cuts of pork, such as center-cut loin chops, can contain less than 1.5 g fat per ounce.
- Both pork and lentils are potentially good sources of selenium.
- This recipe is rich in the cancer-protective vitamins A, C, and folate, providing more than 90 percent, 15 percent, and 30 percent of the DV, respectively.
- High in fiber—37 percent of the DV per serving

PER SERVING

calories	protein	carbohydrates	fat	cholesterol	dietary fiber	saturated fat
364	36 g	22 g	14 g	60 mg	9 g	3 g

% OF CALORIES: 25% carbohydrate, 40% protein, 35% fat

MAJOR SOURCES OF POTENTIAL CANCER FIGHTERS

Phytochemicals: allium compounds, phytic acids, plant polyphenols (flavonoids), protease inhibitors, terpenes (carotenoids, monoterpenes)

MARINATED PORK TENDERLOIN WITH MASHED ORANGE-SCENTED SWEET POTATOES

Gianni Scappin, chef/co-owner, Finch Tavern, Croton Falls, New York

The tenderloin of pork has less than 1.5 grams of fat per cooked ounce (less than a chicken breast), so take a break from chicken and incorporate some variety into your protein selections.

Marinade combinations for pork tenderloin are limitless, making it a very versatile lean meat selection. (See Notes for Gianni's marinade suggestions.)

Serve with Sweet and Sour Cabbage (see Index).

8 servings

PORK

5 garlic cloves, crushed

2 large shallots (about 2 ounces), sliced

2 tablespoons tamari (a Japanese soy sauce)

1 tablespoon Dijon mustard

1 tablespoon sherry vinegar

1 tablespoon canola oil

1½ teaspoons honey

2 tablespoons water

½ teaspoon cracked or coarsely ground black peppercorns

2 fresh rosemary sprigs

1 fresh thyme sprig

2 pork tenderloins (about 2½ pounds), trimmed of all visible fat

salt and freshly ground black pepper

1 teaspoon olive oil

⅓ cup water, dry white wine, veal stock, or White Chicken Stock or Brown Chicken Stock (see Index)

MASHED ORANGE-SCENTED SWEET POTATOES

8 medium sweet potatoes (about 3½ pounds), scrubbed

1 tablespoon olive oil

grated zest of 1 orange

pinch of ground cinnamon

salt

To prepare the marinade, in a rectangular dish, combine the garlic, shallots, tamari, mustard, sherry vinegar, canola oil, honey, water, and cracked pepper. Stir, then add the rosemary and thyme sprigs.

Place the pork tenderloins in the marinade, rolling to make sure they are well coated. Cover with plastic wrap and refrigerate for at least 1 hour. (You can marinate the pork a day in advance.)

Preheat the oven to 350°F. Prick the sweet potatoes with a fork and place on top of a sheet of foil in the oven for 60 to 70 minutes or until very tender. Remove and set aside to cool slightly. Turn the oven temperature up to 375°F.

When the potatoes are almost cooked, begin cooking the pork tenderloin. Wipe the marinade off the pork loin and season with salt and pepper. Heat the olive oil in a large well-seasoned cast-iron or nonstick ovenproof skillet (with a metal handle for transfer into the oven) over medium-high heat. When hot, sear the pork, browning all sides evenly. Transfer the pan to the oven and cook until the pork is only slightly pink in the center, about 15 minutes. Remove the tenderloin from the pan and place on a plate to rest for 5 minutes. Loosely cover with a piece of foil to keep hot.

Remove any fat from the bottom of the sauté pan. Place the sauté pan over medium heat and add the water, wine, or stock while stirring with a wooden spoon to dissolve all particles on the bottom of the pan. Set aside.

Peel the sweet potatoes and put the flesh in a medium bowl. Add the olive oil, orange zest, and cinnamon. Whip with an electric mixer or wooden spoon until well combined. Season to taste with salt.

Spoon the sweet potatoes slightly above the center of each plate. Slice the pork tenderloins into ¾-inch slices on the bias and fan out 4 slices leaning on the sweet potato mound. Top the pork slices with the reserved juices from the sauté pan.

NOTES: Gianni Scappin suggests other marinade combinations:

- 1 tablespoon tamari or teriyaki, 1 teaspoon toasted sesame oil, 2 teaspoons canola oil, grated zest of ½ orange or 1 whole lemon or lime, pinch of ground coriander, 1 tablespoon rice wine vinegar, 2 tablespoons water, and a sprinkle of brown sugar
- grated zest of 1 lemon, 1 tablespoon olive oil, 2 teaspoons herbes de Provence, 3 tablespoons fresh orange juice

These marinade combinations may also be used for lean pork loin chops.

- Fresh rosemary not only adds a wonderful flavor dimension to roasted meat, fish, and vegetables but also contains carnosol, a potent antioxidant.
- Pork is a potentially good source of selenium.
- Sweet potatoes are rich in both beta-carotene and flavor. To maximize sweetness, roast the potatoes at a lower temperature for a longer time and let them cool slightly in their skins before serving.
- Each serving provides almost 250 percent of the DV for vitamin A and more than 50 percent for vitamin C.
- A good source of fiber

PER SERVING OF 5 OUNCES MARINATED PORK TENDERLOIN WITH NATURAL JUICES

calories	protein	carbohydrates	fat	cholesterol	dietary fiber	saturated fat
261	40 g	2 g	9 g	112 mg	0 g	3 g

PER SERVING OF MASHED ORANGE-SCENTED SWEET POTATOES

calories	protein	carbohydrates	fat	cholesterol	dietary fiber	saturated fat
133	2 g	28 g	2 g	0 mg	3 g	0 g

PER SERVING OF MARINATED PORK TENDERLOIN WITH MASHED ORANGE-SCENTED SWEET POTATOES

calories	protein	carbohydrates	fat	cholesterol	dietary fiber	saturated fat
394	42 g	30 g	11 g	112 mg	3 g	3 g

% OF CALORIES: 31% carbohydrate, 44% protein, 25% fat

MAJOR SOURCES OF POTENTIAL CANCER FIGHTERS

Phytochemicals: allium compounds, plant polyphenols (flavonoids), terpenes (carnosol, carotenoids, limonene)

❧ Venison Medallions in Tamarind with Creamy Horseradish Mashed Potatoes

Adam Busby, chef instructor, the Culinary Institute of America at Greystone, St. Helena, California

Venison is a very lean red meat alternative. It cooks quickly and easily and stands up to intense flavors, such as the tamarind and horseradish in this recipe.

The creamy low-fat mashed potatoes can be made with or without horseradish and served with many other dishes.

4 servings

Creamy Horseradish Mashed Potatoes

4 medium potatoes (about 1 pound)
⅔ cup 2% milk
1 tablespoon Lawry's or other creamed horseradish

1 tablespoon unsalted butter
salt and freshly ground black pepper

VENISON

2 tablespoons tamarind concentrate (see Notes)	2 teaspoons peanut oil
¼ cup hot water	salt
2 venison tenderloins (about 1¼ pounds), cut into 8 equal medallions	1 tablespoon crushed black peppercorns
	2 teaspoons aged balsamic vinegar

To make the mashed potatoes, boil the potatoes in salted water until tender, about 20 minutes. Drain, peel, and pass through a food mill or potato ricer into a medium bowl or mash the potatoes with a potato masher.

Heat the milk in the microwave or in a small saucepan until steaming. Add half of the milk, the horseradish, and the butter to the potatoes. Using an electric mixer (or wooden spoon), whip the potatoes until creamy, adding more hot milk as necessary. Season to taste with salt and pepper. Place parchment or wax paper directly on the surface of the potatoes to keep heat in and prevent a skin from forming while you prepare the venison.

To make the venison, whisk the tamarind concentrate and hot water together until smooth. Set aside.

Press the pieces of venison down with the palm of your hand to form 2-inch-thick round medallions. Brush the medallions with the peanut oil and season with salt and crushed peppercorns. Heat a large nonstick or well-seasoned cast-iron pan over medium-high heat; when hot, sear the medallions to brown on both sides, 1 to 2 minutes per side. Reduce the heat to medium and cook until medium-rare, 3 to 5 minutes.

Transfer the venison to a plate and add the tamarind mixture to the sauté pan. Turn off the heat and stir with a wooden spoon to remove all flavorful particles from the bottom of the pan. Add any juices released from the venison to the sauté pan.

Place a mound of horseradish mashed potatoes in the center of each plate. Rest 2 medallions against the mashed potatoes. Spoon the tamarind sauce over the venison and then drizzle with aged balsamic vinegar.

NOTES: Tamarind is a large bean pod native to Asia, India, and North Africa. The pulp, which is concentrated into a paste, is sweet and sour and is used in full-flavored foods, such as chutneys, relishes, and marinades. It is available at Indian and Asian markets and some gourmet specialty stores. If you cannot find tamarind, substitute hoisin sauce, a spicy-sweet sauce made from Asian spices and ground soybeans.

- Mashed potatoes provide more than 10 percent of the DV of vitamin C per serving.
- Horseradish contains cancer-protective glucosinolates and kaempferol, a flavonoid.

PER SERVING OF CREAMY HORSERADISH MASHED POTATOES

calories	protein	carbohydrates	fat	cholesterol	dietary fiber	saturated fat
151	3 g	22 g	6 g	4 mg	0 g	3 g

PER SERVING OF VENISON MEDALLIONS IN TAMARIND

calories	protein	carbohydrates	fat	cholesterol	dietary fiber	saturated fat
203	32 g	3 g	6 g	118 mg	0 g	1 g

PER SERVING OF VENISON MEDALLIONS IN TAMARIND WITH CREAMY HORSERADISH MASHED POTATOES

calories	protein	carbohydrates	fat	cholesterol	dietary fiber	saturated fat
354	35 g	25 g	12 g	122 mg	0 g	4 g

% OF CALORIES: 29% carbohydrate, 40% protein, 31% fat

MAJOR SOURCES OF POTENTIAL CANCER FIGHTERS

Phytochemicals: allium compounds, glucosinolates, plant polyphenols (flavonoids, phenolic acids)

❧ Filet Mignon with Blueberry Barbecue Sauce and Garlic Mashed Potatoes

Robert McGrath, chef/owner, Roaring Fork restaurants, Scottsdale, Arizona, and Austin, Texas

Small portions of juicy red meat can be part of healthy eating. Enjoy the occasional indulgence and make sure the side dishes and condiments add protective nutrients to your meal.

The Blueberry Barbecue Sauce is lower in fat and higher in nutrients than traditional barbecue sauce. Use it in place of standard barbecue sauce for other grilled or seared meats or chicken.

Serve these vegetable-fortified mashed potatoes with other full-flavored entrées.

4 servings

Filet Mignon with Blueberry Barbecue Sauce

¼ cup finely diced onion

1 tablespoon jalapeño pepper,
  seeded and diced

2 teaspoons olive oil

1 pint fresh blueberries

¼ cup water

2 tablespoons rice wine vinegar

1½ tablespoons brown sugar

1 tablespoon Dijon mustard

1 teaspoon unsalted butter

4 4- to 5-ounce filets mignons

1 teaspoon canola oil

salt and freshly ground black pepper

¼ cup blueberries (for garnish)

Garlic Mashed Potatoes

4 medium potatoes (about 1 pound),
  peeled and cut into quarters

¼ cup low-fat or fat-free sour cream

¼ cup Roasted Garlic (see Index) or
  2 teaspoons minced garlic

1 tablespoon unsalted butter

⅓ cup hot 2% milk

¼ cup fresh sweet corn kernels or
  thawed and drained frozen corn
  kernels

2 tablespoons finely diced
  red bell pepper

2 tablespoons finely diced
  green bell pepper

2 tablespoons finely diced red onion

salt and freshly ground black pepper

To prepare the Blueberry Barbecue Sauce, sauté the onion and jalapeño in the olive oil in a medium nonstick skillet over medium-high heat until soft, 3 to 4 minutes. Add the blueberries, water, vinegar, brown sugar, and mustard and stir to combine. Bring to a boil, then reduce the heat and simmer for 15 minutes, stirring often. Remove from heat and stir in the butter. Puree the sauce in a blender or food processor until smooth. Strain through a fine-mesh strainer, using a rubber spatula to push as much sauce as possible through the mesh. Return the sauce to a clean small saucepan to reheat quickly just before serving.

Preheat the oven to 400°F.

To prepare the potatoes, bring 3 quarts of salted water to a boil, add the potatoes, and cook until tender when pierced with a knife, 10 to 15 minutes. Drain thoroughly. Spread the potatoes in a single layer on a nonstick baking pan and roast for 8 minutes to remove moisture. Remove the potatoes from the oven and place in a medium bowl along with the sour cream, garlic, and butter. Using an electric stand mixer or a handheld mixer, begin whipping the potatoes while gradually adding the milk. Stop mixing when all the ingredients have been well incorporated and the potatoes are creamy. Fold in the corn, peppers, and onion and season with salt and pepper to taste. Place a piece of parchment or wax paper directly on the surface of the potatoes to keep heat in and prevent a skin from forming. Set aside.

Preheat the grill.

Brush the filets with the canola oil and season with salt and pepper. Grill to the desired doneness, about 3 to 4 minutes on each side for medium-rare, depending on the thickness of the filets. During the last couple minutes of cooking, brush each filet with about 1 tablespoon of the Blueberry Barbecue Sauce. To sear the filets instead of grilling, heat the canola oil in a medium nonstick skillet and, when almost smoking, add the filets. Brown on both sides, lower the heat, and cook to the desired doneness, a total cooking time of about 8 minutes.

Spoon a mound of mashed potatoes onto the center of the plate. Slice each filet into 4 slices and fan out in front of the mashed potatoes. Spoon the Blueberry Barbecue Sauce over the filets. Sprinkle blueberries around the perimeter.

- Blueberries rank among the highest antioxidant foods.
- Blueberries and potatoes are rich in vitamin C, providing 70 percent of the DV per serving.
- Blueberries also contain ellagic acid, a phytochemical that may help boost enzymes that rid the body of cancer-causing substances.
- Each serving provides more than 110 percent of the DV for vitamin A.
- A good source of fiber

PER SERVING OF BLUEBERRY BARBECUE SAUCE (¼ CUP)

calories	protein	carbohydrates	fat	cholesterol	dietary fiber	saturated fat
115	1 g	18 g	5 g	3 mg	4 g	1 g

PER SERVING OF GARLIC MASHED POTATOES

calories	protein	carbohydrates	fat	cholesterol	dietary fiber	saturated fat
161	5 g	29 g	4 g	9 mg	2 g	2 g

PER SERVING OF FILET MIGNON WITH BLUEBERRY BARBECUE SAUCE AND GARLIC MASHED POTATOES

calories	protein	carbohydrates	fat	cholesterol	dietary fiber	saturated fat
513	41 g	47 g	18 g	162 mg	5 g	6 g

% OF CALORIES: 34% carbohydrate, 34% protein, 32% fat

MAJOR SOURCES OF POTENTIAL CANCER FIGHTERS

Phytochemicals: allium compounds, plant polyphenols (flavonoids, phenolic acids), terpenes (carotenoids)

✿ LIGHTLY SPICED LAMB STEW WITH SPRING VEGETABLES

Laura Pensiero, R.D., co-owner, Gigi Trattoria, Rhinebeck, New York; nutritionist, Strang Cancer Prevention Center

---

The marinade seasoning is exotic but subtle; after seasoning and tenderizing the lamb, it is used to produce flavorful cooking sauce.

This stew is convenient when entertaining because it can be prepared up to a day in advance and reheated. Substitute seasonal vegetables and make it throughout the winter and spring.

Omit the potatoes and serve over whole wheat couscous.

---

6 servings

MARINADE

½ teaspoon ground cumin
¼ teaspoon ground cinnamon
pinch of ground cloves
½ teaspoon ground turmeric
pinch of freshly grated nutmeg

grated zest of ½ lemon
1 teaspoon olive oil
2 pounds leg of lamb, boned, trimmed of all visible fat, and cut into 2-inch cubes

STEW

1 tablespoon plus 1½ teaspoons olive oil
10 small shallots (about 5 ounces), peeled and quartered
2 celery ribs, sliced
1 tablespoon flour
salt and freshly ground black pepper
1 cup fresh orange juice
1 quart White or Brown Chicken Stock (see Index), low-sodium canned broth, or water
1 bay leaf

1½ pounds small Yukon Gold potatoes, peeled and halved or quartered if large
1 small fennel bulb, tough outer layer discarded, sliced into ¼-inch pieces
2 cups cooked and quartered fresh or thawed frozen artichoke hearts
1 cup cooked or drained canned chick-peas (see page 148)
2 tablespoons chopped fresh flat-leaf parsley

To prepare the marinade and lamb, combine all the ingredients in a large bowl; mix well, cover, and refrigerate for at least 1 hour and up to 24 hours.

To prepare the stew, heat 1 tablespoon of the olive oil in a large heavy pot over medium heat. Add the shallots and celery and cook, stirring often, until soft, about 10 minutes.

Sprinkle the vegetables with the flour and stir to incorporate; no lumps should remain. (The stew will end up slightly thickened but still brothy; if you like a more stewlike consistency, add 1 tablespoon more flour to the vegetables.)

Lift the lamb pieces from the marinade, transfer to a large plate, and season with salt and pepper. Reserve the marinade. In a large nonstick skillet, heat the remaining 1½ teaspoons of oil. When almost smoking, add the lamb cubes, in batches if necessary to prevent overcrowding. Sear over high heat, browning the meat evenly on all sides. Remove the lamb and add to the pot with the vegetables. Add the orange juice to the skillet, stirring with a wooden spoon to dissolve the flavorful particles on the bottom of the pan. Add this liquid, along with the chicken stock and bay leaf, to the pot with the lamb and vegetables.

Bring the stew to a boil; immediately reduce the heat so that the mixture simmers gently. Cook for 1 hour, then add the potatoes and continue cooking at a simmer. After another 20 minutes, add the fennel and cook for 10 minutes more. Add the artichokes, chick-peas, and parsley 2 to 3 minutes before serving, then add salt and pepper to taste.

- Each serving provides more than 90 percent of the DV for vitamin C and more than 30 percent for vitamin A and folate.
- Trimmed leg of lamb contains only 2.5 grams of fat per ounce and is a good source of protein and B vitamins and a potentially good source of selenium.
- The peel or zest of citrus fruit contains limonene, which may help boost cancer-fighting enzymes in the body.
- Turmeric contains curcumin, a plant polyphenol that lends yellow color and acts as an antioxidant; it may also play a role in blocking cancer at the initiation stage.
- High in fiber—28 percent of the DV per serving

PER SERVING

calories	protein	carbohydrates	fat	cholesterol	dietary fiber	saturated fat
557	55 g	45 g	17 g	153 mg	7 g	5 g

% OF CALORIES: 32% carbohydrate, 40% protein, 28% fat

MAJOR SOURCES OF POTENTIAL CANCER FIGHTERS

Phytochemicals: allium compounds, phytic acids, plant polyphenols (flavonoids, phenolic acids), protease inhibitors, terpenes (carotenoids, limonene)

Sweet and Sour Braised Brisket

Laura Pensiero, R.D., co-owner, Gigi Trattoria, Rhinebeck, New York; nutritionist, Strang Cancer Prevention Center

This version of the traditional Eastern European dish has a delicious Asian twist. Vary your choice of seasonal vegetables (if they cook relatively quickly, such as snow peas, sugar snap peas, or green beans, add them during the last 5 to 10 minutes of cooking).

6 servings

1 cup sweet and sour sauce
½ cup chili sauce
3 pounds beef brisket, first cut,
    trimmed of all visible fat
salt and freshly ground black pepper
2 teaspoons olive oil
¼ cup rice wine vinegar
¼ cup water

2 tablespoons brown sugar
4 small turnips (about 1 pound),
    peeled
2 medium parsnips (about
    10 ounces), peeled
4 medium carrots (about
    14 ounces), peeled

Combine the sweet and sour sauce and chili sauce in a small baking dish. Coat the brisket with the marinade, cover, and refrigerate overnight.

Preheat the oven to 350°F.

Wipe the marinade from the brisket and season with salt and pepper to taste.

Heat the oil in a large heavy flameproof casserole. Add the brisket to the pan and brown on both sides over medium-high heat. Transfer the brisket to a plate and add the vinegar, water, and brown sugar to the casserole, scraping with a wooden spoon to dissolve any particles on the bottom. Remove from the heat and return the brisket, along with any juices that have accumulated, to the casserole. Cover tightly and roast for 1 hour. Remove the casserole from the oven and surround the brisket with the turnips, parsnips, and carrots. Cover and continue roasting for another 2 hours, until fork-tender, basting 2 to 3 times with the released juices.

Remove the casserole from the oven and place the brisket on a cutting board. Cut it at an angle into ½-inch-thick slices. Place the slices on a serving platter so that they are slightly overlapping and resemble the original shape of the brisket.

Season the juices and vegetables in the casserole with salt and pepper. Quarter the turnips and slice the carrots and parsnips. Place them around the brisket. Spoon the juices over the meat and vegetables and serve.

- First-cut brisket is very lean, containing less than 2.5 grams of fat per ounce. Cook it slowly, covered, and it will become moist and delicious.
- Beef is a potentially good source of selenium.
- Carrots contribute substantial vitamin A: each serving provides more than 150 percent of the DV.
- Turnips and parsnips contribute more than 30 percent of the DV for vitamin C per serving. Like broccoli and cabbage, turnips contain glucosinolates, which may boost enzymes that fight cancer.
- A good source of fiber

PER SERVING

calories	protein	carbohydrates	fat	cholesterol	dietary fiber	saturated fat
490	41 g	47 g	15 g	122 mg	3 g	5 g

% OF CALORIES: 38% carbohydrate, 34% protein, 28% fat

MAJOR SOURCES OF POTENTIAL CANCER FIGHTERS

Phytochemicals: glucosinolates, plant polyphenols (flavonoids, phenolic acids), plant sterols, terpenes (carotenoids, monoterpenes)

Roman-Style Braised Beef and Vegetables over Polenta (*Stracotto alla Romana con Polenta*)

Giuseppe Lattanzi, Va Bene, New York City

This ragu, or thick meat sauce, is heavenly over polenta. Giuseppe also suggests serving it as a flavorful topping for fettuccine.

6 servings

Stracotto

2 pounds boneless beef round or shoulder, trimmed of all fat and cut into 2-inch cubes

salt and freshly ground black pepper

1 tablespoon extra-virgin olive oil

4 celery ribs (about 7 ounces), chopped

3 medium carrots (about 10 ounces), peeled and sliced ½ inch thick

1 medium white onion (about 6 ounces), chopped

4 bay leaves

2 tablespoons flour

1 cup dry white wine

1 28-ounce can tomato puree

¾ cup water

Polenta

3 cups White Chicken Stock or Brown Chicken Stock (see Index), low-sodium canned broth, or water

½ teaspoon salt

1 tablespoon olive oil

1 cup stone-ground yellow cornmeal

Season the meat with salt and pepper to taste. In a large heavy saucepan or Dutch oven, heat the olive oil over medium-high heat. When almost smoking, add half of the seasoned meat and sear over high heat until browned on all sides (you will get better browning by dividing the meat into 2 batches). Remove the meat and reserve on a large plate. Repeat the process with the second batch.

Add the celery, carrots, onion, and bay leaves to the saucepan and cook over medium-high heat, stirring frequently, until they become somewhat soft and are well browned, 8 to 10 minutes. Sprinkle the flour over the vegetables and stir until there are no lumps and the flour is no longer visible. Add the wine, stirring constantly, and cook over high heat for 2 to 3 minutes, then add the tomato puree, water, and meat (and any juices that have been released on the plate) to the saucepan. Cook, covered, over medium-low heat for 2 hours; the meat should be very tender, breaking apart when pressed between 2 fingers. Add salt and pepper to taste.

During the last 30 minutes of cooking, prepare the polenta. In a heavy 2-quart saucepan, combine the stock, salt, and olive oil and bring to a simmer. Slowly add the cornmeal, whisking constantly. Lower the heat and continue stirring with a wooden spoon until the mixture thickens and begins to pull away from the sides of the pan, about 25 minutes.

Divide the polenta among 6 shallow soup bowls and spoon the beef over the top.

- Trimmed beef round is one of the leanest cuts of beef, containing only about 2 grams of fat per ounce (similar to chicken and some types of fish). A higher ratio of the fat is saturated, so moderate how much lean beef you eat. When eaten braised or in a stew, portion sizes tend to be less than when steaks or filets are prepared.
- Moderate intake of lean meat and fish is a good way to get selenium.
- Each serving provides more than 130 percent of the DV for vitamin A and 30 percent for vitamin C.
- High in fiber—more than 30 percent of the DV per serving

PER SERVING OF POLENTA

calories	protein	carbohydrates	fat	cholesterol	dietary fiber	saturated fat
90	2 g	16 g	3 g	0 mg	2 g	0 g

PER SERVING OF STRACOTTO ALLA ROMANA

calories	protein	carbohydrates	fat	cholesterol	dietary fiber	saturated fat
380	42 g	20 g	14 g	73 mg	4 g	4 g

PER SERVING OF ROMAN-STYLE BRAISED BEEF AND VEGETABLES OVER POLENTA

calories	protein	carbohydrates	fat	cholesterol	dietary fiber	saturated fat
470	44 g	36 g	17 g	73 mg	6 g	4 g

% OF CALORIES: 31% carbohydrate, 32% protein, 31% fat, 6% alcohol

MAJOR SOURCES OF POTENTIAL CANCER FIGHTERS

Phytochemicals: allium compounds, plant polyphenols (flavonoids, phenolic acids), plant sterols, terpenes (carotenoids)

BREADS AND DESSERTS

❧ WHOLE WHEAT ROSEMARY ROLLS

Laura Pensiero, R.D., co-owner, Gigi Trattoria, Rhinebeck, New York; nutritionist, Strang Cancer Prevention Center

Serve these fragrant rolls with hearty stews or grilled or roasted chicken or lean pork. They're also great as bread for small sandwiches, such as smoked turkey with a fruit chutney.

24 rolls

1½ ¼-ounce envelopes active dry yeast	3 tablespoons chopped fresh rosemary or 1 tablespoon dried rosemary
3 cups lukewarm water	5 cups whole wheat flour
¼ cup olive oil	2½ cups all-purpose flour
¼ cup honey	1 tablespoon plus 1 teaspoon salt

In a large mixing bowl, stir the yeast into ½ cup of the warm water; let stand until frothy and creamy, about 8 minutes. Stir in the remaining water, the oil, honey, and rosemary. Gradually add the flours and salt to the yeast mixture. Work the ingredients together, then remove the dough from the bowl and place on a work surface lightly dusted with flour. Knead for 10 minutes, until the dough is smooth and springs back when pressed gently.

Place the dough in a lightly greased bowl, cover tightly with plastic wrap, and let rise in a warm (but not hot) place until doubled in size, about 1 hour.

Punch down the dough and shape into 24 rolls, placing them under a clean cloth as they are made to prevent them from drying out. Place the rolls about ½ inch apart on a lightly oiled baking pan. Place a towel over the rolls and let them rise again until almost doubled in size, 20 to 30 minutes.

Preheat the oven to 400°F. Bake the rolls on the middle rack of the oven for 20 to 25 minutes. They should be browned lightly. Let cool slightly on a wire rack. Break the rolls apart and serve warm or at room temperature.

- Carnosol, a phytochemical in rosemary, is a potent antioxidant and may also help increase cancer-fighting enzymes in the body.
- Whole grains, as well as some types of beans and seeds, contain phytic acids, phytochemicals that may help reduce oxidative damage to the body.
- A good source of fiber

PER ROLL

calories	protein	carbohydrates	fat	cholesterol	dietary fiber	saturated fat
155	5 g	28 g	3 g	0 mg	4 g	1 g

% OF CALORIES: 72% carbohydrate, 12% protein, 16% fat

MAJOR SOURCES OF POTENTIAL CANCER FIGHTERS

Phytochemicals: phytic acids, plant polyphenols (flavonoids), protease inhibitors, terpenes (carnosol)

SUNFLOWER AND FLAXSEED BREAD

Laura Pensiero, R.D., co-owner, Gigi Trattoria, Rhinebeck, New York; nutritionist, Strang Cancer Prevention Center

---

The combination of flaxseeds and sunflower seeds gives this whole wheat bread a rich, nutty flavor.

Flaxseed has been part of the human diet for more than 5,000 years, and it has numerous nutritional benefits. It can be used whole in breads, muffins, and cookies or ground in yeast or quick breads, cereals, waffles, cookies, and crackers.

---

2 large loaves

2 ¼-ounce envelopes active dry yeast

3 cups lukewarm water

1 cup ground flaxseed (ground in a clean coffee grinder or small food processor)

2 tablespoons flaxseed oil, olive oil, or canola oil

¼ cup honey

1 tablespoon salt

½ cup sunflower seeds

4 cups whole wheat flour

3½ to 4 cups all-purpose flour

In a large bowl, dissolve the yeast in ½ cup of the warm water and let stand until frothy, about 10 minutes. Add the remaining water, ground flaxseed, oil, honey, and salt and beat until smooth. Add the sunflower seeds and whole wheat flour and beat again, then gradually work in the all-purpose flour. Turn the dough out onto a flat surface dusted with flour and knead for 8 to 10 minutes, until it springs back when pressed gently.

Place the dough in a large lightly greased bowl, cover tightly with plastic wrap, and let rise in a warm (but not hot) place until doubled in size, 30 to 40 minutes. Preheat the oven to 375°F.

Punch down the dough. Divide in half, shape into 2 long, wide loaves, and place on a lightly greased baking sheet or into 2 lightly sprayed 9- × 5-inch loaf pans. Cover with a clean towel and let rise for about 30 minutes.

Bake for about 40 minutes, until lightly browned. The loaves should sound hollow when tapped on the bottom.

- Flaxseed is a terrific source of protective omega-3 fatty acids. It is also high in protein and fiber.
- Sunflower seeds are a potentially good source of selenium.
- Both sunflower seeds and flaxseeds contain isoflavones, phytoestrogens that may lower the risk of certain types of cancer.
- Whole grains, as well as some types of beans and seeds, contain phytic acids, phytochemicals that may help reduce oxidative damage to the body.

PER SERVING (1-INCH SLICE)

calories	protein	carbohydrates	fat	cholesterol	dietary fiber	saturated fat
167	5 g	28 g	4 g	0 mg	4 g	<1 g

% OF CALORIES: 66% carbohydrate, 13% protein, 21% fat

MAJOR SOURCES OF POTENTIAL CANCER FIGHTERS

Phytochemicals: phytic acids, plant polyphenols (isoflavones), plant sterols, protease inhibitors

🌿 SKILLET JALAPEÑO CORN BREAD

Laura Pensiero, R.D., co-owner, Gigi Trattoria, Rhinebeck, New York; nutritionist, Strang Cancer Prevention Center

This tasty quick bread can be made in less than 30 minutes and is the perfect side dish for Robert McGrath's Green Chile Stew or Zarela Martínez's Summer Vegetables in a Creamy Chile Cheese Sauce (see Index) or any other zesty entrée.

Use small nonstick loaf pans or a nonstick muffin pan to make individual corn breads.

10 servings

1 cup all-purpose flour
1 cup yellow cornmeal
¾ teaspoon salt
¼ teaspoon cayenne pepper
2 teaspoons baking powder
½ teaspoon baking soda
1 cup buttermilk
1 large egg

¼ cup olive oil, plus ½ teaspoon for the pan (or use olive oil cooking spray)
2 tablespoons sugar
1 cup canned creamed corn
1 4-ounce can chopped green chiles, undrained

Preheat the oven to 400°F.

In a large bowl, sift together the flour, cornmeal, salt, cayenne, baking powder, and baking soda. In a separate bowl, beat together the buttermilk, egg, ¼ cup olive oil, and sugar, then stir in the creamed corn and chopped chiles and their liquid. Add to the dry ingredients and mix until just combined.

Oil a well-seasoned cast-iron or nonstick skillet and heat on the stove until moderately hot. Add the batter and spread out evenly. Transfer to the oven and bake for 35 to 40 minutes. When a toothpick inserted in the center comes out clean, the corn bread is done. Let cool slightly, then cut into 10 wedges.

- Although corn does not contain substantial amounts of vitamins, it derives its color from the carotenoid lutein, a potent antioxidant.
- Chile peppers contain capsaicin, a phytochemical that may help neutralize carcinogens.

PER SERVING (1-INCH SLICE)

calories	protein	carbohydrates	fat	cholesterol	dietary fiber	saturated fat
178	4 g	27 g	6 g	22 mg	2 g	1 g

% OF CALORIES: 61% carbohydrate, 9% protein, 30% fat

MAJOR SOURCES OF POTENTIAL CANCER FIGHTERS

Phytochemicals: capsaicin, terpenes (carotenoids, monoterpenes)

WALNUT-RAISIN BREAD

Laura Pensiero, R.D., co-owner, Gigi Trattoria, Rhinebeck, New York; nutritionist, Strang Cancer Prevention Center

This bread has a crisp crust and a tender center. Its nutty flavor marries well with cheese or can stand alone as a breakfast bread. Also, try using it for a sandwich of fresh roast turkey, fresh watercress, and a small amount of a soft cheese, such as Brie.

2 loaves

3 cups warm water
1 ¼-ounce envelope active dry yeast
4 cups whole wheat flour
1 tablespoon plus 1 teaspoon salt
¼ cup honey

¼ cup walnut oil
2 tablespoons olive oil
1 cup crushed walnuts
¾ cup raisins
2½ cups all-purpose flour

In a small bowl, combine ½ cup of the water with the yeast. Stir lightly to combine and let sit for 5 minutes.

In a mixer or mixing bowl, combine the whole wheat flour and salt. Make a small well in the center by pushing the flour to the sides. Pour the yeast, remaining water, honey, and walnut and olive oils into the center; mix. Add the walnuts, raisins, and 1 cup of the all-purpose flour and mix. Add the remaining all-purpose flour, ⅓ cup at a time, working the dough together; it should be moist and slightly sticky.

Place the dough on a work surface dusted lightly with flour and knead for 8 minutes, until the dough is soft and elastic (add more flour only if the dough is very sticky).

Place the dough in a large, lightly greased bowl, cover tightly with plastic wrap, and let rise in a warm (but not hot) place until doubled in size, about 1½ hours.

Punch down the dough and shape into 2 oval loaves. Line a baking sheet with parchment paper sprayed lightly with cooking spray. Place the loaves on the baking sheet and let rise until almost doubled in size, about 40 minutes.

Preheat the oven to 375°F. Bake the loaves on the middle oven rack for 40 to 45 minutes, rotating the pan midway through baking; the bread should be browned lightly. Lift off the baking sheet; the loaves should sound hollow when tapped on the bottom.

- Walnuts and raisins contain phenolic acids, which may act as antioxidants and blocking agents against cancer-causing substances. Walnuts and their extracted oil are also a terrific source of protective omega-3 fatty acids and plant sterols.
- Whole grains, as well as some types of beans and seeds, contain phytic acids, phytochemicals that may help reduce oxidative damage to the body.

PER SERVING (½-INCH SLICE)

calories	protein	carbohydrates	fat	cholesterol	dietary fiber	saturated fat
161	5 g	25 g	5 g	0 mg	3 g	1 g

% OF CALORIES: 60% carbohydrate, 11% protein, 29% fat

MAJOR SOURCES OF POTENTIAL CANCER FIGHTERS

Phytochemicals: phytic acids, plant polyphenols (phenolic acids), plant sterols, protease inhibitors

CRANBERRY PECAN BUNDT CAKE

The International Olive Oil Council

Typically, a Bundt cake is made with 2 sticks of butter and 4 eggs, making it a high-cholesterol, high–saturated fat indulgence. This olive oil version has only 20 percent of the cholesterol and less than half of the saturated fat.

14 servings

2½ cups unsifted cake flour

1 tablespoon baking powder

1 teaspoon ground cinnamon

½ teaspoon salt

¼ teaspoon ground cloves

2 large eggs

4 large egg whites

1¾ cups granulated sugar

1¼ cups light olive oil

1 teaspoon vanilla extract

1 cup chopped pecans

¾ cup dried cranberries or other dried fruit, such as chopped figs, prunes, or apricots

1 tablespoon grated orange zest

2 tablespoons confectioners' sugar

Preheat the oven to 325°F. Spray a 10-inch tube or Bundt pan with nonstick cooking spray, then dust with flour. Set aside.

In a medium bowl, sift together the flour, baking powder, cinnamon, salt, and cloves. Set aside. In a large bowl, with an electric mixer on medium speed, beat together the whole eggs, 2 of the egg whites, and the sugar until thick and well blended, about 3 minutes. Reduce the speed to low and gradually add the olive oil. Add the vanilla extract and beat on high for 2 minutes.

Clean and dry the beater(s) of the electric mixer. In a medium bowl, beat the remaining 2 egg whites until soft peaks form. Set aside.

Stir the pecans, dried cranberries, and orange zest into the sugar mixture. Fold the flour mixture into the sugar mixture until just combined. Gently fold the beaten egg whites into the batter. Spoon the batter into the prepared pan. Bake for 30 minutes, then reduce the oven temperature to 300°F and bake for an additional 40 to 45 minutes or until a cake tester inserted in the center comes out clean.

Cool the cake in the pan for 15 minutes. Turn the cake out and cool completely on a wire rack. Transfer the cake to a serving plate and dust with confectioners' sugar.

- Of the total amount of fat, more than 85 percent is protective monounsaturated fat.
- Cranberries contain ellagic acid, a phytochemical that may help boost enzymes that rid the body of cancer-causing substances.
- The peel of citrus (or zest) contains limonene, a phytochemical that may help your body dispose of carcinogens.

PER SERVING

calories	protein	carbohydrates	fat	cholesterol	dietary fiber	saturated fat
409	4 g	43 g	25 g	30 mg	1 g	3 g

% OF CALORIES: 42% carbohydrate, 4% protein, 54% fat

MAJOR SOURCES OF POTENTIAL CANCER FIGHTERS

Phytochemicals: phytic acids, plant polyphenols (flavonoids, phenolic acids), plant sterols, terpenes (monoterpenes, limonene)

LEMON SEMOLINA CAKE

The International Olive Oil Council

Moist and flavorful, this easy-to-prepare cake can be served as a breakfast or tea cake or as a dessert topped with fresh berries.

10 servings

CAKE
2 cups semolina flour or farina
2 cups plain low-fat yogurt
1½ cups granulated sugar
1½ teaspoons baking powder
zest of 1 lemon
6 tablespoons light olive oil
½ cup walnut halves

SYRUP
1 cup granulated sugar
1 cup water
2 teaspoons fresh lemon juice
1 teaspoon grated lemon zest

To make the cake, preheat the oven to 350°F. In a large bowl, combine the flour, yogurt, sugar, baking powder, and zest; mix with a wooden spoon or spatula. Do not use a mixer. Add the olive oil and mix well.

Oil a 12-inch springform pan and pour in the batter. With a table knife, cut about ½ inch into the batter and make 10 to 12 diamond shapes or squares. (The marks will not remain completely visible before baking, but when removed from the oven the cake will be scored.) Arrange a walnut half in the center of each square or diamond shape.

Bake in the preheated oven for about 45 minutes, until golden. Remove the cake from the oven and let cool slightly.

To make the syrup, in a small saucepan, combine all the ingredients. Bring to a boil, reduce the heat, and boil gently until the mixture becomes a fairly thick syrup, about 215°F on a candy thermometer.

Using a sharp paring knife, cut through the scored portions of the cake about 2 inches deep, constantly wiping the knife clean with a kitchen towel. Pour the hot syrup onto the hot cake in the pan. Serve from the pan.

- Of the total amount of fat, more than 65 percent is from protective monounsaturated fat.
- Walnuts contain phenolic acids that act as antioxidants and help rid the body of carcinogens.
- The peel of citrus (or zest) contains limonene, a phytochemical that may help your body to dispose of carcinogens.

PER SERVING

calories	protein	carbohydrates	fat	cholesterol	dietary fiber	saturated fat
447	8 g	77 g	13 g	2 mg	1 g	2 g

% OF CALORIES: 68% carbohydrate, 7% protein, 25% fat

MAJOR SOURCES OF POTENTIAL CANCER FIGHTERS

Phytochemicals: phytic acids, plant polyphenols (phenolic acids), plant sterols, terpenes (monoterpenes, limonene)

🍇 WARM MANGO AND PEAR SOUP WITH FRUIT SORBETS

Charlie Trotter, Charlie Trotter's, Chicago, Illinois

4 servings

MANGO AND PEAR SOUP

1 pound ripe mangoes (about
2 small), peeled, pitted, and
chopped coarse
½ cup ripe pear, peeled, cored,
and diced

¼ cup diced pineapple
2 cups water
¼ cup sugar

FRUIT SORBETS

½ cup diced pear
½ cup diced strawberries
2 tablespoons diced mango
½ cup melon sorbet, store-bought
or homemade (recipe follows)

½ cup banana sorbet, store-bought
or homemade (recipe follows)
½ cup lemon sorbet, store-bought
or homemade (recipe follows)

To make the mango and pear soup, bring the mangoes, pear, pineapple, water, and sugar to a boil. Remove from the heat and let cool for 30 minutes. Puree in a food processor or blender and strain through a fine-mesh strainer into a bowl. Warm just before serving.

To make the fruit sorbets, in a medium bowl, combine the diced pear, strawberries, and mango. Spoon a small mound of the mixed fruit into each bowl. Place a small scoop of each sorbet on the mound of fruit. Pour some of the warmed mango and pear soup over the sorbets in each bowl.

CHEF TROTTER'S BASIC FRUIT SORBET *(4 servings)*

1 cup water
½ cup sugar
2 cups peeled, pitted or seeded, and
diced fruit, such as pear, melon,
strawberries, mango, peach,
raspberries, passion fruit, lemon,
or banana

fresh lemon juice as needed

Combine the water and sugar in a saucepan. Simmer, stirring occasionally, until the sugar dissolves. You should have ½ cup simple syrup. Add the fruit and cook for another minute. Let cool slightly, and then puree the fruit-syrup mixture in a blender or food processor. Taste the fruit syrup and add a touch of lemon juice if necessary to balance the sweetness. Place in an ice cream maker and follow the manufacturer's instructions. The sorbet will keep in the freezer for 3 days.

- Strawberries, mango, and pineapple are all terrific sources of vitamin C—one serving of this delicious dessert provides more than 75 percent of the DV.
- Mangoes' sweet, juicy orange flesh is rich in beta-carotene.
- A good source of fiber

PER SERVING

calories	protein	carbohydrates	fat	cholesterol	dietary fiber	saturated fat
238	1 g	60 g	<1 g	0 mg	3 g	0 g

% OF CALORIES: 97% carbohydrate, 1% protein, 2% fat

MAJOR SOURCES OF POTENTIAL CANCER FIGHTERS

Phytochemicals: plant polyphenols (flavonoids, phenolic acids), terpenes (carotenoids)

STRAWBERRY SOUP

Dieter Schorner, master pastry chef, faculty/chef-instructor, the Culinary Institute of America, Hyde Park, New York

An easy and light summer dessert.

6 servings

3 cups strawberries (about 1 pound), cleaned and trimmed
2½ cups fresh orange juice
¼ cup Grand Marnier

3 tablespoons sugar
½ cup low-fat sour cream
sliced strawberries and fresh mint leaves for garnish

Place 6 bowls in the refrigerator to chill.

Rinse and drain the berries. In a food processor, puree the strawberries with 1 cup of the orange juice until smooth. Transfer the puree to a large bowl and whisk in the remaining ingredients except the garnish, including the remaining orange juice. Cover and refrigerate for at least 1 hour.

To serve, divide the soup among the chilled bowls and garnish with sliced strawberries and mint leaves.

■ Strawberries contain more vitamin C than any other member of the berry family—½ cup provides 70% of the DV.

PER SERVING

calories	protein	carbohydrates	fat	cholesterol	dietary fiber	saturated fat
124	2 g	26 g	<1 g	0 mg	2 g	0 g

% OF CALORIES: 83% carbohydrate, 6% protein, 3% fat, 8% alcohol

MAJOR SOURCES OF POTENTIAL CANCER FIGHTERS

Phytochemicals: plant polyphenols (flavonoids, phenolic acids), terpenes (carotenoids, monoterpenes)

❧ PUMPKIN–ARBORIO RICE PUDDING

Laura Pensiero, R.D., co-owner, Gigi Trattoria, Rhinebeck, New York; nutritionist, Strang Cancer Prevention Center

When stirred during cooking, Italian Arborio rice releases starch, giving it a creamy consistency that is perfect for this low-fat version of rice pudding.

4 to 6 servings

1 quart milk or soy or rice milk
⅓ cup packed brown sugar
1½ teaspoons vanilla extract
1 3-inch (approximately) cinnamon stick or ¼ teaspoon ground cinnamon

dash of ground cloves
1 cup Italian Arborio rice
1 cup unsweetened canned pumpkin puree
⅓ cup raisins

Heat the milk with the brown sugar, vanilla, cinnamon stick, and cloves. When the mixture begins to steam, add the rice and bring to a boil, stirring constantly. Reduce the heat to simmer and cook, stirring often, for 15 minutes. Add the pumpkin puree and raisins and continue cooking, stirring constantly, until the rice is tender and the mixture is creamy, about 5 minutes. Transfer to dessert bowls and serve warm or chilled.

■ Pumpkin is rich in beta-carotene and provides 100 percent of the DV for vitamin A per serving.

PER SERVING (BASED ON 6 SERVINGS)

calories	protein	carbohydrates	fat	cholesterol	dietary fiber	saturated fat
270	5 g	62 g	0 g	0 mg	2 g	0 g

% OF CALORIES: 92% carbohydrate, 8% protein, 0% fat

MAJOR SOURCES OF POTENTIAL CANCER FIGHTERS

Phytochemicals: phytic acids, plant polyphenols (flavonoids, isoflavones), plant sterols, protease inhibitors, terpenes (carotenoids, triterpenes)

🌿 PEACH AND BLUEBERRY CRISP

Laura Pensiero, R.D., co-owner, Gigi Trattoria, Rhinebeck, New York; nutritionist, Strang Cancer Prevention Center

The key to flavor in this easy-to-prepare dessert is using perfectly ripe fruit. Other delicious seasonal combinations include strawberry and rhubarb; apple, walnut, and raisin; mango, apple, and grated ginger.

Try it topped with vanilla frozen yogurt.

6 servings

6 medium peaches, peeled, pitted, and cut into large chunks
2 cups blueberries, rinsed and drained
¼ cup plus 1 tablespoon all-purpose flour
⅓ cup granulated sugar
juice of ½ lemon
½ cup quick-cooking oatmeal
¼ cup packed brown sugar
½ teaspoon ground cinnamon
2 tablespoons melted unsalted butter

Preheat the oven to 375°F. Spray a baking dish or casserole (at least 6-cup capacity) with a canola-oil cooking spray or lightly rub with canola oil.

In a medium bowl, combine the peaches, blueberries, 1 tablespoon of the flour, the granulated sugar, and the lemon juice. Toss with your hands to combine thoroughly. Spread the fruit out in the baking pan.

In a separate bowl, prepare the topping. Mix together the oatmeal, remaining ¼ cup flour, the brown sugar, and the cinnamon. Drizzle with the melted butter, and then rub the topping together between your hands until it resembles a coarse meal. Evenly spread the topping over the fruit and bake for 35 minutes or until the fruit is bubbling and the topping is browned lightly. Remove and let cool slightly. Serve warm or at room temperature.

- Peaches derive their orange color from beta-carotene. They also contain substantial amounts of vitamin C: combined with blueberries, they provide more than 20 percent of the DV per serving.
- Blueberries contain ellagic acid, a phytochemical that may help boost enzymes that rid the body of cancer-causing substances.
- A good source of fiber

PER SERVING

calories	protein	carbohydrates	fat	cholesterol	dietary fiber	saturated fat
261	3 g	49 g	6 g	5 mg	4 g	3 g

% OF CALORIES: 75% carbohydrate, 4% protein, 21% fat

MAJOR SOURCES OF POTENTIAL CANCER FIGHTERS

Phytochemicals: plant polyphenols (flavonoids, phenolic acids), terpenes (carotenoids)

❧ LOW-FAT CHOCOLATE SOUFFLÉ

Laura Pensiero, R.D., co-owner, Gigi Trattoria, Rhinebeck, New York; nutritionist, Strang Cancer Prevention Center

A delicious low-calorie, low-fat "fix" for chocolate lovers and an impressive low-fat dessert for guests. Serve with fresh raspberries, strawberry slices, or Raspberry Sauce (see Index).

8 servings

Soufflé Base
¾ cup plus 2 tablespoons 1% milk
1 tablespoon plus 1 teaspoon
   all-purpose flour
½ teaspoon vanilla extract

1 large egg
3 tablespoons sugar
2 ounces semisweet chocolate,
   cut into small pieces or grated

Soufflé Molds
cooking spray or ½ teaspoon
   melted unsalted butter

3 tablespoons sugar

Whipped Egg Whites
4 large egg whites

2 tablespoons sugar

To prepare the soufflé base, whisk ¼ cup of the milk with the flour in a small bowl, making sure no lumps remain. Place in a small heavy saucepan with the remaining milk and the vanilla and slowly bring to a boil, stirring frequently. Reduce the heat and simmer until the mixture thickens, 1 to 2 minutes.

In a small mixing bowl, beat the egg and sugar together until the mixture is pale yellow and the sugar is well incorporated. Add a small amount of the hot milk mixture (about 2 to 3 tablespoons) and whisk to combine. Add the egg mixture to the milk in the saucepan. Simmer over medium-low heat, stirring constantly. Cook for 1 to 2 minutes, until thick and creamy. Transfer to a large bowl and stir in the chocolate until melted. Set aside and let cool. (The soufflés can be made in advance up to this point.)

Preheat the oven to 400°F.

Spray 8 4-ounce soufflé molds (or ramekins) with a canola oil cooking spray or rub lightly with butter. Add the sugar to the first mold and tilt the mold to coat the bottom and sides evenly. Pour the remaining sugar into the next mold and repeat the process until all molds are dusted lightly with sugar.

To whip the egg whites, using an electric mixer, beat the egg whites to firm peaks and gradually add the sugar. Fold the egg whites into the chocolate until just combined. Do not beat.

Fill the soufflé molds three-quarters full and place on a baking pan. Bake for 9 to 10 minutes, until they have risen and spring back when touched. Serve in the mold or invert onto dessert plates and serve immediately.

PER SERVING

calories	protein	carbohydrates	fat	cholesterol	dietary fiber	saturated fat
113	4 g	19 g	3 g	27 mg	0 g	2 g

% OF CALORIES: 65% carbohydrate, 11% protein, 24% fat

MAJOR SOURCES OF POTENTIAL CANCER FIGHTERS

Phytochemicals: plant polyphenols (phenolic acids)

❧ CREAMY MOCHA AND RASPBERRY "PARFAIT"

Laura Pensiero, R.D., co-owner, Gigi Trattoria, Rhinebeck, New York; nutritionist, Strang Cancer Prevention Center

Tofu never tasted so good. The Mocha Mousse can be made in less than 5 minutes and served on its own, chilled. It can also be served in elegant dessert glasses with the Raspberry Sauce. Or thin the Raspberry Sauce with a touch more orange juice and use with Low-Fat Chocolate Soufflé (preceding recipe).

4 servings

MOCHA MOUSSE

2 10½-ounce containers Mori-Nu lite silken extra-firm tofu (available at natural foods stores and some supermarkets)

3 tablespoons maple syrup

¼ cup packed brown sugar

2 tablespoons Tia Maria or other coffee liqueur

⅓ cup plus 1 tablespoon good-quality unsweetened cocoa powder, such as Ghirardelli, Lindt, or Valrhona

2 teaspoons instant espresso powder

¼ teaspoon ground cinnamon

RASPBERRY SAUCE

2½ cups well-rinsed fresh or thawed frozen raspberries

⅓ cup fresh orange juice

juice of ½ lemon

2 tablespoons granulated sugar

GARNISH

½ cup raspberries	4 fresh mint leaves

To prepare the mousse, combine all the ingredients in the bowl of a food processor and puree until creamy, about 2 minutes. Transfer the mousse to a bowl, cover, and refrigerate.

To prepare the raspberry sauce, combine 1½ cups of the raspberries and the remaining ingredients in the bowl of a food processor and puree until smooth. Strain the raspberry sauce through a fine-mesh strainer (rubbing with a rubber spatula to work through the mesh) into a small bowl. Mix in the remaining 1 cup whole raspberries, cover, and refrigerate for about 15 minutes.

Spoon a 1-inch-deep layer of mousse into tall, narrow parfait glasses or small glass dessert bowls. Top with a layer of raspberry sauce. Repeat, ending with a layer of mousse. Chill for at least 20 minutes. Garnish with some whole raspberries and a mint leaf.

- This dessert is rich in the antioxidant vitamin C: each serving provides 40 percent of the DV.
- Like many other berries, raspberries contain ellagic acid, a phytochemical that may boost enzymes that help rid the body of cancer-causing substances.
- Tofu, the curd of soybean milk, contains numerous cancer-fighting phytochemicals, including protective isoflavones. Each serving provides 8 grams of soy protein.
- A good source of fiber

PER SERVING OF MOCHA MOUSSE

calories	protein	carbohydrates	fat	cholesterol	dietary fiber	saturated fat
133	8 g	20 g	2 g	0 mg	3 g	0 g

PER SERVING OF RASPBERRY SAUCE

calories	protein	carbohydrates	fat	cholesterol	dietary fiber	saturated fat
54	1 g	13 g	0 g	0 mg	0 g	0 g

PER SERVING OF CREAMY MOCHA AND RASPBERRY "PARFAIT"

calories	protein	carbohydrates	fat	cholesterol	dietary fiber	saturated fat
187	9 g	33 g	2 g	0 mg	3 g	0 g

% OF CALORIES: 66% carbohydrate, 17% protein, 12% fat, 5% alcohol

MAJOR SOURCES OF POTENTIAL CANCER FIGHTERS

Phytochemicals: phytic acids, plant polyphenols (isoflavones, flavonoids, phenolic acids), plant sterols, protease inhibitors, terpenes (carotenoids, triterpenes)

SCHAUM TORTE WITH APRICOT-BLUEBERRY COMPOTE

RoxSand Scocos, chef/owner, RoxSand's Restaurant & Bar, Phoenix, Arizona

This classic Austrian dessert can satisfy anyone's craving for sweets while still providing nutrients and sparing fat.

Both the baked meringue and fruit can be prepared one day in advance. Fresh seasonal berries or other fruit can replace the fruit compote.

4 servings

MERINGUE
⅓ cup shelled almonds
½ cup egg whites (3 large eggs)

⅛ teaspoon cream of tartar
¾ cup sugar

APRICOT-BLUEBERRY COMPOTE
2 tablespoons sugar
10 medium apricots (about
    14 ounces), pitted and cut into
    wedges, or ½ pound dried apricots
½ cup fragrant white wine, such as
    gewürztraminer, Riesling,
    sauvignon blanc

½ vanilla bean, split in half
    lengthwise
zest of 1 lemon, sliced into long,
    thick strips
1 cup fresh blueberries (about
    5 ounces)
¼ cup raisins

Place the almonds in a small nonstick skillet over medium-high heat. Cook, tossing or moving the nuts around the pan, until lightly toasted and fragrant, 3 to 5 minutes. Let cool slightly, and then grind in a spice grinder or food processor. Set aside.

Preheat the oven to 250°F.

Line a large baking sheet with a piece of parchment paper. Using a round or heart-shaped cookie cutter, trace 12 separate sketchings of the desired shape onto the paper, about 2 inches apart.

To prepare the meringue, in a dry mixing bowl, beat the egg whites with an electric mixer at low speed. Gradually increase the speed. When the whites are frothy, add the cream of tartar and continue beating. Gradually add the sugar and continue beating until the meringue stands in stiff, shiny (but not dry) peaks, another 3 to 4 minutes.

Fold the ground toasted almonds into the meringue. Transfer the meringue to a pastry bag fitted with a ½- to ¾-inch star or plain tip. Pipe the meringue onto the outlines on parchment paper, making the edges slightly higher than the center by adding an extra rotation. (If you do not have a pastry bag, dollop the meringue onto the paper, then use the back of a spoon to push the meringue away from the center toward the perimeter to form a shape with a rim.) Bake for 1 hour until they are firm and dry but not browned. Let them dry out in the oven as it cools. Gently peel the meringues from the paper (if they stick, they are not done and should be baked longer).

To prepare the fruit compote, heat the sugar in a medium nonstick skillet until it dissolves and begins to brown. Add the apricots and cook for 2 to 3 minutes in the bubbling sugar, then add the white wine, vanilla bean, and lemon zest. Bring to a simmer and cook, covered, for 5 minutes, pouring in a little water if it begins to dry out. Add the blueberries and raisins and simmer for another 2 to 3 minutes, until the fruit is tender. Remove the zest and let the compote cool slightly.

Spoon a small amount of fruit compote into a meringue shell, cover with another meringue, spoon more fruit over the top, and repeat one more time until you have 3 layers.

- Apricots get their orange color from beta-carotene: each serving provides 25 percent of the DV for vitamin A. Along with blueberries, they also provide more than 25 percent of the DV for vitamin C.
- A good source of fiber

PER SERVING

calories	protein	carbohydrates	fat	cholesterol	dietary fiber	saturated fat
367	7 g	70 g	6 g	0 mg	4 g	1 g

% OF CALORIES: 76% carbohydrate, 2% protein, 15% fat, 7% alcohol

Phytochemicals: plant polyphenols (flavonoids, phenolic acids), terpenes (carotenoids, limonene)

APPLE STRUDEL

Jacques Torres, master pastry chef/owner, Jacques Torres Chocolate, Brooklyn, New York; television host, "Chocolate with Jacques Torres" and "Passion for Dessert with Jacques Torres" (The Food Network); dean of pastry arts, the French Culinary Institute, New York City

Crispy and delicious like traditional German strudel, but with less than one-third of the fat and calories.

3 servings

2 tablespoons raisins
2 tablespoons rum
1 large apple, peeled, cored,
   and diced
2 tablespoons chopped walnuts
2 tablespoons granulated sugar
2 tablespoons finely ground
   unseasoned bread crumbs
2 teaspoons fresh lemon juice
¼ teaspoon ground cinnamon

½ vanilla bean, split lengthwise and
   seeds scraped out, or ½ teaspoon
   vanilla extract
zest of ½ lemon
2 phyllo sheets (see Notes)
1 tablespoon plus 1½ teaspoons
   melted unsalted butter
2 tablespoons plus 1½ teaspoons
   confectioners' sugar

Preheat the oven to 400°F.

Soak the raisins in the rum for 5 minutes to rehydrate them.

Place the apple in a mixing bowl with the nuts. Add the granulated sugar, bread crumbs, lemon juice, cinnamon, vanilla bean seeds, drained rum-soaked raisins, and lemon zest. Mix until well combined.

Spread 1 phyllo sheet onto a parchment-covered baking pan. Using a pastry brush, brush evenly with the butter. With a sifter, sprinkle about 1 tablespoon confectioners' sugar over the buttered phyllo sheet. Top with a second phyllo sheet, brush again with butter, and sprinkle with about 1 tablespoon of sifted confectioners' sugar.

Place the apple mixture in a lengthwise row 2 inches from the base of the phyllo rectangle and ending 2 inches from either end. Roll the phyllo dough around the apple mixture (away from you) until you have a long tube. Gently roll the strudel so that the seam end is on the bottom and loosely fold the ends under.

Brush the top of the strudel with butter and sprinkle with the remaining 1½ teaspoons confectioners' sugar. Bake for about 12 minutes, until golden brown. Let cool slightly. Slice into 3 even segments and serve.

NOTES: Phyllo dough can be purchased frozen at many supermarkets. Thaw overnight in the refrigerator before unrolling. Phyllo dough can dry out quickly, making it potentially difficult to work with. Do not remove phyllo from its wrapper until the apple filling is prepared and all equipment is ready. Always cover air-exposed phyllo dough with a slightly moistened clean towel.

- Both apples and walnuts contain phenolic acids, which may act as antioxidants, blocking agents against cancer-causing substances. Walnuts are also good plant sources of protective omega-3 fatty acids.
- Using the peel of citrus in baking is encouraged; it not only lends aroma and flavor but also contains limonene, a phytochemical that may help your body dispose of carcinogens.

PER SERVING

calories	protein	carbohydrates	fat	cholesterol	dietary fiber	saturated fat
242	3 g	34 g	9 g	7 mg	2 g	3 g

% OF CALORIES: 56% carbohydrate, 5% protein, 33% fat, 6% alcohol

MAJOR SOURCES OF POTENTIAL CANCER FIGHTERS

Phytochemicals: phytic acids, plant polyphenols (flavonoids, phenolic acids), plant sterols, terpenes (limonene)

Apple Cake (*Gâteau aux Pommes*)

Robert Bennett, pastry chef/owner, Miel Patisserie, Cherry Hill, New Jersey

---

Delicious, easy to prepare, and full of fruit. Serve warm or at room temperature; goes well with vanilla frozen yogurt.

This cake can be made with pears instead of apples.

---

8 servings

1 teaspoon unsalted butter
1½ cups plus 2 tablespoons
   all-purpose flour
1 cup plus 3 tablespoons sugar
½ teaspoon salt
1½ teaspoons baking powder
3 apples (about 1 pound), peeled,
   cored, and cut into cubes

1 teaspoon ground cinnamon
2 large eggs
¼ cup fresh orange juice
1¼ teaspoons vanilla extract
grated zest of 1 orange
½ cup canola oil

Preheat the oven to 350°F.

Prepare a 6-cup Bundt pan by rubbing it with butter, then sprinkling it with 2 tablespoons flour. Coat evenly, then shake out the excess flour.

In a medium bowl, sift together the remaining 1½ cups flour, 1 cup of the sugar, the salt, and the baking powder and reserve.

In another bowl, combine the apples, remaining 3 tablespoons sugar, and cinnamon and reserve.

In a large bowl, beat together the eggs, orange juice, vanilla, and orange zest with an electric mixer or by hand using a whisk, then pour in the oil and beat until well incorporated. Stir in the dry ingredients, mix, then fold in the apple mixture. Pour the batter into the prepared pan and bake for 1 hour and 5 minutes. Cool for 10 minutes, then invert onto a serving plate.

- Though apples do not contain substantial amounts of vitamins A or C, they are very good sources of fiber and contain protective plant polyphenols.
- Using the peel or zest of citrus in baking is encouraged; it not only lends aroma and flavor but also contains limonene, a phytochemical that may help your body dispose of carcinogens.
- A good source of fiber

PER SERVING

calories	protein	carbohydrates	fat	cholesterol	dietary fiber	saturated fat
296	6 g	45 g	10 g	43 mg	3 g	1 g

% OF CALORIES: 61% carbohydrates, 8% protein, 31% fat

MAJOR SOURCES OF POTENTIAL CANCER FIGHTERS

Phytochemicals: plant polyphenols (flavonoids, phenolic acids), plant sterols, terpenes (limonene)

RASPBERRY AND CHOCOLATE SOY PROTEIN SHAKE

Laura Pensiero, R.D., co-owner, Gigi Trattoria, Rhinebeck, New York; nutritionist, Strang Cancer Prevention Center

A high-protein, low-fat shake for breakfast on the run or a snack—of particular benefit for people who need to maximize their intake of calories and protein.

1 serving

½ cup low-fat raspberry yogurt (4 ounces), dairy or soy
1 cup 1% chocolate milk, dairy or soy
½ cup fresh or frozen raspberries (about 2 ounces)

2 tablespoons soy protein isolate (protein powder; available at natural foods stores)

Combine all ingredients in a blender and puree until the shake is very smooth.

- Each shake contains as much protein as 3 ounces of meat, fish, or poultry—as well as the protective phytochemicals found in soy.
- Raspberries are a good source of ellagic acid, a phytochemical that may help boost enzymes that rid the body of cancer-causing substances.
- High in fiber—20 percent of the DV

PER SERVING

calories	protein	carbohydrates	fat	cholesterol	dietary fiber	saturated fat
241	21 g	36 g	3 g	10 mg	6 g	0 g

% OF CALORIES: 33% carbohydrates, 56% protein, 11% fat

MAJOR SOURCES OF POTENTIAL CANCER FIGHTERS

Phytochemicals: phytic acids, plant polyphenols (flavonoids, isoflavones, phenolic acids), plant sterols, protease inhibitors, terpenes (carotenoids, triterpenes)

Skillet Sweet Potato Pie

Laura Pensiero, R.D., co-owner, Gigi Trattoria, Rhinebeck, New York; nutritionist, Strang Cancer Prevention Center

This deliciously spiced pie can be made with sweet potato or pumpkin puree and contains less than half the fat of traditional pumpkin pie.

8 servings

Filling

2 medium sweet potatoes or 1½ cups
    canned pumpkin puree
2 tablespoons flour
2 teaspoons ground cinnamon
½ teaspoon freshly grated nutmeg
½ teaspoon ground cloves

½ teaspoon ground ginger
¼ teaspoon salt
2 large eggs
½ cup granulated sugar
¼ cup brown sugar
1½ cups evaporated skim milk

CRUST

15 gingersnap cookies	1 tablespoon fresh orange juice
2 tablespoons melted unsalted butter	

Preheat the oven to 350°F.

Bake the sweet potatoes for 1 hour to 1 hour and 15 minutes, until tender when pierced with a knife. Remove from the oven and let them cool to room temperature. Peel away the skin from the potatoes and scoop the flesh into a medium bowl; beat until smooth. (You should have 1½ cups puree.) Set aside.

While the potatoes bake, prepare the crust. Place the gingersnaps in the bowl of a food processor and pulse until coarsely ground. Drizzle in the butter and orange juice and pulse again for 2 to 3 seconds, just to combine.

Spray a 10-inch nonstick skillet with cooking spray or rub with a small amount of canola oil. Transfer the crust to the skillet and evenly spread and press across the bottom to 1 inch up the sides. Place the skillet in the oven for 6 minutes. Remove and set aside.

In a large bowl, combine the flour, cinnamon, nutmeg, cloves, ginger, and salt. Stir to combine. Set aside. In a medium bowl, beat the eggs with the granulated and brown sugars until creamy. Beat in the sweet potato puree. Add the evaporated skim milk, mixing until smooth. Pour the liquid mixture into the bowl with the flour and spices and beat until combined thoroughly. Pour the pie mixture into the skillet with the prebaked crust and bake for 45 to 50 minutes, until set. Remove from the oven and let cool. Refrigerate for at least 2 hours before serving.

Remove the pie from the skillet by loosening the sides: gently run a rubber spatula between the edge of the pie and the skillet. Carefully slide the pie out of the skillet onto a serving plate.

- Sweet potatoes provide enough carotenoids to supply 110 percent of the DV for vitamin A. They also contain substantial amounts of vitamin C, providing more than 20 percent of the DV.
- Nutmeg contains monoterpenes, which may function as antioxidants and help boost cancer-fighting enzymes.

PER SERVING

calories	protein	carbohydrates	fat	cholesterol	dietary fiber	saturated fat
241	7 g	41g	5 g	63 mg	2 g	3 g

% OF CALORIES: 68% carbohydrate, 11% protein, 21% fat

MAJOR SOURCES OF POTENTIAL CANCER FIGHTERS

Phytochemicals: plant polyphenols (flavonoids), plant sterols, terpenes (carotenoids, monoterpenes, triterpenes)

Traditional Christmas Roll (*Bûche de Noël*)

Alain Sailhac, executive vice president and senior dean of studies, the French Culinary Institute, New York City

With delicious Italian meringue and fruit filling replacing buttercream frosting, the fat content of this traditional French Christmas dessert is very low.

12 servings

Sponge Cake
4 large egg yolks

½ cup sugar

4 large egg whites

½ cup plus 2 tablespoons flour, sifted

Filling
⅓ cup black currant jam

1 pint fresh raspberries

1 cup fresh strawberries

2 tablespoons sugar

Meringue
3 large egg whites

¾ cup sugar

1 teaspoon vanilla extract

To prepare the sponge cake, preheat the oven to 400°F. Line a 15¼- × 10½- × 1-inch baking sheet with parchment paper or wax paper (if using wax paper, dust it lightly with sugar).

In a large bowl, beat the egg yolks with 1 tablespoon of the sugar.

Using a kitchen mixer or a handheld electric mixer, whip the egg whites with ¼ cup of the remaining sugar until frothy and thickened. Gradually add the remaining sugar and whip until firm, glossy peaks form, about 5 minutes. Do not overbeat so that the peaks become dry. Fold the egg whites into the yolks using a rubber spatula. Fold the flour into the eggs to combine; do not beat.

Spread the cake batter out on the prepared baking sheet, rotating it so that the batter is spread evenly. Bake for 9 to 10 minutes, until the cake pulls away from the sides and springs back when touched.

Prepare the filling while the sponge cake bakes. Put all the ingredients in a medium nonstick skillet. Simmer until the berry mixture thickens, about 8 minutes. Remove from the heat and set aside.

Trim ¼ inch from all sides of the cake. While the sponge cake is still warm, carefully remove it from the pan (it will be easier to roll if filled while still warm). Peel away the parchment or wax paper and place the cake on a large clean baking sheet. Evenly spread the berry filling on the sponge cake and begin to roll it tightly, starting with a long side. Let cool.

To make the meringue, in a mixer, whip the egg whites with ¼ cup of the sugar. Gradually add the remaining sugar and whip until firm, glossy peaks form, about 5 minutes. At the last moment, add the vanilla extract. Transfer three-quarters of the meringue to a pastry bag fitted with a slanted tip.

Completely cover the cake with meringue by running long, even strips down the top, sides, and ends of the cake. Change to a round pastry tip and refill the pastry bag with the remaining meringue. Make decorative "mushrooms" on the cake by pressing the pastry bag once to form the "stem" and, without moving the bag, squeezing again to form the "cap." Scatter mushrooms on top of the cake.

Increase the oven temperature to 450°F and bake until the meringue is lightly browned, about 5 minutes. Watch it carefully so that it doesn't burn. Slice with a serrated knife and serve.

■ The berry fruit filling replaces the classic buttercream filling and provides vitamin C, as well as carotenoids and protective plant polyphenols.

PER SERVING

calories	protein	carbohydrates	fat	cholesterol	dietary fiber	saturated fat
360	4 g	75 g	2 g	75 mg	2 g	1 g

% OF CALORIES: 90% carbohydrate, 5% protein, 5% fat

MAJOR SOURCES OF POTENTIAL CANCER FIGHTERS

Phytochemicals: plant polyphenols (flavonoids, phenolic acids)

A Sample Week of Menus

The sample menus that follow show that a healthy diet need not be boring or difficult. It's possible to accommodate food preferences and availability, as well as lifestyle, and still follow recommendations to lower the risk of cancer and other diseases.

Here are a few guidelines for using the sample menus:

1. Keep in mind that these menus serve as flexible examples. Note the moderate portion sizes of high-protein foods, the use of soy products as an alternative protein source, the number of servings and variety of types of fruits and vegetables, the limited amounts of added fats (butter, oils, salad dressings, mayonnaise, and other high-fat spreads) and processed foods, and the use and variety of whole grains and legumes.

2. These menus provide the following daily *average* for nutrients:
   - 1,800 calories, 90 grams protein, 60 grams fat per day
   - % calories = 20% protein, 50% carbohydrate, 30% fat
   - 30 to 35 grams dietary fiber per day
   - 4 to 6 vegetable servings plus 2 to 3 fruit servings daily

3. If the calorie level of this plan is too much for you to maintain a healthy weight, adjust the portion sizes of all foods down proportionally. If you require more calories to maintain your desired body weight, try to boost calories with high-nutrient items, such as fruit, whole grains, and legumes, rather than meat, alcohol, and sweets.

4. With the exception of juice and milk, beverages are not included in sample menus. For some healthy drink ideas, check the Index.

5. These menus list serving sizes for adults. With minor adaptations in portion sizes, the menus are appropriate guides for teenagers and children, and unless medically contraindicated, fat intake can be more liberal. Soy products, such as soy milk and yogurt, are provided as options to milk and other dairy. While they have potentially cancer-fighting phytochemicals, low levels of fat, and no saturated fat, many do not contain the same amount of calcium, phosphorus, vitamin D, or B vitamins as their dairy counterparts; you will need to read labels to verify that your soy product selection contributes to your calcium and other needs. Check pages 84–86 to see what your daily calcium requirements are and for a list of selected calcium-rich foods.

6. If you don't care for a particular menu item, try to substitute a nutritionally similar item.

- Substitute tuna, bass, swordfish, or bluefish for the omega-3-rich salmon on the menu for Saturday's lunch.
- For high-protein items, substitute the equivalent amount of another lean protein source.
- When substituting fruits or vegetables, be sure you are selecting not only a vegetable you like but one that is nutrient rich. For example, if you are replacing broccoli, try to stick with the cruciferous family (broccoli, brussels sprouts, cabbage, cauliflower, turnips, rutabagas, collard greens, kale); replace an orange with another citrus fruit, such as a grapefruit.
- If you don't like yogurt, substitute any low-fat or nonfat dairy item.
- Replace one whole-grain breakfast cereal with another that is similar in amounts of fiber, fat, and sugar and look for the word *whole* with the name of the grain on the package or in the ingredient list (for a whole-grain cereal list, see page 55).
- For starches, such as pasta, an equivalent amount (weight) of potatoes, rice, whole grains, or legumes may be substituted. Try to make sure the substituted item does not have high amounts of added fat.

One Week of Menus for Cancer Prevention

Monday

Breakfast
3 small whole wheat pancakes or waffles
1 teaspoon butter or 2 teaspoons canola-based (trans-fat-free) spread
3 tablespoons pure maple syrup
½ cup sliced strawberries
½ cup orange juice

Lunch
Roast turkey sandwich (2 to 3 ounces turkey) on whole wheat bread with
    reduced-fat cheese (if desired), lettuce, tomato, and mustard
1 serving (5 ounces) Broccoli, Potato, and Tomato Salad (see Index)

Afternoon Snack
Small handful of Brazil nuts (about 3 tablespoons)

Dinner
Chicken Cacciatore (see Index)
1 whole wheat dinner roll
Tossed green salad with 2 tablespoons vinaigrette

Dessert or Evening Snack
½ cup fresh raspberries or any other seasonal berry
1 cup low-fat vanilla yogurt or soy-based yogurt

Tuesday

Breakfast
1 cup Cheerios or any other whole-grain cereal (hot or cold)
1 cup 1% milk or 1% soy milk
½ banana
¼ cup dried fruit

Lunch
1 serving Healthy Tuna Salad (see Index) on 2 slices rye bread with sliced
    tomato
Tossed green salad with 1 tablespoon vinaigrette

Afternoon Snack
Handful of low-fat whole wheat crackers
2 tablespoons peanut butter

Dinner
7 ounces cooked pasta with Tomato-Basil Sauce
1 serving Sautéed Spinach with Garlic (see Index)

Dessert or Evening Snack
1 Creamy Mocha and Raspberry "Parfait" (see Index)

Wednesday

Breakfast
½ cup calcium-fortified orange juice
1 poached egg
½ cup 1% cottage cheese

2 slices toasted whole wheat bread
½ pink grapefruit

Lunch
1 cup Black Bean Soup (see Index)
Grilled, poached, or roasted chicken breast sandwich (3 to 4 ounces chicken)
    on whole wheat bread with lettuce, tomato, and low-fat mayonnaise

Afternoon Snack
2 plums
1 handful sunflower seeds

Dinner
1 serving Cauliflower Soup (see Index)
1 turkey or veggie burger on whole wheat roll with lettuce, tomato, ketchup,
    and red onion
1 baked sweet potato

Dessert or Evening Snack
Strawberry Soup (see Index) with ½ cup low-fat vanilla yogurt scooped into
    the center

Thursday

Breakfast
1 cup Müesli or other whole-grain cereal (hot or cold)
1 cup 1% milk or 1% soy milk
½ cup fresh berries

Lunch
1 slice pizza
Tossed salad with lettuce, tomato, and shredded carrot (plus any other desired
    vegetable: broccoli, cucumber, fennel, peppers, etc.)
2 tablespoons vinaigrette
1 cup cubed cantaloupe

Afternoon Snack
1 peach
Small handful of almonds (about 3 tablespoons)

Quick Weeknight Dinner
1 Scrambled Egg Burrito (see Index)
1 cup steamed broccoli drizzled with 2 teaspoons extra-virgin olive oil
1 slice whole wheat toast

Dessert or Evening Snack
2 small oatmeal raisin cookies
1 cup 1% milk or 1% vanilla soy milk

Friday

Breakfast
1 cup oatmeal topped with 2 tablespoons toasted wheat germ
¼ cup raisins
½ banana
½ cup 1% milk or 1% soy milk

Lunch
1 piece skinless, roasted chicken breast (4 to 5 ounces)
½ cup corn kernels or 1 ear corn on the cob
Tossed salad with lettuce, tomato, and shredded carrot (plus any other desired
    vegetable: broccoli, cucumber, fennel, peppers, etc.) and 2 tablespoons
    vinaigrette
1 small whole wheat roll

Afternoon Snack
Small handful of nuts (peanuts, almonds, or walnuts)
1 pear

Japanese Dinner Out
1 serving miso soup
1 serving seaweed salad
2 California rolls
6 pieces sushi (2 tuna, 2 salmon, 2 shrimp)

Dessert or Evening Snack
½ cup green tea ice cream

Saturday

On-the-Go Breakfast
1 cup low-fat yogurt or soy yogurt topped with ½ cup low-fat granola
½ cup berries

Lunch
1 cup vegetable barley soup
1 serving Seared Salmon with Fresh Corn Relish (with or without relish; see Index)
Baby arugula tossed with 1 tablespoon vinaigrette

Afternoon Snack
⅓ cantaloupe
1 small handful almonds (about 3 tablespoons)

Dinner
1 serving Mexican Lasagna (see Index)
Baby greens tossed with 1 tablespoon vinaigrette

Evening Snack
1 serving Peach and Blueberry Crisp (see Index)
⅓ cup vanilla frozen yogurt

Sunday

Breakfast
2 soft-boiled eggs or 1 serving Herbed Vegetable and Parmesan Frittata (see Index)
2 slices whole-grain bread, toasted
1 teaspoon unsalted butter
½ cup 100% fruit juice

Lunch
Caesar salad with 2 tablespoons Caesar dressing (order dressing on the side if dining out), with up to 2 ounces skinless grilled chicken tenders, if desired

Dinner

1 serving Marinated Pork Tenderloin (see Index)

1 baked sweet potato or 1 serving Mashed Orange-Scented Sweet Potatoes (see Index)

1 serving Sweet and Sour Cabbage (see Index)

1 whole wheat dinner roll

Evening Snack

1 serving Apple Strudel (see Index)

Restaurant Dining

Since May 1997, restaurants, bakeries, and delis that make health claims or include nutritional descriptions on their menus must support these claims in compliance with the Nutrition Labeling and Education Act of 1990 (NLEA). Restaurants that include such claims as *low-fat*, *reduced-calorie*, *heart healthy*, and *fat-free* must be able to demonstrate that their menu assertions are consistent with the claim definitions established under NLEA. Unlike processed foods, restaurant menu selections are not required to supply complete nutrition information. Also unlike processed foods, menu items bearing a claim are not held to the same strict standards of laboratory analyses. Other, more economical methods can be used to meet the standard. For example, a restaurant could show that an item was designed to meet the requirements for the claim because it was prepared using a recipe from a recognized health professional association or dietary group or that the nutritional values for the dish were calculated using a reliable nutrition database.

Currently several states are considering legislation that would require fast-food restaurants to display nutrition information on their menu boards and sit-down chain restaurants (with more than ten locations) to present nutrition information, such as calories, fat, sodium, and specified nutrients, on their menus.

The nutrition information provided is only as good as it is accurate, and there are steps you can take to evaluate menu choices. Dining out does not need to be the downfall to an otherwise good day of healthy eating. Here are some general suggestions for menu selections to keep fruit and vegetable intake high and fat intake low.

1. Select menu items that are prepared in the following manner:
    * baked
    * braised

- broiled
- en papillote (sealed in paper or foil and cooked via steam, concentrating flavor)
- grilled
- poached
- roasted
- sautéed (request that minimal fat be used in cooking)
- seared
- steamed
- stewed

2. Consider menu items with these descriptions:
   - au jus (served in its own juices—often better than a stock-based sauce)
   - coulis (served with a strained fruit or vegetable sauce)
   - marinara (spicy tomato sauce that is usually moderate in fat)
   - pilaf (simple and healthy whether rice or another type of grain)
   - Provençal (cooked in the style of southwest France; will include any combination of the following: tomatoes, garlic, onions, capers, anchovies, olives, eggplant, olive oil, and fresh herbs, such as rosemary, thyme, marjoram, oregano, tarragon, or sage)
   - ragout (a classic thick, well-seasoned stew of meat or fish; many restaurants incorporate vegetables or prepare vegetable ragouts)
   - salsa (usually raw vegetables and/or fruits combined with a minimal amount of fat to form a topping, dip, or sauce)

3. Look for entrées served with vegetable accompaniments or select vegetable side dishes.

4. Limit selection of menu items that use these cooking methods:
   - barbecued (The sauce is not inherently unhealthy, but the types and cuts of meat that are typically cooked in this style are usually high in fat. If you know the barbecued item is lean, then it is OK.)
   - blackened
   - charbroiled
   - charcoal-grilled
   - deep-fried
   - fried
   - panfried
   - smoked

5. Limit menu items that have these descriptions:
   - amandine (often misspelled *almondine*; cooked in a style with almonds and usually a lot of butter as well)
   - au gratin
   - batter-dipped
   - béarnaise (a classic French sauce made with a reduction of wine, vinegar, shallots, and tarragon and finished with egg yolks and butter)
   - béchamel (a basic French white sauce made by stirring milk into equal parts of butter and flour)
   - beurre (includes butter, probably a lot of it)
   - breaded (unless oven-baked, the next step is frying; even if the breaded item is sautéed, the bread coating acts as a sponge for fat)
   - creamy (unless otherwise indicated as healthy)
   - crispy
   - croquette (whether made of potato or fish, these oval cylinders are usually deep-fried)
   - en croute (usually signifies food is wrapped in buttery puff pastry)
   - escalloped (a fractured version of the French *escalope*, which refers to a thin piece of meat, a scallop; *escalloped* usually signals a cooking style that includes a sauce for the scallops made of butter and cream)
   - flaky (usually butter or lard worked into flour, producing "flaky" results)
   - fritters (usually deep-fried; can be OK on a limited basis, especially if peanut or olive oil is used to fry)
   - hollandaise (a rich, buttery emulsion sauce typically served with egg dishes, fish, or vegetables)
   - Newburg (usually includes chopped shellfish, cream, eggs, and butter)
   - parmigiana (indicates use of Parmesan cheese, which is not necessarily a problem; however, food served *alla parmigiana* is also typically dredged in flour, eggs, and bread crumbs, then fried or sautéed in a lot of oil, and finally smothered in Parmesan and mozzarella cheese)
   - scampi (unless you request minimal butter and oil, expect a lot)

Here are some tips for ethnic menus. Keep in mind that the lists offer guidance, but they are not exhaustive. You are likely to encounter many foods that do not appear on these lists. In these situations, follow the general menu selection guidelines provided earlier.

Italian

Choose

almost anything made in a wood-burning oven: pizza, fish, meat, and especially vegetables

antipasti (healthy examples include roasted peppers, tomatoes, and bean salads)

cacciatore (usually chicken or fish and vegetables stewed in a tomato sauce)

calamari, sautéed or grilled

cioppino (tomato-based fish stew)

grilled or roasted chicken or fish, simply prepared

minestrone soup or other vegetable or bean soups

mussels served in a marinara or white wine sauce

pasta e fagioli (a flavorful bean and pasta soup)

pasta with clam sauce (request only a moderate amount of olive oil be used)

pasta with tomato and basil or marinara sauce

pasta with vegetables

risotto (This Italian rice with vegetables, fish, or meat can be a healthy balance of carbohydrates and protein as well as a good base for vegetables. The final step of preparation, when a substantial amount of butter or olive oil or Parmesan is stirred in, can be the downfall. Request that this step be omitted.)

vegetable-filled ravioli

vegetable side dishes

Limit or Avoid

alla carbonara (sauce includes eggs, cream, bacon, and Parmesan cheese)

alla parmigiana

cheese-filled baked pastas, such as manicotti, ziti, lasagna, or ravioli

fettuccine Alfredo and other pastas with cream

fried calamari

veal marsala (can be OK, but depends on sauce—often butter is used to emulsify sauce)

veal piccata (can be OK, but depends on sauce—often butter is used to emulsify sauce)

Asian (Japanese, Chinese, Thai)

CHOOSE
California rolls
chicken, shrimp, or vegetable chow mein
hot and sour soup
Hunan shrimp, chicken, or tofu
miso soup
rice, steamed brown or white
seaweed salads
shabu-shabu (beef cooked in a hot broth at the table; usually lean beef is sliced
    paper-thin, helping with portion control)
shrimp or chicken with garlic sauce
shrimp with vegetables
spiced beet salad
steamed or broiled fish
steamed vegetable dumplings
steamed vegetables with rice and side sauces, such as garlic, black bean,
    or brown
stir-fried vegetables or vegetable-chicken or vegetable-fish combinations
sushi hand rolls
sushi or sashimi
sweet and sour shrimp
Szechuan shrimp, chicken, or tofu
teriyaki chicken, fish, or beef with vegetables
Thai chicken
Thai salad
vegetable curries prepared without coconut milk
wonton soup
yakitori (a Japanese term meaning "grilled fowl"; usually small pieces of mari-
    nated chicken that are grilled)
yosenabe (a one-pot meal usually consisting of a combination of chicken, fish,
    shellfish, and vegetables in a broth)

LIMIT OR AVOID
chicken with cashews
coconut soups

curries or soups prepared with coconut milk

egg rolls

fried rice or anything that says *crispy* or *fried*

fried Thai rolls

fried tofu

General Tso's chicken

kung pao chicken

lo mein, beef, chicken, or pork

moo shu, beef or pork

noodles, sautéed or fried

Peking duck

sweet and sour pork

tempura

whole fried fish

Indian

CHOOSE

aam chatni (mango chutney)

aloo bhaji (braised potatoes, tomatoes, and spices)

aloo gobi (braised potatoes, cauliflower, onions, and spices)

aloo mattar gajar (spicy carrots, peas, and potatoes)

aloo paratha (potato-stuffed flatbread)

baingan bharta (roasted eggplant with spices)

basmati rice

chapati (whole wheat flatbread)

chicken or shrimp curry

curried or saffron rice

kachumber (tomato salad)

kali dal (spicy black lentils)

kheer ka raita (cucumber and mint salad)

massor dal (a red lentil stew)

murgh dhansak (chicken with vegetables and lentils)

rajma (translated as "royal beans," this traditional northern Indian dish is a
    combination of red beans, onions, garlic, tomatoes, and spices)

tandoori (select breads, chicken, and fish that have been cooked in the tandoori
    oven)

tomatar jingha (spicy shrimp cooked in tomatoes)
whole roasted fish

LIMIT OR AVOID
anything fried
anything with a cream sauce
anything with ghee (clarified butter)
keema mattar (spicy ground beef with peas)
keema paratha (meat-stuffed flatbread)
pakoras (vegetable fritters)
poori (fried puffed whole wheat bread)
pork, beef, or lamb curries
samosas (meat- or vegetable-filled pastries)

Mexican

CHOOSE
bean soups and salads
cactus salad (Nopalitos cactus, watercress, salad greens, cilantro, and
    vinaigrette)
chicken, seafood, or vegetable tacos (ask for soft tacos, which are not fried)
chicken or turkey mole
fajitas
frijoles (beans, pinto or black)
gazpacho
lime soup
Mexican rice
pan-seared, grilled, or whole-roasted fish served with salsa
pozole (spicy corn stew often containing beans, squash, chiles, and chunks of
    chicken, pork, or beef)
refried beans (prepared with minimal or no fat)
salads with jicama and oranges
vegetable, chicken, or shellfish burritos
vegetable chili

LIMIT OR AVOID
added cheese, guacamole, and sour cream
beef burritos
cheese quesadillas
chiles rellenos
chimichangas
enchiladas
flautas
nachos
taco salads with deep-fried baskets
tamales
tortilla chips (unless they are baked)
tostadas

Fast-Food and Franchise Restaurants

CHOOSE
baked beans or rice and beans
baked potatoes (select vegetable toppings and order other toppings, such as cheese, chili, or sour cream, on the side so that you can spoon on only a small amount)
broiled, grilled, or roasted chicken (skin removed) or fish
broth-based or bean soups made without pork
grilled chicken salad (go light on the dressing)
grilled chicken sandwich (opt for lettuce, tomato, onion, and whatever other vegetable topping is offered)
pita sandwiches or wraps with vegetables and low-fat dressing
rice pilaf, brown rice, or Cajun rice
roasted, boiled, or mashed potatoes (hold the gravy) rather than french fries
rotisserie or roasted chicken (without skin)
salad bars (Select fresh greens, chopped vegetables, low-fat salad dressings, beans, fruit salad, fresh bread, or breadsticks. Limit selections that are drenched in dressing or mayonnaise.)
thin-crust pizza from wood-burning ovens, or even pizzeria-style pizza (Select vegetable toppings and blot any fat from the surface with a napkin. Request less cheese.)

turkey sandwich with mustard, lettuce, and tomato (select higher-fiber breads, such as rye, pumpernickel, whole wheat, or multigrain)

vegetable sides (Many fast-food restaurants now offer vegetable side dishes, such as sautéed spinach, mashed potatoes or mashed sweet potatoes, corn, broccoli, okra, and fruit salad)

LIMIT OR AVOID

almost everything else

Now that you know what to order, here are some quick tips to help keep dining out enjoyable and broaden your healthy selections.

- Eat slowly and enjoy all aspects of the dining experience.
- Fill up on vegetable first courses (antipasto, grilled vegetables, soups, crudités, and so on).
- Restaurants want to please you, so ask questions. Don't order food unless you're sure what is in it and how it's prepared.
- Many restaurants are flexible with preparation methods. Request that the sautéed shrimp be grilled or the sautéed carrots be steamed.
- Look at all choices on the menu and be creative—make combinations to end up with a healthy entrée. For example, if one entrée is served with a healthy sauce or vegetable that appeals to you, request that this be added to or substituted for your choice.
- Go heavier on rice and vegetables and add meat as a topping (more like a condiment). When dining with a companion, order a vegetarian entrée and a meat- or fish-based selection. By dividing them, you and your dining partner will both be closer to appropriate portion sizes.
- Occasionally indulge in your favorite desserts, but limit your portion by sharing with a friend.

6

Prevention

Lifestyle Modifications to Minimize Cancer Risk

ANCER IS A SERIOUS PUBLIC HEALTH PROBLEM. President Richard Nixon declared "war on cancer" in 1971, and since then vast amounts of resources, including time and money, have been spent to win this war. Research has focused primarily on finding a cure for cancer using medical advances. Unfortunately, no magic bullet has been discovered, and we have not been the victors.

An estimated 60 to 80 percent of all cancer could be prevented by simple lifestyle and behavior changes. Some experts believe that the U.S. death rate from cancer could be reduced by as much as 50 percent if these changes were implemented. Prevention of cancer before it occurs is obviously better than trying to treat cancer after it has invaded the body. Cancer screening also plays an important role and can help identify cancer early, when treatment is more successful.

Every day we read in the paper, see in the news, or hear on the radio that "something" causes cancer. All too often these are the results of preliminary studies that fail to be confirmed by other researchers. The proportion of cancer that can be attributed to known cancer-causing agents varies. An individual's perception of what causes cancer also varies. For instance, many people are convinced that food additives are a major cause of cancer, but in fact they are responsible for very few cancer deaths. On the other hand, the benefits of an anticancer diet, one that is high in fruits and vegetables, are well established, but many people fail to modify their diet. This might be because focusing on an outside reason as the cause of cancer is simpler than identifying and changing one's own behavior.

Many factors other than diet are associated with cancer. There are lifestyle changes you can make for a more "cancer healthy" way of life.

Smoking

Smoking accounts for a large proportion of all cancers and about 30 percent of all cancer deaths. Cigarette smoking is the cause of lung, oral cavity, laryngeal, esophageal, bladder, kidney, and pancreatic cancer. Colon and cervical cancer may be related to smoking. Smoking has also been linked to prostate, rectum, stomach, and liver cancer, although the findings are not definitive. The risk of these cancers is increased in people who smoke longer, smoke more, and start at a younger age. In addition, one-quarter to one-third of all heart disease can be attributed to smoking.

It has been established that smoking causes cancer and also depletes the body of antioxidants, which are valuable cancer fighters. The benefits of quitting have been established: 90 percent of lung cancer and one-third of all cancer deaths could be eliminated.

Exposure to environmental tobacco smoke (that is, involuntary or passive smoke) is also a cause of lung cancer in nonsmokers. The increased risk could be as high as 50 percent. It has been estimated that a few thousand people will die each year due to exposure to passive smoke. Users of smokeless tobacco, pipes, and cigars are also at increased risk of developing tobacco-associated cancers.

TIPS TO HELP YOU STOP SMOKING

1. Learn more about the health consequences of smoking by calling the American Lung Association or visiting lung cancer patients at a cancer hospital.
2. Try a smoking-cessation program or support group.
3. If you have already tried to quit smoking and were not successful, try something new, such as the nicotine patch or gum.
4. Make a commitment and try quitting with a friend or relative.
5. Stay positive: smoking is addictive; it's not your fault!
6. Put a picture of a spouse, child, or loved one in your cigarette pack and look at it each time you "light up."
7. Try eating hard candies or gum to keep your mouth "occupied."
8. If you absolutely cannot quit, start cutting back the amount you smoke and don't drink alcohol, which can increase the negative effect of smoking.
9. Don't give up: it usually takes a couple of tries before you quit successfully.

Obesity

Results of the National Health and Nutrition Examination Survey (NHANES) for 1999 and 2000 indicate that a shocking two-thirds (64.5 percent) of the U.S. adult population is overweight (BMI ≥ 25), and almost one-third of the U.S. adult population is obese (BMI ≥ 30). Hundreds of studies have shown that being overweight increases the risk of developing many types of cancer, including kidney, colon, ovarian, endometrial, pancreatic, esophageal, oral, gallbladder, rectal, and breast. Obesity is a risk factor for other diseases as well, such as heart disease, stroke, and diabetes. Further support for the link between being overweight and cancer comes from recent observations that height may be a risk factor for common cancers: breast and colon. The increase in stature that is now being observed parallels the increase in cancer rates over time. It may be that tall stature, a marker of growth rates, is the result of "overnutrition" or excess calories during childhood and adolescence.

Diet and excess calorie intake may directly influence obesity. It is not clear how obesity contributes to the development of cancer, but it is believed that being overweight is related to other risk factors, such as high-fat diets, high-calorie intake, inactivity, being menopausal, adverse hormone levels, and insulin resistance. *Maintaining an ideal body weight is a lifestyle change that everyone can adopt that will help prevent cancer.*

TEN TIPS TO HELP YOU MAINTAIN AN IDEAL WEIGHT

1. See page 21 for information on weight recommendations and calorie requirements.
2. A healthy diet and regular exercise are the two most important factors in weight loss and maintenance.
3. Be sure you are hungry before you eat.
4. A diet low in saturated fats may make it easier to cut calories and eat lots of fruits, vegetables, and grains.
5. Pay attention to fat-free foods—they still contain calories and can make you gain weight if you overindulge.
6. Moderate your intake of alcohol; it contains "empty" calories and may make it hard for your body to control appetite.
7. Stress, boredom, and emotions can contribute to overeating and poor nutrition. Watch for those hard-to-handle situations and develop more beneficial stress fighters.
8. Make a commitment to lose weight and seek nutritional counseling if necessary.

9. Stay positive and be realistic about how much time it will take to lose weight.
10. There is no quick fix; make slow changes to your diet that will become part of your lifestyle.

Physical Activity/Exercise

Individuals who exercise are at reduced risk of developing colorectal cancer and possibly breast, endometrial, and prostate cancer. The evidence supporting the exercise-colorectal cancer link is strong and convincing. With respect to breast, endometrial, and prostate cancer, the results are less conclusive. Increasing our physical activity levels is important from a cancer-prevention standpoint, because colorectal, breast, and prostate cancers are some of the most prevalent cancers in the United States. Inactivity (separate from its contribution to obesity) probably accounts for 3 to 5 percent of all cancer deaths.

We don't fully understand how exercise might protect against cancer, but it may increase immune function, affect hormone and insulin levels, or shorten the stool's transit time through the intestine (reducing exposure to carcinogens). Generally, physically active people are not overweight, and this would also help to decrease risk because obesity is related to many cancers.

The American population has become sedentary, but the benefits of exercise are tremendous. Television, DVDs, and computer games have replaced a walk or bike ride. Exercise that has the most benefit for reducing cancer risk is probably that done at moderate to vigorous levels. To help people make better choices with regard to both exercise and nutrition, the American Cancer Society (ACS) publishes its Nutrition and Physical Activity Guidelines every five years. Another good source of information on this topic is the 1996 Report of the Surgeon General on Physical Activity and Health (U.S. Department of Health and Human Services, Centers for Disease Control and Prevention). In its 2001 guidelines, the ACS suggests that every adult accumulate thirty minutes or more of moderate-intensity physical activity on five or more days of the week. Additionally, forty-five minutes or more of moderate to vigorous activity on five or more days of the week may further reduce the risk of some cancers. Physical activity can be intermittent, such as walking fifteen minutes in the morning and fifteen minutes at lunchtime, as long as it is at least moderately intense. Also, flexibility and strength exercises are recommended. Here are some examples of moderate activity level:

Walking briskly at 3 to 4 mph
Biking at speeds up to 10 mph

Playing Ping-Pong or golf (carrying or pulling clubs)
Fishing (casting from shore)
Canoeing at 2 to 4 mph
Vacuuming, weeding, mowing
House painting

Ten Tips to Help You Start Exercising

1. Be sure to consult your physician before starting an exercise program.
2. Figure out the best time to exercise and schedule an appointment to do it.
3. Work out with a friend; you'll be less likely to skip a day.
4. Have a variety of activities, both indoor and outdoor, so that bad weather doesn't get in the way.
5. Try walking. It's easy, fun, and you can do it almost anywhere and anytime.
6. Exercise while doing other things; for example, ride a stationary bike while watching the news.
7. Physical activity reduces stress and can lift your spirits. If you're in a bad mood, try exercising: everything usually looks better afterward.
8. Try to squeeze an exercise session in between other commitments.
9. Take advantage of friends and family for child care when visiting and go for a walk or run.
10. Stay positive, set realistic goals, and reward yourself often!

Workouts of Moderate Intensity*

basketball (playing a game) for fifteen to twenty minutes
basketball (shooting baskets) for thirty minutes
bicycling five miles in thirty minutes
bicycling four miles in fifteen minutes
dancing fast (social) for thirty minutes
gardening for thirty to forty-five minutes
jumping rope for fifteen minutes
playing touch football for thirty to forty-five minutes
playing volleyball for forty-five minutes
pushing a stroller 1½ miles for thirty minutes
raking leaves for thirty minutes
running 1½ miles in fifteen minutes (ten-minute mile)

---

*U.S. Department of Health and Human Services: Centers for Disease Control and Prevention: A Report of the Surgeon General: Physical Activity and Health 1996.

shoveling snow for fifteen minutes
stairwalking for fifteen minutes
swimming laps for twenty minutes
walking 1¾ miles in thirty-five minutes (twenty-minute mile)
walking two miles in thirty minutes (fifteen-minute mile)
washing and waxing a car for forty-five to sixty minutes
washing windows or floors for forty-five to sixty minutes
water aerobics for thirty minutes
wheelchair basketball for twenty minutes
wheeling self in wheelchair for thirty to forty minutes

Hormones

Hormones, including oral contraceptives and estrogen replacement therapy, have been linked to certain female cancers. These synthetic and natural hormones have regulatory effects on the menstrual cycle and pregnancy and probably increase the risk of some cancers by increasing cell division. Overall, these factors account for about 3 percent of observed cancer deaths.

Oral contraceptives are used to prevent pregnancy and have been associated with a small increased risk of breast cancer in women who are currently using them, probably before the age of forty-five. *Nevertheless, oral contraceptive use does not account for a large proportion of the observed breast cancer cases.* Oral contraceptives have also been shown to increase the risk of liver cancer. But liver cancer is a rare disease, especially in the United States, and does not account for a large proportion of cancer mortality.

A beneficial effect of oral contraceptives (the type that are combination pills containing estrogen and progestin) on ovarian and endometrial cancer has been shown consistently. Five or more years of use reduces the lifetime risk of developing these cancers by as much as 50 percent.

Estrogen replacement therapy is taken for menopausal symptoms, such as hot flashes and vaginal dryness, and in some instances to retard bone loss associated with osteoporosis. *In long-term users (five to ten years or more) estrogen appears to increase the risk of breast cancer.* Short-term use to relieve menopausal symptoms probably does not increase risk significantly. Discuss the risks and benefits associated with estrogen use with a physician.

Factors related to hormone levels increase the risk for some cancers while decreasing the risk for others. Pregnancy (as well as bearing more than one child) appears to protect against breast, endometrial, and ovarian cancer. Breast-feeding may be beneficial for breast and ovarian cancer (probably by decreasing the number of monthly ovulations and related cell divisions). Early age at onset of menstruation and late age at menopause increase the risk of both breast and endometrial cancer, while late age at first pregnancy increases the risk for breast cancer. These increased risks are most likely related to increasing cumulative exposure to estrogens.

It is important to know and understand the hormonal factors that might increase your risk of developing cancer. Adherence to cancer screening guidelines (see Tables 6.1 and 6.2 on pages 351 and 352) and modification of risk factors are even more important.

Occupation

Occupational exposures account for less than 5 percent of all fatal cancers, mainly lung and bladder. Workplace exposure to chemicals and carcinogens can be high, although the absolute number of people exposed tends to be small. Substances identified as human carcinogens include asbestos, formaldehyde, benzene, diesel exhaust, arsenic, vinyl chloride, and radon, to name just a few. However, tobacco smoke is by far the strongest contributor to occupation-associated cancers.

Fortunately, in the United States, the Occupational Safety and Health Act (1970) brought potential occupational hazards to the forefront of attention for both employers and employees. Since the identification of cancer-causing chemicals, the amount of exposure in the workplace has been strictly controlled and regulated. This will likely prevent or reduce the risk of occupation-associated cancers in the future.

Although the number of people who work with or near chemicals is limited, everyone should be aware of chemical exposures at the workplace and their safety profile. Efforts should be made to minimize exposure.

FIVE TIPS FOR MINIMIZING OCCUPATIONAL EXPOSURES

1. Be informed. Ask your employer or human resources manager about chemicals or substances that you are exposed to and any potential hazards; by law they must provide this information.
2. Always wear the appropriate protective clothing, gloves, and eyeglasses.
3. Follow safety rules carefully.
4. If you are exposed to chemicals at the workplace, ask your employer about the possibility of job rotation.
5. Be sure to quit smoking if exposed to workplace chemicals.

Radiation

One of the most common misconceptions is that radiation causes a large proportion of all cancer. Although radiation exposure is a known cause of cancer, only 2 percent of all cancers are estimated to be attributable to radiation, and most of this is from natural sources, such as radon, cosmic rays, and ultraviolet radiation (sunlight). All of us are exposed to this "background" radiation each day.

Ionizing Radiation

Radon is a radioactive gas that is emitted from the earth and is colorless and odorless. In high doses it can cause lung cancer. Most of the radon-induced lung and upper respiratory cancer is seen in underground miners, who are exposed to high levels. Furthermore, it has been shown that exposure to both smoking and radon increases the cancer risk far more than exposure to either one alone. Everyone should know that smoking is hazardous to your health, but it is even riskier in workers exposed to radon. Radon can also accumulate in buildings or homes, but most homes have extremely low levels, and radon is usually found in the basement. Studies have not supported the theory that many cancers can be attributed to radon in the home. Simple home test kits are available to measure radon levels at home.

Radiation exposure and the potential cancer risk from medical x-rays have been studied extensively. It appears that therapeutic radiation (radiotherapy in very large doses to treat a certain condition) does increase the risk for some cancers, such as thyroid, breast, and leukemia. However, diagnostic x-rays (such as those x-rays taken for breast cancer screening—mammography) emit a very low dose of radiation similar to that of dental x-rays, and the immediate benefits for medical use far outweigh any risks. For example, estimates say that mammographic x-rays probably cause less than 1 percent of all breast cancers. This would increase a woman's lifetime risk of developing breast cancer from 13.3 percent (which is the average) to 13.4 percent (with mammography screening).

An increased risk of cancer has been observed in individuals exposed to x-ray sources at the workplace, such as radiologists. All workers should take precautionary measures, such as using protective shields. It is important to know your medical history and exposure to this type of therapeutic radiation. Adherence to cancer screening guidelines is even more important in people exposed to therapeutic radiation.

The media have devoted a lot of attention to "cancer clusters," and an effort has been made to explain increased rates of cancer observed in defined geographical areas. People living near nuclear power plants have been said to have an increased risk of developing cancer. Nuclear *accidents*, such as the one at Chernobyl in 1986, prove that radiation from nuclear materials can cause cancer. However, overall studies have failed to confirm the claim that leukemia rates are higher in people living near nuclear power plants in the absence of any nuclear accident.

Sunlight (Ultraviolet Radiation)

The majority of radiation-induced cancer is caused by the ultraviolet rays from the sun that damage the skin cells. More than 90 percent of skin cancer is caused by sun exposure. The majority of all skin cancers can be prevented by "sun-smart" strategies:

- Avoid or minimize sun exposure, especially during the hours of 10:00 A.M. to 3:00 P.M.
- Use sunscreen, with an SPF of 15 or above.
- Protect exposed parts of the body with clothing.
- Be especially careful to protect children from sunburns.
- Eliminate sunbathing so that you'll have a lot more time for other fun activities! No amount of suntanning is safe. Even "indoor" suntanning in sun beds or with sunlamps is unsafe.
- Instead of sunbathing, try some of the new self-tanning creams, available at cosmetic counters.
- Check any skin growths. A mole or spot that changes in size, shape, or color should be checked immediately by a physician. Most skin cancers are curable when detected early; an important aspect of skin cancer prevention is screening.
- See a physician for regular skin cancer screening, especially if you have fair skin.

Electromagnetic Radiation (Nonionizing Radiation)

Electromagnetic field (EMF) exposure refers to the magnetic fields from power lines and electromagnetic radiation from cellular telephones, video display terminals, and electrical household appliances. These are either extremely-low-frequency fields (power lines and electrical household appliances) or radio-frequency radiation (cellular telephones, microwaves, and other "wireless" devices). The frequency is lower than ionizing radiation or ultraviolet radiation. The amount of radiation emitted from electromagnetic radiation does not have the "energy" to induce a cancer-causing mutation.

Because of the intense public interest in the health effects of EMF exposure, many scientific groups and regulatory agencies have examined the effects on disease, particularly cancer. Some studies have suggested that there may be an effect on childhood leukemia (these often make news headlines), but these studies have been criticized for methodological limitations, and the overall evidence is weak. Because we do not have the technology necessary to study the effects of EMF exposure, and it is not logistically feasible to measure EMF exposure from such common sources as power lines, household appliances, and other electronic devices, long-term EMF exposure cannot be measured accurately. Although there is a possibility of negative health effects from EMF exposure, at this time the evidence is weak and does not support electromagnetic radiation as a significant cause of cancer or any other disease.

Environmental Pollution

We are all exposed to environmental pollutants daily, but fortunately the level of these exposures is low, and they don't appear to cause a significant increase in cancer risk. The overall contribution of environmental pollution, both air and water pollution, to cancer rates is small (probably accounting for only 2 percent of cancer mortality). Smoking, diet, and physical activity level play a much larger role in explaining cancer risk.

Probably the most significant form of air pollution is tobacco smoke, and the effect is not only on smokers but on nonsmokers as well. Air pollution also includes combustion products from industrial emissions, motor vehicle emissions, and heating units and airborne asbestos and radon particles. After observations that city dwellers have increased rates of cancer compared to rural dwellers, urban air pollution was speculated to be responsible for a large proportion of lung cancer. In fact, studies have suggested that only a small amount (less than 1 percent) of lung cancer can be attributed to urban air pollution. The effect of air pollution on risk is increased in those individuals who are smokers. City dwellers who may be exposed to a substantial amount of pollution can minimize outdoor activities during times when traffic volume is heavy and pollution is at its highest.

Pesticides such as DDT, combustion by-products, and industrial products can be passed along into the food chain and can accumulate in the body. Pesticides, some sources have suggested, could be the cause of some forms of cancer. However, the current available evidence is inconclusive and does not support a causal role of these compounds in the development of cancer.

Drinking water may contain known and suspected carcinogens, such as industrial chemicals that seep into the water supply or by-products of the purification process (chlorination). Asbestos, nitrates, radon, pesticides, and metals have all been identified in water supplies, but the levels are extremely low and usually do not present a problem in the United States. The Environmental Protection Agency has rigorous guidelines for hazardous waste disposal, and in the United States water supplies are monitored for many carcinogens. Your drinking water can be tested; an alternative is to use filtered or bottled water.

Most pesticides (99.99 percent) in the American diet are naturally occurring, produced by plants themselves as a defense mechanism against insects, fungi, and predators. They present little danger to our food supply. Some natural substances and chemical substances have been shown to be carcinogenic in animal tests, but there are many uncertainties when relying on animal cancer tests for human prediction. Regulatory agencies use animal studies to formulate policy, and we often do not have human data available. Furthermore, the results from animal studies can be blatantly wrong. For instance, smoke and alcohol, two very potent carcinogens in humans, were not detected as cancer-causing agents in animals for quite some time.

Synthetic (man-made) pesticides used in coloring or preservation have not been shown to be carcinogenic in animal studies. However, a conservative approach would include limiting our exposure to man-made pesticides. This can be done by thoroughly washing produce or buying organically grown products.

Meat and animal products treated with hormones and/or antibiotics have received considerable attention. To date, no link to cancer has been shown. However, aflatoxin, a potent toxin that may be produced when crops are stored improperly, can interact with hepatitis B virus and cause liver cancer. The United States has federal regulations that limit the amount of aflatoxin that can be present in crops.

Infections and Viruses

Viruses are infectious agents, some of which can cause cancer by invading and altering cells in the body to induce or increase the susceptibility to cancer. However, the immune system works effectively against most infectious agents so that serious disease does not occur. Biological agents including viruses contribute to about 5 percent of cancer deaths. Here are the viruses associated with cancer:

VIRUS	CANCER
human immunodeficiency (HIV)	AIDS-related malignancies such as Kaposi's sarcoma
hepatitis B and hepatitis C (common in Asia and Africa)	liver cancer
Epstein-Barr	non-Hodgkin's lymphoma, Hodgkin's disease, nasopharyngeal cancer
human papillomavirus	cervical cancer
human T-cell lymphotropic virus (HTLV-1)	lymphomas and some forms of leukemia
Also:	
Helicobacter pylori (a bacteria, not a virus)	stomach cancer

The overall prevalence of these infections is higher in developing countries than in the United States. Strategies for prevention include avoiding blood exposures, regular Pap screening for women, and vaccination. Improved screening of blood products and use of disposable syringes will help decrease the prevalence of some viruses. The blood supply is currently screened for HIV, hepatitis B and C, and HTLV-1. If you believe you are at risk, discuss precautions, testing, and vaccination with your doctor.

Heredity

The study of hereditary cancers is a relatively new field of research made possible by the technological advances of molecular biology and cancer genetics. Even prior to these advances, cancer clusters within families had been observed.

Overall, having a family history of a particular cancer increases your risk for developing that cancer by about twofold. However, it is not inevitable that you will develop cancer if a family member has the disease. Also, individuals may be susceptible to environmental carcinogens because of their genetic makeup. This increases the role of nongenetic factors in causing cancer.

Most cancers are caused by environmental factors, primarily diet and smoking, or a combination of heredity and environment. Heredity probably accounts for only 5 percent of all cancer mortalities. Know your family history! Increased cancer screening as well as lifestyle and behavior changes are important for individuals with a family history of cancer.

Medical Drugs

Cancer treatment often includes therapy in the form of drugs and radiation. Some chemotherapy drugs and radioactive drugs used in the treatment of cancer and other conditions increase a person's risk of a second malignancy. Immunosuppressive drugs, used in organ transplantation, also increase the risk of cancer because they suppress the immune system, making it vulnerable to precancerous and cancerous cells. It is important to remember that these drugs, although they do carry some increased risk, have been used successfully to cure many people. Anabolic steroids and painkillers that contain phenacetin are also human carcinogens. The amount of overall cancer caused by these drugs is extremely small, probably less than 1 percent.

Stress

Stress has been implicated anecdotally as a cause of cancer; however, there is no scientific evidence to support this. Nor have increased stress levels been shown to decrease survival of patients with cancer. Stress has been associated with other conditions, such as gastrointestinal disorders, infection, hypertension, fatigue, insomnia, impotence, backaches, and headaches. Stress can depress the immune system, and we do know that a healthy immune system is important in fighting cancer. It should be noted that decreasing stress levels will increase the quality of life, which is important for everyone, especially those who are undergoing cancer therapy.

Ten Tips for Keeping Stress to a Minimum

1. Have a support system. Vent your frustrations to friends and relatives.
2. Exercise—it's a great stress buster. Take ten deep breaths or a walk around the block—it really helps!
3. Try not to overeat or drink alcoholic beverages in response to stress; overeating and overimbibing just lead to more stress.

4. Try to remove the source of stress if possible or remove yourself from the stressful situation.
5. Try relaxation/meditation techniques or take a stress management class.
6. Adopt a pet. They are great stress relievers.
7. Engage in a pleasurable hobby or activity.
8. Don't take life too seriously—accept what you can't change.
9. Try not to be a perfectionist and overachiever: set reasonable goals and priorities.
10. If you feel under intense, continuing stress, seek professional counseling. We all need help at certain times in our lives.

Screening

The prevention strategies highlighted in this chapter coupled with screening can make a significant impact on cancer mortality. Screening is the process whereby medical professionals look for disease in people without cancer symptoms. Early detection of cancer can generally ensure a better prognosis because the cancer is diagnosed in a treatable stage, before it has the opportunity to spread to other vital organs.

Many cancer screening tests are available. See Tables 6.1 and 6.2 for the Strang Cancer Prevention Center guidelines for screening.

TABLE 6.1 STRANG CANCER PREVENTION CENTER SCREENING GUIDELINES FOR WOMEN*

Test/Procedure	Age	Frequency
Complete cancer checkup	20–39	Every 3 years
	40 and over	Every year
Clinical breast exam	20–39	Every 3 years
	40 and over	Every year
Breast self-exam	20 and over	Every month
Pap test	18 and over	Every year
Pelvic exam	18 and over	Every year
Mammography	40	Initial baseline screen
	40–49	Every 1–2 years
	50 and over	Every year
Digital rectal exam	40 and over	Every year
Stool occult blood test	50 and over	Every year
Flexible sigmoidoscopy	50 and over	Every 3–5 years
Colonoscopy	50 and over	Every 10 years

*These are guidelines, not rules, and apply only to individuals who do not have symptoms. If you have symptoms, discuss them with your doctor. If you have a personal or family history of any of these cancers, your doctor should discuss individualized screening recommendations with you. A complete cancer-related checkup should also include examination of the skin, mouth, thyroid, lymph nodes, and ovaries. Health counseling should include smoking cessation, weight and exercise management, and nutritional counseling.

TABLE 6.2 STRANG CANCER PREVENTION CENTER SCREENING GUIDELINES FOR MEN*

Test/Procedure	Age	Frequency
Complete cancer checkup	20–39	Every 3 years
	40 and over	Every year
Testicular self-exam	20–40	Monthly
Digital rectal exam	40 and over	Every year
Stool occult blood test	50 and over	Every year
Flexible sigmoidoscopy	50 and over	Every 3–5 years
Colonoscopy	50 and over	Every 10 years
Prostate specific antigen	50 and over	Every year

*These are guidelines, not rules, and apply only to individuals who do not have symptoms. If you have symptoms, discuss them with your doctor. If you have a personal or family history of any of these cancers, your doctor should discuss individualized screening recommendations with you. A complete cancer-related checkup should also include examination of the skin, mouth, thyroid, and lymph nodes. Health counseling should include smoking cessation, weight and exercise management, and nutritional counseling.

Appendix

Nutrition and Cancer Information Resources and Cancer Facts

FOR THOSE INTERESTED in more detailed and current information about cancer research and treatment, this appendix provides contact numbers and websites for several prominent national information centers. It also offers some of the latest statistics about cancer, as well as more information about how cancer studies are researched.

Nutrition and Cancer Information Resources

American Cancer Society: cancer.org
American Dietetic Association: eatright.org
American Heart Association: americanheart.org
American Institute for Cancer Research: aicr.org
Food and Drug Association: fda.gov
Harvard Health Publications: health.harvard.edu/hhp/index.jsp
Harvard School of Public Health: The Nutrition Source: hsph.harvard.edu/
    nutritionsource/index.html
National Cancer Institute: nci.nih.gov
National Institutes of Health: nih.gov
Tufts Nutrition Navigator: http://navigator.tufts.edu

Strang Cancer Prevention Center: strang.org
Tufts Health and Nutrition Letter: healthletter.tufts.edu
USDA: usda.gov
USDA: Food Label and Nutrition: cfsan.fda.gov/label.html

Cooking, Health, and Nutrition

Cooking Light: cookinglight.com/cooking
Eating Well: eatingwell.com
International Olive Oil Council: internationaloliveoil.org
Flax Council of Canada: flaxcouncil.ca
United Soybean Board: unitedsoybean.org

For More Information on Cancer

American Cancer Society: (800) ACS-2345
American Institute for Cancer Research: (800) 843-8114; in D.C. (202) 328-7744
Strang Cancer Prevention Center—Anne Fisher Nutrition Center: (212) 794-4900
National Cancer Institute: (800) 4-CANCER

How Cancer Rates and Risk Factors Are Studied

Epidemiologists try to find a connection between particular foods, nutrients, or vitamins and cancer using different methods. Ecologic or correlational studies compare
the dietary habits and cancer rates of countries or groups of people. Measuring
dietary intake is usually done using per-capita consumption of the country or group,
which is inherently inaccurate. These studies do not take into account other factors,
such as lifestyle habits, that might influence why a particular group got cancer. These
other factors are called potential *confounders*. For example, countries with high rates
of colon cancer also have a high consumption of red meat compared to countries
with low rates of colon cancer. Populations that consume a lot of red meat also tend
to consume less fiber, fruits, and vegetables and tend to exercise less.

Ecologic or correlational studies are further hampered by the fact that a general
diet cannot be linked directly to the person who got cancer. Only the diet and cancer rates of the population as a whole can be assessed. The interpretation of results

PROPORTION OF CANCER DEATHS ATTRIBUTABLE TO SPECIFIC RISK FACTORS

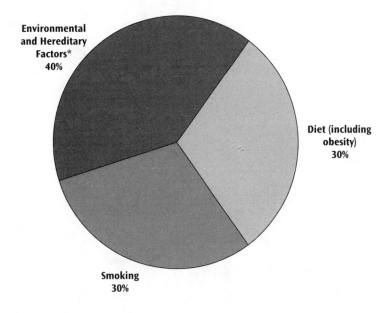

Environmental and Hereditary Factors*
40%

Diet (including obesity)
30%

Smoking
30%

*Environmental and Hereditary Factors:

Inactivity: 5%	Environmental pollution: 2%
Infections and viruses: 5%	Radiation (including sun exposure): 2%
Heredity: 5%	Medical drugs and procedures: 1%
Occupation: 5%	Food additives (salt): 1%
Alcohol: 3%	Other: 8%
Hormones: 3%	

from these studies is limited because of these flaws. However, much of the early data showing a link between diet and cancer was based on these types of studies. The findings were important because they gave some of the first "clues" to the link between diet and cancer.

Cohort studies, consisting of a large number of people, are considered one of the best study designs. Study subjects provide information on their diet by completing a questionnaire or interview. Participants also provide information on other confounding factors that may be related to diet and cancer. The individuals are then followed for many years to see if cancer develops. Repeated assessments (e.g., yearly) of diet can be obtained during this follow-up time period that will help to give a more precise measure of "true" dietary intake. Information on cancer occurrence can be obtained using a questionnaire completed by the study subject, state cancer

Age-Adjusted Cancer Death Rates,* Males by Site, US, 1930-1999

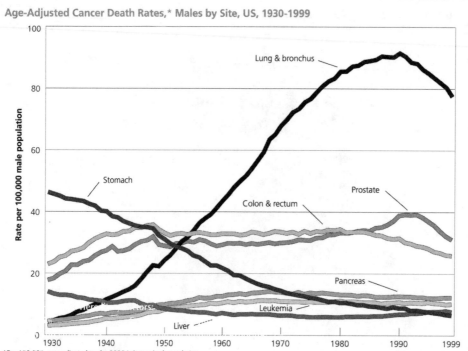

*Per 100,000, age-adjusted to the 2000 US standard population.
Note: Due to changes in ICD coding, numerator information has changed over time. Rates for cancers of the liver, lung & bronchus, and colon & rectum are affected by these coding changes

Source: US Mortality Public Use Data Tapes 1960-1999, US Mortality Volumes 1930-1959,
National Center for Health Statistics, Centers for Disease Control and Prevention, 2002.   American Cancer Society, Surveillance Research, 2003

registries, death certificates, or medical records. Investigators then compare the diets of those who developed cancer to those of people who did not, using mathematical methods called *statistics*. A large number of individuals are needed for this type of study, and the duration of follow-up is long because cancer takes many years to develop. One of the major limitations of this design is the potential for biased or incorrect results if many of the people initially enrolled cannot be located and their cancer status is unknown.

In another type of study design called a *case control study*, persons with cancer are identified using state cancer registries, death records, or hospital records. Individuals identified as having cancer (called *cases*) are asked to complete a questionnaire or are interviewed about their diet and other risk factors prior to their being diagnosed. Subjects without disease (called *controls*) who are similar to the cases are recruited for the study, and the same information is obtained. Statistical methods are then used to compare the diets of these two groups (case versus controls).

Age-Adjusted Cancer Death Rates,* Females by Site, US, 1930-1999

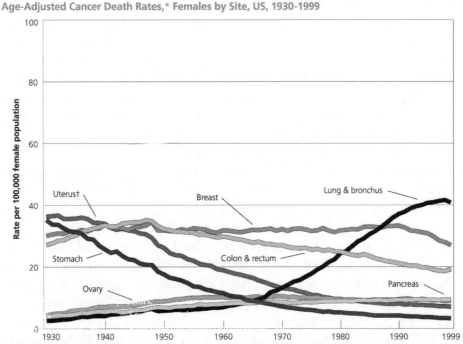

*Per 100,000, age-adjusted to the 2000 US standard population. †Uterus cancer death rates are for uterine cervix and uterine corpus combined.
Note: Due to changes in ICD coding, numerator information has changed over time. Rates for cancers of the liver, lung & bronchus, colon & rectum, and ovary are affected by these coding changes.
Source: US Mortality Public Use Data Tapes 1960-1999, US Mortality Volumes 1930-1959,
National Center for Health Statistics, Centers for Disease Control and Prevention, 2002.   American Cancer Society, Surveillance Research, 2003

Case control studies require fewer numbers of people, and the time needed to complete the study is shorter, compared to the previously described cohort study. However, case control studies have the potential to give biased or inaccurate results because cases with cancer may have predetermined notions about the cause of their disease. They may "recall" their dietary patterns differently than nondiseased controls do, leading to recall bias. For instance, if people with esophageal cancer were asked about their fruit and vegetable intake over the past ten years, they may report their current diet, which is likely to have changed because of their illness. Because of their diagnosis, individuals might be aware of the benefits of eating fruits and vegetables and may over- or underestimate their intake. This is not a problem in a cohort study because information about diet is obtained well in advance of cancer diagnosis. When researchers select the control or comparison group, they may inadvertently choose a group (such as very old subjects or health-conscious individuals) that is more or less likely to eat fruits and vegetables.

Intervention studies (also called *randomized trials* or *experiments*), if conducted properly, can best measure whether a particular factor is beneficial. They do not suffer from the same potential biases as other study designs. In these studies subjects are randomly assigned to one of two groups. For example, depending on the focus of the study, one group may receive a vitamin supplement while the other group receives a placebo (inactive pill). Neither the study subjects nor the investigators know who gets the vitamin versus the placebo. Study participants are then followed for a designated time period and cancer occurrence ascertained.

The well-known studies on beta-carotene supplements and cancer are examples of intervention studies. People were randomly assigned to take beta-carotene, a vitamin thought to protect against some forms of cancer, or a placebo pill and then followed for the occurrence of cancer. Intervention studies are difficult to conduct for several reasons: first, it is hard to get people to comply; second, the amount of time between the diet change and the expected modification of cancer risk is uncertain; third, the amount of change needed to affect cancer risk is probably unknown; and fourth, people who agree to be in a study tend to be healthier, and the dietary change may work only in people who are at high risk for the cancer. The logistics of conducting this type of study make it extremely expensive. Due to ethical considerations, intervention studies are not done on factors thought to be harmful. Nevertheless, even though there are many hurdles to overcome when conducting epidemiologic research, well-conducted studies have been done and valuable information obtained about the role diet plays in cancer prevention.

References

Cancer Facts & Figures—2003. American Cancer Society. 2003: 1–3.

Cancer Prevention and Early Detection Facts and Figures. American Cancer Society. 2002: 1–22; cancer.org/prevent.html.

Cancer Facts & Figures—1997. American Cancer Society. 1997: 1–2.

Cancer Prevention. American Cancer Society. 1997: 1–2; cancer.org/prevent.html.

Position of the American Dietetic Association: Enrichment and fortification of foods and dietary supplements. American Dietetic Association. 1997: 1–8; eatright.org/aenrich-dietsupple.html.

Position of the American Dietetic Association: Food fortification and dietary supplements. *Journal of the American Dietetic Association* 2001; 101: 115–25.

Position of the American Dietetic Association: Food irradiation. American Dietetic Association. 1997: 1–8; eatright.org/airradi.html.

Position of the American Dietetic Association: Health implications of dietary fiber. American Dietetic Association. 1996: 1–5; eatright.org/adietfiber.html.

Position of the American Dietetic Association: Phytochemicals and functional foods. American Dietetic Association. 1997: 1–9; eatright.org/aphyto-chemicals.html.

Position of the American Dietetic Association: Use of nutritive and non-nutritive sweeteners. *Journal of the American Dietetic Association* 1993; 93: 816.

Position of the American Dietetic Association and Dieticians of Canada: Vegetarian diets. *Journal of the American Dietetic Association* 2003; 103: 748–65.

Position of the American Dietetic Association: Vegetarian diets. American Dietetic Association. 1997: 1–6; eatright.org/avegdiets.html.

Position of the American Dietetic Association: Vitamin and mineral supplementation. American Dietetic Association. 1996: 1–13; eatright.org/asupple .html.

Adami, H. O., Day, N. E., Trichopoulos, D., Willett, W. C. Primary and secondary prevention in the reduction of cancer morbidity and mortality. *European Journal of Cancer* 2001; 37(Suppl 8): S118–27.

Adlercreutz, H. Phytoestrogens: Epidemiology and a possible role in cancer protection. *Environmental Health Perspectives* 1995; 103: 103–12.

A food pharmacy: A potpourri of naturally occurring substances that may fight disease. *Eating Well* March–April 1992: 41.

Ames, B. N. What are the major carcinogens in the etiology of human cancer? Environmental pollution, natural carcinogens, and the causes of human cancer: Six errors. *Important Advances in Oncology* 1989; 237–47.

Ames, B. N., Gold, L. S., Willett, W. C. The causes and prevention of cancer. *Proceedings of the National Academy of Sciences* 1995; 92: 5258–65.

Aruoma, O. L., Halliwell, B., Aeschbach, R., et al. Antioxidant and pro-oxidant properties of active rosemary constituents: carnosol and carnosic acid. *Xenobiotica* 1992; 22: 257–68.

Baker, T. R., Piver, M. S. Etiology, biology, and epidemiology of ovarian cancer. *Seminars in Surgical Oncology* 1994; 10: 242–48.

Barnes, S., Peterson, G., Grubbs, C., Setchell, K. Potential role of dietary isoflavones in the prevention of cancer. In Jacobs, M. M., ed. *Diet and Cancer: Markers, Prevention, and Treatment.* New York: Plenum Press, 1994.

Bergan, J. C., Brown, P. T. Nutritional status of "new" vegetarians. *Journal of the American Dietetic Association* 1980; 76: 151–55.

Berkowitz, K. E. Is your coffee habit grounds for health concerns? *Environmental Nutrition* 1994; 17(2): 1–6.

Bloch, A., Thomson, C. A. Position of the American Dietetic Association: Phytochemicals and functional foods. *Journal of the American Dietetic Association* 1995; 95: 493–96.

Blondell, J. M. The anticarcinogenic effect of magnesium. *Medical Hypotheses* 1980; 6: 863–71.

Bray, G. A., Ryan, D. H., eds. *Vitamins and Cancer Prevention.* Pennington Center Nutrition Series. Baton Rouge, La.: State University Press, 1993.

Byers, T., Nestle, M., McTiernan, A., Doyle, C., Currie-Williams, A., Gansler, T., Thun, M. American Cancer Society 2001 Nutrition and Physical Activity Guidelines Advisory Committee. American Cancer Society guidelines on nutrition and physical activity for cancer prevention: Reducing the risk of cancer with healthy food choices and physical activity. *CA A Cancer Journal for Clinicians* 2002; 52: 92–119.

Caloric levels adapted from USDA's Food Guide Pyramid, U.S. Department of Agriculture, Human Nutrition Information Service, April 1992. *Cancer Causes and Control.* 1996; 7: 3–180.

Caragay, A. B. Cancer-preventative foods and ingredients. *Food Technology* 1992; 46: 65–68.

Clairborne, C., Ryan, L. T., Donovan, M. D., eds. *The Professional Chef's Techniques of Healthy Cooking/The Culinary Institute of America.* New York: Van Nostrand Reinhold, 1993.

Clark, L. C., Combs, G. E. Jr., Turnbull, B. W., et al. Effects of selenium supplementation for cancer prevention in patients with carcinoma of the skin. *Journal of the American Medical Association* 1996; 276: 1957–63.

Colditz, G. A. A prospective assessment of moderate alcohol intake and major chronic diseases. *Annals of Epidemiology* 1990; 1: 167–77.

Colditz, G. A., Egan, K. M., Stampfer, M. J. Hormone replacement therapy and risk of breast cancer: Results from epidemiologic studies. *American Journal of Obstetrics and Gynecology* 1993; 168: 1473–80.

Correa, P. Human Gastric Carcinogenesis: A Multistep and Multifactorial Process—First American Cancer Society Award Lecture on Cancer Epidemiology and Prevention. *Cancer Research* 1992; 52: 6735–40.

Cramer, D. W., Harlow, B. L. Author's response to: "Progress in the nutritional epidemiology of ovary cancer." *American Journal of Epidemiology* 1991; 134: 460–61.

Das, S. Vitamin E in the genesis and prevention of cancer: A review. *Acta Oncologica* 1994; 33: 615–19.

Davis, D. L., Muir, C. Estimating avoidable causes of cancer. *Environmental Health Perspectives* 1995; 103(Suppl. 8): 302–6.

Decker, E. A. The role of phenolics, conjugated linoleic acid, carnosine, and pyrroloquinoline quinone as nonessential dietary antioxidants. *Nutritional Reviews* 1995; 53: 49–58.

De Jong, E. H., Oishi, K., Hayes, R. B., et al. Peripheral hormone levels in controls and patients with prostatic cancer or benign prostatic hyperplasia: Results from the Dutch-Japanese case-control study. *Cancer Research* 1991; 51: 3445–50.

Dietary Supplement—Health and Education Act of 1994. U.S. Food and Drug Administration, Center for Food Safety and Applied Nutrition. DSHEA-P.L.-103-471. 1996: 1–4; http://vm.cfsan.fda.gov/-dms/dietsupp.html.

Di Mascio, P., Murphy, M. E., Sies, H. Antioxidant defense systems: the role of carotenoids, tocopherols, and thiols. *American Journal of Clinical Nutrition* 1991; 53: 194S–200S.

Doll, R., Peto, R. The causes of cancer: quantitative estimates of avoidable risks of cancer in the United States today. *Journal of the National Cancer Institute* 1981; 66: 1196–1308.

Friedenreich, C. M., Orenstein, M. R. Physical activity and cancer prevention: etiologic evidence and biological mechanisms. *Journal of Nutrition* 2002; 132(11 Suppl.): 3456S–64S.

Gao, Y. T., McLaughlin, J. K., Blot, W. J., et al. Reduced risk of esophageal cancer associated with green tea consumption. *Journal of the National Cancer Institute* 1994; 86: 855–58.

Garfinkel, L. Overweight and cancer. *Annals of Internal Medicine* 1985; 103: 1034–36.

Garfinkel, L., Boffetta, E., Stellman, S. D. Alcohol and breast cancer: A cohort study. *Preventive Medicine* 1988; 17: 686–93.

Goodwin, T. W., Mercer, E. L. *Introduction to Plant Biochemistry.* Second Edition. Elmsford, N.Y.: Pergamon Press, 1983.

Hamilton, E. M. N., Whitney, E. N., Sizer, E. S. *Nutritional Concepts and Controversies.* Fifth Edition. St. Paul, Minn.: West Publishing Company, 1991.

Harvard Medical School Special Health Report: *Healthy Eating: A Guide to the New Nutrition.* Boston, Mass.: Harvard Health Publications, 2003.

Harvard Report on Cancer Prevention, Volume 1: Causes of Human Cancer. *Cancer Causes and Control.* 1996; 7: 3–58.

Havala, S., Dwyer, J. Position of the American Dietetic Association: Vegetarian diets. *Journal of the American Dietetic Association* 1993; 93: 1317–19.

Helzlsouer, K. J., Block, G., Blumberg, J., et al. Summary of the Round Table Discussion on Strategies for Cancer Prevention: Diet, Food Additives, Supplements, and Drugs. *Cancer Research* 1994; 54(Suppl.): 2044s–51s.

Henson, D. E., Block, G., Levine, M. Ascorbic acid: Biologic functions and relation to cancer. *Journal of the National Cancer Institute* 1991; 83: 547–50.

Herbert, V. Vitamin B-12: plant sources, requirements, assay. In Mutch, P. B., Johnston, P. K., eds. First International Congress on Vegetarian Nutrition. *American Journal of Clinical Nutrition* 1988; 48(3 Suppl.): 852–58.

Herbst, S. T. *The New Food Lover's Companion.* Second Edition. Hauppauge, N.Y.: Barron's Educational Series, Inc., 1995.

Herman C., Adlercreutz, T., Goldin, B. R., et al. Soybean phytoestrogen intake and cancer risk. *Journal of Nutrition* 1995; 125(3 Suppl.): 757s–70s.

Howe, G. R. Dietary fat and breast cancer risks: An epidemiologic perspective. *Cancer Supplement* 1994; 74: 1078–84.

Hrabak, D. A fish oil story: Omega-Ys return to fight heart disease, cancer. *Environmental Nutrition* 1994; 17(7): 1–4.

Hunter, D. J., Spiegehnan, D., Adami, H. O., et al. Cohort studies of fat intake and the risk of breast cancer—a pooled analysis. *The New England Journal of Medicine* 1996; 334: 356–61.

Husten, L. Understanding risk: tricky business. *Harvard Health Letter* 1994; 19(12): 9–12.

International Olive Oil Council. Press Kit 1997.

Katahn, M. *The Tri-Color Diet.* New York: W. W. Norton & Company, Inc., 1996.

Kennedy, A. R. The evidence for soybean products as cancer preventive agents. *Journal of Nutrition* 1995; 125(3 Suppl.): 733s–43s.

Kestin, M., Rouse, I., Correll, R., et al. Cardiovascular disease risk factors in free-living men: comparison of two prudent diets, one based on lactoovovegetarianism and the other allowing lean meat. *American Journal of Clinical Nutrition* 1989; 50: 280–87.

Kris-Etherton, P. M., Hecker, K. D., Bonanome, A., Coval, S. M., Binkoski, A. E., Hilpert, K. F., Griel, A. E., Etherton, T. D. Bioactive compounds in foods: their role in the prevention of cardiovascular disease and cancer. *American Journal of Medicine* 2002; 113(Suppl. 9B): 71S–88S.

Kuczmarski, R. J., Flegal, K. M., Campbell, S. M., et al. Increasing prevalence of overweight among U.S. adults. *Journal of the American Medical Association* 1994; 272: 205–11.

Kushi, L., Giovannucci, E. Dietary fat and cancer. *American Journal of Medicine* 2002; 113(Suppl. 9B): 63S–70S.

Laidlaw, S. A., Swendseid, M. E., eds. *Vitamins and Cancer Prevention.* New York: Wiley-Liss, 1991.

Law, C., Ra'ad, D. Beta carotene's fall from grace draws mixed reactions. *Journal of the National Cancer Institute* 1996; 88: 235–36.

Lew, E. A., Garfinkel, L. Variations in mortality by weight among 750,000 men and women. *Journal of Chronic Diseases* 1979; 32: 563–76.

Mandatory Nutrition Labeling—Final Rule: One of a Series of FDA Regulations Implementing the Nutrition Labeling and Education Act of 1990. Food and Drug Administration. Washington, D.C.: January 6, 1993.

Margen, S. *The Wellness Encyclopedia of Food and Nutrition.* University of California at Berkeley Wellness Letter. Health Letter Associates, 1992.

Marsh, A., Sanchez, T., Michelsen, O., et al. Vegetarian lifestyle and bone mineral density. *American Journal of Clinical Nutrition* 1988; 48: 837–41.

Matanoski, G. M., Elliot, E. A. Bladder cancer epidemiology. *Epidemiologic Reviews* 1981; 3: 203–29.

Messina, M., Barnes, S. The role of soy products in reducing risk of cancer. *Journal of the National Cancer Institute* 1991; 83: 541–46.

Mettlin, C. J. Invited Commentary: Progress in the nutritional epidemiology of ovary cancer. *American Journal of Epidemiology* 1991; 134: 457–59.

Michels, K. B., Willett, W. C. Vitamins and cancer: A practical means of prevention? In DeVita, V. T., Helhnan, S., Rosenberg, S. A., eds. *Important Advances in Oncology.* Philadelphia, Pa.: Lippincott Company, 1994.

Micozzi, M. S., Moon, T. E., eds. *Macronutrients: Investigating Their Role in Cancer.* New York: Marcel Dekker, Inc., 1992.

Mirvish, S. S. Effects of vitamins C and E on N-nitroso compound formation, carcinogenesis, and cancer. *Cancer* 1986; 58: 1842–50.

———. The etiology of gastric cancer: Intragastric nitrosamide formation and other theories. *Journal of the National Cancer Institute* 1983; 71: 631–47.

Moon, R. C., Mehta, R. G. Anticarcinogenic effects of retinoids in animals. *Advances in Experimental Medical Biology* 1986; 206: 399–411.

Napier, K. Fat is everyone's issue. *Harvard Health Letter* 1996; 21(8): 1–3.

———. Green Revolution. *Harvard Health Letter* 1995; 20(6): 9–12.

———. Too Many Vitamins? *Harvard Health Letter* 1996; 21(3): 1–3.

National Cancer Institute Surveillance, Epidemiology, and End Results Program, 1997–99.

National Institutes of Health, National Cancer Institute. *Cancer: Rates and Risks* 1996.

Nelson, R. L., Davis, E. G., Sutter, E., et al. Body iron stores and risk of colonic neoplasia. *Journal of the National Cancer Institute* 1994; 86: 455–60.

Newmark, H. L. Plant phenolics as potential cancer prevention agents. In Back, N., Cohen, I. R., Kritchevsky, D., eds. *Dietary Phytochemicals in Cancer Prevention and Treatment.* New York: Plenum Press, 1996.

Nutrition Labeling and Education Act of 1990 (NLEA).

Nutritionist IV for Windows: Food Labeling Module 1995; First DataBank Division, The Hearst Corporation, 1111 Bayhill Drive, San Bruno, CA 94066.

Parazzini, E., Franceschi, S., Vecchia, C. L., et al. The epidemiology of ovarian cancer. *Gynecologic Oncology* 1991; 43: 9–23.

Pate, R. R., Pratt, M., Blair, S. N., et al. Physical activity and public health. *Journal of the American Medical Association* 1995; 273: 402–7.

Pennington, J. A. T., ed. *Bowes & Church's Food Values of Portions Commonly Used.* Seventeenth Edition. Philadelphia, Pa.: Lippincott, Williams & Wilkins, 1998.

Phillips, R. L., Garfinkel, L., Kuzma, J. W., et al. Mortality among California Seventh-Day Adventists for selected cancer sites. *Journal of the National Cancer Institute* 1980; 65: 1097–1107.

Recommended Dietary Allowances. Subcommittee on the Tenth Edition of the RDAs, Food and Nutrition Board, Commission on Life Sciences, National Research Council. Washington, D.C.: National Academy Press, 1989.

Ressel, G. W. American Cancer Society releases guidelines on nutrition and physical activity for cancer prevention. *American Family Physician* 2002; 66(8): 1555, 1559–60, 1562.

Risch, H. A., Jain, M., Marrett, L. D., et al. Dietary fat intake and risk of epithelial ovarian cancer. *Journal of the National Cancer Institute* 1994; 86: 1409–15.

Ross, R. K., Bernstein, L., Lobo, R. A., et al. 5-alpha-reductase activity and risk of prostate cancer among Japanese and U.S. white and black males. *The Lancet* 1992; 339: 887–89.

Rothman, K. J. *Modern Epidemiology.* Boston: Little, Brown and Company, 1986.

Ruddon R. W., ed. *Cancer Biology.* New York: Oxford University Press, 1995.

Sauber, C. M. The meaning of the word organic. *Harvard Health Letter* 1994; 19(6): 4–5.

Scientists spotlight phytoestrogens for better health. *Tufts University Diet and Nutrition Letter* 1995; 12: 1–5.

Serdula, M. K., Coates, R. J., Byers, T., et al. Fruit and vegetable intake among adults in 16 states: Results of a brief telephone survey. *American Journal of Public Health* 1995; 85: 236–39.

Shamsuddin, A. M. Inositol phosphates have novel anticancer function. *Journal of Nutrition* 1995; 125(3 Suppl.): 725s–32s.

Shils, M. E. Nutrition and diet in cancer management. In Shils M. E., et al., eds. *Modern Nutrition in Health and Disease.* Malvern, Pa.: Lea and Febiger, 1994.

Shottenfeld, D. Principles and applications of cancer prevention. In Shottenfeld D., Fraumeni, J. E. Jr., eds. *Cancer Epidemiology and Prevention.* New York: Oxford University Press, 1996.

Shu, X. O., Gao, Y. T., Yuan, J. M., et al. Dietary factors and epithelial ovarian cancer. *British Journal of Cancer* 1989; 59: 92–96.

Simopoulos, A. P., Herbert, V., Jacobson, B. *Genetic Nutrition: Designing a Diet Based on Your Family Medical History.* New York: Macmillan Publishing Company, 1993.

Singh, M., Lu, J., Briggs, S. P., et al. Effect of excess dietary iron on the promotion stage of 1-methyl-1-nitrosourea-induced mammary carcinogenesis: pathogenetic characteristics and distribution of iron. *Carcinogenesis* 1994; 15: 1567–70.

Slattery, M. L., Schuman, K. L., West, D. W., et al. Nutrient intake and ovarian cancer. *American Journal of Epidemiology* 1989; 130: 497–502.

Steinmetz, K. A., Potter, J. D. Vegetables, fruit, and cancer. II. Mechanisms. *Cancer Causes and Control* 1991; 2: 427–41.

———. Vegetables, fruit, and cancer prevention: A review. *Journal of the American Dietetic Association* 1996; 96: 1027–38.

Stevens, R. G., Beasley, R. P., Blumberg, B. S. Iron-binding proteins and risk of cancer in Taiwan. *Journal of the National Cancer Institute* 1986; 76: 605–10.

Sugimura, T., Shigeaki, S. Mutagens-carcinogens in foods. *Cancer Research* 1983; 43 (Suppl.): 2415s–21s.

Surh, Y. J., Lee, S. S. Capsaicin in hot chili pepper: Carcinogen, co-carcinogen or anti-carcinogen? *Food Chemistry and Toxicology* 1996; 34: 313–16.

Taubes, G. Epidemiology faces its limits. *Science* 1995; 269: 164–69.

Trichopoulos, D., Li, E. P., Hunter, D. J. What causes cancer? *Scientific American* September 1996; 80–87.

Trichopoulou, A., Costacou, T., Bamia, C., Trichopoulos, D. Adherence to a Mediterranean diet and survival in a Greek population. *New England Journal of Medicine* 2003; 348: 2599–2608.

Tzonou, A., Hsieh, C. C., Polychronopoulou, A., et al. Diet and ovarian cancer: A case-control study in Greece. *International Journal of Cancer* 1993; 55: 411–14.

Vecchia, C. L. Nutritional factors and cancers of the breast, endometrium and ovary. *European Journal of Cancer and Clinical Oncology* 1989; 25(12): 1945–51.

Vecchia, C. L., Negri, E., Franceschi, S., et al. Alcohol and epithelial ovarian cancer. *Journal of Clinical Epidemiology* 1992; 45: 1025–30.

Verhoeven, D. T. H., Goldbohm, R. A., van Poppel, G., et al. Epidemiological studies on brassica vegetables and cancer risk. *Cancer Epidemiology, Biomarkers & Prevention* 1996; 5: 733–48.

Watson, R. R., Mufti, S. I., eds. *Nutrition and Cancer Prevention.* New York: CRC Press, 1996.

Wattenberg, L. W. Inhibition of carcinogenesis by minor dietary constituents. *Cancer Research* 1992; 52(Suppl.): 2085s–91s.

Weigley, E. S., Mueller, D. H., Robinson, C. H. *Robinson's Basic Nutrition and Diet Therapy.* Eighth Edition. Upper Saddle River, N.J.: Prentice-Hall, Inc., 1997.

Welland, D. As caffeine controversy rages on, what's a coffee lover to do? *Environmental Nutrition* 1996; 19: 1–6.

Werbach, M. R. Illnesses and the effects of nutrients, toxic metals and food sensitivities: Cancer. In *Nutritional Influences on Illness*. Tarzana, Calif.: Third Line Press, 1993.

Willett, W. C. Diet and breast cancer. *Journal of Internal Medicine* 2001; 249: 395–411.

————. Diet and cancer. *Oncologist* 2000; 5: 393–404.

————. Diet and health: What should we eat? *Science* 1994; 264: 532–37.

————. Diet, nutrition, and avoidable cancer. *Environmental Health Perspectives* 1995; 103(Suppl. 8): 165–70.

————. *Eat, Drink, and Be Healthy*. New York: Free Press, 2001.

————. Harvesting the fruits of research: new guidelines on nutrition and physical activity. *CA A Cancer Journal for Clinicians* 2002; 52: 66–67.

————. Micronutrients and cancer risk. *American Journal of Clinical Nutrition* 1994; 59(5 Suppl.): 1162s–65s.

————. Overview of nutritional epidemiology. In MacMahon B., ed. *Nutritional Epidemiology*. New York: Oxford University Press, 1990.

————. Polyunsaturated fat and the risk of cancer. *British Medical Journal* 1995; 311: 1239–40.

————. Selenium, vitamin E, fiber, and the incidence of human cancer. *Advances in Experimental Medical Biology* 1986; 206: 27–34.

————. The discipline of epidemiology. *Science* 1995; 269: 1325–26.

Willett, W. C., Colditz, G. A., Mueller, N. E. Strategies for minimizing cancer risk. *Scientific American* September 1996; 88–95.

Yamane, T., Takahashi, T., Kuwata, K., et al. Inhibition of N-methyl-N-nitro-N-nitrosoguanidine-induced carcinogenesis by (-)- epigallocatechin gallate in the rat glandular stomach. *Cancer Research* 1995; 55: 2081–84.

Yang, C. S., Wang, Z. Y. Tea and cancer. *Journal of the National Cancer Institute* 1993; 85: 1038–49.

Young, V. R. Soy protein in relation to human protein and amino acid nutrition. *Journal of the American Dietetic Association* 1991; 91: 828–35.

Zemel, M. Calcium utilization: effect of varying level and source of dietary protein. *American Journal of Clinical Nutrition* 1988; 48: 880.

Zhang, L., Cooney, R. V., Bertram, J. S. Carotenoids up-regulate Connexin 43 gene expression independent of their provitamin A or antioxidant properties. *Cancer Research* 1992; 52: 5707–12.

Zheng, W., Doyle, T. J., Kushi, L. H., et al. Tea consumption and cancer incidence in a prospective cohort study of postmenopausal women. *American Journal of Epidemiology* 1996; 144: 175–82.

Ziegler, R. G. Does beta-carotene explain why reduced cancer risk is associated with vegetable and fruit intake? *Cancer Research* 1992; 52(7 Suppl.): 2060s–66s.

About the Contributors

$\sim$&$\sim$ T̲H̲E̲ ̲A̲U̲T̲H̲O̲R̲S̲ ̲W̲O̲U̲L̲D̲ ̲L̲I̲K̲E̲ ̲T̲O̲ ̲T̲H̲A̲N̲K̲ the many extraordinary chefs who have contributed their recipes to this volume, all of whom combine a passionate interest in great taste with foods that are healthful and delicious. The chefs' names appear with the recipes they've created. All chefs were invited to provide a biographical sketch.

MILES ANGELO Miles Angelo credits much of his foundation in modern southwestern cuisine to his early kitchen experience at Sedlar at Abiquiu in Santa Monica, California, under Chef John Rivera. He defined his own place in southwestern cuisine as the executive chef at New York City's Arizona 206. In Portobello Mushroom–Stuffed Chiles Rellenos, Miles combined flavors from the Far East and the Caribbean with indigenous southwestern ingredients, such as corn, chiles, squashes, and beans, to make a perfectly balanced celebration of tastes, textures, and colors. As the executive chef at the exclusive Caribou Club in Aspen, Colorado, Miles creates modern American food while still drawing on southwestern influences. Using the fresh ingredients and game of the Rocky Mountains, his seasonal menus demonstrate the perfect marriage of tradition with contemporary touches.

FRANCESCO ANTONUCCI Born in the beautiful Veneto region of Italy, Chef Antonucci brings us Venetian flavors combined with contemporary infusions and

371

sophistication. After a long career as an acclaimed executive chef at El Touls in Italy, Valentino in Santa Monica, California, DDI Bistro in Trump Tower, and Alo Alo restaurant in New York City, Chef Antonucci teamed up with designer and partner Adam Tihany and opened the original Remi restaurant in New York City. Since 1990, he and Tihany have opened Remi in Santa Monica, California; Mexico City, Mexico; and Tel Aviv, Israel. Additionally, Chef Antonucci has opened two other Manhattan restaurants, Le Zie and Le Zoccole, which serve up cichetti, the tasty bites offered in bars in Venice. He has consistently received both praise and awards from food critics and organizations. Most important, his customers' patronage speaks volumes about the quality and appeal of his cuisine. Chef Antonucci shares with us superb recipes that are both healthful and flavorful.

LIDIA BASTIANICH Born in Istria, at the juncture of Italy and the former Yugoslavia and what is now part of Croatia, Lidia Bastianich grew up surrounded by the delicacies of the Adriatic Sea and fresh ingredients of the region. She also had a grandmother who taught her the secrets of Italian cooking. Lidia opened her first restaurant in Forest Hills, Queens, at the age of twenty-four. In 1981, Lidia opened the acclaimed Felidia, which has received awards and accolades over two decades. She and her son Joseph are now partners in Felidia and Becco restaurants in New York and Lidia's in Kansas City and Pittsburgh. Lidia has authored three cookbooks including *La Cucina di Lidia* (Doubleday, 1990), which weaves history, tradition, and warm memories of her homeland into each recipe. In 1994, Lidia decided to share her home-style ingredients with the rest of the country and created a mail-order company. Her website (lidiasitaly.com) offers a wide selection of fresh Italian ingredients and food products as well as information on her restaurants, travel programs, books, TV programs, and special events. Lidia shares her knowledge of the history of Italian cuisine and the anthropology of food through her writings and on public television. Her current program and corresponding book are titled *Lidia's Italian-American Kitchen* (Knopf, 2001).

ROBERT BENNETT For fourteen years Robert Bennett and his pastry staff of twelve created more than six hundred desserts a week at Philadelphia's most celebrated restaurant, Le Bec Fin. His pastry career began at the New England Culinary Institute, where he stayed on after graduation as a pastry instructor. After three semesters of teaching, he accepted a four-month consulting position at the Jumby Bay Resort in Antigua, West Indies. In 1987, he took a position as one of four pastry chefs at Le Bec Fin and quickly worked his way up to the position of executive pastry chef.

During the last ten years at Le Bec Fin he became actively involved in local pastry organizations, founding the Philadelphia Pastry Society, and has also been recently appointed to the board of directors of the North American Pastry Chefs Association. In 2002 Robert opened his own pastry shop, Miel, an authentic French patisserie, in Cherry Hill, New Jersey.

DANIEL BOULUD Daniel Boulud is one of the most decorated chefs in the world. *Brilliant* and *innovative* are two words frequently used in describing the creations of this chef from Lyons, France. After working in the kitchens of the French masters Georges Blanc, Roger Vergé, and Michel Gurad, Chef Boulud earned accolades and four stars from the *New York Times* during his six years as executive chef at New York City's Le Cirque. In 1992, he left Le Cirque to open Restaurant Daniel. By 1994 he once again received four stars from the *New York Times*. The list of other awards are too long to exhaustively list, but they include: *New York Observer* 4 stars, March 1999; *Daily News* 4 stars, February 1999; *Food Arts* magazine "Silver Spoon Award," December 1998; *Nation's Restaurant News* "Fine Dining Hall of Fame," May 1998; *Wine Spectator* "New York City's Top Food Rating," April 1998; *Zagat Survey* "Top Food Ranking," New York City Restaurants, 1998; *Playboy* magazine, "No. 1: Critic's Choice, The 25 Best Restaurants in America," March 1998; *Gourmet* magazine, "America's Top Tables," No. 1 in New York City, October 1997; Mobil Travel Guide 5 stars, 1997 and 1998. His most recent cookbook is *Daniel Boulud's Café Boulud Cookbook* (Scribner, 1999). In addition to his signature restaurant, Daniel, he owns Café Boulud, which pays homage to the food Chef Boulud grew up with in France and celebrates the food he loves in America, and DB, a modern and casual French-American bistro. Both food critics and customers assert that Restaurant Daniel is the best classic French restaurant in New York and one of the best in the world.

ANTHONY BOURDAIN Anthony is the executive chef at New York's Les Halles. He is also a bestselling author. His memoir *Kitchen Confidential* (Ecco Press, 2001) stemmed from an article he had written for *New Yorker* magazine about life behind the scenes in restaurant kitchens. This world is quite familiar to this veteran chef, who has cooked at some of New York City's finest restaurants, including the Rainbow Room. In 2000 Anthony traveled the globe looking for "the perfect meal." The book and its companion Food Network series, "A Cook's Tour," chronicles his adventures and misadventures on that voyage, including the infamous episode when he ate the live beating heart of a cobra. His satirical thrillers include *Bone in the Throat* (Villard Books, 1995) and *Gone Bamboo* (Villard Books, 1996).

ANTOINE BOUTERIN Born and raised in his family's ancestral farmhouse in Saint-Rémy-de-Provence, Antoine trained at Beaumanière in Les Baux de Provence and the legendary Moulin de Mougins. While serving as the chef de cuisine at Quai d'Orsay in Paris, he came to America on a tour for La Varenne cooking school. By the end of the trip Antoine had fallen for America. In 1982 he took the position as executive chef at New York's Le Périgord; he stayed for twelve years, earning high praise, both for him and for the Provençal restaurant. Over the years awards and recognitions have included "Best Young Chef in France," 1980; "Great Chefs of the East," the Discovery Channel, 1990; and "Chef of the Year," American Tasting Institute, 1998. Antoine has authored three cookbooks, including *Cooking Provence: Four Generations of Recipes and Traditions* (Simon & Schuster Macmillan Co., 1994), as well as several food articles for *Mieux-Etre (Better Living)*. In 1995, he struck out on his own and opened Bouterin in New York's Sutton Place. The dining room fills every night for those who wish to be transported to Provence.

FRANK BRIGTSEN After seven years of training in classic Creole cooking under internationally acclaimed chef Paul Prudhomme, Frank, with his wife and partner, Marna, opened Brigtsen's in March 1986. The following are just a few of the awards and recognition they have received during this time: "Top Cajun Restaurant," 2000 *Zagat Survey*; James Beard Foundation Award for "American Express Best Chef: Southeast" in 1998; "1994 Chef of the Year," New Orleans chapter of Chefs in America; and "Top Ten New Chefs," in 1988, *Food & Wine*. As a chef Frank is hands-on, personally visiting fish markets and vegetable stands and writing daily menus by hand. He is on-site every evening to oversee the preparation of such signature dishes as Rabbit Tenderloin on a Tasso Parmesan Grits Cake with Creole Mustard Sauce and Blackened Yellowfin Tuna with Smoked Corn Sauce and Red Bean Salsa.

DAVID BURKE David is co-owner of the Park Avenue Cafés in New York City and Chicago. He also is vice president of culinary development for The Smith & Wollensky Restaurant Group with restaurants in such cities as Chicago, Miami Beach, New Orleans, Las Vegas, and Washington, D.C. The group also owns The Manhattan Ocean Club, Cité, Moloney and Porcelli, The Post House, and ONEc.p.s. in New York. After graduating from the Culinary Institute of America, David worked in some of the finest kitchens in the United States and Europe, including the River Café, a restaurant where many of America's premier chefs have launched their careers. David also took a pilgrimage through Michelin-starred restaurants in France, where he honed his appreciation for regional specialties. In addition to his busy restaurant operations, David is involved with retail and wholesale distribution of specialty food items that are available under the Park Avenue Café label. His culinary excellence has been recognized by the following awards: *Chef* magazine: Chef of the Year, 1998; First Auggie Award (named for Auguste Escoffier), 1996; Robert Mondavi Culinary Award of Excellence, 1996 and 1997; and Nippon Award of Excellence, 1988.

ADAM BUSBY Adam Busby reaped critical acclaim and industry recognition during his celebrated tenure in the Pacific Northwest kitchens of Bishops, Star Anise, and his own venture, Cascabel. At these restaurants Adam drew on the abundance of ingredients available in the Pacific Northwest to create progressive new American cuisine influenced by classical French technique. In 1997 he left restaurant kitchens to become an educator. As director of the Advanced Culinary Program of the Dubrulle French Culinary School in Vancouver, British Columbia, Adam designed and taught continuing education classes for food professionals. Now at the prestigious Culinary Institute of America at Greystone campus in St. Helena, California, he is a chef instructor in the Advanced Culinary Arts Certificate Program.

MICHAEL CHIARELLO Michael Chiarello takes the splendid ingredients of northern California farms and produces award-winning Italian food at the stylish Tra Vigne restaurant, located in the heart of Napa Valley. Under his direction, Tra Vigne makes its own breads, salami, prosciutto, cheeses, and cured olives and sells them to other local restaurants. Michael has opened four other restaurants since 1994: Bump and Ajax Tavern in Aspen, Colorado, Caffe Museo in the San Francisco Museum of Modern Art, and Tomatina, a casual pizza and pasta restaurant adjacent to Tra Vigne. He has authored five cookbooks, including *Michael Chiarello's Casual Cooking* (Chronicle Books, 2002). He also hosts "NapaStyle" (Fine Living Network) and "Easy Entertaining with Michael Chiarello" (The Food Network). Michael's company, Consorzio Foods, uses local ingredients to produce specialty mustards, flavored oils and vinegars, and vinaigrettes. Michael hopes these retail ingredients help people cook with the same creative force he does. "Our philosophy is convenience without compromise," says Michael.

SCOTT COHEN In 1994, Scott Cohen was awarded the Bronze Medal of the French Vatel Club, honoring him as one of the nation's outstanding young chefs. The road to such recognition began after his high school graduation, when he enrolled in the Culinary Institute of America. He then worked at the Mansion at Turtle Creek in Dallas, the Carlyle Hotel in New York City, and as sous-chef to the late André Gaillard at New York's La Reserve. His training with Gaillard and an apprenticeship at the famed Moulin de Mougins provided him with a solid foundation in classical

French cooking. After earning accolades at the restaurant at the Stanhope Hotel, Scott moved on to head up the kitchen at Las Canarias at La Mansion del Rio in San Antonio, Texas. La Mansion del Rio is one of America's most luxurious and romantic hotels. In this stunning Spanish Colonial building Scott creates American dishes with a southwestern flair and has earned AAA Four Diamond ratings.

ROBERTO DONNA Having made his commitment to the culinary arts at the age of thirteen, Roberto Donna completed four years of training in his native Italy, followed by experiences in England, France, and Switzerland. He is chef and owner of the famous Galileo in Washington, D.C., and owns six other restaurants emphasizing simplicity and freshness. Signature menu items include such specialties as Tomato Risotto with Monkfish and Eggplant and Braised Beef Agnolotti in a Barolo Wine Sauce, served with a small onion tart. In 1996, Roberto won the prestigious James Beard Foundation Award for "Best Chef—Mid-Atlantic Region." Other accolades include induction of Galileo into *Nation's Restaurant News* Fine Dining Hall of Fame, and the DiRoNa (Distinguished Restaurants of North America) Award from 1990 to present. Roberto is the chairman of the Gruppo Ristoratori Italiani, a national organization with the goal of emphasizing authentic Italian food culture in the United States.

DEAN FEARING At the renowned Mansion on Turtle Creek in Dallas, Texas, Dean Fearing merges native ingredients of the Southwest with flavors from around the world to create his own signature southwestern menu. Dean was trained classically at the Culinary Institute of America and began his career at Maisonette in Cincinnati, Ohio. He is inspired by memories of simple backyard barbecues, which he elevates to sophisticated and colorful cuisine, incorporating a variety of homegrown vegetables, herbs, and game. The author of two cookbooks, *The Mansion on Turtle Creek Cookbook* and *Dean Fearing's Southwest Cuisine: Blending Asia and the Americas*, Dean does not hesitate to give away one of his secrets. Says Dean, "I can always create another one."

DIANE FORLEY Diane Forley's interest in food began at an early age with a strong influence from the rich cultural heritage of her family, whose roots spread from Eastern Europe to the Mediterranean, the Middle East, and South America. She has trained with chefs here and in France and has worked at notable places, such as Adrienne's (in Maxim's Hotel) and the River Café and Park Avenue Café in New York City. While pastry chef at the Gotham Bar and Grill, she demonstrated her skills and expertise in pastry arts. Diane's cultural experiences, extensive travels, and avid interests in nutrition and the history of food are the basis for her contemporary American cuisine. She has highlighted her talents at New York's Verbena, a restaurant she launched, for almost a decade. In 1999, Diane met Chef Michael Otsuka at the Masters of Food & Wine event. Their shared passion for food and wine sparked a romance that led to marriage in 2001. Now co–executive chefs and owners of Verbena, they merge their diverse culinary perspectives and combined extensive experience in the restaurant business to the delight of their patrons.

Maria Helm Maria Helm began cooking professionally at age sixteen. After graduating from Union College, where she obtained a liberal arts degree, Maria attended the California Culinary Academy and the Konditeri Tivoli Pastry School in Denmark. For the next seven years she worked, first as a pastry chef and then as executive chef, at the San Francisco Bay Area's Sherman House restaurant. In 1995, Maria moved on to the PlumpJack Cafe, where she received critical praise, including *Food & Wine*'s "Top 10 New Chefs" in 1996. She now provides culinary direction and cooking classes at Robert Sinskey Vineyards, the Napa Valley winery she owns with her husband.

Erasmo "Razz" Kamnitzer Native of Venezuela, Razz Kamnitzer started his culinary career at age seventeen as the assistant manager of the Vegetarian Buffet in Caracas, where he was exposed to healthy cooking. Since that time his career has taken him around the world, and he has cultivated these influences into exotic and well-balanced cuisine. In addition to years of on-the-job training, he attended the National Hotel School of Lausanne in Switzerland and the Culinary Institute of America. Since moving to Arizona in 1980, Razz has owned and operated several restaurants, including Auberge Du Canal, and has performed as chef de cuisine of Etienne's Different Pointe of View at the Pointe Hilton at Tapatio Cliffs, Phoenix. In 1995 Razz opened Razz's Restaurant and Bar in Scottsdale, Arizona, which has received numerous honors, including selection by *Esquire* magazine as one of the "Best New Restaurants" in 1996. His cuisine features herbs, edible flowers, and local fruits and vegetables. Razz was kind enough to provide a delicious, versatile recipe with ingredients that can be found by those of us who don't live near the desert.

Katy Keck Katy Keck began cooking at five years old, using an Easy-Bake oven, and eventually won the blue ribbon in the butter cake division at the local 4-H fair. But cooking became a serious career option only after completion of her MBA at the University of Chicago and a successful career in marketing and finance on Wall

Street. When Katy won the grand prize in the Flavors of France contest for her Marie Brizard chocolate torte recipe, the prize was an apprenticeship at Le Grand Monarue in Chartres, France. She followed this up by interning at three other Michelin-starred restaurants. On returning to the United States, she created Savoir Faire Foods, a consulting business specializing in recipe and new product development and marketing, food and demo styling, and culinary special events. In 1993 Katy and her partner, Richard Barber, opened New World Grill at the Worldwide Plaza in New York City. Her menu is a mix of styles—Asian, French, and southwestern to name a few—and represents a healthful approach to eating out. In 1996, Katy was honored as one of seven national finalists in the *Gourmet* Magazine Evian Healthy Menu Awards. She is featured in the books *Great Women Chefs, New Classic Cocktails,* and *A Woman's Place Is in the Kitchen.* Katy was honored by the 1998–99 Daytime Emmy Awards for contributions to the "Rosie O'Donnell Show."

GIUSEPPE LATTANZI From Sicily to Rome to New York City, the Lattanzi family has perfected its talents, culminating with the contemporary generation's five Lattanzi siblings, all successful restaurateurs. This Roman-Jewish family has been in the restaurant business in New York for more than thirty years. The Lattanzi siblings' New York restaurants include Lattanzi Ristorante, Erminia, Porta Portese, Chelsea, Sumo, Paper Moon, Tevere, and Va Bene. Giuseppe Lattanzi, affectionately called Pipo by staff and friends, oversees Va Bene, an elegant, upscale kosher Italian restaurant. He prides himself on providing classical Roman cuisine in adherence with kosher dietary laws.

BARBARA LYNCH Hard work and immense talent have taken Barbara Lynch to the top of America's culinary scene. While growing up in the housing projects of South Boston, Barbara worked three jobs to help her family with expenses. A high-school home-economics instructor inspired and encouraged her interest in cooking, and she has not looked back since. Barbara credits her six-year combined culinary experience with Michela Larson (Michela's and Rialto) and Todd English (Olives and Figs) for fostering her interest and talent in Italian-style cooking. Her own studies of Italian tradition and cuisine and numerous trips to many of the regions of Italy have further developed her signature style. Barbara realized a dream in opening No. 9 Park in the tony Beacon Hill section of Boston. Over the last few years Barbara has been featured in articles in the *Boston Globe, Boston Herald, Boston* magazine, *Food & Wine, Eating Well,* and *Bon Appétit* and, in 1996, was named among *Food & Wine's* "Top 10 New Chefs." Most recently, the James Beard Foundation named Barbara "Best Chef—Northeast, 2003."

ZARELA MARTÍNEZ Born and raised in Mexico, Zarela Martínez is without a doubt the first lady of Mexican cooking in America. Zarela has brought the tradition, intense flavors, and sophistication of true Mexican cooking to New York City, without a hint of Tex-Mex. At the popular, critically acclaimed Zarela Restaurant you can experience the warmth of her cooking. Zarela Catering allows you to take the flavors home. Zarela shares her traditions and recipes with the rest of the world in *Food from My Heart* (Macmillan, 1992). This autobiography-cookbook was nominated for the prestigious James Beard Award as "Best International Cookbook of the Year." More recently Zarela authored *Zarela's Veracruz* (Houghton Mifflin Co., 2001). She also hosts a public television companion show in which she tours North American viewers through the lush land bordering the Gulf Coast, focusing on the abundant ingredients and how to use them. The ease of preparation and nutritious content of most of her recipes made our selection a difficult but enjoyable process.

ROBERT MCGRATH During Robert McGrath's more than twenty years in the culinary industry he has worked as executive chef of Arrowwood Resort in Westchester, New York; chef de cuisine at the Four Seasons Hotel in Austin, Texas; and chef-owner of Sierra restaurant in Houston, Texas, and chef de cuisine at Windows on the Green, The Phoenician Resort's Southwest-inspired restaurant. In this spectacular setting his culinary magic earned him *Food & Wine*'s "The Ten Best New Chefs in America," 1988; Evian's "Healthy Menu Awards National Winner," 1993, 1994; and numerous James Beard Foundation nominations for "America's Best Chef—Southwest." After leaving Windows on the Green, Robert opened Roaring Fork restaurants in Scottsdale, Arizona, and Austin, Texas. These highly successful "American Western Bistros" earned him "America's Best Chef—Southwest" after seven years of being nominated. In 2000, he published *American West Cooking*.

NICK MORFOGEN Having grown up in the restaurant business, Nick Morfogen admits that cooking was a duty rather than a passion. Training with the late Gilbert La Coze at New York City's Le Bernadin changed his view. After Nick graduated from the Culinary Institute of America in 1987, Gilbert offered him a position and showed him endless creative possibilities. Other strong influences include working with Daniel Boulud at Le Cirque and as sous-chef to Michael Chiarello at Tra Vigne. In 1994, Nick and Michael became partners in the Ajax Tavern in Aspen, Colorado. As the executive chef Nick created an American-style menu with Mediterranean influences. In 1997, Nick moved on to Maxaluna in Boca Raton, Florida. Here he has further defined his flair for Mediterranean cooking, focusing on the soulful flavors of Tuscany. He has received glowing reviews from food critics and customers and in

1996 was named one of the "Top 10 New Chefs in America" by *Food & Wine*. In 1999, Nick joined 32 east in Delray Beach, Florida. Here he has earned countless awards and critical acclaim including two consecutive Golden Spoon Awards. The *Miami Herald* says of Nick's talents "He combines fine, fresh ingredients in new ways and does it so successfully the combination seems inevitable."

MICHAEL OTSUKA Michael Otsuka developed an interest in cooking at the side of his mother and grandmother. He assisted them in preparing the recipes of his Austrian-Jewish and Japanese backgrounds. His professional experience began at the Seventh Street Bistro in Los Angeles where he worked as an apprentice to Joachim Splichal. Michael joined Joachim in his next restaurant, Max au Triangle, in Beverly Hills. Here he was quickly promoted to sous-chef. To round out his culinary background, Michael spent a few years working in Michelin-starred restaurants and hotels in France and Belgium, most notably at the Hotel Negresco in Nice. In 1995, Michael became executive chef at Patina, where he was recognized by the James Beard Foundation, receiving a nomination for "Rising Star Chef." In 1999 at the Masters of Food & Wine event, Michael met Diane Forley, an accomplished chef and culinarian. Their shared passion for food and wine sparked a romance that led to marriage in 2001. At New York's Verbena, where they are co–executive chefs and owners, their diverse culinary perspectives combine to produce innovative and flavorful dishes.

JACQUES PÉPIN As the author of more than fifteen cookbooks, of which almost half provide "healthy" recipes, finding two recipes that contain cancer-fighting foods was not difficult for Jacques Pépin. In addition to being a renowned author, Jacques is a master chef, culinary consultant, and teacher. Like Julia Child, he has taught many Americans the art of French cuisine via television. Jacques has also developed and perfected healthy cooking techniques, sharing them with his reading and viewing audiences. His other forums for culinary instruction include a graduate curriculum in gastronomy, which he oversees at Boston University, and his role as dean of special programs at New York's French Culinary Institute. At the French Culinary Institute Jacques coaches and inspires future chefs through regular culinary demonstrations and student consultations.

MARTA PULINI Marta Pulini began her cooking career in the most important kitchen in Italy—her mother's. Here she learned regional cooking and family recipes that had been passed down through the generations. After marrying and moving to the food capital of Italy, the region of Emilia-Romagna, Chef Pulini created PUMA, a very successful catering business, and later opened La Brasserie in Modena, Italy.

Since her move to New York City in 1989, Chef Pulini has been at the helm of some of New York's finest Italian kitchens. They include Bice in New York and Paris and Le Madri in New York. Chef Pulini is now the corporate chef for Toscorp., a company with Italian restaurants throughout the United States. Chef Pulini gives frequent seminars on Italian cooking and teaches food lovers how to use the best Italian ingredients. She published her first English cookbook, *The Art of Regional Cooking* (Sterling Publishers), in 1995. Chef Pulini believes healthy eating can be easy by avoiding extremes, eating in moderation, and using the freshest ingredients.

MICHAEL ROMANO Union Square Cafe's chef and partner is a native New Yorker with strong family ties in Italy. Michael Romano takes advantage of Union Square Cafe's fortunate location—next door to the city's largest greenmarket. Farm-fresh ingredients of the season, grown by local producers, dominate the Union Square's menu. Michael has forged a unique personal style of contemporary food with French and Italian influences. His straightforward food presentations incorporate robustly flavored, soundly imaginative ingredient combinations. Michael is justifiably considered one of the nation's most talented, trendsetting chefs. Michael and his partner, Danny Meyer, have pioneered an exciting new breed of restaurant, where excellent food and wine are paired with warm hospitality and outstanding value. Together they coauthored *Union Square Cafe Cookbook* (HarperCollins Publishers, 1994). Over the course of his career Michael has earned numerous awards and recognitions, including *Food & Wine* magazine's "Top Ten Chefs in the U.S.A.," the James Beard Foundation nomination for "New York City's Best Chefs," and a profile in *Mastery*, the recently released book featuring interviews with "30 remarkable people."

ALAIN SAILHAC Born close to the Italian-French border in Millau, France, Alain Sailhac grew up surrounded by the fragrances and fresh ingredients of Provence. The influence is evident in his cooking. Alain allows ingredients to speak for themselves, combining them in such a manner so that they complement rather than mask one another. After more than forty years in the culinary arts, during which he gained four stars for New York's Le Cygne and three stars for the world-famous Le Cirque, Alain Sailhac joined the French Culinary Institute (FCI). As the executive vice president and senior dean of studies, he develops the student curriculum, selects first-rate faculty, attracts accomplished guest lecturers, acts as an inspirational student adviser, and has overseen over a decade of growth of this very special culinary environment. Alain lends his hands-on culinary skills developing seasonal menus for L'Ecole, FCI's on-site restaurant, and providing regular cooking demonstrations in the French Culinary Institute's International Culinary Theater and representing FCI throughout the world.

MARTIN SAYLOR After studying cuisine at the Cordon Bleu in France and the Culinary Institute of America, Martin Saylor served in the U.S. Navy. As principal chef to both the Commander of the Seventh Fleet and Deputy Commander in Chief of U.S. Forces in Europe, he traveled extensively throughout Asia and Europe. Although he is known for his American-inspired cuisine with bold and well-defined flavors, the influences of his travels are subtly apparent. Following his naval service, he was chef to then Secretary of the Treasury James A. Baker III. From 1994 to 1997 Martin succeeded the unforgettable Patrick Clark as the chef at the prestigious Hay-Adams Hotel in Washington, D.C. In 1999, he opened Butterfield 9, also in Washington, D.C. Butterfield 9 was nominated as "Best New Restaurant" in 2000, and Martin has been nominated for "Best Chef" by the Restaurant Association of Metropolitan Washington for 2001. His achievements also include the James Beard House award as one of the "30 Best Chefs in America" and *Food & Wine* magazine's award-winning apprentice chef.

GIANNI SCAPPIN Gianni Scappin has long been one of the most respected interpreters of regional Italian cuisine in the United States. As the corporate chef for Manhattan restaurateur Pino Luongo's Toscorp., he ensured the excellence of the food at Le Madri, Coco Pazzo, Tuscan Square, and Luongo's seven other restaurants. Food journalists and dining critics applaud Gianni's skill in creating menus and dishes with robust, earthy flavors, balanced by a sophistication to please even the most demanding diners. Under his guidance Le Madri was twice among the top two Italian restaurants in New York in Gault Millau's *Best of New York*. At Le Madri, Gianni befriended actor Stanley Tucci, a regular at the restaurant. Tucci was producing the film *Big Night*, an affectionate look at how two brothers struggle to operate an Italian restaurant in New Jersey during the 1950s. Tucci would come into the kitchen to watch Gianni's moves to give the kitchen scenes in the film a more authentic flavor. The friendship also led to *Cucina & Famiglia*, a cookbook Scappin coauthored with Tucci's mother, Joan, which features traditional Italian home dishes as well as recipes from the movie. In 2002, Gianni and Stanley Tucci partnered in the restaurant business, opening Finch Tavern in Croton Falls, New York. The menu highlights farm-fresh products offered by skilled artisans of the Hudson Valley and demonstrates the skills and culinary passions of its operators.

DIETER SCHORNER Born in Rehau, Germany, Dieter Schorner began his career in pastry as an apprentice at the age of fifteen. After studying at Coba Institute in Basel,

Switzerland, he went on to work at some of the finest restaurants in Europe. At age twenty-seven he became the chef patissier and chef confiseur at the acclaimed Savoy Hotel in London, England. Since arriving in the United States in 1968, Dieter has held executive pastry chef positions at such renowned restaurants as New York City's Le Cirque, Tavern on the Green, and La Côte Basque. Le Cirque owner Sirio Maccione has referred to Dieter Schorner as "the best in the world." In 1988, *Time* magazine called him the best pastry chef in the United States. In 1988, Dieter opened Patisserie Café Didier in Washington, D.C. This café consistently received accolades, such as "best breakfast" in Washington, D.C., and in 1997, a 26-out-of-30 food rating by *Zagat Survey*. Additionally, *Money* magazine rated the café as one of the best breakfast places in America. Dieter now shares his expertise and career achievements with students as a faculty member at the Culinary Institute of America.

RoxSand Scocos RoxSand Scocos is owner and executive chef at RoxSand's Restaurant & Bar in Phoenix, Arizona, and has won numerous awards including the James Beard Foundation "Best Chef—Southwest Region" in 1997. Known for her fusion cuisine—the art of bridging a variety of cooking techniques and flavors—she focuses on the future of food in our society and understands the importance of food choices and health. RoxSand remarks, "Since both the health of our children and the environmental future of the planet are at stake, it is our duty as chefs to send an urgent message about sustainable food choices." She demonstrates this by including 100 percent organic products in her menu, when possible.

Jimmy Sneed Chef Jimmy Sneed's culinary initiation came at Le Cordon Bleu cooking school in Paris, where he had a job translating for American students. It was here that he was exposed to classic French cooking techniques and launched his culinary career. He returned to the States to begin six years in training with master chef Jean-Louis at the Watergate restaurant in Washington, D.C. With a firm grasp of French cooking, Jimmy has been able to create "modern American cuisine" with a French flair. Now chef and proprietor at the Frog and the Redneck in Richmond, Virginia, Jimmy serves fresh seasonal products from local growers with simple sophistication and a touch of savoir faire. In 1995, he earned a James Beard Foundation nomination for "Best Chef—Mid-Atlantic Region."

André Soltner In the 1960s, Master Chef André Soltner brought French haute cuisine to New York. During the next thirty years, as chef-proprietor of New York's Lutece, his commitment and dedication to the quality of his classic French cooking never wavered. Loyal patronage was gained through not only superb food, but also the impeccable service and charm that remained consistent in the dining room.

Among his many awards and accolades are the Grande Medaille d'Or, Academie Culinaire de France, and the James Beard Foundation's Lifetime Achievement Award. André has served for more than twenty years as the Délegué Général of the Master Chefs of France. Although semiretired, André shares his more than fifty years of cooking experience with aspiring chefs at the French Culinary Institute in New York. Here he is able to instill his firm belief that the classics are the foundation for culinary success.

JACQUES TORRES After completing his apprenticeship at La Frangipane, a small pastry shop near his hometown of Bandol, France, Jacques Torres began the swift climb to his current status as one of the world's most acclaimed pastry chefs. In 1980, he began an eight-year working relationship with Jacques Maximin at the famous Hotel Negresco. From 1980 to 1983, he went back to school on his days off to earn the degree of master pastry chef. In 1986, Jacques was awarded the prestigious Meilleur Ouvrier de France medal, the youngest chef to earn the distinction. One year after coming to the United States, in 1988, he joined New York's famous Le Cirque, where cooking for presidents, kings, and celebrities is part of every workday. Jacques is dedicated to sharing his passion for the art of pastry; his training and teaching are ongoing at the French Culinary Institute, where he was appointed dean of pastry arts in 1996. In January 1998, Jacques starred in a twenty-six-episode public television series entitled "Dessert Circus with Jacques Torres." The companion cookbook, *Dessert Circus: Extraordinary Desserts You Can Make at Home* (Morrow Cookbooks, 1998), was nominated for a 1999 James Beard award. In 1999, he created the second television series and wrote the companion cookbook, *Dessert Circus at Home* (William Morrow, 1999). Jacques now hosts two shows on TV's Food Network ("Chocolate with Jacques Torres" and "Passion for Dessert with Jacques Torres"), is working on a third book, and has designed and built his own chocolate manufacturing plant, Jacques Torres Chocolate in Brooklyn, New York, where he is currently indulging in his chocolate fantasies on a daily basis.

JERRY TRAUNFELD After many years of culinary experience, including four as the executive chef at the Alexis Hotel in Seattle, Washington, Jerry Traunfeld had the opportunity to combine his longtime passions for gardening and cooking: in 1990, he accepted the chef's position at the Herbfarm. This unique restaurant is surrounded by acres of kitchen gardens and serves only one exquisite seating of a nine-course menu each night. Jerry's herb-infused seasonal menus use the magnificent ingredients of the Northwest and have made the Herbfarm one of the most coveted restaurant reservations in the country. He shares more than two hundred of his best recipes in *The Herbfarm Cookbook* (Scribner, 2000).

CHARLIE TROTTER Charlie Trotter began his culinary career in 1982. Since 1987, when he opened his elegant Chicago townhouse restaurant, Charlie Trotter's, he has soared to the top of America's culinary community. Charlie Trotter's is one of only a handful of U.S. restaurants to have earned five Mobil stars and five AAA diamonds and to have been inducted into the internationally renowned Relais & Chateaux. Charlie has also been named America's "Best Chef—Midwest" and has received nine nominations for awards by the James Beard Foundation, including "Outstanding Restaurant"(2000) and "Outstanding Chef" (1999). *Wine Spectator* named Charlie Trotter's "The Best Restaurant in the World for Wine & Food" (1998) and "America's Best Restaurant" (2000). As an innovator of cuisine, Charlie expands on classic French traditions and uses the freshest possible ingredients and imagination to produce recipes that blend the flavors of the world. To our benefit, Charlie's recipes use many fresh fruits and vegetables; his book *Charlie Trotter's Vegetables*, a narrative on vegetable cuisine in America, contains stunning photographs to accompany each recipe.

MING TSAI Ming Tsai began his cooking career at his family's Chinese restaurant as a teenager in Dayton, Ohio. This led him to Paris, where he studied at the Cordon Bleu. He then returned to the United States and obtained a master's degree in hotel administration from Cornell University. At Santacafe in Santa Fe, New Mexico, Ming launched his career with a unique approach to fusion cooking by merging southwestern and Asian cuisine and earned a *Zagat Survey* food rating of 27 out of 30. In 1998, he opened Blue Ginger in the Boston suburb of Wellesley, Massachusetts. Ming's East-meets-West cooking has garnered many awards since, including three stars from the *Boston Globe*, "Best New Restaurant" from *Boston* magazine, and, in 2002, Ming won the James Beard Foundation "Best Chef—Northeast." Additionally, his Food Network cooking show, "East Meets West, Cooking with Ming Tsai," won an Emmy Award in 1998, and his cookbook by the same name is now in its fifth edition.

NORMAN VAN AKEN As the father of South Florida's New World Cuisine, Norman Van Aken has ushered in a concept of global cuisine and has led the way for many other successful chefs. Johnson & Wales University awarded him an honorary doctorate for his innovative career achievements. He currently cooks, consults, and lectures internationally on New World Cuisine while still overseeing his award-winning restaurant, NORMAN'S, in Coral Gables, Florida. His culinary philosophy is "to create a marriage of the raw and rustic with the classic and intellectual in a celebration of the various places we live." This is New World Cuisine. Norman has authored four cookbooks, including the Julia Child/IACP-nominated *Norman's New World Cuisine* (Random House, 1997) and more recently *New World Kitchen: Latin and Caribbean Cuisine* (HarperCollins Publishers, 2003). In 1996, he won the James Beard Perrier Joliet Award for "Best Chef—Southeast." Other awards include the Robert Mondavi Award and the Food Arts Silver Spoon.

SUSAN WEAVER During her almost twenty years with the Four Seasons Hotel organization, Susan Weaver accumulated such critical acclaim as winning a top-ten finalist spot in the Bocuse d'Or and becoming the only female finalist in the Prix Culinaire International Pierre Tattinger. In 1994, she was selected as the U.S.A. Hotel Chef of the Year. Her incredible career began when she was backpacking in Europe. During a period of time in which she worked as a dishwasher and vegetable peeler on the small island of Corsica, her passion for the kitchen was born. After returning to the United States, Susan worked and studied under the world-renowned chef Fernand Gutierrez, who provided her with the foundation of classic technique. Susan's style is "alternative" cuisine (sophisticated and elegant, yet relatively low in fat, sodium, and cholesterol)—a style of cooking she helped pioneer more than a decade ago.

CHARLES WILEY The delicious creations of Charles Wiley, executive chef at Elements Restaurant at the Sanctuary at Camelback Mountain in Paradise Valley, Arizona, embody culinary simplicity and innovative modern character. Charles's self-taught skills are predominantly the product of thirty years cooking experience, although he has studied formally under Madeline Kamman at the Beringer Vineyards School for American Chefs. While executive chef at the Boulders in Carefree, Arizona, Charles perfected skills in creating spa and lighter fare. He also received numerous awards and accolades including *Food & Wine*'s "Top 10 New Chefs." In keeping with the desires of the "healthy clientele" at Elements, Charles creates foods that are spare in fat with robust and intense flavor derived from fresh local ingredients and spices instead of butter or cream. His unpretentious dishes might be called simple; however, the quiet touches speak volumes.

Index